# The Scottish Criminal Courts in Action

**Alastair L Stewart** QC, BA, LLB

Sheriff of Tayside, Central and Fife at Dundee,
Temporary Judge in the Court of Session
and the High Court of Justiciary

Second edition

Butterworths
Edinburgh
1997

| United Kingdom | Butterworths, a Division of Reed Elsevier (UK) Ltd, 4 Hill Street, EDINBURGH EH2 3JZ and Halsbury House, 35 Chancery Lane, LONDON WC2A 1EL |
| --- | --- |
| Australia | Butterworths, SYDNEY, MELBOURNE, BRISBANE, ADELAIDE, PERTH, CANBERRA and HOBART |
| Canada | Butterworths Canada Ltd, TORONTO and VANCOUVER |
| Ireland | Butterworth (Ireland) Ltd, DUBLIN |
| Malaysia | Malayan Law Journal Sdn Bhd, KUALA LUMPUR |
| New Zealand | Butterworths of New Zealand Ltd, WELLINGTON and AUCKLAND |
| Singapore | Reed Elsevier (Singapore) Pte Ltd, SINGAPORE |
| South Africa | Butterworth Publishers (Pty) Ltd, DURBAN |
| USA | Michie, CHARLOTTESVILLE, VIRGINIA |

The moral right of the author has been asserted. A CIP Catalogue record for this book is available from the British Library.

ISBN 0 406 99943 0

Typeset by Phoenix Photosetting, Chatham, Kent
Printed and bound in Great Britain by
Redwood Books, Trowbridge, Wiltshire

# Preface

Since the appearance of the first edition there have been substantial changes in the field of Scottish criminal procedure, caused most notably by the passing of the Criminal Justice (Scotland) Act 1995. Paradoxically, this legislation is scarcely mentioned in the new edition, because no sooner had it been passed than its provisions were consolidated into the Criminal Procedure (Scotland) Act 1995, which is now the principal statute governing procedure in the Scottish criminal courts. It is this latter Act which provides the great bulk of statutory references in this edition. There has been other important legislation since the appearance of the first edition as well as a considerable amount of case law affecting the subject matter of the book. By 1996 the first edition had accordingly become dangerously out of date and a second edition was clearly required. Butterworths took the initiative in asking whether I would be willing to prepare this edition, and it was an invitation which I was glad to accept.

The format of the new edition is essentially the same as that of the first. The first two chapters again narrate the cases of David Balfour and Nicol Jarvie with appropriate amendments to take account of changes in the law. I have, for the sake of convenience following my own move from Aberdeen to Dundee, transferred Duncairn, its inhabitants and its police force from Grampian to Tayside. I trust that lovers of Lewis Grassic Gibbon will not be offended! The various forms referred to in the first two chapters are now grouped together at the end of the sections of the text in which they are first mentioned. I hope that this will make reference to them easier. The other chapters follow the same pattern as in the first edition, subject, I am afraid, to considerable expansion in some cases because of legislative changes.

I have followed essentially the same policy as with the first edition so far as citation of authorities is concerned. I have made no attempt to be exhaustive but I have tried to refer to as many recent cases as possible.

I wrote the first edition with the primary aim of providing a textbook for students taking the Diploma in Legal Practice although, as I said in the preface, I hoped that it might also be of some assistance to practitioners. I have been surprised and, I must confess, gratified to learn that the book has in fact been used by the profession. In the hope that this new edition too will be of some value outside academic circles, I have put rather more detail into it than might be justified in a book directed solely at students. I trust that in attempting to provide a book which will be useful to the two classes of reader, I have not succeeded in making it unacceptable to either.

An unexpected and unwelcome complication was introduced into the preparation of this edition by the passage in the spring of the Crime and Punishment (Scotland) Act 1997. This statute, which provides for some fairly radical changes in procedure, received the royal assent just before the manuscript of this edition had to be sent off to the publishers. At that date it was uncertain which, if any, of its provisions would actually be brought into force. I attempted to deal with the problem caused by this uncertainty by describing the principal provisions of the Act in an appendix to the main text with appropriate cross-references. To my dismay, just as I was completing the checking of the proofs, I learned that the first commencement order under the Act was being made and that certain sections would come into effect on 1 August 1997. I have endeavoured, with what success I am not quite sure, to take account of the order in both the appendix and the main text. I apologise for the inevitable inelegancies which this last-minute paper and paste job has caused.

As with the first edition I owe an immense debt of gratitude to many people. The staff of Butterworths have offered encouragement and helpful advice. My colleagues in Dundee, the sheriff clerk's staff there and the Tayside Police have been of considerable assistance. Mrs Pauline Meldrum, court liaison social worker in Dundee Sheriff Court for the City of Dundee Social Work Department, provided the social enquiry report for David Balfour. As in the case of her counterpart in Aberdeen who provided the equivalent report for the first edition, I cannot but be amazed at the powers of invention and imagination which she has displayed. Miss Lorna Fleming read most of the text from a student's point of view and made many useful comments.

It is appropriate that I should again acknowledge my debt to Sheriff Gordon for his editing of Renton and Brown's *Criminal Procedure according to the Law of Scotland*. The sixth edition which appeared so astonishingly soon after the passage of the 1995 legislation proved to be of as much assistance with this edition as its predecessor was with the first.

Mr Michael E Monro, who assisted me so greatly with the first edition, was persuaded to undertake the same thankless task for this edition also. He read the whole text apart from the appendix and was responsible for preparing all the defence forms for the first two chapters. Mr Alan W Kempton, procurator fiscal depute in Dundee, performed the same function from the prosecution side. He too read the whole text with the exception of the appendix and either prepared or procured all the prosecution and police forms. Both Mr Monro and Mr Kempton made countless suggestions for the improvement of the text. Time and again they prevented me from falling into serious error. I find it difficult to thank them both enough for all they have done.

Finally, I must express my gratitude to my wife for being prepared, over the months spent in preparation of this book, to share her life with me with my word processor.

No doubt, despite all the help which I have had, there will be errors and omissions in the text. For these I, of course, accept entire responsibility.

As with the first edition, the names of all persons (with the exception of that of Lord Mackay of Drumadoon who was Lord Advocate at the beginning of 1997 and whose name I have used in the indictment in the case of *David Balfour*) and places mentioned in the first two chapters are imaginary, and, that exception apart, have no relation to any person, living or dead.

I have attempted to state the law as it was at the end of April 1997 with a few later additions.

Alastair L Stewart
Sheriffs' Chambers
Sheriff Court House
Dundee

*July 1997*

# Contents

# List of forms

# Table of statutes

# Table of orders, rules and regulations

# Table of cases

# List of abbreviations

**Statutes**

| | |
|---|---|
| 1975 Act | Criminal Procedure (Scotland) Act 1975 (c 21) |
| 1984 Act | Mental Health (Scotland) Act 1984 (c 36) |
| 1993 Act | Prisoners and Criminal Proceedings (Scotland) Act 1993 (c 9) |
| 1995 Act | Criminal Procedure (Scotland) Act 1995 (c 46) |
| 1997 Act | Crime and Punishment (Scotland) Act 1997 (c 48) |

**Statutory instrument**

1996 Rules   Act of Adjournal (Criminal Procedure Rules) 1996, SI 1996/513

**Law reports**

| | |
|---|---|
| Adam | Adam's Justiciary Reports 1894–1919 |
| All ER | All England Law Reports 1936– |
| Arkley | Arkley's Justiciary Reports 1846–48 |
| Couper | Couper's Justiciary Reports 1868–85 |
| Crim App Rep | Criminal Appeal Reports (England) 1908– |
| Crim LR | Criminal Law Review (England) 1954– |
| Irv | Irvine's Justiciary Reports 1851–68 |
| JC | Justiciary Cases 1917– |
| QB | Law Reports, Queen's Bench Division (England) 1891–1901, 1952– (year precedes) |
| RTR | Road Traffic Reports 1970– |
| SCCR | Scottish Criminal Case Reports 1981– |
| SCCR Supp | Scottish Criminal Case Reports Supplement 1950–80 |
| SC (J) | Justiciary Cases in Session Cases 1907–16 |
| SLT | Scots Law Times 1893– |
| White | White's Justiciary Reports 1885–93 |
| WLR | Weekly Law Reports (England) 1953– |

**Books**

| | |
|---|---|
| Alison *Principles* | Archibald Alison *Principles of the Criminal Law of Scotland* (1832) (reprinted 1989) |
| Alison *Practice* | Archibald Alison *Practice of the Criminal Law of Scotland* (1833) (reprinted 1989) |
| *Gane and Stoddart* | C H W Gane and C N Stoddart *Criminal Procedure in Scotland: Cases and Materials* (2nd edn, 1994) |
| *Gordon* | G H Gordon *The Criminal Law of Scotland* (2nd edn, 1978) (Supplement 1984) |

| | |
|---|---|
| *Hume* | David Hume *Commentaries on the Law of Scotland, Respecting the Description and Punishment of Crimes* (2 vols, 1797) (reprinted 1986) |
| *Macdonald* | J H A Macdonald *The Criminal Law of Scotland* (5th edn, 1948) (reprinted 1986) |
| *Nicholson* | C G B Nicholson *The Law and Practice of Sentencing in Scotland* (2nd edn, 1992) |
| *Renton and Brown* | R W Renton and H H Brown *Criminal Procedure according to the Law of Scotland* (6th edn, 1996 by G H Gordon) |

# CHAPTER 1

# THE CASE OF DAVID BALFOUR

## HM ADVOCATE v DAVID BALFOUR: DETENTION, ARREST, JUDICIAL EXAMINATION AND COMMITTAL

At two o'clock in the morning of Saturday, 27 July 1996, John Henry Starr was in St Mary's Street, Duncairn outside the Flamingo Night Club when he was stabbed twice in the right arm. The precise circumstances of how this came about were to be the subject of considerable dispute at a later date. An ambulance was called and Mr Starr was taken to hospital, where his injuries were treated. The police had arrived at the scene just before the ambulance, and an officer took a brief statement from Mr Starr before the ambulance left. As his wounds were quite deep the doctor wished him to remain in hospital for at least the rest of the night, but Mr Starr was unwilling to do so and discharged himself.

The police made immediate investigations in the area of St Mary's Street, and about 2.20 am PC McIntyre detained a slightly built young man called David Balfour. David was aged nineteen. He had been in trouble with the law before but not for anything terribly serious. When he was seventeen he had been fined £25 in the sheriff court for possessing an offensive weapon (a piece of wood which he had picked up in the course of a skirmish between two groups of youths). Then, a year later, he had been fined £15 in the district court for breach of the peace. Only six weeks ago he had again appeared in the district court on a charge of breach of the peace. He had pleaded guilty, but the youth who was charged with him had pleaded not guilty. Trial had been fixed for the co-accused and sentence had been deferred on David until the trial date. He had been released on bail.

PC McIntyre told David that he was being detained under section 14 of the Criminal Procedure (Scotland) Act 1995 on suspicion of having assaulted John Starr by stabbing him a short time previously in St Mary's Street, and that he was not obliged to say anything other than to give his name and address. At that stage David said 'It was him or me'. He was then taken the short distance to Divisional Police Headquarters in John Street. There the appropriate forms (see pp 8, 9) were completed. David was told of his right to have a solicitor or any other named person informed of his detention, but said that he did not want to. This was not a very sensible thing for David to do, but he was not particularly bright and did not yet realise what a serious position he was in. He was then searched and his fingerprints were taken. In his left jacket pocket was found a penknife the blade of which bore reddish brown stains.

David was placed in a cell for about two hours and then two CID officers, DC Black and DC White, came to see him. They introduced themselves to him and told him that they were inquiring into the stabbing of John Starr about which he had been detained. They then asked David if he was willing to be interviewed 'on tape'. David said that he was, and the three of them went to one of the rooms which contained equipment for tape-recording interviews with suspects.

The tape of the interview was later transcribed, and it ran as follows:

Time injection 5.05 am

DC BLACK: The time is 5.07 am on Saturday 27 July 1996. I am DC Angus Black and this other detective officer present is DC Tom White, both of the CID, Tayside Police. At this time we are in interview room no 2 within the Divisional Police HQ, John Street, Duncairn. What is your full name?

ACCUSED: David Balfour.

DC BLACK: What is your date of birth?

ACCUSED: 23 November 1976.

DC BLACK: So that means you're nineteen, David?

ACCUSED: Yes.

DC BLACK: What's your occupation?

ACCUSED: Unemployed.

DC BLACK: And your address?

ACCUSED: 19 Gairn Street.

DC BLACK: And that's in Duncairn?

ACCUSED: Yes.

DC BLACK: Now, David, we're going to ask you some questions about an assault which happened outside the Flamingo in St Mary's Street about two o'clock this morning. You're not bound to answer any question, but if you do your answers will be tape-recorded and noted and may be used in evidence. Do you understand?

ACCUSED: Yes.

DC BLACK: Now, David, when you were detained by the uniformed officer, he says that you said 'It was him or me'. Do you agree with that?

ACCUSED: Yes.

DC BLACK: And when you were searched you had in your pocket a knife with what looked like blood on the blade. What do you have to say about that?

ACCUSED: This guy came at me so I used the knife in self-defence.

DC BLACK: Just a minute. Who's 'this guy'?

ACCUSED: I dinna ken his name except that his mates call him Starry.

DC BLACK: OK, so what happened?

ACCUSED: I was just walking along the street when he came at me with his hand up. I thought he was going to hit me. I minded I had the knife in my pocket, so I took it out. I only meant to frighten him, but he kept coming, so I hit him with it. I didnae mean to hurt him.

DC BLACK: What happened then?

ACCUSED: I ran off. The polis got me just a few minutes later.

DC BLACK: OK David, I'm now going to charge you, but before I do so I must caution you that you don't need to say anything in answer to the charge, but anything you do say will be noted and may be used in evidence. Do you understand that?

ACCUSED: Yes.

DC BLACK: All right then. The charge against you is that on 27 July 1996 in St Mary's Street, Duncairn outside the premises known as the Flamingo Night Club, you did assault John Henry Starr, unemployed, c/o Tayside Police, John Street, Duncairn, and stab him repeatedly on the arm with a knife or similar instrument to his severe injury. Do you understand the charge?

ACCUSED: Aye.

DC BLACK: Have you anything to say?

ACCUSED: It was self-defence.

DC BLACK: OK. This is DC Black. I'm terminating the interview with David
Balfour at 5.17 am on Saturday 27 July 1996.

Time injection: 5.15 am

DC Black then told David that he was now being arrested for the crime with
which he had just been charged. Another form was completed (see p 10). David
was again given the opportunity to have information about his arrest given to a
solicitor or any other named person, but again, foolishly, he declined. He was then
locked up in a cell until Tuesday morning. Normally he would have appeared in
Court on Monday, but, unfortunately for him, that was a local holiday, and there
was no court sitting.

On Tuesday he was taken to the sheriff court along with other persons who had
been arrested during the weekend. While in the cells at the court he received a
copy of a petition containing the charge against him together with a paper containing statements alleged to have been made by him to or in the presence of police
officers (see pp 11–13). He was told that he was entitled to see the duty solicitor.
By this time David had at last realised that he was in a serious position, and he
decided that he did want to see a solicitor. Thus it came about that he met
Margaret McKenzie, who was an associate with one of the bigger legal firms in
Duncairn and who had considerable experience of criminal cases in both the sheriff and district courts. When Miss McKenzie heard that David wished her to appear
for him she spoke to Jack Forbes, the procurator fiscal depute who was dealing
with custodies that day and asked him whether there was to be a judicial examination and whether the Crown was opposing bail. Mr Forbes answered both questions in the affirmative.

David had an interview with Miss McKenzie which lasted about fifteen minutes.
During that time he explained to her what had happened in the early hours of
Saturday morning. She said that, if what he had told her was true, he should plead
not guilty to the charges against him, and David agreed that he would do so. She
explained that, as he was on petition and not on a summary charge, he would not
actually make any plea when he first appeared in court that day. What would happen was that he would be taken before a sheriff for 'judicial examination'. There
he would be asked questions by the procurator fiscal. She advised him to answer
the questions as fully as possible. She explained self-defence in simple terms and
emphasised how important it was that he gave an account of what Starr had done,
and how afraid he had been that Starr was going to attack him. Miss McKenzie also
confirmed with David that the statements made by him to the police had been correctly recorded.

David asked if he would be able to get out on bail, and Miss McKenzie said that
she would apply for bail on his behalf, but that she had been told that bail was to
be opposed by the Crown. She obtained some details from David about his personal background and his previous criminal record. She asked him if he had a solicitor who would act for him at his trial. David said that he did not have any other
solicitor, and would she please be his lawyer? Miss McKenzie agreed and said that
she assumed that David would want to apply for legal aid. She produced a legal aid
form and filled it in on the basis of the information given to her by David who then
signed it (see pp 14, 15). At the same time she completed a bail application form
(see p 16).

About half an hour later David, now handcuffed to a policeman, was taken into
a small room which seemed to be very crowded. There was a big table on which

lay a tape recorder. At the far end of the table sat the sheriff. On his left was a woman wearing a gown (the sheriff clerk depute, Miss Grant), and on her left sat Miss McKenzie also wearing a gown. Opposite Miss McKenzie was a youngish man, who was similarly gowned (Jack Forbes, procurator fiscal depute). David was asked by Miss Grant if he was David Balfour and, having said that he was, he was told by the sheriff to sit down. He sat at the end of the table with Miss McKenzie on his right.

Miss McKenzie told the sheriff that she appeared for David, and that he 'made no plea or declaration'. Mr Forbes said that he wished to have David judicially examined. Miss Grant pressed the button to start the tape recorder running, and what now follows is the transcript of the proceedings at the judicial examination:

SHERIFF CLERK: Judicial examination of David Balfour in the presence of Sheriff Walter Scott at Duncairn Sheriff Court on 30 July 1996 commencing at 11.45 am.

SHERIFF: Mr Balfour, you are here for what is called a judicial examination, the purpose of which is to give you an opportunity to say anything which you may wish about the charge against you. Have you received a copy of a petition containing one charge?

ACCUSED: Yes, sir.

SHERIFF: Do you understand the charge?

ACCUSED: Yes.

SHERIFF: Have you also received a piece of paper which gives details of statements alleged to have been made by you to police officers?

ACCUSED: Yes.

SHERIFF: Have you had an opportunity of discussing all these matters with your solicitor?

ACCUSED: Yes.

SHERIFF: You are now going to be asked some questions by Mr Forbes, this gentleman sitting here, who is a procurator fiscal depute. You are not obliged to answer any of the questions, and you may consult with Miss McKenzie before deciding whether or not to answer any question. If you do answer a question, your answer will be recorded on the tape recorder which you see on the table in front of you. Evidence of your answers may be given at your trial. If you decide not to answer any question and, at your trial, you say anything which you could have said today in answer to that question but chose not to, then that may be commented on at your trial and may go against you. If in answering any question you disclose what appears to be a defence to the charge against you, the procurator fiscal must, so far as reasonably practicable, investigate that defence. Do you understand?

ACCUSED: Yes, sir.

SHERIFF: Yes, Mr Forbes.

PFD (PROCURATOR FISCAL DEPUTE): Obliged to your lordship. Is your full name David Balfour?

ACCUSED: Yes.

PFD: Is your date of birth 23 November 1976?

ACCUSED: Yes.

PFD: Are you employed?

ACCUSED: No.

PFD: Is your home address 19 Gairn Street, Duncairn?

ACCUSED: Yes.

PFD: Now, you have received a copy of a petition containing one charge. That states that on 27 July 1996 at about 2 am in St Mary's Street, Duncairn outside the premises known as the Flamingo Night Club, you did assault John Henry Starr, c/o Divisional Police Office, John Street, Duncairn, and did stab him repeatedly on the arm with a knife or similar instrument to his severe injury, and you did commit this offence while on bail, having been granted bail on 10 June 1996 at Duncairn District Court. Do you understand the charge?

ACCUSED: Yes, sir.

PFD: Do you deny the charge?

ACCUSED: Well, I did hit him with the knife, but it wasn't repeatedly, and I only did it because he was coming at me.

PFD: How many times did you strike him with the knife?

ACCUSED: Twice at the most.

PFD: You said that he was coming at you. Did he have anything in his hand?

ACCUSED: I thought he did, but I wasn't sure. I couldn't see very clearly as it was dark.

PFD: Do you have any further explanation or comment to make with regard to the matters in that charge?

ACCUSED: I thought he was going to attack me. I was scared. I was defending myself.

PFD: Do you deny being granted bail on 10 June 1996 at Duncairn District Court?

ACCUSED: No, sir.

PFD: Please now turn to the paper with the statements allegedly made by you. The first statement is said to have been made by you at 2.20 am in George Street, Duncairn when you were detained by PC McIntyre. Do you deny then saying: 'It was him or me'?

ACCUSED: I said that. It was true.

PFD: The second statement is alleged to have been made by you at Divisional Police Headquarters in Duncairn at about 5.10 am on the same day when you were being interviewed by DC Black and DC White. It is alleged that you said: 'This guy came at me so I used the knife in self-defence.' Do you deny saying that?

ACCUSED: No. I admit it.

PFD: It is alleged that you then said: 'I was just walking along the street when he came at me with his hand up. I thought he was going to hit me. I minded I had the knife in my pocket, so I took it out. I only meant to frighten him, but he kept coming, so I hit him with it. I didnae mean to hurt him.' Do you deny saying that?

ACCUSED: I'm not sure of the exact words, but I said something like that.

PFD: Do you have any comment which you wish to make about the circumstances in which you made these statements?

ACCUSED: What do you mean?

PFD: Well, do you want for instance to suggest that there was anything unfair about the way in which you came to make these statements?

ACCUSED: Oh, no.

PFD: Thank you, my lord. I have no further questions.

SHERIFF: Miss McKenzie, do you have any questions?

SOLICITOR: No thank you, my lord.

SHERIFF: That concludes this judicial examination.

SHERIFF CLERK: This judicial examination is concluded at 12.01 pm, Mary Grant, clerk of court.

Miss Grant then switched off the tape recorder, and the following exchange took place:

PFD: My lord, I move that the accused be committed for further examination.

SOLICITOR: My lord, I would ask that my client be released on bail. I place before the court a bail application.

PFD: Bail is opposed, my lord.

SHERIFF: I suggest, Miss McKenzie, that I hear the Crown's reasons for opposing bail and then I'll hear what you have to say. Mr Forbes.

PFD: Bail is opposed for two reasons. First, the accused is on bail already. Secondly, he has a conviction in September 1994 for an analogous offence, a contravention of the Prevention of Crime Act 1953, section 1.

SHERIFF: That is being in possession of an offensive weapon?

PFD: Yes, my lord. It would now be section 47 of the Criminal Law (Consolidation) (Scotland) Act 1995.

SHERIFF: Have you any information as to what the weapon was? And what sentence was imposed?

PFD: I am sorry, my lord, but I don't know what the weapon was. The sentence was a fine of £25.

SHERIFF: That suggests that the court did not take a terribly serious view of the offence, doesn't it?

PFD: Perhaps, my lord. In any event, there remains the fact that he is on bail already – bail granted only some six weeks ago.

SHERIFF: In the district court?

PFD: Yes. I have nothing further to add.

SOLICITOR: My lord, my client lives with his parents. He is unemployed at present but has recently worked as a builder's labourer and would hope to obtain a similar job in the near future. I cannot deny that my client is on bail at present, but I would suggest that your lordship should take into account that he has no previous convictions for breach of bail, and that the bail order concerned is from the district court. I understand that my client pleaded guilty to a breach of the peace charge there and sentence was deferred for the trial of a co-accused. It is perhaps rather surprising that he was not simply ordained to appear. So far as the offensive weapon charge is concerned, that was a bit of a tree branch which my client picked up in the course of a fracas involving two lots of youths. As your lordship has pointed out, the court did not apparently take a very serious view of it and there was no order for forfeiture of the weapon. In my submission there would be no prejudice to the public if your lordship were to grant bail.

SHERIFF: Mr Forbes, is there anything further that you wish to say?

PFD: No, my lord, except that if your lordship is prepared to grant bail the Crown would wish to have an additional condition in the form of a curfew. That would be to the effect that the accused does not leave his house between the hours of 10 pm and 7 am.

*Miss McKenzie spoke to David for a moment.*

SOLICITOR: My lord, my client has no objection to the proposed additional condition.

SHERIFF: In my opinion this is a case where I would not be justified in refusing bail. Stand up please, Mr Balfour. You will be committed for further examination and will be released on bail on the following conditions. There are the standard conditions which are, first, that you must attend court on any date when you are told to attend. Secondly, you must not commit any offence while on bail. Thirdly, you must not interfere with witnesses or in any way obstruct the course of justice. Fourthly, you must make yourself available for the purposes of enabling inquiries or a report to be made in the event of your being convicted of the offence with which you are charged. There is an additional condition to the effect that between now and the disposal of the case you must not leave your home between the hours of 10 pm and 7 am. Do you understand these conditions?

ACCUSED: Yes, sir.

SHERIFF: Do you accept them?

ACCUSED: Yes.

SOLICITOR: My lord, I have a legal aid application which I would ask your lordship to consider now.

SHERIFF: (*Having looked at form*) Yes, Miss McKenzie, in view of the fact that your client is unemployed, he is certainly entitled to legal aid. I shall grant your application.

David was then taken back to the court cell and, a short time later, was released, having been served with a full copy of the petition and with his bail order (see p 17). Before he left the court building he again saw Miss McKenzie, who told him that he would in due course receive a copy of the transcript of the judicial examination and, later, would be served with an indictment. She asked him to contact her when he received the transcript.

Some ten days later both David and Miss McKenzie received the copy of the transcript. David telephoned Miss McKenzie and made an appointment to see her. What happened at their meeting will be described below.

## Form 1: Detention Form A

**TAYSIDE POLICE**                                                              [11]
F.  *(b)* E Division                          *(c)*  Ref.No.  2012/96
                                         P.F. Ref.No.
**CRIMINAL PROCEDURE (SCOTLAND) ACT, 1995**
**STATEMENT  TO BE COMPLETED BY OFFICER DETAINING SUSPECT UNDER SECTION 14**    | A |
In terms of the Criminal Procedure (Scotland) Act 1995, Section 14,
I        Andrew McIntyre PC E 7592        (designation of detaining officer)
detained    David Balfour
of        19 Gairn Street, Duncairn
             **Telephone : NOT KNOWN** (address of suspect)
at *(d)*     02.20 (Time) on *(e)* 27 July 1996
at *(f)*     George Street, Duncairn                    (place detention commenced)

Has the suspect been detained on the same grounds in pursuance of any other enactment?    /NO
If yes, quote statute and section ...........................................................
Previous detention commenced at (time)........ on (date)................. and concluded at
(time)........ on (date).
Note cumulative detention time must not exceed 6 hours

At the time the above named was so detained I informed him that I was detaining him
under Section 14 of the Criminal Procedure (Scotland) Act 1995; that because
(State circumstances giving rise to suspicion)

        He answered description of man sought re stabbing nearby a short time before

I suspected that he had committed an offence punishable by imprisonment, namely
(State general nature of offence (g))

        Assault by stabbing

that the reason for his detention was to enable further investigations to be carried
out and that he was under no obligation to answer any question other than to give
his name and address. When detained the above named d̶e̶c̶l̶i̶n̶e̶d̶x̶t̶o̶x̶c̶o̶m̶m̶e̶n̶t / stated

        "It was him or me"

(If statement lengthy, use separate sheet(s); each sheet to be signed by detainee and officers concerned).
I thereafter took the above named to    Divisional Police HQ, Duncairn
and timed his arrival there at *(h)*    02.29 hrs

Signature of Detaining Officer *Andrew McIntyre PC 7592* Corroborating Officer *G Smith PSE 7841*
**PROCEDURE ON DETENTION UNDER SECTION 14**
Detention accepted by station or other officer: YES/N̶O̶    Signature *G. Smith PSE 7841*
Name____George Smith____    Number___PS E 7841___    Time_02.29__ hrs.
NOTE : If detention is accepted complete form as appropriate. If detention is rejected
proceed either to release or arrest suspect and complete form on page B or C).
**STATEMENT TO DETAINEE BY STATION OR OTHER OFFICER**
It has been reported to me that you have been detained under Section 14 of the Criminal
Procedure (Scotland) Act 1995. I must inform you that you are under no obligation to answer
any question other than to give your name and address.        Time *(k)* 02.31 hrs.
What is your name ?    David Balfour
What is your address ? 19 Gairn Street, Duncairn

            Telephone :
What is your date of birth ? *(l)* 23.11.76
The above named declined to comment

(If statement lengthy, use separate sheet(s); each sheet to be signed by detainee and officers concerned).

Signature of Station or Other Officer *G. Smith PSE 7841* Corroborating Officer *Andrew McIntyre PCE 7592*.

## Form 2: Detention Form B

**TAYSIDE POLICE**
Document Serial No:                                                                [11]

<u>DETAINEE NOT UNDER 16 YEARS OF AGE (ADULT)</u>

Name Of Detainee :   David Balfour

[ B ]

**INTIMATION TO SOLICITOR AND NAMED PERSON**
You are entitled to have intimation of your detention and of the place where you are being
detained sent to a solicitor and to one other person reasonably named by you.
Do you wish to have such intimation sent to a Solicitor?   *(m)* **NO**      Time *(n)* 02.36 hrs

If *YES*, name & address of named/duty solicitor (if solicitor not named, intimation to duty
solicitor to be offered)

            Telephone :
Name of person giving intimation                              (    ) Time *(s)*      hrs.
If no contact or more than one contact with solicitor, note reason ........................
........................................................................................

Do you wish to have such intimation sent to
one other person (ie. other than a Solicitor)?      *(q)* **NO**      Time *(r)* 02.36 hrs
If *YES*, name and address of person named

            , Telephone :
Name of person giving intimation                              (    ) Time *(s)*      hrs.

If no contact or more than one contact with such person, note reason ....................
........................................................................................
(If some delay in sending intimation to solicitor or other person is necessary in the
interest of the investigation, the prevention of crime or the apprehension of offenders,
specify the reason for such delay)   *(t)* .............................................
........................................................................................

You may now be questioned and searched, your fingerprints, biological samples and other
impressions may be taken.  You may be taken elsewhere for these processes to be completed.
                                                       Time *(u)* .02.40.hrs.
Signature of Station or Other Officer *G. Smith PS*   Corroborating Officer *Andrew McIntyre*
                                    E7841                                  PCE 7592.

**MOVEMENT OF DETAINEE**
The detainee was thereafter moved to (other police station, premises or place) ...........
..................................................................   Time ...............
For the purpose of ......................................................................
........................................................................................
Subsequent movements of the detainee to be recorded in the detaining officers notebook

**\*RELEASE FROM DETENTION**
You are being released from detention
and are now free to leave these premises                    Time *(v)*.............
Reason for release           \* Grounds for detention no longer exist.
                             \* Detainee has been detained for a period of six hours.

**\*ARREST** Up to now you have been detained under Section 14 of the Criminal Procedure
(Scotland) Act, 1995. You are now under arrest.            Time *(y)*............ 05.18 hrs

**FURTHER DETENTION UNDER ANOTHER ENACTMENT**
Up to now you have been detained under section 14 of the Criminal Procedure (Scotland) Act
1995. You are now to be detained under (specify statute and section) .....................
........................................................................................

Signature of Station or Other Officer *G. Smith PS*   Corroborating Officer *Andrew McIntyre*
                                    E7841                                  PCE 7592.

## Form 3: Arrest Form

**TAYSIDE POLICE**                                                      [12]
Document Serial No:
Date  27.7.96          <u>**ARREST - RIGHTS OF ACCUSED**</u>      Ref.No.  2012/96
NOTE: PARTS A and B are to be completed for all arrests.PART C is to be completed for accused NOT UNDER 16 years only (ADULT).
      PART D is to be completed for accused UNDER 16 years only (CHILD)

---

**A.** Name        David Balfour
   Date of birth  23.11.76

---

**B.** Informed of right to have solicitor informed                    Time 05.20 hrs.
      Solicitor requested ?                                            NO
      If YES, name & address of solicitor requested

         ,
         , ,
         , ,
         Telephone :
   Informed by (rank,no.& name)                                       Time        hrs.

      If contact not made, note reason .........................................................

      If solicitor attends, time of arrival ................. time of departure .............

---

**C.** Informed of right to have reasonably named person informed      Time 05.21 hrs.
      Reasonably named person requested?                               NO
      If YES, name and address of person requested
                                              ,                              ,
                                              ,                              ,

               Telephone :

   Informed by (rank,no.& name)                                       Time        hrs.

      If contact not made, note reason ..........................................................
      ...........................................................................................
      If some delay in sending intimation is necessary in the interest of the investigation,
      the prevention of crime or the apprehension of offenders, note reason for such delay
      ...........................................................................................

---

**D.** Informed re police duty to inform parent/guardian ..............................................
      If contact not made, note reason ...........................................................

      If parent/guardian attends, time of arrival ............::.. time of departure .............

      Name, if different from above ...............................................................
      (A parent/guardian MUST be permitted access to accused unless there is reasonable cause to suspect that he/she has been
      involved in the same alleged offence, in which case he/she MAY be permitted access.  The nature and extent of any access is
      subject to any restriction essential for furtherance of the investigation or well-being of the child).

      Duration of access                   From ............. To .............

      Nature and extent of access (if restricted note reason) ................................
      ...........................................................................................

      Note any request made by parent/guardian ..................................................
            Signature of Station Officer       *G. Smith  PsE 7841*
            Signature of Corroborating Officer  *Andrew McIntyre PcE7592.*

## Form 4: Petition

**F.10**

96500720

30 July 1996

UNTO THE HONOURABLE THE SHERIFF OF TAYSIDE, CENTRAL AND FIFE AT DUNCAIRN

THE PETITION OF George William Brown

PROCURATOR FISCAL OF COURT FOR THE PUBLIC INTEREST

HUMBLY SHEWETH

That from information received by the Petitioner, it appears, and he accordingly charges,

DAVID BALFOUR    (Unemployed)
19 GAIRN STREET
DUNCAIRN

Date of Birth:   23.11.76

that

on 27 July 1996 at St Mary's Street, Duncairn, outside the premises known as the Flamingo Night Club, **DAVID BALFOUR** did assault John Henry Starr, care of Divisional Police Office, John Street, Duncairn and did strike him repeatedly on the arm with a knife or similar instrument to his severe injury and he did commit this offence while on bail, having been granted bail on 10 June 1996 at Duncairn District Court.

*Jack Forbes*
Procurator Fiscal Depute

In order, therefore, that the said Accused may be dealt with according to Law,

MAY it please your Lordship to grant Warrant to Officers of Law to search for and apprehend the said Accused DAVID BALFOUR

and meantime, if necessary, to detain him in a police station house or other convenient place and to bring him for examination in respect of the above charge(s); thereafter grant Warrant to imprison him within the Prison of Duncairn therein to be detained for further examination or until liberated in due course of Law: Further, to grant Warrant to search the person, repositories, and domicile of the said Accused, and the house or premises in which he may be found, and to secure, for the purpose of precognition and evidence, all writs, evidents, and articles found therein tending to establish guilt or participation in the crime(s) foresaid, and for that purpose to make patent all shut and lockfast places; and also to grant Warrant to cite Witnesses for precognition and to make production for the purposes foresaid of such writs, evidents, and articles pertinent to the case as are in their possession: Further, to recommend to the Judges of other Counties and Jurisdictions to grant the Warrant of Concurrence necessary for enforcing that of your Lordship within their respective territories; or to do further or otherwise as to your Lordship may seem meet.

According to Justice, &c.

*Jack Forbes*
Procurator Fiscal Depute

## Form 5: Petition warrant

DUNCAIRN:   30 July 1996. -The Sheriff having considered the foregoing Petition, grants Warrant to Officers of Law to search for, apprehend, and bring for examination the said Accused DAVID BALFOUR and meantime, if necessary, to detain him in a police station or other convenient place, as also to search, secure, and cite for precognition and to open shut and lockfast places, all as craved: Further, recommends Judges of other Counties and Jurisdictions to grant any Warrant of Concurrence necessary for enforcing this Warrant within their respective territories.

Walter Scott.

For further
Examination                                      19  .-The Sheriff having again considered this Petition, and the said Accused

No
Declaration

having intimated that           do           not desire to emit a Declaration, on the motion of the Procurator Fiscal, grants Warrant to imprison the said Accused in the Prison of           therein to be detained for further examination.

For further
Examination

                                      19  .-The Sheriff having again considered this Petition and the Declaration of the Accused

Declaration

on the motion of the Procurator Fiscal, grants Warrant to imprison the said Accused in the Prison of therein to be detained for further examination.

Bail

                          19  .-The Sheriff, on the motion of the Agent of the said Accused and of consent of the Procurator Fiscal, admits the said Accused to bail, and grants Warrant for liberation from Prison on                          finding Caution for further examination or trial in common form, under the penalty of £ sterling.

For trial

                          19  .-The Sheriff having again considered this Petition, on the motion of the Procurator Fiscal grants Warrant to imprison the said Accused

in the Prison of                                      , therein to be detained until liberated in due course of Law.

For trial

                          19  .-The Sheriff having again considered this Petition and letter in terms of Section 76 of the Criminal Procedure (Scotland) Act 1995, granted by the Agent of the said Accused

Letter under
Section 76

No
Declaration

and the said Accused having intimated that           do           not desire to emit a Declaration, on the motion of the Procurator Fiscal grants Warrant to imprison the said Accused in the Prison of therein to be detained until liberated in due course of Law.

For trial

                          19  .-The Sheriff having again considered this Petition, Declaration of the said Accused

Letter under
Section 76

and letter in terms of Section 76 of the Criminal Procedure (Scotland) Act, 1995, granted by the Agent of the said Accused, on the motion of the Procurator Fiscal grants Warrant to imprison the said Accused in the Prison of                          , therein to be detained until liberated in due course of Law.

Declaration

*Form 6: Extrajudicial statement by accused*

Criminal Procedure (Scotland) Act 1995, Section 36(3)

Extrajudicial statement allegedly made by

(Name):          David Balfour

(Address):       19 Gairn Street
                 Duncairn

to or in the hearing of Officers of Police, namely the
officers undermentioned

---

Date(s), Time(s) and     At 2.20 am, on 27 July 1996 in George Street, Duncairn,
Place(s) made            when detained by PC McIntyre, he said:

"It was him or me"

At Divisional Police Headquarters, in Duncairn, at about
5.10 am on 27 July 1996 when being interviewed by
DC Black in connection with an assault by stabbing John
Henry Starr, care of Divisional Police Headquarters,
Duncairn on 27 July 1996 in St Mary's Street, Duncairn
he said:

"This guy came at me so I used the knife in self-
defence."

"I was just walking along the street when he came at me
with his hand up.  I thought he was going to hit me.
I minded I had the knife in my pocket, so I took it out.
I only meant to frighten him, but he kept coming so I
hit him with it.  I didnae mean to hurt him."

*Freddie Kempton.*

Procurator Fiscal Depute

*Form 7: SLAB application form for legal aid in solemn criminal proceedings*

### SCOTTISH LEGAL AID BOARD
APPLICATION TO THE COURT FOR LEGAL AID IN
SOLEMN CRIMINAL PROCEEDINGS
OR UNDER SECTIONS 23(1)(b) AND 30(1) OF
THE LEGAL AID (SCOTLAND) ACT 1986

## SOLEMN

**PART A - THE APPLICANT**

1. Applicant's personal legal aid reference number (if known)

2. Applicant's National Insurance number (if known)          Y Z 3 6 8 4 2 1 B

3. ✓ Male          Female          4. ✓ Single          Married          Divorced          Widowed

5. ✓ Mr          Mrs          Miss          Ms          *Enter below any other title preferred for use in correspondence*

6. Applicant's forename(s)          DAVID

7. Applicant's surname          BALFOUR

    **PLEASE NOTE:** The information asked for in questions 8-12 is needed so that we can be sure we
    never confuse your records with those of someone else having the same name.

8. Applicant's surname at birth if different from surname above          9. Maiden surname of applicant's mother
                                                                          STEVENSON

10. Date of   *Day   Month   Year*        11. Age last          12. Place of   *Town, city or district*
    birth     2 3 | 1 1 | 1 9 7 6         birthday   1 9       birth          DUNCAIRN

13. Usual home address
    *Use a separate line for each part of the*          19 Gairn Street
    *address, just as if you were addressing an*        DUNCAIRN
    *envelope. Please include the postcode to*
    *ensure that mail reaches you as soon as*
    *possible.*
                                          14. Postcode          DU10   6RT

**PART B - THE CASE**   *To be completed by the solicitor*

1. The court is the        District Court                                  2. Procurator Fiscal's Reference
                      ✓   Sheriff Court   at   DUNCAIRN                        9 6 5 0 0 7 2 0
                           High Court

3. Case category   Please say how many charges have been brought against the applicant under each of the following categories:
                   e.g for two charges of assault - 2 Assault

|   1 Assault | Attempted Murder | Breach of the Peace | Criminal Justice (Scotland) Act |
|---|---|---|---|
| Culpable Homicide | Drugs offences | Embezzlement | Fraud |
| Housebreaking | Murder | Police(Scotland) Act | Possession of offensive weapon |
| Road Traffic | Sexual offences | Theft of motor vehicle | |
| Theft | Robbery | Other (specify) | |

4. Names of any co-accused          None

5. Has the applicant previously applied for legal aid in this case?          Yes          ✓ No
                                                                                       *Legal aid case reference number*

    If Yes, please state the legal aid case reference number (if known)
    Please explain why another application for legal aid is now being made:

6. Has the applicant any rights or facilities which might assist in the defence of
   this case? *e.g. from insurers, employer, trade union, motoring organisation, etc.*          Yes          ✓ No
   If Yes, please give details and explain why an application has been made for legal aid.

## PART C - FINANCIAL STATEMENT

The court has to decide if you can meet the cost of your case without undue hardship to yourself or your dependants. Full information must be given about your own means. You do not have to say anything about the means of your spouse or anyone else, but you should say if someone is getting a state benefit for you.

**EMPLOYMENT STATUS**

1.  employed    ✓ unemployed    self-employed
    student      company director    retired

**CAPITAL (To the nearest pound)**

2. Cash (coin, banknotes, cheques)    £..............
3. Money in Bank    £..............
   Building Society    £..............
4. Shares in    £..............
5. a. Land at    £..............
   b. House (other than your main house)
      at    £..............
   c. Timeshare at    £..............
6. Loan secured over above property
   owed to..............
   £..............
7. Other capital  *Say what this is*
   ..............
   ..............   £..............
   £..............
8. Money due by applicant (e.g. expenses
   regularly met from savings)
   *Say what these are*
   ..............   £..............
   ..............   £..............

**PERSONS DEPENDENT ON APPLICANT**

9. Do you support a spouse?    ☐ Yes  ☑ No
10. Number of dependent children under 11    ☐
11. Number of dependent children aged 11 to 15    ☐
12. Number of dependent children aged 16 or 17    ☐
13. Number of dependants aged 18 or over    ☐

**WEEKLY INCOME (from all sources)**

14. Child Benefit    £..............
15. Any other state benefits    *Say what these are*
    a. Job Seekers Allowance    £ 35.00
    b. ..............    £..............
16. Address of benefit office
    Thistle Street
    Duncairn
17. Pay or Sick Pay from work (including overtime, commission,
    bonuses, but after deducting tax, National Insurance, etc.)    £ Nil
18. Name and address of any employer(s)
    ..............
    ..............
19. Drawings from business if self-employed or in partnership    £ Nil
20. Student grant    £ Nil
21. Money from any other source including maintenance    £ Nil
    *Say what this is.*

**TOTAL WEEKLY INCOME**    £ 35.00

**WEEKLY PAYMENTS DUE BY APPLICANT**

22. Rent or Board and Lodgings    £ 10.00
23. Mortgage (including any endowment or life policies linked
    to the mortgage)    £ Nil
24. Council Tax/Community Charge    £..............
25. Maintenance paid to
    (name)..............    £   "
    (name)..............    £   "
26. Other payments due to be made    *Say what these are*
    a. Hire Purchase Agreement    £ 5.00
    b. ..............    £..............

**TOTAL WEEKLY EXPENDITURE**    £ 15.00

## PART D - DECLARATION BY APPLICANT  *IF YOU KNOWINGLY MAKE A FALSE STATEMENT YOU MAY BE PROSECUTED*

I declare that the information given in this application is true and complete to the best of my knowledge and belief. I give my permission for the Scottish Legal Aid Board to make enquiries of any other persons or bodies as it may consider necessary in relation to this application. I authorise such other persons or bodies to provide such information as may be required by the Board. I apply for legal aid and wish the solicitor named below to act for me.

Signature of applicant  *David Balfour*    Date signed  30.7.96

## PART E - DETAILS OF SOLICITOR ACTING (PLEASE PRINT)

1. Practitioner's
   code number   5 | 9 | 6 | 3 | 4 | 1

2. Branch
   code   –

3. Your reference   MEM

Name   MARGARET E. McKENZIE

Firm   Messrs. D. Russell & Co.,

Address  4 Exchequer Street
         DUNCAIRN
         DX DU33

Postcode  DY12 7RT

### DECLARATION BY SOLICITOR

4. I am giving criminal legal aid until
   this application is determined, by
   virtue of the automatic legal aid
   provisions of section 22 of the Legal
   Aid (Scotland) Act 1986.    Yes    No

   I confirm that I have agreed to act on behalf
   of the applicant if legal aid is granted.

   *Margaret McKenzie*
   Signature of solicitor

   30.7.96    Date

## PART F - DECISION OF COURT

✓ Legal aid granted for solemn proceedings

Legal aid granted under section 23(1)(b)
*Summary proceedings, where, following conviction, the court
is considering a first custodial sentence for the applicant*    Legal aid refused

Legal aid granted under section 30(1)
*Contempt of Court proceedings*

Clerk of Court  ..............

Date of Decision  30.7.96

## Form 8: Bail petition

SHERIFFDOM OF  TAYSIDE, CENTRAL & FIFE AT DUNCAIRN

The Petition of  DAVID BALFOUR
presently a prisoner in the Prison of Duncairn


HUMBLY SHEWETH
that on 30th July,       1996, the Petitioner was committed to the Prison of
Perth,    therein to be detained (for further examination) till liberated in
due course of law on a Petition at the instance of the Procurator Fiscal of
Court, charging him with the crime of
assault to severe injury committed while on bail


The said crime is      bailable and the Petitioner is innocent of it

May it therefore please your Lordship to grant warrant for the Petitioner's
liberation, so far as detained on said charge on his finding bail to the
satisfaction of the Clerk of Court on such conditions as your Lordship shall
appoint.

According to Justice
*Macqoub McKenzie*
Solicitor
Agent for Petitioner.

A.  1)    DUNCAIRN,
          Having considered the foregoing Petition and heard the Petitioner's
      Solicitor and the Procurator Fiscal Depute thereon finds the crime with which
      the Petitioner is charged bailable and Grants Warrant for his liberation on
      the conditions specified in the separate bail order attached hereto, said
      conditions having been accepted by the Petitioner.


                                                    Sheriff.


    2)    DUNCAIRN,
          Having considered the foregoing Petition and heard the Petitioner's
      Solicitor and the Procurator Fiscal Depute thereon.  Refuses to admit the
      Petitioner to Bail.


                                                    Sheriff.


    3)    DUNCAIRN,
          Having considered the foregoing Petition and heard the Petitioner's
      Agent and the Procurator Fiscal Depute thereon finds the crime with which
      the Petitioner is charged bailable and Grants Warrant for his liberation on
      his acceptance before the Court of the conditions specified in terms of
      separate bail order appended hereto, said conditions not having been
      accepted by the Petitioner.


                                                    Sheriff.

Form 9: Bail order granting release

POLICE NO: 2012/96
PF REF NO: 96500720

UNDER THE CRIMINAL PROCEDURE (SCOTLAND) ACT 1995

DUNCAIRN SHERIFF COURT

DATE OF ORDER      30-JULY-96

ACCUSED      DAVID BALFOUR

DATE OF BIRTH      23-NOV-76

ADDRESS      19 GAIRN ROAD    Citation to appear at any diet
               DUNCAIRN        relating to the offence(s)
                                    charged and any other document
                                    or intimation shall be sent
                                    to this address

OFFENCE(S)      ASSAULT TO SEVERE INJURY COMMITTED WHILE ON BAIL

The Court granted bail and imposed the following conditions namely:-

(a)    That the Accused appears at the appointed time at every diet, including every continuation of a diet relating to the offence(s) charged of which due notice is given.

(b)    That the Accused does not commit an offence while on bail.

(c)    That the Accused does not interfere with witnesses or otherwise obstruct the course of justice in relation to this case.

(d)    That the Accused be available for the purpose of enabling inquiries or a report to be made to assist the court in dealing with this case.

(e)    That the Accused does not leave his home between the hours of 10 p.m. and 7 a.m.

The above conditions having been accepted, the Court authorised the Accused's release.

*Mary Groat*

CLERK OF COURT

CERTIFICATE THAT COPY HAS BEEN GIVEN TO ACCUSED

I ACCEPT THE FOREGOING CONDITIONS, AND ACKNOWLEDGE RECEIPT OF A COPY OF THIS ORDER.

ACCUSED

I certify that a copy of the foregoing Bail Order was given to the said Accused by me on this date.

SIGNATURE AND DESIGNATION          Date

## HM ADVOCATE v DAVID BALFOUR: PREPARATION BY CROWN, INDICTMENT, PREPARATION BY DEFENCE

Because David had been allowed bail, there was no immediate urgency about proceeding with preparation of the prosecution case against him, as there would have been had he been remanded in custody. In the latter event strict time limits would have applied, as is described in chapter 4.

At this stage the procurator fiscal's office did not have full witness statements but only a summary of the evidence made by the police. The police were therefore instructed by Mr Forbes to obtain full statements from the witnesses, and this they did. When the full statements had been sent to the fiscal's office Mr Forbes read through them. He was satisfied that there was a good case, and instructed that precognitions of the witnesses should be obtained. A precognition officer in the fiscal's office then interviewed each witness and produced a full precognition of the case. This, with a copy of the petition, was in due course sent to the Crown Office in Edinburgh, with a request for instructions from Crown Counsel.

In the Crown Office the precognition was read by one of the advocates-depute. He considered that this was a case which should be prosecuted. Although a knife had been used and the injuries inflicted were not trivial, the advocate-depute did not consider that the crime was likely to attract a higher sentence than a sheriff could impose. He accordingly marked the papers 'Proceed sheriff and jury', rather than instructing indictment in the High Court.

These instructions were returned to the fiscal's office in Duncairn on 20 December 1996, where they again landed on the desk of Jack Forbes. Mr Forbes prepared an indictment containing a charge which was virtually the same as that in the petition. The indictment had appended to it a list of productions, the documentary ones being referred to as 'productions' and the others being called 'labels'. There was also appended to the indictment a list of witnesses. Mr Forbes confirmed that the case should be put down for the jury sitting at Duncairn Sheriff Court beginning on Monday 10 March 1997 with a first diet on 20 February. He gave instructions for a copy of the indictment and its accompanying lists together with a notice showing David's previous convictions to be served on David in good time for that sitting.

On 17 January 1997 a policeman called at David's house. David was at home – he had unfortunately not managed to obtain a job yet – and the officer handed him the service copy of the indictment, the annexed lists and the notice of previous convictions, together with a notice calling on him to appear at the sheriff court for the first diet on 20 February 1997 at 10 am and for trial at 10 am on 10 March 1997. (See pp 23–27 for copies of the papers which David received and p 28 for a copy of the execution of service and citation.) The officer also served on David a statement of uncontroversial evidence relating to the evidence of the doctor who had treated John Starr in hospital (see p 29). This stated the injuries which Mr Starr had received and said that they had been caused by a sharp pointed instrument, such as a knife. Also on 17 January Miss McKenzie received from the procurator fiscal a copy of the indictment and of all the other papers served on David together with copies of the Crown documentary productions. The forensic scientists' report (Production 4) stated that the stains on David's knife (Label 1) were human blood and that it was of the same group as that of a sample taken from Mr Starr (Label 2). This came as no surprise to Miss McKenzie. She was glad to receive the indictment such a long time before the first diet. She had just been about to write to the procurator fiscal asking to be provided with a provisional list of witnesses. The fiscal would normally have complied with such a request once he had received instructions from Crown Office.

David had already appeared again in the district court for his deferred sentence. The justice had taken a lenient view of the breach of the peace and had fined David £25, payable at £5 per fortnight.

As mentioned above, David had also already had a meeting with Miss MacKenzie a short time after service of the transcript of the judicial examination. At that meeting she took a full statement from him about himself and about the events of 27 July. She asked him if there were any witnesses who might be able to give evidence to help him, and David gave her the name of his friend Alan Stewart, who had been with him that night. David did not know Alan's address, so Miss McKenzie told him to see Alan and get him to arrange an appointment with her. She told David that, after the indictment had been served, she would get statements from the prosecution witnesses and would then see him again. On the basis of the statement which David had given to her Miss McKenzie prepared a precognition. This is it:

### Precognition of David Balfour

My full name is David Balfour. I am unemployed. I live with my parents at 19 Gairn Street, Duncairn. I am nineteen years old (dob 23/11/76).

I have one conviction for possessing an offensive weapon. That was in September 1994. I was fined £25. I have two district court convictions for breach of the peace. I was fined £15 in 1995, and in June of this year I had sentence deferred for the trial of a co-accused. I am due to go back to court for that in November.

I left school when I was sixteen. I was unemployed for about six months and then got a job as a builder's labourer. I was made redundant at the end of last year (1995). I have not had a job since then. My only income is jobseeker's allowance.

I don't go out much – only at weekends.

On Friday 26 July 1996 I went out for the evening. I was alone. I went to the Red House pub about 9 pm and there I met Alan Stewart, a friend of mine I know from playing in the same football team a couple of years ago. I don't know Alan's address. In the Red House I had about three pints of lager. Alan had the same. We stayed there till closing time at 11 pm and then went to Sandy's Night Club in High Street. We stayed there till about 1.50 am. I had another three pints to drink there. I was not drunk, just happy. I had more to drink than usual that night. I usually can't afford to drink very much, but my dad had given me some money from a win he had had on the lottery. Alan had more to drink than me. I should say he was drunk.

We left Sandy's at 1.50 am and started to walk to St Mary's Street where there is a taxi rank. As we approached the Flamingo two men came out. I knew one as 'Starry'. I had met him a few times in pubs. I didn't like him much. He is very loud mouthed and has a reputation as a hard man. I know that he got the jail for assault a couple of years ago. I think that he has other convictions. I didn't know the other man. Starry saw me and started running towards me. He was shouting. It was something like: 'I'll get you, you wee bastard.' I don't know why he would want to attack me. I hardly know him. He had his right hand up in the air as if he was going to strike me. I don't know if he had anything in his hand. I was scared. I didn't think of running away. He was too close. I remembered that I had a knife in my pocket. It was just a penknife. I always carry a penknife. It's just a habit. I pulled out the knife and opened it. I just meant to scare him. He kept coming at me and I struck out with the knife at his arm. I think I hit him twice. He fell down. I ran away. I don't know what happened to Alan.

I didn't know what to do. I still had the knife. I sort of wiped it and put it back in my pocket. I walked about for a bit. I saw the police. One of them yelled at me. I tried to run away but he caught me. I said to the police 'It was him or me.' I was taken to the police station where they found the knife in my pocket. I was interviewed by two detectives and I told them that I had stabbed Starry but that it had been in self-defence.

As soon as she had received her copy of the indictment Miss McKenzie instructed the inquiry agents whom she used as precognoscers to obtain precognitions from the Crown witnesses. She asked them to obtain a precognition from the hospital doctor as well as the other witnesses. She had reservations about accepting his evidence as contained in the statement of uncontroversial evidence which had been served on David along with the indictment. She thought that he might be able to provide evidence favourable to the defence. Therefore, in order to preserve David's position, she served on the procurator fiscal a notice challenging the facts contained in the statement of uncontroversial evidence (see p 30). Miss McKenzie did not, however, instruct the inquiry agents to precognosce the forensic scientists. She was prepared to accept that their report was accurate and did not consider that they would be able to provide any additional evidence. A little less than three weeks after instructing the inquiry agents Miss McKenzie received the precognitions. The one which concerned her most was, of course, that of Mr Starr. It was in the following terms:

### Precognition of John Henry Starr

My full name is John Henry Starr. I am unemployed. I live at 76 Riverside Terrace, Duncairn. I am 26 years old. I have a criminal record. I have sixteen previous convictions including some for assault. I am not prepared to give you details.

On 26 July 1996 I went to the Flamingo Night Club about 11 pm. I had previously been drinking in several different pubs. I had had about eight pints. In the Flamingo I had another couple of drinks. I can't remember what I had to drink. I met up with Bill Brown (witness). At about 2 am we decided to go home. We went out of the door of the Flamingo into the street. I saw two youths coming towards us. I knew one of them by sight, but I do not know his name (accused). I waved at him. I was being friendly. Suddenly, for no reason, he rushed at me, and I saw that he had a knife in his hand. I put my arm up to protect my face and he stabbed me in the arm. He stabbed me twice. I did not realise I had been stabbed until I saw the blood. I fell to the ground. An ambulance took me to hospital. My injuries were cleaned and stitched. The doctor wanted me to stay in hospital, but I refused and got a taxi home. I have had a bit of trouble with my arm since then. It is stiff and it aches at times. I have difficulty moving my fingers.

I don't know why the accused should attack me. I have nothing against him. I would recognise him again.

**Note.** *This witness is a heavily built man. He was not inclined to be co-operative. I would describe his attitude as truculent.*

The precognition from William Brown gave a similar account of events. The note appended to it indicated that he also had not been a willing witness. He too admitted to having a criminal record but was coy about disclosing details.

The precognition from the doctor at the hospital indicated that the two stab wounds to Starr's arm had been deep, penetrating the muscle. They were in the front of the arm. He had lost a substantial quantity of blood, but there had been no reason to think that complications would be likely. Starr had not returned to the hospital since the incident. The doctor's opinion was that a good deal of force would have been required to make such deep wounds with a small knife. The injury could equally well have been caused by the knife being lunged at the arm, or by the arm being brought down onto the knife. The doctor also said that Starr had been fairly heavily under the influence of alcohol when admitted to hospital and that he had been truculent and uncooperative. The terms of this precognition confirmed Miss McKenzie's view that the doctor should be a witness at the trial.

In the case of the police officers Miss McKenzie had, following normal practice, required to obtain the permission of the Chief Constable to have them precognosced. The precognition from PC McIntyre told how he had received a description of Starr's alleged attacker over his personal radio, had seen a man answering that description (the accused) about a quarter of a mile from the locus at about 2.20 am, had given chase and had detained the accused, who had said: 'It was him or me.'

The precognitions from DC Black and DC White gave an account of their interview with David as contained in the transcript reproduced at pages 2, 3.

Miss McKenzie arranged a further appointment with David. She told him what the precognitions of the Crown witnesses said. David agreed that he was not disputing the terms of the forensic scientists' report. Miss McKenzie advised David that he should not agree the medical evidence and David accepted her advice, thus formally instructing her not to withdraw the challenge to the notice of uncontroversial evidence. Miss McKenzie then asked David some searching questions about his own statement. David stuck to his story. Miss McKenzie had heard nothing from David about his witness, Alan Stewart, and she asked David if he had seen him. David said he had not yet been able to find him. Miss McKenzie emphasised the importance of continuing the search. 'You see, David, even though you, as the accused, don't need corroboration, it always helps if you have someone to support your evidence.'

Miss McKenzie then went on to talk about another very important matter. 'As you know, David, I'm a solicitor. Now, I would be perfectly entitled to appear for you at your trial, as solicitors are allowed to take jury trials in the sheriff court. But your case is a serious one, and I was thinking that we might be better to bring counsel in.' 'You mean a QC?' 'Well, not actually a QC, who is a senior member of the Bar. I was thinking of a junior advocate. I think you would get legal aid approval for counsel all right. What do you say?' David agreed that counsel should be brought in.

Miss McKenzie immediately applied to the Scottish Legal Aid Board for permission to employ junior counsel, using the appropriate form (see pp 31, 32) and enclosing a copy of the indictment. Her application was granted a week later and she then telephoned Edinburgh and spoke to Mr McTaggart, the advocates' clerk of whose 'stable' Robert MacGregor was a member. Mr MacGregor, who had been a member of the Faculty of Advocates for six years, was free to come to Duncairn for the trial on 10 March. He was going to be in Duncairn on other business shortly before the first diet, so Miss McKenzie arranged for him to have a consultation with David then. She prepared a full set of instructions for Mr MacGregor and sent it off to him in Parliament House, Edinburgh. The instructions consisted of: the indictment with its attached lists; the schedule of previous convictions; the precognitions of the Crown witnesses and David's own precognition; and the copy of the forensic scientists' report. The covering letter confirmed the arrangements for the consultation and attendance at the trial. It also stated that the case was on legal aid.

A few days before the date of the consultation Miss McKenzie saw Alan Stewart, David's witness with whom he had at last succeeded in making contact. Miss McKenzie produced a precognition from his statement. It supported David's evidence in all essentials. About the same time Miss McKenzie received from the procurator fiscal a draft joint minute agreeing the terms of the forensic scientists' report (see p 33).

The consultation took place on 17 February in Miss McKenzie's office. Mr MacGregor went through David's account of events with him and questioned him closely about it. David stuck to his story. Mr MacGregor was particularly anxious to find out whether David could make any suggestion about why Starr should attack him. Eventually David conceded that, the last time he had seen Starr in a pub, he had had a bit of an altercation with him – and he had given Starr some cheek. Starr had been very annoyed with him, but had taken no action at that time, just saying that he would get him later. This would have been about two weeks before 27 July.

Before the end of the consultation Mr MacGregor obtained formal instructions from David that a special defence of self-defence should be lodged on his behalf together with a notice that the defence intended to attack Starr's character. Counsel also confirmed that the evidence of the hospital doctor who had treated Starr should not be agreed. However, he did accept that the terms of the scientists' report could be agreed.

Following the consultation Miss McKenzie instructed a sheriff officer to cite Alan Stewart to attend as a defence witness on 10 March.

*Form 10: Indictment against David Balfour*

**SHERIFF AND JURY**

First Diet:   20 February 1997 at 10 am

Trial Diet:   10 March 1997 at 10 am

DAVID BALFOUR, born 23.11.76, whose domicile of citation has been specified as 19 Gairn Street, Duncairn,

you are Indicted at the instance of The Right Honourable THE LORD MACKAY OF DRUMADOON, Her Majesty's Advocate, and the charge against you is that

on 27 July 1996 in St Mary's Street, Duncairn, District of Duncairn, you DAVID BALFOUR did assault John Henry Starr, care of Tayside Police Divisional Headquarters, John Street, Duncairn, and did stab him repeatedly in the arm with a knife or similar instrument to his severe injury and you did commit this offence while on bail, having been granted bail on 10 June 1996 at Duncairn District Court.

**BY AUTHORITY OF HER MAJESTY'S ADVOCATE**

*Freddie Kempton.*

**PROCURATOR FISCAL DEPUTE**

*Form 11: List of productions*

LIST OF PRODUCTIONS

| | | |
|---|---|---|
| PRO NO | 1 | Transcript of Proceedings at Judicial Examination and Execution of Service |
| | 2 | Transcript of Interview at Police Office, Duncairn on 27 July 1996 and execution of service |
| | 3 | Medical Records |
| | 4 | Joint Report by Kenneth Duff, Forensic Scientist, CChem, MRSC and Fiona McDougall, Forensic Scientist, BSc (Hons), MSC, both care of Police Forensic Science Laboratory, Tayside Police Divisional Headquarters, Duncairn, dated 20 December 1996 and notice is hereby given in terms of Section 281(2) of the Criminal Procedure (Scotland) Act 1995 that the Crown intends to call only said Kenneth Duff to give evidence in respect of this joint report |
| | 5 | Extract Minute containing Bail Order |
| LABEL NO | 1 | Knife |
| | 2/3 | Blood Samples |
| | 4 | Tape |

## Form 12: List of witnesses

LIST OF WITNESSES

1. JOHN HENRY STARR,
   care of Tayside Police Divisional Headquarters, John Street, Duncairn

2. WILLIAM BROWN,
   3 North Street, Duncairn

3. JOHN WATSON, MB, ChB,
   care of Royal Infirmary, Duncairn

4. ANDREW MCINTYRE, Constable E7592,
   Tayside Police Divisional Headquarters,
   John Street, Duncairn

5. ANGUS BLACK, Detective Constable,
   Tayside Police Divisional Headquarters,
   John Street, Duncairn

6. THOMAS JAMES WHITE, Detective Constable,
   Tayside Police Divisional Headquarters,
   John Street, Duncairn

7. KENNETH DUFF, Forensic Scientist,
   care of Police Forensic Science Laboratory, Tayside Police Divisional Headquarters, John Street, Duncairn

8. FIONA MCDOUGALL, Forensic Scientist,
   care of Police Forensic Science Laboratory, Tayside Police Divisional Headquarters, John Street, Duncairn

## Form 13: Notice of previous convictions

F.14

DAVID BALFOUR, within designed   TAKE NOTICE that in the event of your being convicted under the indictment to which this notice is attached, it is intended to place before the Court the following previous conviction(s) applying to you.

| Date | Place of Trial | Court | Offence | Sentence |
|------|----------------|-------|---------|----------|
| 1994 11 February | Duncairn | Sheriff | Con. Prevention of Crime Act 1953, Section 1 | Fined £25 |
| 1995 8 March | Duncairn | District | Breach of the Peace | Fined £15 |
| 1996 10 June | Duncairn | District | Breach of the Peace | Sentence Deferred until 4 October 1996 |

Date ...15/1/97............   Procurator Fiscal *depute*.... *Freddie Kempton*.

## Form 14: Notice to accused to appear

F37/3                                                                96500720

**NOTICE TO ACCUSED TO APPEAR**

Under the Criminal Procedure (Scotland) Act 1995

**NOTICE TO ACCUSED IN TERMS OF SECTION 66**

To:   DAVID BALFOUR, 19 Gairn Street, Duncairn

TAKE NOTICE THAT YOU MUST APPEAR at the Sheriff Court, Duncairn on 20 February 1997 at 10.00 am for a first diet and on 10 March 1997 at 10.00 am for a diet of trial at which you will be required to answer to the indictment to which this Notice is attached.

Served on the .17.th........ day of .January..1997...........
by me .John..F..Boyd..D.H.Q..Duncairn..................
by .handing..it..personally..to..said..David..Balfour....
.......................................................

..........John..F..Boyd...PC..E.9612....
(Signature of Officer of Law effecting service)

...John Donaldson.. PC.F.1912
(Signature of witness to service)

## Form 15: Execution of service of indictment

F37/3                                                                96500720

**EXECUTION OF SERVICE OF INDICTMENT AND
OF CITATION OF ACCUSED**

(To be returned to the Procurator Fiscal)

Under the Criminal Procedure (Scotland) Act 1995

I, .... John F. Boyd PC E 9612 D.HQ Duncairn .............
on ...17 January 1997 ............................. duly served on
DAVID BALFOUR, 19 Gairn Street, Duncairn the Indictment against him, with a notice to
appear attached to it for a first diet in the Sheriff Court, Duncairn at 10.00 am on
20 February 1997  and for a diet of trial in said court at 10.00 am on 10 March 1997
This I did by  handing it personally to said David Balfour.
...............................................................................

.... John F. Boyd PC E 9612 ....
(Signature of Officer of Law effecting service)

.... John Davidson PC E 7912
(Signature of witness to service)

## Form 16: Statement of uncontroversial evidence

IN THE SHERIFF COURT

OF TAYSIDE, CENTRAL AND FIFE

AT DUNCAIRN

STATEMENT OF UNCONTROVERSIAL EVIDENCE

by

The Procurator Fiscal at DUNCAIRN

in

HER MAJESTY'S ADVOCATE

against

DAVID BALFOUR

TAKE NOTICE:

(1)  That the facts listed below have been identified by me as uncontroversial and capable of being agreed in advance of trial under Section 258 of the Criminal Procedure (Scotland) Act 1995.

(a)  at around 2.25 am on 27 July 1996, the complainer referred to in the charge on the Indictment, namely John Henry Starr, attended at Duncairn Royal Infirmary for treatment;

(b)  said John Henry Starr was diagnosed by John Watson, MB, ChB, as bleeding profusely from 2 stab wounds to the front aspect of his right forearm;

(c)  said wounds were cleaned and stitched;

(d)  said wounds were consistent with having been inflicted by Crown Label production number 1, a knife.

(2)  That a failure to challenge any of the foregoing facts within seven days of the date of service of this notice will result in the unchallenged facts being treated by the court as having been conclusively proved unless the court makes a direction under subsection (6) of Section 258 of the above-mentioned Act.


*Freddie Kempton* .


Procurator Fiscal Depute

*Form 17: Notice of challenge of facts*

Sheriffdom of Tayside, Central and Fife at Duncairn

NOTICE of CHALLENGE of FACTS

specified and referred to in statement under Section 258(2) of the Criminal Procedure (Scotland) Act 1995

by

DAVID BALFOUR, 19 Gairn Street, Duncairn

in causa

HER MAJESTY'S ADVOCATE

against

DAVID BALFOUR

NOTICE IS HEREBY GIVEN that the following facts specified and referred to in the statement of uncontroversial evidence under Section 258(2) Criminal Procedure (Scotland) Act 1995 served on the Panel, David Balfour, on 17th January, 1997 in terms of Section 258(3) of said Act are challenged by me:-

1 (a)   On 27th July, 1996 at approximately 2.25a.m. the complainer referred to in the charge, John Henry Starr, attended at Duncairn Royal Infirmary for treatment.

(b)   Said John Henry Starr was diagnosed by Dr. John Watson, MB, ChB, as bleeding profusely from two stab wounds to the front aspect of his right forearm.

(c)   The wounds were cleaned and stitched by Dr. Watson.

(d)   The wounds were consistent with being inflicted by Crown label production number 1, a knife.

MARGARET E. McKENZIE,
Solicitor,
D. Russell & Co.,
4 Exchequer Street,
DUNCAIRN
Agent for the Panel,
David Balfour

*Form 18: SLAB application form for employing junior counsel*

**SCOTTISH LEGAL AID BOARD**
APPLICATION FOR AUTHORITY FOR EMPLOYMENT
OF COUNSEL OR EXPERT WITNESSES, OR FOR
UNUSUAL OR UNUSUALLY EXPENSIVE WORK

**SANCTION**

## PART A - THE APPLICATION

1. Please give the legal aid case reference number to which this application relates   83/13/645321/ED

2. Please give the date of notification by the Board of the grant of legal aid

| Day | Month | Year |
|-----|-------|------|
| 0 6 | 0 8 | 1 9 9 6 |

3. Applicant's forename(s)   DAVID

4. Applicant's surname   BALFOUR

5. Applicant's personal legal aid reference number (if known)   B A L F O D 9 8 0 7 2 7 0 0 1 5

6. Applicant's National Insurance number (if known)   Y Z 3 6 8 4 2 1 B

## PART B - THE CASE

1. Please describe the proceedings in relation to which Board authority is sought
   *e.g. Sheriff court action for divorce, High Court murder trial*

   Sheriff & Jury trial for charge of assault to severe injury with aggravation of bail.

2. Please indicate the stage presently reached in those proceedings

   Indictment has been served. First diet 20th February, 1997, trial diet 10th March, 1997.

3. Please state the date when the case is next in court   *e.g. for debate, proof, trial, etc.*

| Day | Month | Year |
|-----|-------|------|
| 2 0 | 0 2 | 1 9 9 7 |

## PART C - DETAILS OF SOLICITOR MAKING THIS APPLICATION

1. Practitioner's code number   5 9 6 3 4 1

2. Branch code   —

3. Your reference   MEM

Name   MARGARET E. McKENZIE

Firm   Messrs. D. Russell & Co.

Address   4 Exchequer Street,
DUNCAIRN

DX DU33

Postcode   DY12 7RT

---

*USE THIS FORM FOR ALL PROCEEDINGS
COVERED BY THE FOLLOWING
LEGAL AID TYPES*

- civil legal aid
- legal aid for children
- criminal legal aid
- legal aid for contempt of court

Page 2

## PART D - SANCTION FOR COUNSEL

1. In the case of solemn criminal proceedings at first instance, are these proceedings

    ✓ before a sheriff and jury?                              in the High Court of Justiciary?

2. Please indicate whether sanction has already been given for

    one junior                two juniors              senior acting alone         senior acting with junior

3. Please indicate whether it is now sought to have sanction for

    ┗ one junior              two juniors              senior acting alone         senior acting with junior

4. Please indicate whether it is proposed to instruct counsel for

    a note or opinion          a consultation          drafting or revising papers     a preliminary plea, debate
                                                                                        or like hearing

    ✓ the trial or proof       an appeal               other *please specify*

5. Please give detailed reasons for the request now made

    (a)   The accused has been indicted on a very serious charge.

    (b)   Complicated special defence of self defence plus also the intention by the
          accused to attack the character of the complainer.

    (c)   Although the accused has no record of such, if convicted he may well receive
          a lengthy custodial sentence.

    (d)   Due to the complicated matters of law it is submitted that the accused should
          be represented by an experienced Advocate.

---

PLEASE ATTACH A COPY OF THE MOST UP-TO-DATE PLEADINGS, INDICTMENT OR COMPLAINT ETC.

**Signature of solicitor**   *Margaret McKenzie*          **Date**   4th February,1997

*Form 19: Joint minute of agreement*

UNDER THE CRIMINAL PROCEDURE (SCOTLAND) ACT 1995

SHERIFF COURT OF TAYSIDE, CENTRAL AND FIFE AT DUNCAIRN

JOINT MINUTE OF AGREEMENT

in causa

HER MAJESTY'S ADVOCATE

against

DAVID BALFOUR

Forbes, Procurator Fiscal Depute for the Crown and McKenzie, Solicitor, for the Accused concur in stating to the Court that the following facts are agreed and should be admitted in evidence:

that the findings contained in the Joint Report by Kenneth Duff and Fiona McDougall (Crown Production Number 4) are true and accurate to the effect that the blood on the knife (Crown Label Number 1) and the blood sample from the Complainer (Crown Label Number 3) are both of blood groups O MN Rh+:

IN RESPECT WHEREOF

*Jack Forbes*
Procurator Fiscal Depute

*Margaret S. McKenzie*
Solicitor for the Accused

# HM ADVOCATE v DAVID BALFOUR: FIRST DIET

On 20 February David attended court for the first diet. Although he had been cited for 10 am his case was not in fact called until nearly 11 as there were several other first diets before his. Mr MacGregor was not available to attend the first diet, so David was represented by Miss McKenzie. As with all cases on indictment the proceedings at the first diet were recorded on tape, and the following is a transcript of that recording:

BEFORE SHERIFF LAWSON
FOR THE CROWN: Mr Forbes, Procurator Fiscal Depute, Duncairn.
FOR THE ACCUSED: Miss McKenzie, Solicitor, Duncairn.
CLERK OF COURT: Miss Mary Grant.

CLERK: Call the diet, Her Majesty's Advocate against David Balfour. Are you David Balfour?—Yes.

MISS McKENZIE: My Lord, I appear for the panel. He pleads not guilty and I am lodging a special defence of self-defence together with a notice of intention to attack the character of the complainer. I also lodge a list of defence witnesses containing the name of one witness. *(See pp 35–37 for the documents lodged.)*
SHERIFF: Do I take it therefore that this case will proceed to trial?
MISS McKENZIE: Most certainly, my lord.
SHERIFF: What is the state of preparation of the defence case?
MISS McKENZIE: We are fully prepared. The defence witness has been cited. I have instructed counsel and although he is not here today, he has confirmed that he will be available for the trial.
SHERIFF: Thank you, Miss McKenzie. Mr Forbes, is the Crown ready to proceed to trial?
PROCURATOR FISCAL DEPUTE: Yes, my lord. The Crown witnesses have all been cited. There are two matters about which I should like to be clear. The first is that my friend has served a notice challenging the statement of uncontroversial evidence which was served on her client. I should be grateful if she could inform me whether she is still challenging that evidence. The second is that I sent to her a draft joint minute. I wonder whether she is prepared to agree its terms.
MISS McKENZIE: My lord, so far as the statement of uncontroversial evidence is concerned I am insisting on my notice of challenge. In the opinion of both myself and counsel it is necessary for the defence that Dr Watson should give evidence. However, I *am* prepared to agree the terms of the joint minute.
SHERIFF: I take it that both sides have complied with the terms of section 257(1) of the Act? [*This section lays an obligation on each party to identify facts which are not likely to be disputed and to seek agreement about them—see below at p 129.*]
PROCURATOR FISCAL DEPUTE: My lord, there is no other evidence which I have been able to identify where I see any possibility of agreement.
MISS McKENZIE: I agree with that.
SHERIFF: Very well. That appears to be all that we can do at this stage.
CLERK: David Balfour, the case is continued to the trial diet on 10 March 1997 at 10 am. Your bail is continued.

On 28 February Miss McKenzie had a final consultation with David.

*Form 20: Notice of special defence*

Sheriffdom of Tayside, Central & Fife at Duncairn

**N O T I C E**

of

SPECIAL DEFENCE

in terms of Section 78(1) Criminal Procedure (Scotland) Act 1995

<u>in</u> <u>causa</u>

HER MAJESTY'S ADVOCATE

against

DAVID BALFOUR

McKENZIE for the Panel, David Balfour states that the Panel pleads not guilty to the charge libelled against him and specially and without prejudice to the said plea states that if he did assault the complainer, John Henry Starr, he was acting in self defence, he having first been assaulted or threatened by the said John Henry Starr.

IN RESPECT WHEREOF

MARGARET E. McKENZIE,
Solicitor,
4 Exchequer Street,
Duncairn
<u>Agent for Panel</u>

*Form 21: Notice of intention to attack character of complainer*

### Sheriffdom of Tayside Central & Fife at Duncairn

**N O T I C E**

in terms of Section 78 (1) Criminal
Procedure (Scotland) 1995

on behalf of

**DAVID BALFOUR**

<u>in causa</u>

**HER MAJESTY'S ADVOCATE**

against

**DAVID BALFOUR**

McKENZIE for the Panel, David Balfour, states that the Panel pleads not guilty to the charge and specially and without prejudice to the said plea intimates that evidence may be led by or on behalf of the Panel or by any Crown witness to attack the character of the complainer, John Henry Starr.

IN RESPECT WHEREOF

MARGARET E. McKENZIE,
Solicitor,
4 Exchequer Street,
DUNCAIRN
<u>Agent for the Panel</u>

*Form 22: List of defence witnesses*

Sheriffdom of Tayside, Central & Fife at Duncairn

**LIST OF DEFENCE WITNESSES**

in <u>causa</u>

**HER MAJESTY'S ADVOCATE**

against

**DAVID BALFOUR**

1. Alan Stewart, 67E Glebe Street, Duncairn.

IN RESPECT WHEREOF

MARGARET E. McKENZIE,
Solicitor,
4 Exchequer Street,
Duncairn
<u>Agent for the Panel</u>

## HM ADVOCATE v DAVID BALFOUR: TRIAL

David's trial began at 10 am on 10 March 1997. Before the sheriff came into court Miss Grant, the sheriff clerk depute who was clerking the trial, spoke briefly with the members of the public who had been cited to attend for jury service and who were sitting in the public benches of the courtroom. The potential jurors had in fact all received along with their jury citations a leaflet which explained what would happen in court, but Miss Grant assumed, probably correctly, that some of them had not read the leaflet very carefully. She explained to them that fifteen of them would be selected to sit on the jury. Miss Grant told the potential jurors the name of the accused, the name of the alleged victim of the assault and the place and date where it was alleged to have taken place. She told them that it was very important that none of those selected to sit on the jury should know any of the persons involved in the case or anything about it in advance of the evidence. She said that if any of them had such knowledge and was selected to sit on the jury, he or she should say so immediately and would be excused.

The sheriff came onto the bench and Miss Grant started the tape recorder which would record everything said during the trial. The following is a transcript of the tape-recording of the trial:

BEFORE SHERIFF LAWSON AND A JURY
FOR THE CROWN: Mr Forbes, Procurator Fiscal Depute, Duncairn
FOR THE ACCUSED: Mr MacGregor, Advocate, instructed by Miss McKenzie, Solicitor, Duncairn
CLERK OF COURT: Miss Mary Grant

CLERK: Call the diet, Her Majesty's Advocate against David Balfour. *(David took his place in the dock.)* Are you David Balfour?—Yes.
COUNSEL: My lord, I appear for Mr Balfour. He adheres to his plea of not guilty, and to the special defence which was lodged at the first diet.
SHERIFF: Thank you. Miss Grant, please empanel a jury.
CLERK: Will the ladies and gentlemen whose names I call please come forward and take their seats in the jury box?

*On the clerk's table was a glass jar containing slips of paper, on each of which were written the name and jury list number of a member of the jury panel. Earlier both the prosecution and the defence had been provided with a list of assize (as the list of jurors is called) giving the names and addresses of those summoned for jury service. Miss Grant began to empanel the jury by picking out a slip of paper at random and calling out the name and number written on it. Each juror took a seat in the jury box as his or her name was called out. When all fifteen jurors (nine women and six men) had been balloted Miss Grant asked them to stand up as she called their names. She then called the name of each juror in turn, beginning with the fifteenth to be empanelled and ending with the first. All were then standing.*

CLERK: Ladies and gentlemen, the accused is indicted at the instance of Her Majesty's Advocate, and the charge against him is *(she then read out the charge in the indictment substituting 'he' for 'you' wherever it occurred)*. The accused has lodged a special defence which is in the following terms *(she read out the special defence)*. Will you please take the oath? Raise your right hands. Do you swear by Almighty God that you will well and truly try the accused and give a true verdict according to the evidence?

THE JURY: I do.

CLERK: Please be seated.

SHERIFF: Ladies and gentlemen who have been selected to sit on this jury, I am now going to adjourn the court for a short time so that you may take off your coats and make yourselves comfortable. You have heard the charge against the accused read out to you. I ask that during the adjournment each of you thinks very carefully whether there is any reason why you should not be on a jury to try this case. If you think that there is any such reason, then please let me know as soon as you come back to court, and you may be excused. Those ladies and gentlemen who have not been selected to sit on this jury, I must ask you to remain for a little longer.

*The court adjourned for approximately 15 minutes. On its resumption –*

SHERIFF: Ladies and gentlemen of the jury, may I take it that you all are quite satisfied that there is no reason why you should not try this case? (*No juror indicated otherwise.*) Those ladies and gentlemen who have been summoned here today for jury service, but have not been selected to serve on this jury, are now free to go, if you wish. I must thank you for your attendance here today in performance of the very important public duty of making yourselves available for jury service. Your services will not be required again at this sitting as there are other ladies and gentlemen coming tomorrow morning. If you have any expenses to claim arising out of your attendance here, please go to the sheriff clerk's office, where your claims will be attended to. If you wish to leave, would you please do so now? (*The unempanelled jurors left. The sheriff turned to the jury.*) Ladies and gentlemen, before we start the trial I should like to say a few words to explain the procedure to you, as it may be that it will be strange to some of you. The first advice which I would give you is to forget anything of criminal trials which you may have seen on television. Most trials shown on television are English or American, and our procedure is quite different. In any event real life is rather unlike what is portrayed on television. In Scotland we do not have any opening speeches; we just go straight into the evidence. Evidence for the prosecution will be presented to you by Mr Forbes, the gentleman sitting on my right, who is a procurator fiscal depute. Each witness in turn will be asked questions by Mr Forbes and may then be asked further questions by Mr MacGregor. He is the gentleman in the wig sitting on my left, and he is appearing as counsel for the accused, Mr Balfour. After Mr MacGregor has asked a witness questions Mr Forbes has a limited right to ask further questions to clarify any points raised in cross-examination. This process of examination by Mr Forbes, cross-examination by Mr MacGregor and re-examination by Mr Forbes goes on with each witness until all the evidence for the Crown has been led. There may then be evidence led for the defence. That is a matter for the defence to decide. If defence evidence *is* led, the same process takes place except that this time it is Mr MacGregor who starts off and Mr Forbes who cross-examines. When all the evidence has been completed Mr Forbes will address you on behalf of the Crown, and Mr MacGregor will address you on behalf of Mr Balfour. I shall then charge you, that is to say I shall give you such directions in law as I consider appropriate in this case. You will then retire to consider your verdict. That may sound rather complicated, ladies and gentlemen, but I think that you will find that it all falls into place. I would remind you that you have taken an oath to decide the case according to the evidence. Please now listen carefully to the evidence as it is presented before you.

PROCURATOR FISCAL DEPUTE: My lord, my first witness is number one on the Crown list, John Henry Starr.

JOHN HENRY STARR (SWORN)
EXAMINED BY THE PROCURATOR FISCAL DEPUTE: Is your full name John Henry Starr? Do you live at 76 Riverside Terrace, Duncairn and are you presently unemployed?—Yes.

How old are you?—26.

Now, Mr Starr, I want to take you back to the early hours of the morning of Saturday 27 July last year. I think that something happened to you then?—Yes. I got stabbed in the arm.

Whereabouts did this happen?—Outside the Flamingo in St Mary's Street.

Just tell us what happened.—Well, it was about two o'clock. We'd just come out of the Flamingo – me and Bill Brown – when I saw this guy I kind of knew. I gave him a wave – just to say hi! to him. The next thing I knew he ran at me and I saw that he had a knife in his hand. I put my hand up to protect my face, and he stabbed me in the arm. I fell down.

Would you recognise this man again?—Yes. That's him sitting there (indicating accused).

What happened then?—I'm not sure. I think I may have passed out. The next thing I remember is speaking to a policeman. Then an ambulance came and took me to DRI (*Duncairn Royal Infirmary*). I saw a doctor there who stitched up my cuts. He wanted me to stay in hospital, but I didn't want to stay, so I got a taxi home.

How many times were you stabbed?—Twice.

Do you have any problems with your arm now?—It's a bit stiff and sore, and I can't move my fingers very well.

Was there any reason why the accused should attack you?—No. I didn't do anything to him.

*It is now the turn of counsel to cross-examine the witness. In doing so he will challenge the witness's version of events and put to him David's version. He will also seek to attack the witness's credibility and suggest that he is a man of bad character and, in particular, of violence. The attack on character raises a risk for David as we shall see later. Counsel starts, however, by trying to show that the witness had had a lot to drink.*

CROSS EXAMINED BY MR MacGREGOR: How much had you had to drink that night, Mr Starr?—A few pints. I don't remember how many.

Hadn't you had at least ten pints? Eight before you went to the Flamingo and another two while you were there?—It's possible, but I wasn't drunk. I can hold my drink.

Why did you discharge yourself from hospital?—I don't like hospitals.

Did you go to your own doctor about your injuries?—No.

Isn't it the case that there's nothing wrong with your arm now?—I've told you. It's sore and stiff and I can't move my fingers properly.

Why didn't you go to your doctor then?—I don't like doctors, in hospital or anywhere else.

Do you remember meeting my client in a pub, the Green Man, about the middle of July last year?—I could have done. I've seen him a few times.

Didn't he give you a bit of cheek and weren't you very annoyed?—He was cheeky, but I wasn't worried. I just told him to go away.

Didn't you say that you would get him for it?—I don't think so.

And isn't that exactly what happened outside the Flamingo on 27th July? Didn't you run at him with your hand raised, shouting that you were going to get him?—I've already told you. Nothing like that happened. It was him who came at me.

You've got a record for violence, haven't you?—What if I have?

How many convictions for assault do you have?—Do I have to answer that?
BY THE COURT: I'm afraid that you must.—Well, I've been done three times for assault.
CROSS EXAMINATION CONTINUED BY MR MacGREGOR: What sentences did you get for your assault convictions?—I got fined twice, and the last time I got 60 days.

So, it would be fair to describe you as a man of violence?—I don't agree.

Well, that will be something that the jury may have to decide. Would you say that you were an honest man?—I've got convictions for theft if that's what you're getting at. But that doesn't mean I'm telling lies here.

Isn't the truth of the matter that you went for my client, and he had no option but to defend himself?—That's rubbish.

Why should he attack you?—I don't know.

He's much smaller than you, isn't he?—You can see that, but he had a knife.

*Counsel decides to leave it at that. He has not shaken the witness in his account of the actual events − he had not really expected to do so − but he has obtained an admission of a large amount of drink having been taken, and he has sown in the jury's minds the idea that the witness is a violent man. Mr Starr will certainly not appear lily-white in the eyes of the jury.*

JOHN WATSON (SWORN)
EXAMINED BY THE PROCURATOR FISCAL DEPUTE: Is your name John Watson, and are you a medical practitioner with the qualifications MB ChB?—Yes.

What is your age?—26.

What is your present post?—I am a casualty officer in the Accident and Emergency Department of Duncairn Royal Infirmary.

Did you hold that post at the end of July last year?—Yes.

Please have before you Production No 3. (*The court officer handed Mr Starr's hospital records to the witness.*) Are these the records relating to a patient who was admitted by you in the early hours of Saturday 27 July 1996?—Yes.

Do you recollect the case?—Vaguely.

Please refresh your memory from the records. The patient's name was John Starr?—Yes.

What was his condition when you first saw him?—He was bleeding profusely from two incised wounds in his right forearm − the anterior aspect. He was conscious. I thought he was drunk.

By the anterior aspect do you mean the front of the arm?—Yes.

What position would the arm have been in when he was struck if his assailant had been in front of him?—In that event I think that his arm must have been raised.

As if to defend himself? (OBJECTION BY Mr MacGREGOR on the ground that the question is leading. Question withdrawn.)

What did you consider had caused his injuries?—A sharp object with a point. Something like a small knife.

Please look at Label No 1. (*The court officer handed him the knife.*) Could that have caused the injuries?—Yes, certainly.

How deep were the wounds?—It is difficult to be precise, but they appeared to be quite deep. They had certainly penetrated the muscle.

Are you able to say how much force would have been required to inflict these wounds if the knife you have before you was the weapon used?—Quite a lot of force, I think, given the depth of the wounds and the relatively small size of the knife.

What treatment did you give Mr Starr?—His wounds were cleaned and sutured. I wanted to detain him as he appeared to have lost a lot of blood, but he discharged himself from hospital against medical advice.

Do you consider it likely that his injuries will have left him with any permanent ill effects?—I don't think so, but I can't be sure as I saw him for such a short time.

How would you describe the injuries – serious, trivial or what?—Well, they certainly weren't trivial, but they were not life-threatening.

CROSS-EXAMINED BY MR MacGREGOR: Could his arm have been raised as if to strike a blow when he received the injuries?—That is possible. All I can say is that, if he were struck from the front, then I think that his arm must have been raised in such a way as to present the front of it to his assailant.

You concluded that a fair amount of force must have been used, to judge from the depth of the wounds. At least part of the force, if indeed not all, could have consisted in Mr Starr bringing his arm down to strike at my client, couldn't it?—Yes, that is quite possible.

I know that doctors are reluctant to categorise the gravity of injuries, but I wonder if you could help me a little. You say the injury was not trivial. You wouldn't say that it was severe, would you?—Well, severity is not really a term that we use very much in medicine. We are more concerned as to whether life is endangered.

You formed the impression that Mr Starr was drunk. On what basis?—He smelt strongly of alcohol. His speech was slurred. He was unsteady on his feet. He was unco-operative.

You say he was unco-operative. In what way?—He was truculent. He swore at me and the nurse and wouldn't keep still when I was examining his injuries.

RE-EXAMINED: Apart from the smell of alcohol, the other things about which you have told us could have been caused by shock? (OBJECTION BY MR MacGREGOR on the ground that the question is leading.)

BY THE COURT: Yes, Mr Forbes, you really must remember that leading questions are just as impermissible in re-examination as in examination-in-chief. I shall sustain the objection.

RE-EXAMINATION CONTINUED BY THE PROCURATOR FISCAL DEPUTE: You say that part of the force required to cause the wounds could have been Mr Starr bringing his arm down. What if his arm had been held still?—In that event all the force must have come from the strength of the blows.

WILLIAM BROWN (SWORN)
EXAMINED BY THE PROCURATOR FISCAL DEPUTE: Is your full name William Brown, and do you live at 3 North Street, Duncairn?—Yes.

How old are you?—25.

Are you a friend of John Starr?—Yes.

Were you and he together during the early hours of Saturday, 27 July last year?—Yes.

Where were you?—We were in the Flamingo. I met Starry there.

What time did you leave?—About two o'clock.

Did something happen when you got outside?—Yes.

Just tell us about it in your own words—Well, we came out into the street, and I saw these two geezers walking along the road. Starry like waved at them, and then the wee guy just ran at him and stuck this dirty great knife into his arm. I couldn't believe what was happening.

Do you see in court the person you've described as 'the wee guy'?—Yes, that's him there (indicating the accused).

What happened then?—I was sort of confused, but I think that Starry fell down and the wee guy ran away. I went back into the Flamingo and got one of the bouncers to phone for an ambulance. I could see that Starry was bleeding badly.

Did Mr Starr say or do anything, so far as you could see, that might have caused the accused to attack him?—No, not at all. He just gave him a friendly wave.

CROSS-EXAMINED BY MR MacGREGOR: Mr Brown, are you a good friend of Mr Starr?—Well, I've known him since we were at school.

How often do you usually see him?—Most weekends.

So you'll have seen him quite often since last July?—Aye.

Tell me, have you spoken at all about what happened that night?—Oh no, I know you mustn't talk about a case that's coming to court.

Of course, you have quite a lot of experience of courts, don't you?— Well, I've been in them a few times.

Have you ever been in the dock?—Yes.

Were you convicted?—Yes, but I wasn't guilty.

*Mr MacGregor has no detailed information about Brown's criminal record, and therefore decides to take this line of cross-examination no further.*

How much had you had to drink that night?—Just a few pints.

How many is 'just a few'?—Maybe about seven or eight. I can't remember.

Were you drunk?—Oh no, just happy.

Isn't the truth of the matter that you were very drunk indeed?—That's not true at all.

Were you able to give the police a description of what had happened?—Yes, and I told them what like the guy was that did the stabbing.

You've described the weapon used as 'a dirty great knife'. Look at Label No 1, please. Would you describe that as a 'dirty great knife'?—No. The knife I saw was much bigger than that.

So that couldn't be the knife that was used to stab your friend?—I don't think so. I suppose it could have been. The light wasn't that good.

So you're not so sure now about the knife. Could you perhaps be mistaken too about who started the trouble?—Oh no. There's no mistake about that.

Isn't it the case that it was Starry who ran at my client as if he was going to attack him?—No, I don't think it happened like that.

You don't *think* it happened like that. Are you not sure?—Now you're getting me confused. It happened like I told you.

And you're still asking us to believe that you and Mr Starr have never discussed the case together?—Yes.

Even although you've been seeing each other every weekend since? Do you really think that's credible?

BY THE COURT: Surely that's a matter for the jury, Mr MacGregor?

MR MacGREGOR: I apologise, my lord. Of course it is. I'm afraid I got carried away. I have no more questions for this witness.

ANDREW McINTYRE (SWORN)

EXAMINED BY THE PROCURATOR FISCAL DEPUTE: Is your full name Andrew McIntyre, and are you a constable of Tayside Police stationed at Duncairn?—Yes.

How old are you and how many years' police service do you have?—I am 33 years old and I have fourteen years' service.

In the early hours of 27 July last year were you on duty on mobile patrol in Duncairn, and did you receive a message about an incident in St Mary's Street?—Yes.

What time was this?—Just after 2 am.

What did you do?—The message gave a description of the man who was suspected of committing an assault outside the Flamingo, so I decided to tour the streets and see if there was anyone about answering that description.

Did you see anyone who did answer the description?—Yes, in George Street I saw a young man walking along the street. When he saw me he ran away, but I chased after him and I caught him.

Do you see that young man in court?—Yes, there in the dock. (Pointing at the accused.)

What happened then?—I informed him that I was detaining him under section 14 of the Criminal Procedure (Scotland) Act on suspicion of assault and that he didn't need to say anything but that if he did it could be used in evidence.

What do you mean by section 14 of the Criminal Procedure (Scotland) Act?—That allows me to detain someone if I have reason to suspect he has committed a crime.

Did he say anything?—He said 'It was him or me'.

What happened then?—I took him to the police office. When I got him there I searched him, and in his pocket I found a knife, which appeared to be bloodstained.

Please look at Label No 1. Is that the knife?—Yes.

CROSS-EXAMINED BY MR MacGREGOR: What state was the accused in when you came across him?—He was out of breath, as if he had been running. And he seemed frightened. He had been drinking, but I did not think that he was very drunk.

Apart from running away when he first saw you, did he make any attempt to obstruct you?—Oh no. In fact he was thoroughly co-operative.

ANGUS BLACK (SWORN)

EXAMINED BY THE PROCURATOR FISCAL DEPUTE: Is your full name Angus Black, and are you a detective constable in the Tayside Police, stationed at Duncairn?—Yes.

How old are you and how many years' police service do you have?—I am 40 years old and I have 21 years' police service.

In the early hours of 27 July last year did you interview a man called David Balfour in interview room no 2 at Divisional Headquarters in Duncairn? And was that in connection with an alleged assault which had taken place some time earlier?—Yes.

Do you see in court the man who you interviewed?—Yes, that's him there. (Pointing at the accused.)

Please have before you Label No 4 and Production No 2. Is the Label a tape recording of your interview, and is the Production a transcript of that interview?—Yes.

If my learned friend, Mr MacGregor, has no objection, I would ask you to read out the transcript. *(Mr MacGregor indicated that he had no objection, and the witness then read out the transcript reproduced at pp 2, 3.)*
NO CROSS-EXAMINATION

PROCURATOR FISCAL DEPUTE: My lord, that is the last witness I intend to lead. However, I would ask your lordship's clerk to read out the joint minute. I would also ask her to read out the transcript of the judicial examination.

SHERIFF: Ladies and gentlemen. The parties have agreed certain evidence which has been incorporated into a document called a joint minute. I am going to ask my clerk to read that document out to you. I am also going to ask her to read out the transcript of the accused's judicial examination. A judicial examination takes place when an accused first appears in court and it gives an accused an opportunity to say anything he wishes about the charge against him, especially with regard to any defence which he wishes to put forward.

*(Miss Grant then read out the terms of the joint minute (see p 33) and the transcript of the judicial examination (see pp 4, 5)*

PROCURATOR FISCAL DEPUTE: My lord, that is the case for the Crown.

MR MacGREGOR: My lord, I intend to call my client and one other witness. I now call Mr Balfour.

DAVID BALFOUR (SWORN)
EXAMINED BY MR MacGREGOR: Is your full name David Balfour, do you live at 19 Gairn Street, Duncairn, and are you twenty years old?—Yes.
Do you have a job?—No, I'm unemployed at present, but I hope to get a job soon.
Do you know John Starr?—I don't know him well, but I've met him a few times in pubs. I call him Starry.
Did you ever see him in the Green Man?—Yes, I've seen him there several times.
Is there any particular time that you remember?—Yes. About a fortnight before he was stabbed I saw him in the pub, and he got angry with me. He said that he would get me.
Was there any particular reason for that?—Well, I suppose that I was a bit cheeky to him, but I didn't mean any harm.
Let me now come to the evening of 27 July last year. What did you do then?—I went to the Red House. That's a pub. I met Alan Stewart there. He's a friend of mine. We stayed till closing time, and then we went to Sandy's Night Club.
How long did you stay there?—Until about ten to two.
What happened then?—We went out into the street and walked towards the taxi rank in St Mary's Street. Outside the Flamingo I saw Starry and another man. Starry came at me, shouting he was going to get me. I was scared.
What did you do?—I remembered that I had a knife in my pocket, so I pulled it out. He kept coming so I held out the knife. I just meant to frighten him, but when he didn't stop I stuck the knife into his arm.
How was he holding his arm?—It was up above his head. I thought he had something in his hand, but I wasn't sure. When I cut him he fell down.
What happened then?—I ran away, and the polis caught me.

Please look at Label No 1. Do you agree that that is your knife and that it was stained with Starr's blood?—Yes.

I think that you don't dispute any of the evidence given by the police as to what you said when you were caught or in the police station?—That's right.

Why didn't you run away when Starr came at you?—He was too close, and I thought he could run faster than me as he's much bigger.

CROSS-EXAMINED BY THE PROCURATOR FISCAL DEPUTE: How much had you had to drink that night?—About six pints.

Were you drunk?—No. I maybe wasn't completely sober, but I wasn't really drunk.

You say that you did not have time to run away?—That's right.

Can you explain then how you had time to open the knife?—I don't know. I just did.

Isn't it the case that you had time to open the knife because it wasn't Mr Starr who came at you but you who went for him?—That's not true. I wouldn't go for him. He's much bigger than me, and he's got an evil reputation.

PROCURATOR FISCAL DEPUTE: My lord, at this stage I have a motion to make which it would be appropriate to deal with outwith the presence of the jury.

SHERIFF: Ladies and gentlemen, Mr Forbes wishes to address me on a point of law, so I must ask you to withdraw. (*The jury left the jury box.*) Yes Mr Forbes.

PROCURATOR FISCAL DEPUTE: My lord, I move you to allow me to cross-examine the accused as to his criminal record and character in view of the attack which he has made on the character of the complainer, John Starr. I refer your lordship to the terms of section 266(4)(b) of the Criminal Procedure (Scotland) Act 1995.

SHERIFF: Mr MacGregor, do you oppose that motion?

MR MacGREGOR: Yes my lord, indeed I do. I am, of course, familiar with the terms of the section to which my friend has referred your lordship, but I would remind your lordship that it was clearly laid down in the Seven Judge case of *Leggate v HM Advocate* that your lordship has a very wide discretion in the matter and that the fundamental test is fairness. The case is reported in 1988 SCCR at page 391 and in 1988 SLT at page 665. With your lordship's permission I shall refer to the SCCR report, which I have immediately available. That case was, of course, considering the terms of section 141(1)(f)(ii) of the 1975 Act, but the terms of the 1995 Act in this regard are virtually identical with those of the earlier Act, and, in my submission, the case is entirely in point. I refer my lord to the rubric at the foot of page 391 and the top of page 392: 'Held. . . (2) that a trial judge has a wide discretion to refuse to allow an accused to be cross-examined on his character, that the fundamental test in exercising that discretion is one of fairness having regard both to the position of the accused and the public interest in bringing wrongdoers to justice, and that a significant factor in the exercise of the discretion is whether the questions asked of the Crown witnesses were integral and necessary to the defence or were a deliberate attack on the character of the witness.' I submit, my lord, that the questions which I asked of Mr Starr, although they may have been an attack on character, were also necessary to the defence. I submit also that it would be very unfair to the accused to allow his character to be put in issue. He has a very trivial criminal record. It is such that I should have no concern about your lordship's having knowledge of it, but I should be afraid that a jury might be unduly prejudiced if they were to get to learn about it.

SHERIFF: Mr MacGregor, if you are unconcerned about my knowing your client's record, perhaps you would tell me what it is.

MR MacGREGOR: Certainly, my lord. In 1994 he was convicted of being in possession of an offensive weapon, which sounds relatively serious. However, the weapon concerned was only a piece of wood, and the court clearly took a not very serious view of the offence as it imposed a fine of only £25. In 1995 he was fined £15 for a breach of the peace, and in June last year he pleaded guilty in the District Court to another breach of the peace, for which he was eventually fined £25. I submit, my lord, that the prejudicial effect of allowing this record to go before the jury would far outweigh the very necessary task of the defence to show that the complainer is a man of violent disposition. I therefore ask your lordship to refuse my friend's motion.

SHERIFF: Mr Forbes, what do you say?

PROCURATOR FISCAL DEPUTE: My lord, in my submission what the defence did here was not essential for the presentation of their case, but was quite simply an attack on the character of the complainer. As far as fairness is concerned, I am sure that your lordship would give sufficient directions to the jury to ensure that they would not be unduly prejudiced by the disclosure of the accused's criminal record. I have nothing further to add.

SHERIFF: In my opinion, it would be unfair to allow the jury to hear details of the accused's criminal record. He has not been convicted of any crime implying dishonesty, so his creditworthiness would not be impugned by allowing reference to his record. He might, however, be shown, in the eyes of some members of the jury, to be a violent person because of the offensive weapon charge, and I consider that that might give a misleading impression and could be very prejudicial to the defence. Accordingly I shall refuse the Crown motion. Please bring the jury back into court.

*(The jury was brought back into court.)*

CROSS-EXAMINATION BY THE PROCURATOR FISCAL DEPUTE CONTINUED: If you thought that you had done nothing wrong, why did you run away?—I was scared about what I had done. I thought that they wouldn't believe me.

But you are now asking the ladies and gentlemen of the jury to believe you?—Yes, because I am telling the truth.

You knew perfectly well that Starr didn't have any weapon in his hand, didn't you?— I wasn't sure then, but I think now that he probably hadn't.

RE-EXAMINED BY MR MacGREGOR: Is what you have told us today in any way different from what you told the police or what you said at judicial examination?—No, sir.

ALAN BRECK STEWART (SWORN)

EXAMINED BY MR MacGREGOR: Is your full name Alan Breck Stewart, do you live at 67A Glebe Street, Duncairn, and are you nineteen years old?—Yes, Sir.

Are you employed?—No.

Are you friendly with David Balfour, who is sitting there in the dock?—Yes. I've known him for a few years.

Were you with Mr Balfour in the late evening of Friday, 26 July, and the early hours of Saturday, 27 July, last year?—Yes. We met in the Red House. I had got there before him. He came in about nine o'clock.

How much had you had to drink before Mr Balfour arrived?—Probably a couple of pints.

How much did you have to drink after he came?—I think three or four pints and a couple of nips.

What time did you leave the Red House?—I'm not sure, but I think it must have been after eleven. We went on to Sandy's.

Did you have some more to drink there?—Yes, I think I had another couple of drinks.

How would you describe your state by this time?—I was pretty well on, but I wasn't falling about.

Did you leave the night club with Mr Balfour?—Yes.

What happened when you got outside?—Well, I saw these two men coming and one ran at David. David defended himself and the man fell.

Let's take this a bit more slowly. First of all. Where did this happen?—Near the taxi rank.

Is that in St Mary's Street?—Yes.

Did you know the man who came at David?—I knew him as Starry. I'd seen him around.

Now, tell us slowly and clearly what happened.—Like I told you, he ran at David. He had his arm up. I thought he had something in his hand. He was shouting something about getting David.

What did David do?—He backed off a bit and then took something out of his pocket. I thought it was a nail file or something like that. And he stuck it into Starry's arm. That's all I saw, because I ran away then.

Why didn't David run away?—I don't know. I think that it just happened too fast.

CROSS-EXAMINED BY THE PROCURATOR FISCAL DEPUTE: Mr Stewart, if I've understood your evidence correctly, you must have had about ten pints to drink during the evening. Is that right?—I wasn't just drinking pints.

Were the shorts you drank singles or doubles?—Probably doubles. That's what I usually have.

So you must have had the equivalent of at least ten pints?—I suppose so. Do you think that your recollection is really clear?—I reckon so. I got such a fright when I saw what was happening that I sobered up.

You say you don't know why David didn't run away. He could easily have done so, if he'd wanted, couldn't he?—I don't know. I was scared. I guess he was scared too.

In fact are you really certain that it was the man who ran at David? Wasn't it the other way round, that David ran at the man?—No, I'm quite sure about that.

Have you talked about this case to the accused at all?—No. I've hardly seen him since last July.

MR MacGREGOR: My lord, that is the case for the defence.

SHERIFF: Ladies and gentlemen, that is all the evidence in the case. It is just after one o'clock, so we'll now adjourn for lunch. You will be taken to a local hotel and given lunch there. You should not discuss the case. You have heard all the evidence, but you have not heard speeches or my charge, so it is too early to be making up your minds in any way yet. The court will sit again at 2.15.

AFTER THE ADJOURNMENT

PROCURATOR FISCAL DEPUTE: May it please your lordship. Ladies and gentlemen of the jury, it is now my privilege to address you on behalf of the Crown. In what I have to say to you I may deal a little with the law which you will have to apply to the case, but anything I say about the law is subject to correction by his lordship, and you must accept what he says about the law.

I accept that the burden of proof is on the prosecution and that the standard of proof which the prosecution must reach is proof beyond reasonable doubt, which is a very high standard of proof. I submit, however, ladies and gentlemen, that the Crown has achieved that standard of proof in this case and that you should therefore find the accused guilty of the crime with which he is charged.

He is charged with assault, which needs no definition by me. As I understand the line the defence has taken, the accused is not denying that he struck Mr Starr with a knife. He is saying that he was *entitled* to do it because he was acting in self-defence. Now, ladies and gentlemen, subject as always to correction by his lordship, I understand the law to be that a person may use violence to defend himself only in certain special circumstances. First, he must have a reasonable fear that he is being attacked. Secondly, he must have no other means of escape. And thirdly, the retaliation he uses must not be excessive.

In the present case, even if you accept the defence version of what happened – and I shall, at the end of the day, be inviting you to reject it – you could not, in my submission, hold that the accused had been acting in self-defence. I say this for two reasons. First, he could have run away. Secondly, the retaliation which he used was grossly excessive. So far as running away is concerned, he had time to take the knife from his pocket and to open it. Surely he could better have spent that time by taking to his heels. He retaliated with a knife. There is not a shred of evidence that Mr Starr had a weapon at all. Therefore, for the accused to use a weapon was far in excess of anything that may have been required to protect himself. I urge you, ladies and gentlemen, to reject self-defence.

But I suggest that you should never even get to the stage of considering self-defence, because you should not accept the basic premise on which it depends, namely that it was Mr Starr who attacked the accused. I submit to you that you should accept the evidence of Mr Starr and Mr Brown and find it proved that what happened here was an unprovoked attack by the accused on Mr Starr. You may ask what motive the accused would have had for such an attack, but, as I am sure his lordship will direct you, the Crown does not have to prove motive. I would remind you that the accused had had a lot to drink. Perhaps his passions were simply inflamed by liquor. It is true that Mr Starr also had had a good deal to drink, but he is an older man and, you as men and women of the world may think, might therefore be able to hold his drink better than the accused.

It is not disputed, ladies and gentlemen, that the accused was on bail at the time when he stabbed Mr Starr, so if you find him guilty of assault you must also find proved that part of the charge which says that he was on bail at the time.

Ladies and gentlemen, I do not think that I need detain you any longer. I submit that, whatever view you may take of the facts, your clear duty here is to find the charge proved. I therefore confidently ask you to return a verdict of guilty as libelled.

SHERIFF: Thank you, Mr Forbes. Mr MacGregor.

MR MacGREGOR: Thank you, my lord. Ladies and gentlemen, it is now for me to address you on behalf of David Balfour, the accused in this case. I would begin by reminding you of a cardinal principle of our law: every person is presumed innocent until proved guilty. So you must not say to yourselves, as I am sure you will not, that, just because my client is in the dock, he must be guilty. As my friend has already reminded you, the burden of proof is on the prosecution. And I would add that that is still so, even though the accused is putting forward a special defence of self-defence, as I am sure his lordship will direct you.

My friend has asked you to accept the evidence of Mr Starr and Mr Brown in this case. I ask you to reject their evidence as being unworthy of any credit at all. I would remind you that both have criminal records, including, in Starr's case, a conviction for violence which attracted a prison sentence. It is clear from the evidence that both were considerably under the influence of alcohol. Look at the respective sizes of Starr and of my client, and ask yourselves whether it is likely that my client would deliberately attack Starr. I suggest to you that you should be satisfied that the initial attack came from Starr. The only question which you have to ask yourselves therefore is whether anything my client did was done in self-defence.

I agree in general terms with my friend's statement of the criteria which are essential for self-defence, but I disagree with him in his suggestion that these have not been established.

If you accept my client's version of events, he was attacked by a much bigger man who had threatened him on a previous occasion. He therefore had every reason to fear for his own safety. What was he to do? The learned procurator fiscal depute suggests that he should have run away. Perhaps in an ideal world he would have done so, but, ladies and gentlemen, we are dealing here with real life where decisions have to be taken in the heat of the moment. You must not weigh things too finely. Should Mr Balfour have taken the risk of being pursued by a bigger and more powerful man? The fiscal criticised him for having time to take out and open his knife. But ladies and gentlemen, you probably all know how easy it is to open a penknife – it doesn't take a moment. I submit to you that that criticism by the fiscal is quite unjustified. And again my friend suggested that there was no evidence that Starr was armed. I put it to you that my client had every reason to suspect that he *was*. Mr Balfour told you himself that he *thought* he might be. The fact that he did not say that he was *sure* demonstrates his honesty to you, in my submission. Mr Stewart also raised the possibility of Mr Starr having a weapon. The question is not, ladies and gentlemen, whether he *did* have a weapon, but whether my client genuinely *thought* that he did. I suggest to you that he had every reason for thinking that. In that event, to use a knife himself was in no way excessive retaliation. It was a perfectly reasonable thing to do.

Ladies and gentlemen, my friend did not detain you long. Nor shall I. I submit to you that this is a clear case of a frightened young man acting legitimately in defence of his own skin against an attack by a larger and older drunken lout. I confidently ask you to find my client not guilty.

SHERIFF: Thank you, Mr MacGregor.

Ladies and gentlemen, we now come to the final stages of this case. As I explained at the beginning, I must now charge you.

The first thing which I must tell you is about our respective functions. It is for me to deal with the law, and you must accept whatever I may say about the law. Your province is the facts. You and you alone are the masters of the facts. The facts have nothing to do with me, and if, in the course of anything I say to you, I give any indication of a view I may have formed on the facts (which I hope I will not) you should ignore it, because the facts are no business of mine. It follows from that, that it is your recollection of the evidence which counts, not mine or Mr Forbes' or Mr MacGregor's. If anything any of us says about the evidence differs from your recollection, it is yours that counts and not ours.

What I have to say next is merely intended to assist you with how you may care to approach the facts in this case. If you do not agree with any suggestion I may make, please feel perfectly free not to follow it.

Credibility is clearly an important issue in this case. That is entirely for you. It is for you to decide which witnesses to believe and which witnesses to disbelieve. It is perfectly possible for you to accept part of a witness's evidence and to reject part; or you may accept it all or reject it all. Remember, though, that if you reject a witness's evidence on any matter, you are not entitled to assume that the opposite of what he said is in fact what happened.

How you decide questions of credibility is really a matter of applying your common sense to the evidence, but there are certain factors which you may find it helpful to consider. What, for instance, was the witness's demeanour when he was giving his evidence? Did he appear comfortable or did he seem evasive? You should, of course, make allowances for the fact that a witness may feel nervous and overawed by being in court. What does a witness have to gain by not telling the truth? You may think that a witness would be unlikely to tell lies without a good reason for doing so. Well, what might be the reason? Was the witness's evidence consistent with other evidence in the case? Was it internally consistent? In other words was each part of his evidence consistent with the other parts? These, ladies and gentlemen, are all pointers which you may or may not find helpful in assessing credibility.

Another factor which you should bear in mind when assessing a witness's evidence is reliability. You see, a witness may be doing his very best to tell the truth, but he may simply not remember things very well. This may be because a long time has passed since the events which he is describing, or it may be because his vision at the time was blurred because he was drunk or because he simply did not have a very good view. So, ladies and gentlemen, you should consider carefully the credibility and reliability of all the witnesses.

I now turn to the directions in law which I must give you, and I remind you that you *must* accept the law from me. It may be that some of what I say about the law has already been said to you by either Mr Forbes or Mr MacGregor, and, if that is so, I apologise for repeating it, but I must do so as it is I who must direct you in the law.

The first direction is about the burden of proof. In a criminal trial such as this, the burden of proof rests fairly and squarely on the prosecution. It is not for an accused person to prove anything. In this case the accused has lodged what is called a special defence, but that does not mean that he has to prove anything. All it means is that he is founding on a defence of a sort that he must give notice of to the Crown. That is the only special thing about the defence. Put another way, an accused person is presumed innocent until proved guilty. This is a fundamental principle of our law, and you must always have it in mind.

The next direction which I must give you is about the standard of proof which the Crown must satisfy. It is a very high standard: proof beyond reasonable doubt. What that means is that, if, after considering all the evidence, you are left with a reasonable doubt about the guilt of the accused, the benefit of that doubt must go to the accused, and you will acquit him. What is meant by a reasonable doubt? Well, it is not some airy-fairy, speculative doubt. Nor, on the other hand, does the law require that the Crown proves its case to a mathematical certainty. Human frailty being what it is, that would be impossible. Reasonable doubt is a doubt which is the result of your exercising your reasoning faculties on the evidence. You might care to look at it this way. Supposing that you had an important decision to make in your own life, either at home or at work. You would weigh all the factors both for and against the line of action which you might take. If, having done that as carefully as you could, you still were unable to reach a decision on the matter, you would have, I suggest, a reasonable doubt. If you have that sort of doubt about the guilt of the accused, you must, as I have said, give the benefit of that doubt to him and acquit.

Now I must tell you about what is called corroboration, although it is not, I think, a very controversial issue in this case. According to the law of Scotland, no person can be convicted of a crime such as we are dealing with here on the evidence of only one witness, no matter how credible or reliable you may think that witness is. There must be evidence from at least two separate sources pointing at the guilt of the accused. In other words, the Crown must prove every essential fact by the evidence of more than one witness. In this case there are really only two essential facts: that the crime was committed; and that it was the accused who committed it. What I have said applies only to the Crown case. The accused does not require to be corroborated. I don't think that, in the context of the present case, I need to say anything further about corroboration.

I now pass from general directions, such as you would get in any criminal trial, to deal with this specific case.

The only charge on the indictment is a charge of assault. An assault is a deliberate attack on the person of another. Sometimes an attack which would otherwise be an assault is excusable, and the attack does not amount to an assault. That is the situation where a person acts in self-defence. In the present case the accused does not deny attacking Mr Starr, but he says that the attack was justified because he was defending himself. Remember, as I have said, it is not for the accused to prove anything. The proper way to look at it is that, the possibility of self-defence having been introduced by the defence, the onus is on the Crown to negative it.

Now I must tell you what is meant by self-defence. There are three requirements if what would otherwise be an assault is to be justified. First, the accused must reasonably be afraid that he is in immediate danger of being seriously injured. It is not necessary that the basis for his fear be factually well founded, provided that it is reasonable. Thus, in the present case, you should consider whether or not there was any reasonable basis for the accused's saying (if you believe him) that Mr Starr had a weapon. Secondly, there must be no other reasonable means of escape. If a person can avoid an attack by running away, he must do so. He must not remain and resist by force. Thirdly, the retaliation used must not be cruelly excessive. It should not be more than is necessary for his own safety. Now you must not weigh any of these factors in too fine a scale. You must make due allowance for the heat of the moment and the state of fear which the accused may be in.

I now turn to deal very briefly with the evidence in the case. I do not intend to rehearse it to you as it will be very fresh in your minds, and, in any event, it is not the function of a Scottish judge in a jury trial to go through all the evidence. First of all, a general point: you will give just as careful attention to the evidence for the defence as to that for the Crown. Turning to the more specific: if you believed the evidence of Mr Starr and Mr Brown (and therefore rejected the evidence of the accused and Mr Stewart), it is difficult to see how you could do anything other than find that the accused was guilty of assault, because these witnesses spoke of an attack for no reason at all. As Mr Forbes said, it is the law that the Crown does not have to prove motive.

If you believed the accused's evidence, you would have to consider whether he was acting in self-defence, using the test I've just told you about. If you concluded that he *was* acting in self-defence, you would acquit. If the accused's evidence raised a reasonable doubt in your mind, equally you would acquit, as you would not then be satisfied of his guilt beyond reasonable doubt. You will note that I have referred only to the accused's evidence, and that is because, as I have told you, the accused does not require to be corroborated. Mr Stewart did, however, also give evidence for the defence, and you will consider his evidence as well.

If you came to the conclusion that the accused was not acting in self-defence (and whether or not you do is for you alone to decide), you might consider whether there had been any provocation. The difference between self-defence and provocation is that self-defence is a complete answer to the charge, while provocation is consistent with guilt, but might be reflected in sentence. I emphasise that you would consider provocation only if you were going to return a verdict of guilty of assault.

There are two other matters which I should mention before I tell you about the verdicts which you may return.

The first is this. The charge alleges that Mr Starr was assaulted 'to his severe injury'. Has the Crown proved that the injury was severe? That is entirely a matter for you. You will take account of the medical evidence and of what Mr Starr himself said in reaching your conclusion. You would also be entitled to take account of the fact that Mr Starr did not seek any further medical attention for his injury after his discharge from hospital. One way of looking at it might be: supposing that you yourself suffered an injury like this, would you be inclined to call it severe? If you are not satisfied that the injury has been proved to be severe but you do find that the charge of assault has been proved you would find the accused guilty under deletion of the word 'severe'.

The second matter, which I must mention, is that the charge alleges that the accused was on bail at the time he assaulted Mr Starr. The fact that he was on bail at the relevant time has not been challenged, and I therefore direct you that, if you find the accused guilty of assault, you must find that the part of the charge alleging that he was on bail has been proved.

As you probably know, there are three verdicts open to a jury in Scotland. These are: guilty, not guilty, and not proven. If your verdict were to be guilty, you would have to decide whether the injury had been proved to be severe, and you might consider the question of provocation. The other two verdicts are both verdicts of acquittal, and both have exactly the same effect in law. They both mean that the accused is for ever more free from the charge against him.

You may reach your verdict either unanimously or by a majority. There is just one proviso to that. There must be at least eight of you in favour of a verdict of guilty before you could return that verdict. You see, there are fifteen of you in the jury. You might be split, for example, seven for guilty, five for not guilty, and three for not proven. In that event, the largest number among you would be in favour of a verdict of guilty, but that would be a minority of the jury as a whole. In such an event you would have a majority for acquittal, and it would be for you to decide which of the two possible verdicts your acquittal verdict would be.

I suggest that the first thing you do when you go to the jury room is to elect one of your number as foreman. He or she will have two functions. One will be to act as chairman while you are discussing the case, and the other will be to tell my clerk what your verdict is when you return to court. When you come back my clerk will ask your foreman to stand up and will ask if you have reached a verdict. You will then be asked what your verdict is and whether it is unanimous or by a majority.

Ladies and gentlemen, will you please now retire and consider your verdict, which I can take at any time.

*The jury retired at 3.30 pm.*

*Upon their return at 4.45 pm:*

CLERK OF COURT: Ladies and gentlemen, have you reached a verdict?

FOREMAN OF THE JURY: We have.

CLERK OF COURT: What is your verdict?

FOREMAN OF THE JURY: Guilty of assault but not to severe injury, and we find that the accused was provoked.

CLERK OF COURT: Is that unanimous or by a majority?

FOREMAN OF THE JURY: Majority.

CLERK OF COURT: Your verdict will now be recorded.

SHERIFF: Ladies and gentlemen, my clerk will now write down your verdict and will read it back to you for you to confirm that it is correct.

CLERK OF COURT: Ladies and gentlemen, is this a true record of your verdict? The jury by a majority finds the accused guilty of the charge under deletion of the word 'severe' and under provocation.

FOREMAN OF THE JURY: Yes.

PROCURATOR FISCAL DEPUTE: My lord, I move for sentence. I produce a notice of previous convictions to which no exception has been taken. The accused's personal circumstances so far as known to me are that he is nineteen years of age, single, unemployed and lives with his parents. He was arrested on 27 July, as your lordship has heard, and he appeared in court from custody on 30 July when he was released on bail. I move for forfeiture of the knife, which is Label No 1.

SHERIFF: Thank you Mr Forbes. Mr MacGregor, your client is under 21. I think before we can go any further I shall have to have a social enquiry report.

MR MacGREGOR: I am in your lordship's hands. Might I with respect submit that your lordship should ask for a community service assessment to be included in the social enquiry report? And I move that my client's bail be continued. I should say that my client has no objection to forfeiture of the knife.

SHERIFF: Very well, I shall order forfeiture of the knife, and I shall ask for the report which you have suggested. I am prepared to continue bail. Stand up, Mr Balfour. You will continue to be on bail, and I remind you that it is a condition of your bail that you must make yourself available to the social worker who will wish to see you in order to prepare the report I have asked for. Do you understand?

ACCUSED: Yes, sir.

CLERK OF COURT: Case adjourned for social enquiry report until 10 am on 7 April 1997. Bail continued.

SHERIFF: Ladies and gentlemen, I have to thank you for your services on this jury and for the careful consideration which you have given to this case. I should explain that, because the accused here is under 21, I really have to obtain reports before I can decide what is the appropriate sentence. This is why I have not been able to sentence him today in your presence as I might otherwise have done. I am glad to tell you that your services will not be required any more at present as we have a fresh panel of jurors coming tomorrow. If you have any expenses to claim arising out of your attendance here today, my clerk will advise you what to do. May I now wish you good day?

# HM ADVOCATE v DAVID BALFOUR: SENTENCE

On 7 April David appeared in court again. In the meantime he had been interviewed by a social worker, and a social enquiry report had been prepared (see pp 57–59). Miss McKenzie and David had had a brief meeting at the end of the previous week at Miss McKenzie's office in order to bring Miss McKenzie up to date with David's personal details. Before the court started Miss McKenzie went through the report with David, and confirmed that there was no factual statement in it with which he disagreed. Miss McKenzie was going to make the plea in mitigation on David's behalf herself as Mr MacGregor was not available. She had sat through the trial and knew as much about the case as Mr MacGregor would have done. When the case called in court the proceedings took the following form:

CLERK OF COURT: Call the indictment, Her Majesty's Advocate against David Balfour. Are you David Balfour?

ACCUSED: Yes.

MISS McKENZIE: My lord, I appear for the accused. I take it that your lordship has had an opportunity to read the report?

SHERIFF: Yes, Miss McKenzie.

MISS McKENZIE: I submit that the report is reasonably favourable. My client's personal circumstances are fully detailed in it. So far as the previous convictions are concerned, your lordship will see from the social enquiry report that the accused was ultimately fined £25 in respect of the breach of the peace for which sentence was deferred in the district court. The fine has been paid in full. Unless your lordship wishes any further information, I do not want to add anything to what is said in the report with the exception of one very recent development. He has been fortunate enough to obtain a job starting next week if he is at liberty to take it. I have myself been in contact with his prospective employers and have confirmed that the offer of a job is genuine and definite. The employers are aware of the circumstances of this case, as my client has made no attempt to conceal his unfortunate situation. He will be employed as a builder's labourer at a weekly wage of approximately £110 net. From that he will pay to his parents board of £40 per week, and the only other regular commitment which he will have is a club payment of £15 per week.

So far as the facts of the case are concerned, your lordship, of course, heard all the evidence. I submit that the assault of which my client was convicted is not nearly as serious as it appeared at first sight. The jury deleted the reference to severity of injury, and they also found that the accused had been provoked.

As your lordship sees, the report recommends a period of probation with a condition of community service. I submit, with respect, that that would be a disposal which would do justice to the accused on the one hand and to the interests of society on the other.

SHERIFF: Thank you, Miss McKenzie. (*After taking time to consider.*) Stand up please, Mr Balfour. You have been found guilty of a serious crime, but I accept that there were mitigating factors to which I am entitled to give weight. As I am sure you are aware, anyone who carries and uses a knife can usually expect to receive a sentence of custody. However, in your case, because of the mitigating factors to which I have referred, I am prepared to accept the recommendations in the report. I intend to make a probation order for a period of two years with the standard conditions and one additional one. The standard conditions are: that, throughout the period of probation, you will be under the supervision of a social worker; you must obey any directions given to you by the social worker; you must attend for appointments with him or her as required; you must notify your social worker of any change of address; you must not commit any offence while on probation. The additional condition is that you will perform 120 hours unpaid work. You will be told where and when to attend for your work appointments. You must attend punctually and you must perform the work efficiently. You must also keep your supervising social worker informed of the hours when you are working at your normal job and of any changes therein. This is so that your unpaid work may be fitted in with your paid work. Either you or your supervising social worker may apply to the court at any time for a review of the probation order. I must tell you that if you are in breach of probation by failing to abide by any of the conditions which I have described to you, you will be brought back to court and dealt with as if you had not been placed on probation, and that, in your case, would almost certainly mean a custodial sentence. Do you understand?

ACCUSED: Yes.

SHERIFF: And do you accept probation on that basis?

ACCUSED: Yes.

CLERK OF COURT: David Balfour, you have been placed on probation for two years with a condition of performing 120 hours unpaid work.

*Form 23: Social enquiry report*

# DUNCAIRN COUNCIL

**Social Work**

**Kinord House, West Road**
**Duncairn DY12 7QR**

**Tel 01222 003456**
**Fax 01222 006543**

**Case no:** 6031983

## SOCIAL BACKGROUND AND
## COMMUNITY SERVICE REPORT

**Surname:** BALFOUR          **Date of Birth:** 23.11.76

**Forenames:** DAVID          **Occupation:** Unemployed

**Address:** 19 Gairn Street , Duncairn          **Marital Status:** Single

**Offence:** Assault by stabbing committed while on bail

**Date of court appearance:** 7.4.97

---

## BASIS OF REPORT

Mr Balfour has been interviewed twice, once in the company of his parents. He has also attended this office to read over his report. I have had access to full SCRO information.

## FAMILY & HOME CIRCUMSTANCES

Mr Balfour lives at the above address with his parents and younger brother (17 yrs). The area of the home is one of mixed social standards but the house is well furnished and maintained. A transfer to another area has been applied for because it would provide a more healthy environment for both boys. To date the application has been unsuccessful.

Both of Mr Balfour's parents are working, mother only part-time. The family seem to have a strong work ethic.

Mr Balfour is welcome to remain at home for as long as he wishes and is not at present considering making alternative living arrangements.


## PERSONAL HISTORY

Mr Balfour has lived in the area all his life and at the present address for some seventeen years. Education was at local schools where he encountered no problems until his final year at secondary school. At this time and for no apparent reason Mr Balfour lost all interest and began truanting on a regular basis. This was not serious enough to bring him to the attention of the Children's Hearing System but he did leave school in December 1992 without obtaining formal qualifications.

On leaving school Mr Balfour was unemployed until June 1993 when he found work in the building industry. He was made redundant in December 1995 and has remained unemployed since, although he has an interview on APRIL 1st and should have the result by his court appearance on APRIL 7th. This work is also as a builder's labourer.

When Mr Balfour was interviewed alone he was able to speak more openly about relationships, and it emerged that he feels somewhat neglected and ignored by his parents. It seems his brother had an illness and as a result his parents gave him more attention. The feeling has persisted and I would speculate that this is the reason for Mr Balfour's failure to take full advantage of his final year of education. His self-esteem suffered further when his brother did well at school and secured a more prestigious job. These matters have never been discussed within the family.

Mr Balfour does little with his spare time other than socialising with friends and helping with household tasks. He denies taking illegal drugs but I am concerned about his alcohol intake. Whilst he states that drinking is not a problem, Mr Balfour admits that this and previous offences occurred after he had been drinking.

Mr Balfour's income is from benefits at present but could alter if he obtains employment. He has been paying his parents £10 per week for board.

Any monetary penalty could be paid at modest weekly instalments.


## ATTITUDE TO THE OFFENCE AND OFFENDING BEHAVIOUR

Mr Balfour does not see alcohol as a factor in his present offence. He thought he was about to be attacked by a man running towards him and claims he was defending himself. Whilst he shows no particular remorse he now reflects he should have run away.

With regard to re-offending he presents as low to medium risk in view of his stable home background and relatively modest previous offending pattern. Factors which do indicate a future risk are: alcohol misuse, lack of real remorse or victim empathy, denial of responsibility, and lack of self-esteem. These are issues which could form the basis of a work plan within the context of probation supervision.

## COMMUNITY SERVICE

Mr Balfour has been assessed as suitable to perform community service, is willing to do so and there is a vacancy available. Work would be supervised in terms of National Objectives and Standards for Social Work Services in the Criminal Justice System.

## CONCLUSION AND RECOMMENDATION

Mr Balfour presents as an angry, immature young man with some emotional problems stemming from his feeling of neglect by parents. His stable home background is a positive feature as is his keenness to obtain employment. Mr Balfour has no doubt of the seriousness of this offence and the fact that he could lose his liberty.

I have outlined areas at work within the context of probation and Mr Balfour understands the limitations and implications of such an order. I therefore respectfully recommend that Mr Balfour is made the subject of probation coupled with a condition that he perform hours of unpaid work in the community, to mark the serious nature of the offence.

*P. Malcolm.*
..............................................
Ms P Malcolm, Social Worker
Criminal Justice Services (Duncairn)

3 April 1997

PM/AB

# CHAPTER 2

# THE CASE OF NICOL JARVIE

## THE PROCURATOR FISCAL, DUNCAIRN v NICOL JARVIE: SEARCH, ARREST, FIRST COURT APPEARANCE

On Saturday 8 June 1996 Mr James Todd left his second floor flat at 56 Constitution Street, Duncairn at 11 am. He returned home about 5 pm to find that the door had been forced open. The only thing missing was a video cassette recorder which Mr Todd had bought only one week previously. Mr Todd called the police. A uniformed officer came to see him very quickly and, later the same evening, he was interviewed by Detective Constables John Reid and Stephen Watson. DC Reid noted Mr Todd's statement in his notebook. Mr Todd gave the officers the receipt which he obtained when he bought the VCR. This gave its serial number.

During the afternoon of 13 June DC Reid received an anonymous telephone call to the effect that the stolen video cassette recorder was in a flat at 10B Duncry Close, Duncairn, the occupier of which was Nicol Jarvie. DC Reid had had some previous acquaintance with Mr Jarvie, who was aged 26 and had a record for crimes of dishonesty including more than one conviction for theft by housebreaking, so he was not altogether surprised by the information given to him. He decided to ask the procurator fiscal's office to apply to the sheriff for a warrant to search the Jarvie flat. He took to the fiscal's office a brief written report of the facts of the case. The duty procurator fiscal depute prepared a petition applying for a search warrant (see p 63). DC Reid went straight from the fiscal's office to the sheriff court and there saw Sheriff Lawson in his chambers. He explained the circumstances of the case to the sheriff who agreed to grant the search warrant.

At about 6 pm the same day DC Reid and DC Watson went to 10B Duncry Close. They knocked at the door, and it was opened by Mr Jarvie. DC Reid showed him the search warrant and Mr Jarvie asked the officers to come into the house. There they carried out a thorough search. Underneath the bed in the only bedroom of the flat they found a video cassette recorder which they were able to identify from its serial number as that stolen from Mr Todd. DC Reid told Mr Jarvie that he believed the VCR to be stolen, and cautioned him that he was not obliged to say anything but that, if he did, it would be noted and could be used in evidence. He then asked him if he had any explanation for the presence of the VCR under the bed. To this Mr Jarvie replied 'It's just a spare in case my other one packs up'. DC Reid then asked Mr Jarvie how he had got it, and Mr Jarvie said 'I bought it from a guy in a pub'. Thereafter he refused to say anything more. In the living room of the flat there was a VCR attached to the television set. That VCR appeared to be reasonably new, but the police did not test it to see whether it worked.

DC Reid then told Mr Jarvie that he was being arrested on a charge of theft by housebreaking on 8 June 1996 at 56 Constitution Street, Duncairn. He again cautioned him and asked if he had anything he wished to say in reply to the charge. Mr Jarvie replied that he did not. He was then taken to Divisional Police Headquarters in Duncairn and locked up in a cell overnight. He was told that he had a right to have a solicitor informed of his arrest, but decided not to avail himself of it.

The following morning the police report of the case (which consisted at this stage of only a summary of the evidence) went to the procurator fiscal's office, where Susan Stuart, the procurator fiscal depute dealing with custody cases that day, decided that it should be the subject of a summary complaint in the sheriff court. The complaint was prepared (see p 64) and about 11 am Mr Jarvie, who had been taken to the sheriff court, was served with the complaint together with a notice of previous convictions (see p 65).

The legal aid duty solicitor in the sheriff court was Kenneth Liberton, the court partner in a small firm in Duncairn. He had a brief interview with Mr Jarvie, who instructed him that he wished to plead not guilty. Mr Liberton asked him if he had a lawyer of his own. Mr Jarvie said that his regular lawyer was Robert Seymour and that he was wanting Mr Seymour to appear for him at his trial. Mr Liberton knew that Mr Seymour was a partner in the firm in Duncairn which did more criminal defence work than any other. He told Mr Jarvie that he would appear for him in court that day, and Mr Jarvie could then contact Mr Seymour in order to arrange for him to appear at his trial. Mr Jarvie asked Mr Liberton to apply for bail on his behalf. Mr Liberton said that he would do so, but advised Mr Jarvie not to be too optimistic in view of his previous record. However, when Mr Liberton spoke to Miss Stuart just before the case called in court, she said that the Crown was not opposing bail.

About noon Mr Jarvie was taken into court handcuffed to a police officer. Sheriff Walter Scott was on the bench, and Miss Stuart was the depute fiscal taking the court. Matters proceeded as follows:

CLERK OF COURT: Are you Nicol Jarvie?
ACCUSED: Yes.
MR LIBERTON: My lord, I appear for the accused as duty solicitor. He has instructed me to tender a plea of not guilty. I move for bail. I should say that, in any further proceedings, Mr Jarvie will be represented by Mr Seymour.
CLERK OF COURT: Mr Jarvie, do you confirm that you wish to plead not guilty?
ACCUSED: Yes.
PROCURATOR FISCAL DEPUTE: My lord, I move your lordship to fix intermediate and trial diets. I have no objection to the accused being granted bail.
SHERIFF: Very well. Mr Jarvie, you will be released on bail on the following conditions. First, you must attend court on the dates which you will be told. You will be given two dates, and you must attend on the first of these dates. If the case is not then disposed of, you must attend on the second date also. The second condition is that you do not commit any offence while on bail. The third condition is that you do not interfere with witnesses or in any way obstruct the course of justice. And the fourth condition is that in the event of your being convicted of the charge you will make yourself available to enable any reports to be prepared. Do you understand these conditions?
ACCUSED: Yes.
SHERIFF: Do you accept them?

ACCUSED: Yes.

CLERK OF COURT: (*After having confirmed with Miss Stuart that the trial date did not coincide with the leave dates of the police witnesses, which were noted in the police report.*) Intermediate diet 6 September 1996 and trial diet 11 October 1996, both at 10 am. Bail granted.

Mr Jarvie was then taken back to the court cells where, in due course, he was served with his bail order. He was then released from custody.

Outside the court Mr Liberton spoke briefly to Mr Jarvie. He told him that he (Mr Liberton) would give Mr Seymour the service copy complaint and notice of previous convictions. He advised Mr Jarvie to contact Mr Seymour as soon as possible. 'Remember that you've got to apply for legal aid within fourteen days from today.'

On Miss Stuart's return to the office she took steps to instruct the officer in charge of the case, DC Reid, to prepare full witness statements, and this was done. As this was only a summary case the Crown witnesses were not precognosced. The fiscal conducting the trial would do so on the basis of the police statements.

*Form 24: Application for search warrant*

## UNDER THE CRIMINAL PROCEDURE (SCOTLAND) ACT 1995

## IN THE SHERIFF COURT OF TAYSIDE CENTRAL AND FIFE AT DUNCAIRN

## THE PETITION OF GEORGE WILLIAM BROWN PROCURATOR FISCAL DUNCAIRN

DUNCAIRN
13 June 1996

**HUMBLY SHEWETH THAT:-**

*1.* On 8 June 1996, the second floor flat at 56 Constitution Street Duncaim was broken into and a video cassette recorder was stolen therefrom;

*2.* There is reason to believe that said video cassette player can be found at the flat at 10B Duncry Close, Duncairn, occupied by Nicol Jarvie;

**THE PETITIONER THEREFORE CRAVES THE COURT**
to grant Warrant authorising John Reid, Detective Constable of Tayside Police, based at Duncairn or any other police officer of Tayside Police, to enter into said dwellinghouse at **10B DUNCRY CLOSE, DUNCAIRN** and any repositories pertaining thereto or pertaining to said Nicol Jarvie and to search said dwellinghouse and repositories and seize and remove said video cassette player and any other writs, evidents & articles found there, tending to establish guilt or guilty participation in said crime of theft by housebreaking, and for that purpose, to open all shut and lockfast places or to do further or otherwise as to your Lordship may seem meet.

ACCORDING TO JUSTICE

*Susan Smith*

Procurator Fiscal Depute

DUNCAIRN 13 JUNE 1996: The Court having considered the foregoing petition, grants warrant as craved.

**Sheriff**

## Form 25: Complaint against Nicol Jarvie

<u>F.1</u>                                                                                                     C

| Names of Accused | Date of Disposal | Sentence (if any) |
|---|---|---|
|  |  |  |
|  |  |  |
|  |  |  |

96500107

Under the Criminal Procedure (Scotland) Act, 1995

IN THE SHERIFF COURT OF TAYSIDE, CENTRAL AND FIFE AT DUNCAIRN

The COMPLAINT of the PROCURATOR FISCAL against

NICOL JARVIE                                    Date of Birth:  1.3.70
10B DUNCRY CLOSE
DUNCAIRN

The charge against you is that

on 8 June 1996 you did break into the second floor flat at 56 Constitution Street, Duncairn, occupied by James Todd and steal therefrom a video cassette recorder.

*Susan Smart*

Procurator Fiscal Depute

Apprehension
and Search                                  19  .-The Court grants Warrant to apprehend the
said Accused and grants warrant to search the person, dwellinghouse, and repositories of said
Accused and any place where they may be found and to take possession of the property
mentioned or referred to in the Complaint and all articles and documents likely to afford evidence
of guilt or of guilty participation.

SHERIFF

Diet                                        19  .-The Court Assigns
              19  , at       .m., within the SHERIFF Court-House,
                    as a Diet in this case.

Clerk of Court.

## Form 26: Notice of previous convictions

F.19

NOTICE OF PREVIOUS CONVICTIONS APPLYING TO

NICOL JARVIE

In the event of your being convicted of the charge(s) in the Complaint it is intended to place before the Court the following previous conviction(s) applying to you.

| Date | Place of Trial | Court | Offence | Sentence |
|------|----------------|-------|---------|----------|
| 1988<br>17 June | Duncairn | District | Theft | Admonished |
| 20 October | Duncairn | District | Theft | Fined £50 |
| 1989<br>18 August | Duncairn | Sheriff<br>Summary | Theft by Opening Lockfast Places<br>Theft | Probation 1 Year |
| 1990<br>8 January | Duncairn | Sheriff<br>Summary | Theft<br>Con. Police (S) Act 1967 Section 41(1)(a) | Fined £50<br>Fined £50 |
| 15 August | Duncairn | District | Breach of the Peace | Fined £40 |
| 1991<br>29 May | Duncairn | Sheriff<br>Summary | Con. Road Traffic Act 1988, Section 178(1)(a) | Fined £100, Licence Endorsed |
| 23 August | Duncairn | Sheriff<br>Summary | Theft by Housebreaking | 60 Hours<br>Community Service Order |
| 1992<br>15 June | Duncairn | Sheriff<br>Summary | Theft by Housebreaking and Opening Lockfast Places | 30 Days Imprisonment |
| 1993<br>12 February | Duncairn | District | Breach of the Peace<br>Assault | Fined £75 |
| 1994<br>30 September | Duncairn | Sheriff<br>Summary | Theft<br>Fraud | Fined £100<br>Fined £50 and £100<br>Compensation Order |
| 1995<br>6 June | Duncairn | Sheriff<br>Summary | Attempted Housebreaking and Opening Lockfast Places With Intent | 120 Hours Community Service Order |
| 20 December | Duncairn | Sheriff<br>Summary | Theft by Houserbreaking | 3 Months Imprisonment |

# THE PROCURATOR FISCAL, DUNCAIRN v NICOL JARVIE: DEFENCE PREPARATION, INTERMEDIATE DIET

As soon as he left the court Mr Jarvie made an appointment to see Mr Seymour on Tuesday 18 June. At this meeting Mr Seymour (who had meanwhile received the service copy complaint and notice of previous convictions from Mr Liberton) took a brief statement from Mr Jarvie. He also completed a legal aid application form which he got Mr Jarvie to sign (see pp 69–72). In his statement Mr Jarvie said that he knew nothing about the housebreaking on 8 June. He had not even been in Duncairn that day as he had been visiting a friend in Edinburgh. As for the VCR, he had, as he had told the police, bought it from a man in a pub. The date of the transaction was, so far as he could remember, 8 June. He did not know the name of the seller, but had been assured by him that the sale was legitimate. He had paid £120. It was true that he already had a VCR, but it was rather old and had not been working very well. He had been thinking of replacing it.

Mr Seymour submitted the legal aid application to the Scottish Legal Aid Board together with a copy of the complaint, the notice of previous convictions and a note of the address of the office where he signed on for benefit. About a week later he received a legal aid certificate. He then wrote to the procurator fiscal's office and requested a list of the Crown witnesses in Mr Jarvie's case. Shortly afterwards he received the list which contained only three names: Mr James Todd (the owner of the VCR), DC John Reid and DC Stephen Watson. Mr Seymour decided to obtain the two police officers' statements first. He thought that they might provide him with enough information to make it unnecessary for him to interview Mr Todd. He was well aware of the reluctance of many victims of crime to co-operate with defence lawyers.

Mr Seymour, following the usual practice, wrote to the Chief Constable requesting statements from the two police witnesses. In due course he received these. DC Reid's statement was in the following terms:

### Statement of John Turnbull Reid

I am John Turnbull Reid. I am a detective constable in the Tayside Police stationed at Duncairn. I am 29 years old and have ten years' police service.

On 8 June 1996 at 7 pm I attended at the second floor flat at 56 Constitution Street, Duncairn occupied by James Todd. I was accompanied by DC Watson. I took a statement from Mr Todd. He told me that he had been away from the house from 11 am to 5 pm and had discovered the break-in on his return. I saw that the front door had been forced open, apparently by bodily pressure. The lock was broken. Mr Todd informed me that the only item missing was a VCR which he had bought one week previously. He showed me the receipt for it which gave the serial number of the VCR and showed that it had cost £430. I took possession of the receipt (Production No 1). I arranged for members of the Identification Branch to attend and examine the premises for fingerprints. I understand that this examination proved negative.

On 13 June about 3 pm I was at Divisional Headquarters when I received a telephone call from a man who refused to give his name. He said that he had heard that I was dealing with the break-in at 56 Constitution Street and that the stolen VCR was in Nick Jarvie's flat at 10B Duncry Close. I asked him how he knew, but he rang off.

I obtained a search warrant and at 6 pm on the same day, accompanied by DC Watson, I went to Jarvie's flat. We were admitted by Jarvie who was alone in the flat. It consists of one bedroom, living room, bathroom and kitchen. We carried out a search and found a VCR under the bed in the bedroom. I checked the serial number and found that it corresponded with that on the receipt given to me by Mr Todd. I had already seen that there was another VCR in the living room. It was attached to the television. I did not check that it was working, but it looked reasonably new to me. I cautioned Jarvie and asked him to account for his possession of the VCR under the bed. He said: 'It's just a spare in case my other one packs up'. I then asked Jarvie where he had got it. He said: 'I bought it from a guy in a pub'. He refused to answer any further questions. I cautioned and charged him with theft by housebreaking, to which he made no reply. I then arrested him and took him to Divisional Headquarters where he was locked up. I took possession of the VCR (Label No 1).

I can identify Jarvie.

DC Watson's statement was in similar terms.

Mr Seymour decided that he did not require to obtain a precognition from Mr Todd. He wrote to Mr Jarvie asking him to make an appointment to see him as soon as possible, and in due course an appointment was made for 14 August.

At that meeting Mr Seymour went over with Mr Jarvie the statements which he had obtained from the police officers and told him that the prosecution had a strong case against him.

'You were in possession of this VCR fairly soon after it had been stolen, and the fact that it was under the bed may be sufficient in the way of suspicious circumstances to raise a presumption that you stole it.'

'I've told you already that I know nothing about the break-in. I was in Edinburgh all that day.'

Mr Seymour asked for the name and address of the friend in Edinburgh whom Mr Jarvie had been visiting, and was given the name Stewart Green of 65 Niddrie Mains Road. Mr Jarvie was certain that Mr Green would be willing to give evidence on his behalf.

Having discussed the case further, Mr Seymour prepared a precognition for Mr Jarvie as follows:

### Precognition of Nicol Jarvie

I am Nicol Jarvie. I live at 10B Duncry Close, Duncairn. I am 26 years old. I am unemployed.

I know nothing about the housebreaking at 56 Consitution Street, Duncairn on 8 June 1996.

On 7 June 1996 I travelled to Edinburgh by bus to visit my friend, Stewart Green, 65 Niddrie Mains Road. I arrived in Edinburgh about 7 pm and went immediately to Stewart's house. We both then went out for a drink. We started off in a pub and ended up at a party somewhere. I don't know the address. We got back to Stewart's house about 1 am. The next morning we did not get up until 10. Stewart and I had something to eat and then went out for a drink and to the bookie's. We were in the pub until about 5 pm. I then caught the bus back to Duncairn.

I got back to Duncairn about 7 pm. I went home and had something to eat. I then went to my local, the Rowan Tree. I got there about 9 pm. I got talking to a guy I'd never met before. He told me he had a VCR to sell. He was needing money badly. My own VCR had been playing up a bit so I was interested in this one. I asked him if it was legit and he said it was. He asked for £150, and I said that I'd give him £120. I'd been lucky on the horses that afternoon, so I had the money. He agreed to accept £120. We then went outside to a van. The VCR was in the back of the van. I took it and gave him the £120. He then drove off in the van. I haven't seen him since.

I can't really describe the guy. He was quite ordinary looking, aged about 35. The van was green, I think. I don't remember what make it was.

I took the VCR home and put it under my bed. My old one seemed to be working OK, so I really didn't give it a thought until the police came round. I agree that I told the police that I'd bought it from a guy in a pub and that it was a spare in case my other one packed up.

I had no idea the VCR was stolen. If I had, I would not have touched it. I have been trying to go straight since I got out of jail in February.

Mr Seymour reminded Mr Jarvie that he had to be in court for the intermediate diet on 6 September and said that he would write to Mr Green in order to ask him for a statement. He did so, but had received no reply by 6 September.

On 6 September Mr Jarvie attended the intermediate diet court in which there were about 40 cases due to call. He arrived a little before 10 am. He looked for Mr Seymour to ask him if he had heard from Mr Green. However, Mr Seymour had six other cases calling that morning and was too busy to speak to Mr Jarvie and tell him about Mr Green's failure to communicate. Eventually Mr Jarvie's case called.

CLERK OF COURT: Intermediate diet. Nicol Jarvie. Are you Nicol Jarvie?

ACCUSED: Yes.

MR SEYMOUR: My lord, I appear for Mr Jarvie. He adheres to his plea of not guilty. The case is fully prepared with the exception of a statement from one witness. I can at this stage indicate that my client will be pleading an alibi. He maintains that from about 7 pm on 7 June until about 5.30 pm on 8 June he was in Edinburgh and that from about 5.30 pm until 7 pm on the latter date he was on a bus between Edinburgh and Duncairn. A witness, Stewart Green of 65 Niddrie Mains Road, Edinburgh, will be called to prove the alibi. I move your lordship to continue bail.

SHERIFF LAWSON: Thank you Mr Seymour. (*Addressing Kenneth Patrick, the procurator fiscal depute*) Mr Patrick, is the Crown prepared?

PROCURATOR FISCAL DEPUTE: Yes, my lord. All the witnesses have been cited.

SHERIFF: Is there any evidence which can be agreed? What about the householder's evidence?

MR SEYMOUR: I am prepared to agree the evidence of Mr Todd, my lord.

PROCURATOR FISCAL DEPUTE: I am obliged to my friend. I shall have a joint minute prepared.

SHERIFF: Very well.

CLERK OF COURT: Case continued to the trial diet on 11 October at 10 am. Bail continued.

After leaving court Mr Seymour spoke to Mr Jarvie and told him he had not heard from Mr Green. Mr Jarvie said that Green was not very good at answering letters, but that he (Jarvie) had spoken to him on the telephone and he had confirmed that he would be willing to attend as a witness. Mr Seymour said that he would issue him with a citation to attend and would have an interview with him before the trial started.

That same day Mr Seymour sent instructions to sheriff officers in Edinburgh to cite Green as a witness for the trial. In due course he received from the sheriff officers an execution of citation showing that Green had personally received the citation. Mr Seymour put the execution of citation in his file so that he could take it to court on the date of the trial. If Green failed to attend Mr Seymour would be able to produce the execution as evidence that he had been properly cited. About ten days after the intermediate diet Mr Seymour received from the fiscal a draft joint minute which set out the terms of Mr Todd's evidence. Mr Seymour checked it and returned it to the fiscal's office with a letter saying that it was correct.

*Form 27: SLAB application form for legal aid in summary criminal proceedings*

| | |
|---|---|
| **SCOTTISH LEGAL AID BOARD** | **SUMMARY** |
| APPLICATION FOR LEGAL AID IN SUMMARY CRIMINAL PROCEEDINGS | |

**PART A - THE APPLICANT**

1. Applicant's personal legal aid reference number (if known)

2. Applicant's National Insurance number (if known)

    Y Z 8 2 4 5 7 9 D

3. ✓ Male    Female    4. ✓ Single    Married    Divorced    Widowed

5. ✓ Mr    Mrs    Miss    Ms    *Enter below any other title preferred for use in correspondence*

6. Applicant's forename(s)    NICOL

7. Applicant's surname    JARVIE

PLEASE NOTE: The information asked for in questions 8-12 is needed so that we can be sure we never confuse your records with those of someone else having the same name.

8. Applicant's surname at birth if different from surname above    9. Maiden surname of applicant's mother

     N/A          ROBERTS

10. Date of birth   *Day Month Year*   1 5 0 3 1 9 7 0    11. Age last birthday   2 6    12. Place of birth   *Town, city or district*   DUNCAIRN

13. Usual home address
*Use a separate line for each part of your address, just as if you were addressing an envelope. Please include your postcode to ensure that mail reaches you as soon as possible.*

     10B Duncry Close
     DUNCAIRN

     14. Postcode    DU12   7LB

15. Name and address for correspondence
*The Board may have to write to you. If you do not wish mail to be addressed using the first forename and surname and address above, please say here how you wish mail to be addressed.*

     *Forename*
     *Surname*

     As above

     16. Postcode

17. Daytime telephone number      01683 449286

18. Occupation, trade or profession
*Even if not now in work*      Unemployed labourer

---

Use this form only where a plea of NOT GUILTY has been tendered in a summary procedure case.

A copy of the complaint, containing the charge(s) against the applicant, should be submitted with this form. If the applicant is working, the last payslip should also be submitted.

> **This application must be lodged with the Board within 14 days of the first diet at which the plea of not guilty was tendered.**
> **The Board may consider a late application if there is a special reason for doing so.**

Page 2

**PART B - THE CASE** - *To be completed by the solicitor*

1. Was there a special urgency grant of legal aid in this case?                    Yes      ✓No

   If Yes, please give the date and reference number of this grant
                    Day   Month   Year                              *Legal aid case reference number*
                    |  |  ,  |    |  |  |  |

2. **Case category**    Please indicate the nature of the charge. Where more than one charge is involved, please
                 indicate the most serious charge by ticking one, and only one, of the following boxes

   | Assault | Breach of the Peace | ✓Criminal Justice (Scotland) Act | Drugs offences |
   |---|---|---|---|
   | Embezzlement | Fraud | Housebreaking | Police (Scotland) Act |
   | Road Traffic | Robbery | Possession of offensive weapon | Sexual offences |
   | Theft of motor vehicle | Theft | Other (specify) | |

                                                           Day   Month   Year
3. Date when the plea of NOT GUILTY was tendered          1|4  |0|6  |1.9|9|6

                                                           Day   Month   Year
4. Date of any intermediate diet fixed                    0|6  |0|9  |1|9|9|6

                                                           Day   Month   Year
5. Date set for the trial (if known)                      1|1  |1|0  |1|9|9|6

6. The court is the   Sheriff Court at   DUNCAIRN          ~~District Court at~~

7. The Procurator Fiscal's reference number for this case is        9 6 |5|0|0|1|0|7|  |

8. Names of any co-accused   None . . . . . . . . . . . . . .

9. Has the applicant previously applied for legal aid in this case?        Yes      ✓ No

   If Yes, please state the legal aid case reference number (if known)    *Legal aid case reference number*
   Please explain why another application for legal aid is now being made

   . . . . . . . . . . . . . . . . . . . . . . . . . . . . . . . . . . . . . . . . . . . . . . . . . . . .

10. Has the applicant any rights or facilities which might assist in the defence of
    this case? *e.g. from insurers, employer, trade union, motoring organisation, etc.*        Yes      ✓ No

    If Yes, please give details and explain why an application has been made for legal aid

    . . . . . . . . . . . . . . . . . . . . . . . . . . . . . . . . . . . . . . . . . . . . . . . . . . . .

11. If the applicant is in custody, please state where, and in what circumstances
    *e.g., on remand, already serving a sentence, non-appearance warrant, etc.*

    . . . . . . . . . . . . . . . . . . . . . . . . . . . . . . . . . . . . . . . . . . . . . . . . . . . .

12. **Interests of justice**

    In determining whether it is in the interests of justice that criminal legal aid be made available, the Board must take into account
    certain factors specified in section 24(3) of the Legal Aid (Scotland) Act 1986. These statutory factors are detailed on the next page.

    If it is felt that any of the statutory factors (a) - (d) on page 3 apply, it will be helpful to give a relevant explanation against that factor where it
    appears on page 3. (If a statement by the applicant is submitted and deals with various matters, it is <u>not</u> sufficient merely to state against any
    particular factor "See statement".)

    Information about factor (e) (the defence), or about factor (f) (remanded in custody pending trial) may be given at paragraph 13 on the next page,
    or in a separate statement, if that is preferred. Any separate statement must also be signed and dated by the applicant.

    **Please give as much information as possible to assist the Board in deciding whether it is in the interests of justice for the applicant
    to be given legal representation.**

Page 3

**PART B - THE CASE (Continued)**

**12. Interests of Justice (Continued)** *Full information should be provided for each factor which applies in this case*

a. The offence is such that if proved it is likely that the court would impose a sentence which would deprive the accused of his liberty or lead to loss of his livelihood.

Yes. The accused has a substantial schedule of previous convictions, including his last conviction being the maximum sentence of imprisonment in summary proceedings. He has also had in the past probation which was breached and also Community Service. If convicted custody is almost inevitable.

b. The determination of the case may involve consideration of a substantial question of law, or of evidence of a complex or difficult nature.

Yes. There is the question whether the accused being in recent possession of the stolen item would entitle the court to draw the inference that he had stolen or reset it. There is case law on that matter. In addition the accused maintains a defence of alibi.

c. The accused may be unable to understand the proceedings or to state his own case because of his age, inadequate knowledge of English, mental illness, other mental or physical disability or otherwise.

Yes. The accused is of low level of intellect and also has a severe alcohol problem.

d. It is in the interests of someone other than the accused that the accused be legally represented.

Yes. The complainer in this case whose evidence may be agreed by Minute of Admission.

e. The defence to be advanced by the accused does not appear to be frivolous.
   In my opinion the defence (summarised at 13 below)    ✓ is not frivolous        is frivolous

f. The accused has been remanded in custody pending trial.                    Yes              ✓ No

**13. State here the nature of the defence to be advanced to the charge(s). Specify any charge(s) in relation to which a plea of guilty has been, or will be, tendered. Also state here any other factors or additional information which may assist the Board in determining the application. If you are submitting a separate statement, this must also be signed and dated by the applicant.**

The accused maintains that at the time of the actual housebreaking libelled he was in Edinburgh. He has a defence witness to confirm his alibi. If he was not in Edinburgh at the time of the offence he was on a public service vehicle returning to Duncairn. The accused attended at a public house at Duncairn upon his return and there purchased the VCR. He paid £120 for it which would indicate that the transaction was an honest one and the accused is therefore not even guilty of reset. He is adamant and told the police according to his precognition that he had an alibi and also his possession of the stolen item, although recent, was possession in good faith.

Page 4

## PART C - FINANCIAL STATEMENT

The Board has to decide if you can meet the cost of your case without undue hardship to yourself or your dependants. Full information must be given about your own means. You do not have to say anything about the means of your spouse or anyone else, but you should say if someone is getting a state benefit for you. The Board may make enquiries to verify information given.

**EMPLOYMENT STATUS**

1. employed ✓   unemployed   self-employed
   student   company director   retired

**CAPITAL (To the nearest pound)**

2. Cash (coin, banknotes, cheques) £ NIL
3. Money in Bank £ NIL
   Building Society £ NIL
4. Shares in £ NIL
5. a. Land at £ NIL
   b. House (other than your main house) at £ NIL
   c. Timeshare at £ NIL
6. Loan secured over above property owed to £ NIL
7. Other capital   *Say what this is* £ NIL
   £ NIL
8. Money due by applicant   (e.g. expenses regularly met from savings) *Say what these are* £ NIL
   £ NIL

**PERSONS DEPENDENT ON APPLICANT**

*What dependants (if any) do you yourself actually support (either wholly or partly)?*

9. Do you support a spouse?   | | Yes  |✓| No
10. Number of dependent children under 11   ( )
11. Number of dependent children aged 11 to 15   ( )
12. Number of dependent children aged 16 or 17   ( )
13. Number of dependants aged 18 or over   ( )

(name) . . . . . . . . . . . . . . . . .
(name) . . . . . . . . . . . . . . . . .
(name) . . . . . . . . . . . . . . . . .

**INCOME (from all sources)**

14. Child Benefit
    ☐ per week ☐ per 2 weeks ☐ per 4 weeks   £
15. Any other state benefits   *Say what these are*
    a Unemployment Benefit
    ☐ per week ☑ per 2 weeks ☐ per 4 weeks   £ 72.00
    b
    ☐ per week ☐ per 2 weeks ☐ per 4 weeks   £
16. Address of benefit office
    Thistle Street
    Duncairn
17. Pay or sick pay from work (including overtime, commission, bonuses, but after deducting tax, National Insurance, etc.)
    ☐ per week ☐ per 2 weeks ☐ per month ☐ per year   £
18. Name and address of any employer(s)
19. Drawings from business if self-employed or in partnership
    ☐ per week ☐ per 2 weeks ☐ per month ☐ per year   £
20. Student grant
    ☐ per week ☐ per 2 weeks ☐ per month ☐ per year   £
21. Money from any other source including maintenance
    *Say what this is*
    ☐ per week ☐ per 2 weeks ☐ per month ☐ per year   £

**PAYMENTS DUE BY APPLICANT**
Please do not include general living expenses, such as food, gas/electricity, clothes, petrol, etc.- a standard allowance will be given for these items.

22. Rent or Board and Lodgings
    ☐ per week ☐ per 2 weeks ☐ per month ☐ per year   £
23. Mortgage (including any endowment or life policies linked to the mortgage)
    ☐ per week ☐ per 2 weeks ☐ per month ☐ per year   £
24. Council Tax/Community Charge
    ☐ per week ☐ per 2 weeks ☐ per month ☐ per year   £
25. Maintenance paid to
    (name)
    ☐ per week ☐ per 2 weeks ☐ per month ☐ per year   £
    (name)
    ☐ per week ☐ per 2 weeks ☐ per month ☐ per year   £
26. Other payments due to be made   *Say what these are*
    HP 15: Gas £10: Electricity £10
    ☐ per week ☑ per 2 weeks ☐ per month ☐ per year   £ 25.00

## PART D - DECLARATION BY APPLICANT *IF YOU KNOWINGLY MAKE A FALSE STATEMENT YOU MAY BE PROSECUTED*

I declare that the information given in this application is true and complete to the best of my knowledge and belief. I give my permission for the Scottish Legal Aid Board to make enquiries of any other persons or bodies as it may consider necessary in relation to this application. I authorise such other persons or bodies to provide such information as may be required by the Board. I apply for legal aid and wish the solicitor named below to act for me.

Signature of applicant   *Nicol Jarvie*   Date signed   18.6.96

## PART E - DETAILS OF SOLICITOR ACTING (PLEASE PRINT)

1. Practitioner's code number   1 2 3 4 5 1
2. Branch code   –

3. Your reference   RS

   Name   ROBERT SEYMOUR
   Firm   Messrs Davidson & Young
   Address   7 North Street
   DUNCAIRN
   DX DU27
   Postcode   DU19 7YT

### DECLARATION BY SOLICITOR

4. As the applicant is in custody, I am giving criminal legal aid until this application is determined, by virtue of the automatic legal aid provisions of section 22(1)(d) of the Legal Aid (Scotland) Act 1986.   Yes   No

I confirm that I have agreed to act on behalf of the applicant if legal aid is granted.

*Robert Seymour*
Signature of solicitor
18.6.96
Date

# THE PROCURATOR FISCAL, DUNCAIRN v NICOL JARVIE: TRIAL, VERDICT AND SENTENCE

On 11 October at 10.30 am the 'call over' of cases set down for summary trial that day took place before Sheriff Walter Scott. The reason why they did not call at 10 am, as they should have done, was that Sheriff Scott had two cases to deal with which had been adjourned for sentence from trials which had taken place four weeks previously. There were nine trials all together in the call over. Of these four pleaded guilty and were disposed of. In two others the accused had failed to turn up, so the Crown moved for a warrant to apprehend. In one an essential Crown witness had been suddenly taken ill, so the trial was adjourned to a later date. In the case of Mr Jarvie and one other case the pleas of not guilty were adhered to. The other trial proceeded first, which was a great relief to Mr Seymour as he had not yet had an opportunity to interview Mr Green, although the latter *had* appeared in response to his citation.

While the other trial was proceeding Mr Seymour spoke to Mr Green and obtained a brief statement from him. This confirmed what Mr Jarvie had said about the time of his arrival in and departure from Edinburgh, although Mr Green was somewhat vague about what had happened during the period in between.

Mr Seymour had already prepared a 'list of defence witnesses' as a courtesy for the court, and he now gave three copies of this list to the court officer, so that he, the sheriff and the fiscal could each have one. The 'list' contained only the one name, that of Mr Green.

At 12.15 the other trial finished and Mr Jarvie went into the dock. The Crown was represented by Susan Stuart, the depute fiscal who had originally dealt with the case (although this was purely coincidental), and Mr Jarvie was, of course, represented by Mr Seymour. The clerk of court was Mr Harrison. The trial proceeded as follows:

CLERK: Trial of Nicol Jarvie. Are you Nicol Jarvie?

ACCUSED: Yes.

SOLICITOR: My lord, my client adheres to his plea of not guilty. I would remind your lordship that, at the intermediate diet, I gave notice of a special defence of alibi. (*Mr Seymour repeated the terms of the alibi.*)

PROCURATOR FISCAL DEPUTE: My lord, there is a joint minute dealing with the evidence of the householder, Mr Todd. I lodge that now. (*Miss Stuart handed the joint minute, which she and Mr Seymour has earlier signed, to Mr Harrison who passed it up to the sheriff – see p 79.*) My first witness is DC Reid.

## JOHN TURNBULL REID (SWORN)

EXAMINED BY THE PROCURATOR FISCAL DEPUTE: Are you John Turnbull Reid, a detective constable of Tayside Police?—Yes.

What are your age and length of service?—29 years old and ten years' police service.

In the evening of Saturday 8 June this year were you instructed to attend at a flat at 56 Constitution Street, Duncairn in connection with an alleged theft by housebreaking?—I was.

What time did you get there?—About 7 pm.

What did you find?—The front door of the flat had clearly been forced. The Yale lock was broken. The jamb had been torn away from the woodwork. I saw the householder, Mr Todd, who informed me that a VCR was missing. He gave me the receipt for it.

Please look at Production 1. Is that the receipt?—Yes.

Did you arrange for a search to be made for fingerprints?—Yes. It proved negative.

What was your next involvement with the case?—I received certain information as a result of which I obtained a search warrant for the flat at 10B Duncry Close. That was on 13 June. I went there about 6 pm.

Please look at Production 2. Is that the search warrant?—It is.

Was anyone with you?—Yes, my colleague, DC Watson. He had also been with me at the flat on the 8th.

What happened when you went to Duncry Close?—We knocked at the door, and it was opened by the accused.

When you say 'the accused', is that someone who is in court?—Yes. That's him there. (*The witness pointed at the accused.*)

What happened then?—I showed him the search warrant, and he let us in. We then searched the flat.

Did you find anything of significance?—Yes. Under the bed in the bedroom we found a VCR with the same serial number as was on the receipt.

Please look at Label 1. Is that the VCR you found?—Yes.

Was there any other VCR in the flat?—Yes. There was one attached to the television in the living room.

What did you do when you found the VCR under the bed?—I cautioned the accused and asked him if he could account for it being there.

Did he say anything?—May I be allowed to refer to my notebook?

Did you make the note at the time?—Yes.

SHERIFF: Mr Seymour, have you any objection?

MR SEYMOUR: No, my lord.

SHERIFF: Please do consult your book.

THE WITNESS: The accused said: 'It's just a spare in case my other one packs up.' I then asked him where he had got it, and he said: 'I bought it from a guy in a pub.' He refused to say anything more.

What happened then?—I cautioned and charged the accused, and he made no reply. I then arrested him and took him to police headquarters.

CROSS-EXAMINED BY MR SEYMOUR: Was Mr Jarvie obstructive in any way?—Oh no. Not at all.

Was the VCR concealed?—Well, it was right under the bed. You couldn't see it without either getting down on the floor or moving the bed.

Did you test the other VCR, the one attached to the TV?—No.

So far as you know, it may have been on its last legs?—I suppose so, but it looked fairly new and, if it wasn't working properly, I don't understand why it was still attached to the TV and the other one was under the bed.

Is it the case that, apart from finding the VCR in his flat, you found no other evidence to connect my client with this crime?—That's correct.

There is no suggestion that he was seen hanging around the locus on the day of the break-in?—No, sir.

*DC Watson was then called to give evidence, and his examination-in-chief and cross-examination proceeded in virtually the same way as that of DC Reid. At the conclusion of DC Watson's evidence Miss Stuart closed the Crown's case.*

MR SEYMOUR: My lord, I have a submission to make in terms of section 160 of the 1995 Act. In my submission there is no case to answer in respect that there is insufficient evidence in law to prove that my client committed the crime charged or any other crime of which he could competently be found guilty on this charge. The only evidence implicating him is that the stolen VCR was found in his flat. No doubt my friend will seek to found on the doctrine of recent possession, but, in my submission, while the property may indeed have been recently stolen, there is nothing in the way of criminative circumstances surrounding my client's possession, and, as your lordship is well aware, the existence of such circumstances is essential before the doctrine can be prayed in aid.

SHERIFF: What about the fact that the VCR was found under a bed? Is that not suspicious?

MR SEYMOUR: In my submission, no. That is neutral. I don't think that I can usefully add anything to what I have said.

PFD: My lord, in my submission there are criminative circumstances here. There is, as your lordship has said, the fact that the VCR was found under a bed. That is surely an unusual place to keep such an object. There is also the fact that there was another VCR in the house, apparently being used normally as it was attached to the TV. I think that I am also entitled to found on the explanation given by the accused as to how he came into possession of it. Buying from a man in a pub is just about as hackneyed an excuse as saying it fell off the back of a lorry. Certainly, I submit that the three factors taken together are more than ample to provide criminative circumstances, which, together with the possession, raise a presumption of guilt. It is, of course, open to the accused to rebut that presumption.

MR SEYMOUR: I have nothing to add.

SHERIFF: In my opinion there is a case to answer here. I agree that the place where the VCR was found together with the fact that there was another VCR apparently in use in the house amount to criminative circumstances. It may well be that the explanation given by the accused as to how it came into his possession is also a criminative circumstance. I reject the defence submission. Mr Seymour, do you wish to lead evidence?

MR SEYMOUR: Yes, my lord. Might I suggest that, that as it is now 12.50, your lordship hears the defence case after lunch?

SHERIFF: Certainly. I shall adjourn until two o'clock.

*When the court resumed after lunch Mr Seymour called Mr Jarvie to give evidence.*

NICOL JARVIE (SWORN)
EXAMINED BY MR SEYMOUR: Is your full name Nicol Jarvie, do you live at 10B Duncry Close, Duncairn, and are you 26 years old?—Yes, sir.

Mr Jarvie, where were you on Saturday, 8 June this year?—I was in Edinburgh until about half past five. I had gone there the night before. I didn't get back to Duncairn until about seven.

Where were you staying in Edinburgh?—With my friend, Stewart Green. He lives in Niddrie.

Were you with him the whole time you were in Edinburgh?—Yes. We went to a pub and then a party the night I got there. We went to the pub again at dinner time on the Saturday and stayed there until I left apart from going to the bookie's next door.

What time did you leave Edinburgh?—My bus was about 5.30.

What time did you get back to Duncairn?—About seven.

What did you do when you got back to Duncairn?—I went home and had something to eat. I then went out to the Rowan Tree. That's my local.

What happened there?—A man spoke to me and asked me if I wanted to buy a video. I was interested because mine wasn't working very well. He wanted £150, but I offered him £120 and he accepted. He had the video in his van. We went out and I collected it and took it home.

Do you know this man's name?—No.

Had you seen him before?—No, I don't think so.

Have you seen him since?—No.

How did you come to have £120 on you?—I'd had a bit of luck with the horses that afternoon in Edinburgh.

Why did you put the VCR under the bed?—I didn't want it to be too obvious in case anybody saw it and decided to pinch it. I found that my old one was still working OK.

Did you have no suspicion about being offered the VCR in a pub by a stranger?—Oh no. People often buy and sell things in that pub. I asked the guy if it was legit, and he assured me it was. The only reason he was selling it was that he was hard up.

CROSS-EXAMINED BY THE PROCURATOR FISCAL DEPUTE: What did you do in Edinburgh on the Friday night?—We went to a pub and then to a party.

Which pub?—I don't know.

Where was the party?—I don't know. I don't know Edinburgh that well.

When did you get back to your friend's house?—About one.

What time did you get up the next day?—About ten.

What was the name of the pub you went to on the Saturday?—I can't remember.

Was it the same one as the night before?—No.

Which betting shop did you go to?—William Hill.

What horses did you back that day?—I don't remember.

What sort of bet was it?—A three horse accumulator.

What did you put on?—About a fiver.

How much did you win?—I can't remember exactly, but it was about £150.

Are you surprised to hear that the VCR had been bought only a week previously for £430?—I don't really know the value of these things.

If that was the price, then you were getting it very cheaply paying only £120, weren't you?—I suppose so.

How much did you pay for your own VCR?—I don't remember. I think it was about a couple of hundred quid.

And you weren't at all suspicious?—No.

Aren't you just making all this up?—No.

Isn't it the case that you came into possession of that VCR by breaking into Mr Todd's flat and stealing it?—No. As God's my witness I was in Edinburgh that day.

Or, if you didn't steal it, didn't you get it from the thief knowing very well that it was stolen?—I had no idea it was stolen. If I had, I wouldn't have touched it.

*Miss Stuart sat down pretty well satisfied with her cross-examination. She felt that, by concentrating on the details of the alleged alibi, she had exposed Mr Jarvie's rather patchy knowledge of what he had been supposed to be doing in Edinburgh. Mr Seymour did not re-examine. He also realised that Miss Stuart's cross had been effective, and he had no desire to get Mr Jarvie into deeper trouble.*

STEWART GREEN (SWORN)

EXAMINED BY MR SEYMOUR: Is your full name Stewart Green, do you live at 65 Niddrie Mains Road, Edinburgh, and are you 27 years old?—Yes.

Do you have a job?—I'm a dealer.

Do you know Mr Jarvie, who is sitting there? (*Indicating the dock*)—Yes.

How long have you known him?—About five years.

Does he ever come to visit you in Edinburgh?—Yes. Quite often.

Please take your mind back to a Friday near the beginning of June this year. Did Mr Jarvie come to see you then?—Yes, it was the first Friday in June, the 7th, I think. He came to my house about quarter past seven.

What did you do then?—We went out to the pub and then on to a party.

What time did you get home?—About five o'clock.

What did you do the next day?—We got up about twelve, had something to eat and went out to the pub.

Did you go anywhere else apart from the pub?—Yes. The bookie's.

What time did Mr Jarvie leave to go home?—About half five.

CROSS-EXAMINED BY THE PROCURATOR FISCAL DEPUTE: What pub did you go to on the Friday night?—The Edinburgh Arms.

What pub did you go to on the Saturday?—The same one. It's my local.

What bookie did you go to?—Harrower's.

Did Mr Jarvie have a bet?—Yes. He won some money.

How much?—About £25 I think.

What sort of bet did he have?—I think it was a double.

Are you sure you're remembering the right weekend?—Yes.

Are you an honest man?—I think so.

Have you been convicted of perjury?—Yes, but that was a long time ago. I told a lie in court because I was scared of getting beaten up.

Aren't you telling lies now in order to protect your friend?—No. I'm telling the truth. He was with me that weekend.

What sort of dealer are you, Mr Green?—General dealer.

Do you ever deal in video cassette recorders?—Sometimes.

RE-EXAMINED BY MR SEYMOUR: When were you convicted of perjury?—When I was sixteen.

What was the sentence?—I had sentence deferred for a year for good behaviour, and then I was admonished.

*Mr Seymour decided not to ask any questions directed at the discrepancies between Mr Green's evidence and that of Mr Jarvie. He feared that if he did so, even more damage might be done to the defence case.*

MR SEYMOUR: My lord, that is the case for the defence.

PFD: My lord, in my submission there is sufficient evidence here for your lordship to infer that the accused is guilty as libelled. I found on the doctrine of recent possession. Your lordship has already held that there is enough evidence for that doctrine to operate. In my submission the accused's explanation of his possession should be rejected as utterly incredible. I would remind your lordship of the discrepancies between the evidence of the accused and that of his witness. They differed as to times, names of places and the nature of bets. I suggest that the whole alibi is simply concocted. It is not without significance, perhaps, that Mr Green is a dealer who deals occasionally in VCRs. I invite your lordship to find the charge proved. At the very least, if your lordship is not satisfied that there is sufficient evidence of the accused's involvement in the actual theft, I submit that your lordship must find him guilty of reset of the VCR, which your lordship is aware is a competent verdict on a charge of theft. I would press, however, for a verdict of guilty as libelled.

SHERIFF: Thank you Miss Stuart. Mr Seymour.

MR SEYMOUR: My lord, in my submission you should accept my client and Mr Green as witnesses worthy of credit. It is true that there were discrepancies between them, but does this not demonstrate that they have not put their heads together to concoct a story? Had they done so, surely they would have made a better job of it. I suggest that your lordship should have no difficulty in accepting that my client could not have committed the housebreaking as he was in Edinburgh at the time. So far as the circumstances of his coming into possession of the VCR are concerned, again surely he would have made up a better story if he had been trying to manufacture one. It may seem strange for him to buy a VCR in a pub, but, as your lordship knows, strange things do happen. And if he paid £120 for it, that is still a substantial amount of money. If he had said that he paid only £10, then that really would have been incredible. On the whole matter I urge your lordship to find my client not guilty or, at the very least, to find the charge not proven.

SHERIFF (*after a few minutes' consideration*): I accept that there are cases where discrepancies between the evidence of witnesses reinforce credibility, but that is when the discrepancies are relatively few and of a minor character. In the present case the discrepancies between the accused and Mr Green are so numerous that I cannot accept their evidence as credible. I accordingly reject the alibi. Equally, I have found unworthy of belief the accused's evidence of how he came into possession of the VCR. I accordingly reject that evidence also. This means that the accused has completely failed to rebut the presumption of guilt created by his possession of the recently stolen VCR in criminative circumstances. Although there may be nothing else to connect him with the actual housebreaking, I am entitled under the doctrine of recent possession to find him guilty of the crime charged. I have rejected his alibi as false, and this reinforces my view that I should find him guilty as libelled, which I now do.

PFD: My lord I produce a schedule of previous convictions.

MR SEYMOUR: These are admitted. I must accept, my lord, that my client has a bad record for dishonesty. However, he has kept out of trouble, apart from the present offence, since his release from prison in February.

SHERIFF: That's not very long, Mr Seymour.

MR SEYMOUR: Not perhaps for you or me, my lord, but quite long for my client. I would remind your lordship that, contrary to what happens all too often in housebreaking cases, there was no suggestion here of the house being ransacked or vandalised. My client is unfortunately unemployed. He is single and has no dependants. He receives benefit of £72 per fortnight. His rent is paid direct. He has the usual household expenses. I appreciate that a custodial sentence must be a possibility, but I would strongly urge your lordship to consider a financial penalty or, alternatively, to ask for a community service report.

SHERIFF (*after some consideration*): Stand up please, Mr Jarvie. You have been found guilty of a serious crime. You have previous convictions for dishonesty. In my opinion a fine would be an unrealistic disposal. Given your record and the gravity of the offence, a fine would be quite inappropriate. You received a sentence of community service not that long ago, and that clearly did not have the desired effect of discouraging you from offending. I'm afraid that I can see no alternative to a sentence of imprisonment. Looking to your record and the nature of the crime, I should be perfectly justified in imposing a sentence of six months. I am, however, with some hesitation prepared to restrict it to a period of four months.

## Form 28: Joint minute of agreement

96500107

UNDER THE CRIMINAL PROCEDURE (SCOTLAND) ACT 1995
SHERIFF COURT OF TAYSIDE, CENTRAL AND FIFE AT DUNCAIRN

JOINT MINUTE OF AGREEMENT
RE
GEORGE WILLIAM BROWN
PROCURATOR FISCAL, DUNCAIRN       COMPLAINER
against
NICOL JARVIE       ACCUSED

Shaun Butler, Procurator Fiscal Depute and Robert Seymour, Solicitor for the Accused concur in stating to the Court that the following fact(s) are agreed and should be admitted in evidence

1.      on 8 June 1996 at approximately 11 am, the second floor flat at 56 Constitution Street, Duncairn was locked and secured by the occupier, namely James Todd;

2.      at that time the front door of said flat was undamaged and Crown label production number 1 (video cassette recorder) was within said house;

3.      at approximately 5 pm on 8 June 1996, said John Todd returned to said house and discovered that (i) said house had been broken into, entry having been obtained by forcing open and damaging said front door and (ii) said video cassette recorder had been stolen;

4.      the estimated cost of repairing said door was £45; and

5.      the cost of said video cassette recorder when purchased one week prior to said theft was £430, conform to Crown production number 1 (sales receipt) which relates to said purchase.

In respect whereof


*Shaun Butler*

PROCURATOR FISCAL DEPUTE

*Robert Seymour*

FOR THE ACCUSED

CHAPTER 3

# FROM CRIME TO COURT

## INTRODUCTION

The investigation of crime in Scotland is carried out by the police. The public prosecution of crime is the responsibility of the Lord Advocate, who acts, at the local level, through the procurator fiscal service. In theory the police act on the instructions of the procurator fiscal in investigating crime[1], but nowadays it is relatively rare for the fiscal to be personally concerned in the investigation of a case except for such serious crimes as murder.

The first part of this chapter is concerned with the powers which the police have to question, detain, arrest and search, all or any of which may be a preliminary to an accused person's appearing before a court. It should, however, be remembered that the great majority of criminal cases are summary prosecutions where the accused is simply cited to attend court without having been detained or arrested, and where there has been no search carried out. A person may be cited without ever having been charged, although the majority of those cited will have been charged. Citation will be described below in the chapter dealing with summary prosecution (chapter 6). The second part of this chapter is concerned with the role of the solicitor prior to a case actually coming to court.

## PART 1: THE POLICE INVOLVEMENT

### Questioning by the police

The police have a right to ask questions of any person whom they believe to be a witness to a crime[2]. If police inquiries are only at the stage of investigation, and suspicion has not focussed on any person, the police do not require to administer any form of caution to a person questioned by them. While it is the moral duty of a citizen to assist the police, a person is, generally speaking, under no legal obligation to answer questions apart from the obligation of a potential witness to give his name and address[3]. There is, however, under certain statutes an obligation to give information to the police when required by them to do so[4].

---

1  See *Smith v HMA* 1952 JC 66 at 71, 1952 SLT 286 at 288, per Lord Justice-Clerk Thomson.
2  *Bell v HMA* 1945 JC 61, 1945 SLT 204; *Chalmers v HMA* 1954 JC 66, 1954 SLT 177; *Thompson v HMA* 1968 JC 61, 1968 SLT 339.
3  1995 Act, s 13(1)(b). See below at pp 85, 86.
4  Eg Prevention of Terrorism (Temporary Provisions) Act 1989, s 18; Road Traffic Act 1988, s 172. The position under the Civic Government (Scotland) Act 1982, s 58 (being in possession of tools and failing to demonstrate that possession is not for the purpose of theft) is less certain. See *Docherty v Normand* 1996 SCCR 701, 1996 SLT 955 in which it was held that there was no time limit set as to when an explanation could be given.

Once suspicion has focussed on a particular person he will probably be detained under section 14 of the Criminal Procedure (Scotland) Act 1995 (for which see the next section of this chapter), but it is possible that a suspect may be questioned without having been detained. In any event, the common law rules about the admissibility in evidence of answers to questions apply equally whether or not the suspect has been detained[1]. These rules will therefore be examined now.

It used to be thought, on the basis of *Chalmers v Her Majesty's Advocate*, that the law made inadmissible any answers given by a suspect to police questioning[2]. If that was indeed ever the law, it is clear that it is no longer so. Later cases have emphasised that the only test of admissibility is 'fairness', by which is meant both fairness to the accused person and fairness to the interests of the public[3]. A statement made in answer to a question will be admissible if it was fairly obtained. Whether questioning has been fair in any particular case depends on its own facts. Factors which, it has been suggested, may be relevant, are: the age of the suspect[4]; his mental capacity[5]; his physical state[4]; the length of time during which he has been in a police station[6]; whether or not he has been cautioned[7] (although a caution is not essential[8]); and the nature of the questioning[9]. The fact that the person being questioned is a suspect is only one other factor to be taken into account in assessing fairness[10]. Evidence of answers to questions will usually be excluded only if the police have clearly indulged in intimidation, threats, inducement or cross-examination[11]. However, to make answers to questions inadmissible it is not necessary that there be any actual bullying or pressure designed to break the will of the suspect or to force from him a confession against his will[12]. As we shall see when the procedure in a jury trial is examined, the law now favours the jury being the arbiter of what is fair or unfair and not the judge[13], but in an extreme case the judge should himself take the decision to exclude evidence of the questioning[14].

A person who is to be charged should always be cautioned to the effect that he is not obliged to say anything in answer to the charge, but that anything he does say will be noted and may be used in evidence. This is what is popularly known as 'a common law caution'. An answer to the charge made following upon such a caution is normally admissible in evidence. If the charging of the accused is tape-recorded, as it may be, for example, following a tape-recorded interview, the caution should refer to the fact of tape-recording as well as to noting.

1  1995 Act, s 14(7)(a).
2  *Chalmers v HMA* 1954 JC 66, 1954 SLT 177.
3  *Miln v Cullen* 1967 JC 21, 1967 SLT 35; *Hartley v HMA* 1979 SLT 26.
4  *Chalmers v HMA* 1954 JC 66, 1954 SLT 177.
5  *Hartley v HMA* 1979 SLT 26; *HMA v Gilgannon* 1983 SCCR 10.
6  *Thompson v HMA* 1968 JC 61, 1968 SLT 339; *Hartley v HMA* 1979 SLT 26; *HMA v Gilgannon* 1983 SCCR 10.
7  *Tonge v HMA* 1982 JC 130, 1982 SCCR 213, 1982 SLT 506; *Wilson v Heywood* 1989 SCCR 19.
8  *Pennycuick v Lees* 1992 SCCR 160, 1992 SLT 763.
9  *Lord Advocate's Reference No 1 of 1983* 1984 JC 52, 1984 SCCR 62, 1984 SLT 337; *HMA v Mair* 1982 SLT 471; *Codona v HMA* 1996 SCCR 300, 1996 SLT 1100.
10  *Miln v Cullen* 1967 JC 21, 1967 SLT 35; *Tonge v HMA* 1982 JC 130, 1982 SCCR 213, 1982 SLT 506.
11  *Lord Advocate's Reference No 1 of 1983* 1984 JC 52, 1984 SCCR 62, 1984 SLT 337: *HMA v Mair* 1982 SLT 471; *Harley v HMA* 1995 SCCR 595, 1996 SLT 1075; *Stewart v Hingston* 1996 SCCR 234; *Codona v HMA* 1996 SCCR 300, 1996 SLT 1100.
12  *Codona v HMA* 1996 SCCR 300, 1996 SLT 1100, a case where a 14-year-old girl was questioned for three and a half hours during which time she was asked nineteen times whether she had kicked the deceased. The appeal court held that the questioning was so clearly unfair that the trial judge should not have allowed the jury to hear evidence of an admission of kicking ultimately made by the girl.
13  See below at p 169.
14  *Harley v HMA* 1995 SCCR 595, 1996 SLT 1075; *Codona v HMA* 1996 SCCR 300, 1996 SLT 1100.

Once a suspect has been charged he should not be further questioned by the police, and answers given to questioning at that stage may be inadmissible in evidence[1]. However, anything said by an accused person which is truly voluntary is admissible[1]. If a person who has been charged indicates that he wishes to make a voluntary statement, it is accepted practice that the statement should be noted by an officer who is unconnected with the case[2]. The statement should be written out by the officer, read over to or by the accused, and then signed by him and by the officer.

## Detention under section 14 of the Criminal Procedure (Scotland) Act 1995

Until the coming into force of section 2 of the Criminal Justice (Scotland) Act 1980 (the predecessor of section 14 of the 1995 Act) on 1 June 1981 a police officer had generally no legal right to detain a person suspected of committing a crime unless he had arrested him, although a person who was asked to 'assist the police with their inquiries' may very well have been unaware of this fact. Section 14 gives a constable[3] limited powers of detention where he has 'reasonable grounds for suspecting that a person has committed or is committing an offence punishable by imprisonment'[4]. Having detained the person the constable must take him 'as quickly as is reasonably practicable to a police station or other premises'[5]. The police station need not be that nearest to which the suspect was detained[6].

Detention is for a maximum period of six hours and must conclude at the end of that period or (if earlier) when the detainee is either arrested, or detained in pursuance of some other enactment or subordinate instrument, or where the constable no longer has grounds for suspecting that he has committed or is committing an offence punishable by imprisonment[7]. The detainee must be informed that his detention has been terminated immediately that in fact happens[7]. If a person is in fact detained for more than six hours, that does not invalidate anything lawfully done during the six-hour period[8].

Once a person has been released from detention under section 14 he may not again be detained on the same grounds or grounds arising out of the same circumstances[9]. If a person has previously been detained under another enactment and is then detained under section 14(1) on the same grounds or on grounds arising from the same circumstances as these which led to his earlier detention, the period of six hours under section 14(1) is reduced by the length of the earlier detention[10].

When a person is detained under section 14 the detaining officer must inform him of his suspicion, of the general nature of the offence of which he is suspected and of the reason for his detention[11].

---

1 *Stark and Smith v HMA* 1938 JC 170, 1938 SLT 516; and see below at p 89.
2 *Tonge v HMA* 1982 JC 130 at 147, 1982 SCCR 313 at 350, 1982 SLT 506 at 517, per Lord Cameron.
3 'Constable' means any police officer up to and including a chief constable: Police (Scotland) Act 1967, ss 3(1), 51(1), as applied by the 1995 Act, s 307(1).
4 1995 Act, s 14(1). For an example of 'reasonable grounds for suspicion', see *Wilson v Robertson* 1986 SCCR 700.
5 1995 Act, s 14(1).
6 *Menzies v HMA* 1995 SCCR 550, 1996 SLT 498.
7 1995 Act, s 14(2).
8 *Grant v HMA* 1989 SCCR 618, 1990 SLT 402.
9 1995 Act, s 14(3).
10 1995 Act, s 14(4), (5).
11 1995 Act, s 14(6).

Certain matters must be recorded. These are: (a) the place where detention begins and the police station or other premises to which the detainee is taken; (b) any other place to which the person is, during detention, thereafter taken; (c) the general nature of the suspected offence; (d) the time when detention begins and the time of arrival at the police station or other premises; (e) the time when the detainee is informed of his right to refuse to answer questions and to request (under section 15(1)(b) of the Act) intimation of his detention to be given to a solicitor and another person; (f) the time when such request is (i) made and (ii) complied with; (g) the time of his release from detention or, if appropriate, of his arrest[1]. The Act contains no provisions as to how these matters should be recorded. In practice police forces have forms which are used[2], but it has been held that entries in police notebooks are sufficient[3]. In the same case the High Court specifically reserved its opinion on what the legal effect would be of a failure to record.

A constable may ask a detainee questions relating to the suspected offence, but the general rules of admissibility of evidence apply to any answers given[4]. In the case of serious crime a tape recorder is frequently used to record the questioning of a person who has been detained[5] (as in the case of *David Balfour*). The type of recorder used includes a time injection system and provides for two copies of the tape of the interview. The recording is therefore virtually immune from being tampered with. A transcript of a recording of an interview between an accused person and a police officer, if appropriately certified by the transcriber, is sufficient evidence of the making of the transcript and of its accuracy, provided that it has been served on the accused not later than fourteen days prior to the trial and he has not challenged its accuracy[6]. If the transcript is not served timeously or if the accused challenges its accuracy, the person who made the transcript may be called as a witness and, if he is, his evidence is sufficient evidence of the making of the transcript and of its accuracy[7]. This means that his evidence does not require to be corroborated and not, of course, that his evidence on accuracy may not be challenged. Even if the accuracy of the transcript is not in question, it may be to the advantage of the defence to insist on the tape being played in order that the jury, sheriff or justice may hear how the police actually asked the questions and how the accused answered them. A tape-recorder is available in all courts so that the tape may be played. If no transcript of the tape recorded interview has been lodged (as is almost invariably the case in summary prosecutions) the court is not entitled to *insist* on one being provided, although a summary trial may be adjourned with a *request* that such a transcript be made available[8]. The defence solicitor may, in such a case, be provided with a copy of the tape by the procurator fiscal on request (and usually also on payment of a fee).

Although a constable is empowered to ask questions of a detainee, the latter has the right not to answer any question other than to give his name and address. The constable must inform him of this right both on detaining him and on arrival at the

1  1995 Act, s 14(6).
2  See the case of *David Balfour* at pp 8, 9.
3  *Cummings v HMA* 1982 SCCR 108, 1982 SLT 487.
4  1995 Act, s 14(7)(a). For the general rules of admissibility in evidence of answers to police questions see the first section of this chapter.
5  The tape-recording of interviews is almost invariably carried out only by CID and not by uniformed officers. If, as sometimes happens, even in the case of serious crime, the CID do not become involved in the investigation of the crime, then it is most unlikely that any interview of a suspect will be tape-recorded. Some police forces record interviews on video as well as on audio.
6  1995 Act, s 277(1), (2).
7  1995 Act, s 277(4).
8  *McGlennan v McLaughlin* 1992 SCCR 454.

police station or other premises[1]. If the detainee is to be questioned, it may not be sufficient simply to advise him of this right. It is desirable also to give the normal common law caution, ie that he is not obliged to answer any question, and that, if he does so, his answer will be noted down and may be used in evidence[2], although a failure to caution will not necessarily be fatal to the admissibility of any statement made[3].

A detainee is subject to the same powers of search as he would be if he had been arrested[4]. Although it is not specifically stated, this almost certainly means search of the individual rather than search of premises. It is an open question whether the right to search includes a right to put the detainee on an identification parade[5]. In any case where an identification parade is held, the suspect (whether a detainee under section 14 or not) is entitled to have the legal aid duty solicitor attend on his behalf[6]. Indeed, he is entitled to have a solicitor of his own choice attend who will be paid under the legal aid scheme[7].

Where a suspect has been detained and released at the end of a detention period, it is competent for a sheriff, at a later stage, to grant a warrant to detain him further for the purpose of holding an identification parade, but the period of detention should be limited to what is necessary for holding such a parade[8].

The detainee may have his fingerprints and palmprints taken and 'such other prints and impressions of an external part of the body as the constable may, having regard to the circumstances of the suspected offence, ... reasonably think it appropriate to take'[9]. It is provided that, subject to very limited exceptions, the records of such prints and impressions must be destroyed immediately following a decision not to institute criminal proceedings or on the conclusion of such proceedings otherwise than on a finding of guilt[10]. However, there is no sanction provided for a failure to destroy the records. A police officer of the rank of inspector or above may authorise a constable to take from a detainee certain samples such as hair, nails, blood (by means of a swab only) and saliva[11].

A constable is entitled to use reasonable force in detaining a person and in searching him under section 14(7)(b)[12] or obtaining prints, impressions or samples under section 18(2) and (6)[13].

---

1  1995 Act, s 14(9).
2  *Tonge v HMA* 1982 JC 130, 1982 SCCR 213, 1982 SLT 506.
3  *Scott v Howie* 1993 SCCR 81, in which it was held that the requirement laid down by s 14(9) of the 1995 Act (that a detainee should be informed of his right not to answer questions) was purely procedural and did not determine the admissibility of evidence.
4  1995 Act, s 14(7)(b). For powers to search on arrest see below at p 89.
5  *Renton and Brown* at para 6–14 suggest that an identification parade may be an extension of the right to search. The *Stair Memorial Encyclopaedia* vol 17, para 606 and *Gane and Stoddart* at p 159 disagree, arguing that, if parading a suspect had been intended to follow detention, it would have been specifically provided for as is the taking of fingerprints. It is submitted that the latter view is to be preferred.
6  Legal Aid (Scotland) Act 1986, s 21(4)(b) and Criminal Legal Aid (Scotland) Regulations 1987, SI 1987/307, reg 5(1)(a).
7  Legal Aid (Scotland) Act 1986, s 21(4)(b).
8  *Archibald v Lees* 1994 SCCR 97, 1995 SLT 231.
9  1995 Act, s 18(2). This subsection has been amended by the 1997 Act, s 47 which came into force on 1 August 1997. See the Appendix below at p 317. For the use to which fingerprints may be put see *HMA v Shepherd* 1997 SCCR 246.
10  1995 Act, s 18(3), (4), (5).
11  1995 Act, s 18(6). See p 192 below.
12  1995 Act, s 14(8).
13  1995 Act, s 18(7). This subsection has been amended by the 1997 Act, s 47 which came into force on 1 August 1997. See the Appendix below at p 317.

It is the practice at least in certain police forces to photograph detainees. There is no specific statutory authority for this but it might be argued that it is covered by the provisions of section 18(2) referred to above.

Certain rights are given to the detainee under section 15 of the 1995 Act. If he is an adult (ie over sixteen years old), he is entitled to have intimation of his detention and of the place where he is being detained sent to a solicitor and one other person reasonably named by him[1]. The reference to reasonableness probably means that the police are not obliged to contact a person unless he is in the reasonably close vicinity of the police station and an unduly expensive telephone call is not required. Such intimation must be made without delay or 'where some delay is necessary in the interest of the investigation or the prevention of crime or the apprehension of offenders, with no more delay than is so necessary'[1]. Although it is not explicitly stated, it seems to be clearly implied that it is the police officer responsible for the detention who is to be the judge of when delay is necessary. The detainee must be informed of this entitlement on arrival at the police station or other premises[2]. He should subsequently be informed whether his solicitor has been advised of his detention and whether information has been given to the other named person.

There are also provisions in section 15[3] relating to the detention of a child (defined as a person under sixteen years of age)[4]. These will be discussed below in chapter 10.

The Prevention of Terrorism (Temporary Provisions) Act 1989 provides for what it calls 'detention' of suspected persons under section 14, although 'detention' appears to be used here to mean custody following arrest. The Criminal Justice (Scotland) Act 1980 provides[5] rules relating to intimation to solicitors and others in respect of arrest and detention under the 1989 Act, but the details of these are outwith the scope of a textbook such as this.

Other statutes also provide for detention in certain circumstances[6].

## Detention under section 13 of the Criminal Procedure (Scotland) Act 1995

Before we leave the subject of detention it should be noted that, under section 13 of the 1995 Act, there is conferred on a constable what might be described as a very limited right of detention, to enable identification of a suspect or witness to a crime. Section 13(1) empowers a constable to require a person to give his name and address if the constable has 'reasonable grounds for suspecting that (he) has committed or is committing an offence'[7]. The constable may also 'ask him for an explanation of the circumstances which have given rise to the constable's suspicion'[7]. There is a similar power with regard to the requirement to provide a name and address in respect of a potential witness to the offence[8]. The constable must

1  1995 Act, s 15(1)(b).
2  1995 Act, s 15(2)(a).
3  1995 Act, s 15(4), (5).
4  1995 Act, s 15(6).
5  1980 Act, ss 3A, 3B, 3C and 3D.
6  Eg Misuse of Drugs Act 1971, s 23(2)(a) (detention of person for purpose of searching him for possession of drugs); Criminal Law (Consolidation) (Scotland) Act 1995, s 26 (detention in connection with drug smuggling offences).
7  1995 Act, s 13(1)(a).
8  1995 Act, s 13(1)(b).

explain to the suspect or witness the general nature of the offence[1]. In both cases the power may be exercised either at the locus of the offence or at any place where the constable is entitled to be. The constable may require a suspect to remain with him while he notes any explanation given by the suspect and/or until his name and address have been verified provided that this can be done quickly[2]. He may use reasonable force to ensure that the suspect remains with him[3], so to that extent may detain him. There is no power to 'detain' a potential witness. The suspect or the potential witness who fails without reasonable excuse to provide his name and address or, in the case of the suspect, fails to remain with the constable if required to do so, is guilty of an offence[4]. A constable may arrest a suspect if he has reasonable grounds for suspecting that he has committed an offence under section 13(6)[5]. The provisions of section 13 (unlike those of section 14) are not confined to offences punishable by imprisonment.

## Arrest

### (a) General

A person is arrested when he is forcibly detained (using that word in a non-technical sense), which may or may not involve actual physical restraint. Arrest is, at least in legal theory, a more drastic step than detention[6]. As has been described above, there is a strict time limit to detention under section 14 of the 1995 Act. A person who has been arrested must be brought before a court with due expedition, but there is no general statutory limit[7]. A failure to bring an arrested person before a court timeously does not vitiate subsequent proceedings[8]. Arrest is generally considered to require more in the way of evidence against a suspect than detention, where only 'reasonable grounds for suspecting' are necessary, but it is common for a person merely to be detained where there is ample evidence to justify arrest.

### (b) Arrest with warrant

A warrant to arrest is most commonly granted in respect of a crime which is likely to be tried under solemn procedure. The initiating writ in such a case is the petition (see the case of *David Balfour* at pp 11, 12). It runs in the name of the procurator fiscal, narrates the crime alleged to have been committed, and craves the court to grant a warrant to apprehend and, usually, also to search. The petition is almost invariably presented to a sheriff, although probably any magistrate having

---

1   1995 Act, s 13(5).
2   1995 Act, s 13(2), (3).
3   1995 Act, s 13(4).
4   1995 Act, s 13(6). The offence is punishable, in the case of a suspect, by a fine not exceeding level 3 on the standard scale, and, in the case of a potential witness, by a fine not exceeding level 2 on the standard scale.
5   1995 Act s 13(7).
6   See *Forbes v HMA* 1990 JC 215, 1990 SCCR 69.
7   Police (Scotland) Act 1967, s 17 (1) provides that it is the duty of any police officer 'to take every precaution to ensure that any person charged with an offence is not unreasonably and unnecessarily detained in custody'. The 1995 Act, s 135(3), (4) provides that a person arrested under a summary warrant in terms of the Act, at common law or under other statutory powers, must, where practicable, be brought before a competent court not later than the first day after arrest which is not a Saturday, Sunday or court holiday.
8   *Robertson v Thom* 1993 JC 1, 1992 SCCR 916 sub nom *Robertson v MacDonald* 1993 SLT 1337.

jurisdiction in the area where the crime was committed has power to grant a warrant[1]. The sheriff usually grants the warrant without further inquiry as the procurator fiscal (or, more commonly, the depute fiscal dealing with the case) who has signed the petition is presumed to be acting responsibly and to have satisfied himself that there is evidence of sufficient quality to justify arrest. If an accused person is arrested without a warrant (see below), a petition is presented to the sheriff as soon as possible, usually when the accused first appears before the sheriff. The warrant is then granted. This is what happened in the case of *David Balfour*.

A warrant may also be granted in respect of a summary complaint, but this is relatively rare as most summary complaints proceed by way of citation of the accused. The 1995 Act provides that a judge of the court in which a complaint is brought (who may be a sheriff or a justice or stipendiary magistrate in the district court) has power, on the motion of the prosecutor, 'to grant warrant to apprehend the accused where this appears to the judge expedient'[2]. Typical situations where a warrant to apprehend might be granted in a summary prosecution are: where the accused's whereabouts are unknown; where the accused has failed to respond to citation; where it is necessary to have the accused fingerprinted; where it is necessary to place him on an identification parade; where he is likely to abscond; where the case would be time-barred if citation proceeded in the normal course; or where the accused is in custody in another jurisdiction.

### (c) Arrest without warrant

Arrest without warrant has long been accepted as part of the common law of Scotland, although its scope and limitations are somewhat ill-defined. Contrary to the situation in England and Wales, in Scotland offences are not divided between 'arrestable' (ie those where arrest without warrant is permitted) and 'non-arrestable' or between felonies and misdemeanours. Arrest itself being a serious step, it might have been thought that arrest without warrant required especial justification and that the onus of proof would be on the arrester. However, it has been held in the Outer House of the Court of Session that the onus is on a person alleging unlawful arrest to prove that it was unreasonable and unnecessary[3].

A private citizen has a right to arrest without warrant if he witnesses a serious crime[4], but must hand the arrested person over to a police officer as soon as possible[5].

A constable may arrest without warrant where, for example, he has seen a crime committed or where the suspect is pointed out to him running from the locus. Other circumstances which may justify arrest without warrant are the gravity of the offence, the fact that the suspect is in hiding and about to abscond or if he is of no fixed abode[6]. If the suspect can simply be charged and then released for citation, or if there is no prejudice caused by the officer's waiting until a warrant to apprehend has been obtained, arrest is not justified[7].

---

1 *Hume* II, 77; Alison *Practice* p 121; *Macdonald* p 198. But see the 1995 Act, s 34(2) which appears to envisage that an application for a petition warrant should always be presented to a sheriff.
2 1995 Act, s 139(1)(b). The form of warrant should be as provided in the 1996 Rules, r 16.5(1).
3 *Henderson v Moodie* 1988 SCLR 77, 1988 SLT 361, sub nom *Henderson v Chief Constable, Fife Police.*
4 *Hume* II, 76; Alison *Practice* p 119; *Macdonald* p 197. For examples of cases where the concept of arrest by a private citizen is discussed, see *Codona v Cardle* 1989 SCCR 287, 1989 SLT 791 and *Bryans v Guild* 1989 SCCR 569, 1990 SLT 426.
5 *McKenzie v Young* (1902) 10 SLT 231.
6 *Peggie v Clark* (1868) 7 M 89.
7 *Leask v Burt* (1893) 21 R 32; *Somerville v Sutherland* (1899) 2 F 185, 7 SLT 239.

Arrest without warrant is in certain circumstances authorised in respect of a large number of statutory offences. Probably that most frequently encountered in practice is in terms of the Road Traffic Act 1988, section 6 (where arrest is for the limited purpose of subjecting the suspect to a breath test or of obtaining a sample from him in terms of section 7 of the 1988 Act), but there are other offences under the Road Traffic Act and under such statutes as the Misuse of Drugs Act 1971 and the Civic Government (Scotland) Act 1982[1]. An arrest without warrant for a statutory offence is legal if the constable has reasonable grounds for belief that the offence has apparently been committed, provided that that conclusion is honestly reached[2].

### (d) Procedures after arrest

An arrested person may have fingerprints and other prints taken from him in the same way as a detainee[3] and he may also have other samples taken from him[4].

As has already been noted, an arrested person should be brought before a court as soon as possible[5]. He may, pending his appearance in court, be detained in a police station, police cell or other convenient place[6]. He has a right to have intimation of his arrest and whereabouts sent to a solicitor[7] and to have a private interview with the solicitor prior to his appearance at judicial examination or in court[8]; and he must be informed of these rights[9]. An arrested adult is also entitled to have intimation of his arrest and whereabouts sent to one other named person but that is subject to a proviso that such intimation may be delayed if delay is 'necessary in the interest of the investigation or the prevention of crime or the apprehension of offenders'[10]. The time of the making of the request for intimation and the time of compliance with it must be recorded[11]. It may be noted that there is no sanction against a failure to comply with any of these rights of intimation. No doubt the general rule of 'fairness' would be applied, and evidence obtained following a failure to intimate would be admissible if it were considered by the court that it had not been unfairly obtained[12]. A person arrested on a charge of murder, attempted murder or culpable homicide has the right at this stage to call on the services of the duty solicitor under the legal aid scheme, and the duty solicitor must act for him until he is released on bail or fully committed[13]. A person arrested on any other charge is not entitled to the services of the duty solicitor at this stage (unless he is to be placed on an identification parade[14]) but is so entitled on his appearance in

---

1  For a fuller, although not completely comprehensive, list see *Renton and Brown* para 7–09.
2  *McLeod v Shaw* 1981 SCCR 54, 1981 SLT (Notes) 93 – a case of an alleged offence under the Road Traffic Act 1972, s 5(2), ie being drunk in charge of a motor vehicle.
3  1995 Act, s 18(2). See p 84 above.
4  1995 Act, s 18(6). See p 92 below.
5  See p 86 above.
6  1995 Act, s 135(2), which applies to summary cases. Although there is no specific provision in the 1995 Act for cases on petition, the usual form of petition warrant provides for detention in a police station or other convenient place.
7  1995 Act, s 17(1)(a).
8  1995 Act, s 17(2).
9  1995 Act, s 17(1)(b). In a petition case judicial examination may be delayed for up to 48 hours after arrest to allow time for the attendance of a solicitor (s 35(2)).
10  1995 Act, s 15(1)(a). As has already been noted, the provision about delay applies also in the case of persons detained under s 14: see p 85 above.
11  1995 Act, s 15(3).
12  Cf the comments on 'fairness' in connection with the admissibility of statements to the police at p 81 above. See also *Bell v Hogg* 1967 JC 49, 1967 SLT 290.
13  Criminal Legal Aid (Scotland) Regulations 1987, SI 1987/307, reg 5(1)(b).
14  Criminal Legal Aid (Scotland) Regulations 1987, reg 5(1)(a).

court on petition[1] and for his first appearance in court from custody or as an under-taker on summary complaint[2]. The advice of a solicitor at the stage of arrest may, however, be paid for under the advice and assistance provisions of the legal aid leg-islation[3] if the arrested person is financially eligible.

At common law an arrested person may be searched by the police[4], and this can include physical examination[5] and the taking of fingerprints[6]. The corollary of these rights of the police after arrest is that such searches are usually unlawful before arrest, although an exception may be made in a case of emergency, in which case the test of 'fairness' will be applied[7].

There is no general rule that the police may not question a person who has been arrested, provided that the questioning is not unfair[8]. An admission made by an arrested person to the police, if made voluntarily, is admissible in evidence. 'It is not the law that after a man has been cautioned and charged, there must be no con-tact whatever between him and police officers. What the law seeks to do is to pro-tect the arrested person against unfair pressure and against the inducement to emit statements against his interest'[9]. There is, of course, no reason in principle why the arrested person should not be questioned about matters unconnected with the crime with which he has been charged.

### (e) Release after arrest

An arrested person normally remains in custody until his appearance in court, but the police have powers, in the case of a charge which is likely to be tried summar-ily, to release following arrest. The person who is to be released may give an undertaking (signed by him) that he will attend a specified court on a given date[10]. This date is normally no more than fourteen days after the date of the undertaking. Release on undertaking is the normal practice in cases involving drinking and dri-ving under the Road Traffic Act 1988. Alternatively, an arrested person may be released without any undertaking[10], in which case he might be put on honour to attend a specified court at a specified time. This is very rare, and he would more probably simply be cited to attend court in normal course. A person who has been released on undertaking and who fails to attend court is guilty of an offence[11].

If an 'undertaker' fails to appear in the specified court at the specified time the case will not call, and the court will almost certainly subsequently grant a warrant for his arrest so that the case will commence as a custody case. A charge of failing to attend as an undertaker will most probably either be added to the original charges in the complaint or will be brought as a separate complaint.

The procurator fiscal may also direct the release of an arrested person before his appearance in court if he considers that further inquiries require to be made before the case calls in court, whether on petition or summary complaint.

1 Legal Aid (Scotland) Act 1986, s 22(1)(b).
2 Legal Aid (Scotland) Act 1986, s 22(1)(c).
3 Legal Aid (Scotland) Act 1986, s 6.
4 *Jackson v Stevenson* (1897) 2 Adam 255, 24 R (J) 38, 4 SLT 277.
5 *Forrester v HMA* 1952 JC 28, 1952 SLT 188.
6 *Adair v McGarry* 1933 JC 72, 1933 SLT 482.
7 *Bell v Hogg* 1967 JC 49, 1967 SLT 290.
8 *Johnston v HMA* 1993 SCCR 693, 1994 SLT 300.
9 *Fraser and Freer v HMA* 1989 SCCR 82 at 91, per Lord Justice-General Emslie.
10 1995 Act, s 22(1).
11 1995 Act, s 22(2).

## Search

### (a) General

As a general rule a person may not be searched (unless he has been detained or arrested) nor may premises be searched, unless a court has granted a warrant for that purpose. The same principles apply to both searches of persons and searches of premises. A search without warrant may, however, take place if the individual to be searched or the occupier of premises to be searched gives consent[1].

### (b) Search without warrant

Certain statutes[2] make provision for search of premises and persons without warrant. Such statutes usually provide that, before carrying out a search, the police officer concerned must have 'reasonable grounds for suspecting' that an offence under the statute is being or has been committed. There is no need for the officer to obtain the consent of the person who is to be searched[3].

At common law search of premises (and of persons) without warrant may be justified on the ground of urgency[4].

### (c) Search with warrant

At common law a search warrant may be granted by any justice (which includes a sheriff[5]) and may be executed throughout Scotland[6]. Some statutes specify that only a sheriff may grant a warrant[7]. Under certain statutes a magistrate must take evidence on oath before he grants a search warrant[8]. Intimation to the alleged offender of an application for a search warrant is not appropriate unless the statute provides for such intimation[9]. In the case of a search warrant at common law intimation is the norm but is not appropriate if its effect would be to give the alleged offender an opportunity to remove the evidence and thus defeat the purpose of the granting of the warrant[10].

A search warrant must be dated[11] and signed by the person granting it[12]. There is no need for anyone to have been charged or arrested before a search warrant can be granted[13]. All that is necessary is that the person applying for the warrant (usually the procurator fiscal) should have reasonable grounds for suspecting that a crime has been committed. The application for the warrant should state what the crime is and, if known, the name of the alleged perpetrator. The view has been

---

1 *Davidson v Brown* 1990 JC 324, 1990 SCCR 304, 1991 SLT 335.
2 Eg Misuse of Drugs Act 1971, s 23(2) (illegal drugs); Civic Government (Scotland) Act 1982, s 60 (stolen property); Criminal Law (Consolidation) (Scotland) Act 1995, s 48(1) (offensive weapon). For a more detailed examination see *Renton and Brown* para 7–24.
3 *Chassar v Macdonald* 1996 SCCR 730.
4 *HMA v McGuigan* 1936 JC 16, 1936 SLT 161; *Bell v Hogg* 1967 JC 49, 1967 SLT 290. For a more recent example see *Edgley v Barbour* 1994 SCCR 789, 1995 SLT 711.
5 1995 Act, s 307(1).
6 1995 Act, s 297(1).
7 Eg Public Order Act 1936, s 2(5).
8 Eg Misuse of Drugs Act 1971, s 23(3).
9 *Harris* 1993 SCCR 881, 1994 SLT 906 sub nom *Harris, Complainer*.
10 *Mellors v Normand (No 2)* 1996 SCCR 657, 1996 SLT 1146.
11 *Bulloch v HMA* 1980 SLT (Notes) 5; *HMA v Welsh* 1987 SCCR 647, 1988 SLT 402.
12 *HMA v Bell* 1984 SCCR 430. It is probably not essential that the granter of the warrant be named or designed in it: *HMA v Strachan* 1990 SCCR 341 (Sh Ct).
13 *Stewart v Roach* 1950 SC 318, 1950 SLT 245.

expressed that a search warrant would not normally be justified if the offence is to be prosecuted summarily[1].

It is competent for the procurator fiscal to apply for a search warrant to recover evidence relating to a statutory offence without anyone having been charged, unless the statute concerned excludes this expressly or by necessary implication[2]. It is also competent for the procurator fiscal to apply for a warrant at common law to inspect and copy entries in banker's books before proceedings have commenced; there is no need for him to proceed under the Bankers' Books Evidence Act 1879[3]. When the warrant is to search premises it must adequately identify the premises, but this may be done by reference to a designation in the application for the warrant[4].

A warrant to take a blood sample from a person suspected of committing a crime but not charged may be granted if the circumstances are special and where the interests of the individual are outweighed by the public interest[5]. The scope of any warrant granted should be no wider than is necessary to achieve its purpose[6].

Where an ex facie valid warrant is founded upon as ground for a search, a sheriff cannot review the granting of it, although the High Court has power to suspend an illegal search warrant[7]. Where, therefore, it is desired to challenge the validity of a search warrant in a trial in the sheriff court, whether solemn or summary, an application must be made to the High Court for that purpose. The appropriate procedure is by bill of suspension prior to the trial[8].

As a general rule, once a person has been committed for trial under solemn procedure or had a trial diet fixed under summary procedure, the prosecutor cannot carry out any further search of the accused's person or of premises in connection with the crimes or offences charged. However, a warrant for further search will be granted in exceptional circumstances[9]. A warrant may be granted even after service of an indictment[10]. In such cases intimation of the application for the warrant should be made to the accused in order that he may be heard on the matter.

## (d) Evidence obtained by irregular search

If evidence has been obtained irregularly, either without a warrant or by the officer exceeding the scope of the warrant, it may not necessarily be inadmissible. It is a question of circumstances in each individual case and of fairness. 'Whether any given irregularity ought to be excused depends upon the nature of the irregularity

---

1 *Mellors v Normand* 1995 SCCR 313 at 318D, per Lord Justice-General Hope giving the opinion of the court.
2 *MacNeill, Petr* 1984 JC 1, 1984 SCCR 450, 1984 SLT 157.
3 *Normand, Complainer* 1992 JC 108, 1992 SCCR 426, 1992 SLT 478.
4 *Bell v HMA* 1988 SCCR 292, 1988 SLT 820.
5 *Morris v MacNeill* 1991 SCCR 722, 1991 SLT 607. See also *Begley v Normand* 1992 SCCR 230.
6 *Walker v Lees* 1995 SCCR 445, 1995 SLT 757.
7 *Allan v Tait* 1986 SCCR 175.
8 *Stuart v Crowe* 1992 JC 46, 1992 SCCR 181, 1993 SLT 438.
9 *HMA v Milford* 1973 SLT 12 (warrant granted after full committal to take blood sample in case of alleged rape); *Lees v Weston* 1989 SCCR 177, 1989 SLT 446 (warrant granted after full committal to take fingerprints in case of allegedly being concerned in the supply of Class A drugs); *Currie v McGlennan* 1989 SCCR 466, 1989 SLT 872 (warrant granted to hold an identification parade after full committal in a case of murder); *Williamson v Fraser* 1995 SCCR 67, 1995 SLT 777 (warrant granted to take fingerprints after summary trial had been fixed); cf *McGlennan v Kelly* 1989 SCCR 352, 1989 SLT 832, where, in a case of alleged rape, a warrant to obtain samples of pubic hair was refused partly because of the lapse of time between samples having previously been obtained and the presentation of the petition to obtain the further samples.
10 *Frame v Houston* 1991 JC 115, 1991 SCCR 436, 1992 SLT 205.

and the circumstances under which it was committed"[1]. If, in the course of a search under a warrant granted in respect of an offence, a suspicious article is found which appears to implicate the accused in a different offence, that article may be admissible in evidence at a trial for the latter offence. However, it will be admissible only provided that the search was not random[2]. In this connection it is, in certain jurisdictions, not uncommon for an application for a common law search warrant for stolen property to be accompanied by an application for a search warrant under the Misuse of Drugs Act 1971, thus widening the scope of any search carried out.

### (e) Intimate body searches

There are no reported cases in Scotland dealing with intimate body searches at common law, but there seems to be no good reason why the general principles explained above should not apply to such searches. By analogy with the case of *Hay v Her Majesty's Advocate*[3], a warrant authorising the search should be obtained unless the matter is one of great urgency.

In terms of recent legislation a constable may take certain samples from a person who has been either arrested or detained under section 14[4] provided that he has the authority of an officer of a rank no lower than that of inspector[5]. The samples which may be taken are: (a) a sample of the hair of an external part of the body other than pubic hair; (b) a sample from a fingernail or toenail or from under such a nail; (c) a sample of blood or other body fluid, body tissue or other material obtained from an external part of the body by means of swabbing or rubbing; (d) a sample of saliva or other material from the inside of the mouth obtained by means of swabbing[5]. The constable may use reasonable force to obtain such samples[6].

# PART 2: THE SOLICITOR'S INVOLVEMENT

## General

In most cases, whether under solemn or summary procedure, a solicitor is unlikely to become involved until after the case is in court. However, as we have already seen, a person who has been arrested has a right to have a solicitor informed of that fact and a right to have a private interview with the solicitor[7]. A person detained under section 14 of the 1995 Act has a right to have a solicitor informed of that fact[8], although he has no right to a private interview with the solicitor. In these cases the information given to the solicitor by the police is likely to be little more than the details of the charge as given in the detention or arrest forms[9]. The solic-

---

1 *Lawrie v Muir* 1950 JC 19 at 27, 1950 SLT 37 at 40, per Lord Justice-General Cooper. See also *MacNeil v HMA* 1986 SCCR 288 and *Innes v Jessop* 1989 SCCR 441, 1990 SLT 211.
2 *Tierney v Allan* 1989 SCCR 334, 1990 SLT 178; *Innes v Jessop* 1989 SCCR 441, 1990 SLT 211.
3 *Hay v HMA* 1968 JC 40, 1968 SLT 334, in which it was held competent to take impressions of a suspect's teeth, a warrant having been granted by a magistrate prior to arrest.
4 1995 Act, s 18(1).
5 1995 Act, s 18(6).
6 1995 Act, s 18(7).
7 1995 Act, s 17(2).
8 1995 Act, s 15(1)(b).
9 See the forms in the case of *David Balfour* at pp 8–10 above.

itor is under no obligation to attend on the accused or detainee or to act for him. A person charged with murder, attempted murder or culpable homicide has a right to call on the services of the duty solicitor under the legal aid scheme, and, in this case, the duty solicitor *must* act for him until he is released on bail or fully committed[1]. Another situation where the duty solicitor *must* become involved is where a person is to be placed on an identification parade. The duty solicitor must attend the parade on behalf of the suspect if called upon to do so by him[2]. A suspect may also have the solicitor of his choice attend an identification parade under the legal aid scheme[3].

A solicitor should abide by the terms of the Code of Conduct for Criminal Work approved by the Law Society of Scotland[4]. This contains ten articles and represents 'the norm of acceptable professional behaviour'[5]. Particular attention should be paid to the provision which prohibits a solicitor acting for more than one accused in the same case[6].

## The solicitor and the detainee

If a solicitor is told that a detained person has asked that he be informed of his detention and whereabouts, he may very well decide to attend at the police station or other premises where the detainee is being held. What should he do when he gets there?

As a general rule the solicitor should try to speak to the officer in charge of the case in order to find out from him as much as possible about it: what the alleged crime is and where, when and how it was perpetrated. He should find out if the detainee has said anything to the police, whether incriminating or exculpatory. He should inquire whether any real evidence incriminating his client has been found. How much information the solicitor will actually be given will depend on the attitude of the officer concerned. Many policemen are extremely reluctant to say more than they absolutely have to. Having obtained such information as he can, the solicitor should, if permitted to do so, interview his client.

The advice which the solicitor will give to his client will obviously depend on the circumstances. If the client confesses his guilt to the solicitor, the latter may very well advise him to make a full statement to the police. If the detainee denies guilt, the solicitor may wish to inquire whether there is any particular line of defence, eg alibi, incrimination or self-defence. In the event that there is, he may again advise his client to make a full statement to the police. If the solicitor advises his client to make a statement, the advice should include a recommendation that the statement should, if possible, be tape-recorded and, in fact, this is almost invariably now done as a matter of course. On the other hand, he may advise that, as he is fully entitled to do, the detainee should say nothing beyond giving his name and address.

1 Criminal Legal Aid (Scotland) Regulations 1987, SI 1987/307, reg 5(1)(b).
2 Legal Aid (Scotland) Act 1986, s 21(4)(b), and Criminal Legal Aid (Scotland) Regulations 1987, SI 1987/307, reg 5(1)(a).
3 Legal Aid (Scotland) Act 1986, s 21(4)(b).
4 (1996) 41 JLSS 468.
5 Ibid, introduction.
6 Ibid, art 2.

The solicitor should ensure that his client is not detained for longer than permitted under section 14.

## The solicitor and the client who has been charged

The above comments about what the solicitor should do on arrival at the police station apply equally in the case of a solicitor called to see someone who has been arrested and charged.

When a person has been charged, the police should ask him no further questions[1]. However, it may still be in his interests, having received legal advice, to make a full statement to the police. If the solicitor advises him to do so, and that advice is accepted, the solicitor should inform the officer in charge of the case of his client's wish. He should request that an officer who is not connected with the case note his client's statement[2], and that, if possible, the statement should be tape-recorded. There is no reason, in principle, why the solicitor should not be present when his client makes his statement. Unwillingness on the part of the police for the solicitor to be present or to have a statement tape-recorded may be a matter for adverse comment by the defence at a later stage.

## The solicitor and the identification parade

If there is an eye-witness to a crime, the police may wish to hold an identification parade in order to see whether the witness is able to identify the suspect. The suspect is placed in a line with a number of other persons, and the parade is viewed by the witness. It is usual nowadays for the parade to be viewed by means of a one-way screen, so that the suspect does not see the witness.

An arrested person may be placed on an identification parade[3]. He has no legal right to refuse, but, for obvious practical reasons, if he were unwilling, there would be little point in holding a parade. If an arrested person were to refuse, the police would be entitled to have him viewed by witnesses in circumstances which might very well be less favourable to him than those of an identification parade, although care must be taken about any form of identification other than at a parade[4].

The function of the solicitor attending a parade on behalf of his client is to ensure that the parade is conducted fairly and that his client is not prejudiced, whether because of the composition of the parade or for any other reason. The solicitor is also present as an observer, and, in the event of any dispute about the conduct of the parade, he would be able to give evidence of what occurred. Legal representation is especially important if a one-way screen is used as then the witnesses cannot be seen by the suspect. If such a screen is used, the solicitor is at the same side of the screen as the witness viewing the parade and the police officer conducting it. This officer is always one unconnected with the case. The solicitor should listen to and note any conversation between the officer and each witness viewing the parade.

1 *Stark and Smith v HMA* 1938 JC 170, 1938 SLT 516.
2 See p 82 above.
3 *Adair v McGarry* 1933 JC 72, 1933 SLT 482. In exceptional circumstances a warrant to hold an identification parade may be granted even after full committal: *Currie v McGlennan* 1989 SCCR 466, 1989 SLT 872.
4 *Howarth v HMA* 1992 SCCR 364.

The Scottish Home and Health Department has laid down rules for the conduct of identification parades[1]. Although these rules have no statutory force, a failure to observe them would be a matter for comment by the defence, and might well render any identification made less valuable to the Crown case.

The solicitor attending a parade should check that those in the line-up are, so far as possible, similar in age and build to his client. The solicitor may object to the composition of the parade. He should ensure that his client is not wearing any particularly distinctive clothing. If his client has facial hair, he should request that as many of the stand-ins as possible are similarly adorned.

The solicitor should satisfy himself that a witness who has viewed the parade has no opportunity to communicate with a witness who has still to do so. He should note carefully what words, if any, are used by a witness who points out his client or any other person on the parade.

If the solicitor is in any way dissatisfied with the parade, he should inform the officer in charge of the parade of his dissatisfaction and should request that his comments be recorded in the report of the parade. He should, of course, make a note himself of such matters as well as keeping a full record of what happened at the parade.

Although strictly outwith the scope of this chapter as it would normally occur after an accused person has appeared in court, it is convenient here to note that an accused (in practice his solicitor) has a right to ask the sheriff to direct the prosecutor to hold an identification parade[2]. The sheriff may grant the application only if (a) an identification parade has not already been held at the prosecutor's instance, (b) the prosecutor has refused or unreasonably delayed holding a parade after being requested to do so by the accused, and (c) the sheriff considers that the application is reasonable[3]. The prosecutor must be given an opportunity to be heard[3]. Accordingly, the necessary preliminary to an application to the sheriff is a formal request to the fiscal that he hold a parade. In the only case on this subject which has been reported to date[4] the sheriff held that an identification parade took place only when the accused was actually placed in a line-up, whether or not any witnesses actually attended. Two abortive attempts to hold parades which had been cancelled because witnesses refused to attend were therefore not parades within the meaning of the section.

1  The rules for the conduct of identification parades are conveniently set forth in *Gane and Stoddart* at pp 160–2.
2  1995 Act, s 290. The application is in the form of a petition in terms of the 1996 Rules, r 28.1.
3  1995 Act, s 290(2).
4  *Wilson v Tudhope* 1985 SCCR 339 (Sh Ct).

# CHAPTER 4

# SOLEMN PROCEDURE: BEFORE THE TRIAL

## INTRODUCTION

Solemn procedure is the name given to the form of criminal procedure in which an accused, if he goes to trial, is tried before a jury. Other names for the procedure are 'petition procedure' and 'procedure on indictment'. These are used because the initiating writ in solemn procedure is a petition, and an indictment is the document containing the charge(s) on which the accused goes to trial. The case of *Her Majesty's Advocate v David Balfour* described in chapter 1 is an example of such procedure. The trial may take place in the High Court of Justiciary or in a sheriff court. The initial procedure is, however, identical in the early stages, whichever court the accused is ultimately tried in. Solemn procedure is governed by Part VII of the Criminal Procedure (Scotland) Act 1995. The other form of procedure, which involves trial without a jury, is called summary procedure. It is illustrated by the case of *Nicol Jarvie* described in chapter 2, and will be the subject of a later chapter.

In this chapter and the next we shall examine the progress of a solemn case in the sheriff court from the time when the accused first appears before a sheriff to the conclusion of the trial when the jury returns its verdict. The different procedure adopted latterly when an accused is to be tried in the High Court will also be noted. First, however, it is appropriate to discuss the composition, jurisdiction and powers of the two courts of solemn jurisdiction.

## THE HIGH COURT OF JUSTICIARY

The High Court is both a court of first instance and a court of appeal. In this chapter we are concerned only with its original jurisdiction, ie as a court of trial.

The High Court can try any crime triable under solemn procedure, unless its jurisdiction is specifically excluded by statute. Its powers of punishment are unlimited, unless defined by statute.

The permanent judges of the High Court (Lords Commissioners of Justiciary) are the same individuals as the judges of the Court of Session[1], headed by the Lord Justice-General (who is, in his civil capacity, Lord President of the Court of Session)[2]. Retired Court of Session judges may be appointed by the Lord President to sit as judges in the High Court 'to facilitate the disposal of business'[3]. At the time

1  1995 Act, s 1(2).
2  1995 Act, s 1(1).
3  Law Reform (Miscellaneous Provisions) (Scotland) Act 1985, s 22.

of writing, such judges (somewhat scurrilously but affectionately known as 'moth-balls') are frequently asked to sit in the High Court, especially in its appellate capacity. Temporary judges of the Court of Session[1] may also sit as judges of the High Court. Temporary judges are appointed from among the senior ranks of sheriffs and practising Queen's Counsel. The Chairman of the Land Court has also been appointed as a temporary judge. There are usually about ten temporary judges at any one time. Temporary judges do not sit in the High Court in its appellate capacity. By direction of the Lord Justice-General, they preside at trials only in Edinburgh and Glasgow and do not try cases of murder or rape. When sitting in the High Court a temporary judge does not wear the robes of a High Court judge but those of a Queen's Counsel.

For the purposes of a criminal trial a High Court judge will normally preside alone, but, in cases of difficulty or importance, it is competent for more than one judge to sit for part or the whole of a trial[2].

Members of the Faculty of Advocates and solicitor advocates have the right of audience in the High Court. Solicitor advocates are solicitors who have undergone specialised training to equip them to appear before the supreme courts in Scotland[3]. Most solicitor advocates are qualified to appear in either the High Court of Justiciary or the Court of Session. A very small number are qualified to appear in both. At the time of writing there are more than 50 solicitor advocates who have the right to appear in the High Court.

The prosecution case in the High Court is conducted by Crown Counsel (usually an advocate depute[4] but, on occasions, one of the Law Officers[5]).

The High Court, as a court of first instance, may sit anywhere in Scotland[6]. Until about 1980 the High Court sat only in certain old-established circuit towns and a case would be tried in the circuit town nearest to the locus of the crime. In more recent years the High Court has sat in many more sheriff court buildings, and it is not uncommon for a case to be tried in a place many miles from the locus of the crime, even though this may cause considerable inconvenience to witnesses and others. The reason for this is very often the need to bring a case to trial before the expiry of the 110-days time bar[7] but it may also be because a case requires particular conditions of security which would not be available in the local court. There is provision for a case to be transferred from one venue of the High Court to another on the motion of the prosecutor[8].

Only in the High Court may cases of treason, murder, rape and breach of duty of magistrates be tried[9]. The High Court also has exclusive jurisdiction in the case of certain statutory offences.

The territorial jurisdiction of the High Court extends throughout Scotland, and to its territorial waters (including ships in these waters). In cases of cross-border

---

1 Appointed in terms of the Law Reform (Miscellaneous Provisions) (Scotland) Act 1990, s 35(3) and Sch 4, paras 5–11.
2 1995 Act, s 1(5).
3 Solicitors (Scotland) Act 1980, s 25A: applied to the High Court by the 1995 Act, s 301(1).
4 Advocates depute are appointed by the Lord Advocate to conduct prosecutions in the High Court and to consider cases reported by procurators fiscal to the Crown Office. They are either members of the Faculty of Advocates or solicitor advocates.
5 The Scottish Law Officers are the Lord Advocate and the Solicitor General for Scotland.
6 1995 Act, s 3(2).
7 See below at p 119.
8 1995 Act, s 2(3).
9 1995 Act, s 3(6).

crimes (eg a fraud perpetrated in one country and taking effect in another) the High Court has jurisdiction if the 'main act' took place in Scotland[1].

In certain cases, both at common law and by statute, the High Court (and unless its jurisdiction is excluded by some rule of law, the sheriff court too) has jurisdiction over crimes committed outwith Scotland. The most important[2] of these are as follows:

(1)  Piracy. This is a crime according to the law of nations (*jure gentium*). It is triable wherever the pirates are found[3].

(2)  Treason. This may be tried in Scotland irrespective of where the treasonable acts were committed[4]. The procedure and rules of evidence in a trial for treason are the same as those in a trial for murder[5].

(3)  'Any British citizen or British subject who in a country outside the United Kingdom does any act or makes any omission which if done or made in Scotland would constitute the crime of murder or of culpable homicide shall be guilty of the same crime and subject to the same punishment as if the act or omission had been done or made in Scotland'[6]. Under this section a person may be proceeded against in any sheriff court district in which he is arrested or is in custody[7] or in such sheriff court district as the Lord Advocate may determine[8].

(4)  'Any British citizen or British subject employed in the service of the Crown who, in a foreign country, when acting or purporting to act in the course of his employment, does any act or makes any omission which if done or made in Scotland would constitute an offence punishable on indictment shall be guilty of the same offence, and subject to the same punishment, as if the act or omission had been done or made in Scotland'[9]. Again the accused may be proceeded against in any sheriff court district in which he is arrested or is in custody[10] or in such sheriff court district as the Lord Advocate may determine[11].

(5)  Crimes committed on British ships on the high seas irrespective of the nationality of the accused, and crimes committed by a British subject on a British ship in a foreign port[12].

(6)  A thief who has committed theft in any other part of the United Kingdom may be tried in Scotland for that crime if he is found in Scotland in possession of the stolen property[13]. Similarly, if a person receives in Scotland property stolen elsewhere in the United Kingdom, he may be dealt with (for reset) in

---

1  *Macdonald* p 192. In the case of *Laird v HMA* 1984 SCCR 469, 1985 SLT 298, the High Court appears to have gone further and held that it is sufficient for jurisdiction in Scotland in a fraud case that the initial fraudulent pretence was made in Scotland, even though the practical consequences occurred in England. See also *Clements v HMA* 1991 JC 62, 1991 SCCR 266, 1991 SLT 388, a case concerning the supply of drugs where the accused were caught with drugs in Scotland but virtually all the activities involving the drugs took place in England. It was held that the High Court had jurisdiction.
2  For an exhaustive list see *Renton and Brown* paras 1–22 to 1–40.
3  *Hume* II, 48; *Macdonald* p 192. For a rare modern example of a charge of piracy see *Cameron v HMA* 1971 JC 50, 1971 SLT 202, 333.
4  *Hume* II, 50.
5  1995 Act, s 289.
6  1995 Act, s 11(1).
7  1995 Act, s 11(3)(a).
8  1995 Act, s 11(3)(b).
9  1995 Act, s 11(2).
10  1995 Act, s 11(3)(a).
11  1995 Act, s 11(3)(b).
12  Merchant Shipping Act 1894, s 686.
13  1995 Act, s 11(4)(a).

the same way as if the property had been stolen in Scotland[1]. The converse does not, however, apply: a person who receives in England property stolen in Scotland cannot be convicted of reset[2].

# THE SHERIFF COURT

Scotland is divided into six sheriffdoms[3]. With the exception of the sheriffdom of Glasgow and Strathkelvin (in which there is only the one sheriff court) every sheriffdom is divided into a number of sheriff court districts. In each district is a sheriff court which is manned by one or more sheriffs. In each sheriffdom there is also a sheriff principal. Although the sheriff principal has an appellate function in civil cases, his criminal jurisdiction is identical with that of a sheriff. The sheriff principal also has important administrative functions[4].

As in the High Court, provision has been made for assistance to be provided by temporary members of the judiciary. An advocate or solicitor of at least five years' standing may be appointed to be a temporary sheriff[5]. A temporary sheriff has the full powers of a sheriff. Most temporary sheriffs sit for only a few days each month, although there are some who sit virtually full-time. At the time of writing there are considerably more temporary sheriffs than there are permanent sheriffs, and the sheriff court relies increasingly on temporary assistance, especially for the disposal of criminal business. Such extensive use of temporary sheriffs has given rise to a certain amount of criticism and unease, not least because a temporary sheriff does not have the same security of tenure in his office as does a permanent sheriff. A temporary sheriff's commission is at the disposal of the Secretary of State who may recall it at any time[6]. That of a permanent sheriff may be revoked only after a joint report by the Lord Justice-General and Lord Justice-Clerk has stated that the sheriff is unfit for office[7] and the Secretary of State, on receipt of that report, has made an order removing the sheriff from office[8]. Such an order is made by statutory instrument and is subject to annulment by resolution of either House of Parliament[9].

Both solicitors and advocates have the right of audience in the sheriff court. The prosecution case is usually conducted by the procurator fiscal or one of his deputes, although on very rare occasions Crown Counsel may appear.

The court in which proceedings in any particular case will be commenced is normally that for the district in which is situated the place where the crime is alleged to have been committed[10]. The 1995 Act contains detailed rules governing

1  1995 Act, s 11(4)(b).
2  *Roy v HMA* 1963 SLT 369.
3  The sheriffdoms are: Grampian, Highland and Islands; Tayside, Central and Fife; Lothian and Borders; Glasgow and Strathkelvin; North Strathclyde; South Strathclyde, Dumfries and Galloway. Most of these names are based on the names of the regional authorities created by the Local Government (Scotland) Act 1973. Even though these regions were abolished by the Local Government etc (Scotland) Act 1994, the names of the sheriffdoms have been retained.
4  For example in connection with summoning jurors. See below at pp 139–140.
5  Sheriff Courts (Scotland) Act 1971, s 11(2), (3)(b).
6  1971 Act, s 11(3).
7  1971 Act, s 12(1).
8  1971 Act, s 12(2).
9  1971 Act, s 12(3).
10 There is provision for the prosecutor to apply to the sheriff to have a case transferred from the court of one district to the court of another district in the same sheriffdom: 1995 Act, s 83(1).

the territorial jurisdiction of the sheriff in cases where the normal rule does not apply[1]. These are not entirely easy to understand, and there is a certain amount of apparent duplication between one section and another. The following are the most important rules:

The territorial jurisdiction of the sheriff includes 'all navigable rivers, ports, harbours, creeks, shores and anchoring grounds in or adjoining' the sheriffdom[2]. In certain cases two or more courts may have concurrent jurisdiction[3]. If a crime is committed partly in one sheriff court district and partly in another, the accused may be indicted in the court of either district as the Lord Advocate directs[4]. If crimes connected with each other are committed in different sheriff court districts, the accused may be indicted in the sheriff court of any of these districts[5]. A similar rule applies if several crimes are committed in succession in different sheriff court districts[6]. These provisions apply equally whether the sheriff court districts are in the same or different sheriffdoms. Indeed, it is strongly arguable that, if the districts are within the same sheriffdom, the provisions are unnecessary, as a sheriff has jurisdiction throughout the whole sheriffdom and not only in the district of the court to which he is appointed[7]. In any event, specific provision is made for an offence committed in one sheriff court district to be tried in any other sheriff court district of the same sheriffdom[8].

We have already noted that, in the case of certain crimes committed abroad, proceedings may be taken in Scotland, and that these proceedings are commenced in the court of the district where the accused is arrested or is in custody[9].

Any crime triable on indictment may be tried in the sheriff court with the exception of those for which the High Court has exclusive jurisdiction, either at common law or by statute[10]. The sentencing powers of the sheriff are limited. The maximum sentence which he may impose is one of three years' imprisonment[11], although the maximum sentence for a statutory offence may be less, in which case it is the statutory maximum which applies. However, the sheriff may remit a convicted person to the High Court for sentence if he considers that his powers of punishment are inadequate[12]. On indictment a sheriff has power to impose an unlimited fine, unless, of course, a maximum fine is prescribed by statute.

1  1995 Act, ss 4, 9, 10.
2  1995 Act, s 4(1).
3  When sheriffdoms or sheriff court districts are separated by a stretch of water, the courts of both have jurisdiction over the stretch of water (1995 Act, s 9(1)). Under s 9(2) both courts have jurisdiction if a crime is committed on or near the boundary of their districts. In the case of a crime committed on a moving vehicle or vessel, any court through whose district the vehicle or vessel has passed has jurisdiction (s 9(3)).
4  1995 Act, s 10(1), 2(a). Although the section uses the world 'indicted', its provisions are clearly intended to apply also to the procedure prior to actual indictment.
5  1995 Act, s 10(1), 2(b). See also s 9(4).
6  1995 Act, s 10(1), 2(c). See also s 9(4).
7  Sheriff Courts (Scotland) Act 1971, s 7; *Kelso District Committee v Fairbairn* (1891) 3 White 94; *Tait v Johnston* (1891) 18 R 606.
8  1995 Act, s 4(2). See *Howdle v Beattie* 1995 SCCR 349, 1995 SLT 934.
9  1995 Act, s 11. See above at p 98.
10  See above at p 97.
11  1995 Act, s 3(3). This will increase to five years if the 1997 Act, s 13 comes into force. See the Appendix at p 318 below.
12  1995 Act, s 195.

# FIRST EXAMINATION

The charge in a case brought under solemn procedure is almost invariably first formulated in a petition at the instance of the procurator fiscal[1]. The accused may be arrested on the basis of the warrant contained in the petition, or he may have been arrested previously without a warrant[2], or he may simply have been asked to attend court on a specified date, having been served with a copy of the petition. This latter procedure is common in cases where there has been a long period of investigation, for example embezzlement. It has been held that where a case is put on petition, the proceedings (for the purpose of a statutory time bar) commence when a petition warrant is granted[3].

The accused's first appearance on petition is always before the sheriff, even though the case may ultimately be tried in the High Court. It is in private[4]. This appearance is known as 'first examination', and any subsequent appearance is known as 'further examination'[4]. If there is more than one accused on the petition each must appear separately before the sheriff at either first or further examination[4].

An accused appearing on petition is entitled to the services of the duty solicitor under the legal aid scheme up until the time when he is released on bail or fully committed, or his application for legal aid is granted or refused, whichever of these events is the earlier[5]. An accused is, of course, under no obligation to be represented by the duty solicitor. He may choose to have his own solicitor. As we shall see below[6], an accused is entitled to apply for legal aid, nominating a solicitor of his choice, as soon as he has been committed or released on bail. If legal aid is applied for and granted at first examination, it will cover everything which the solicitor has done that day, including interviewing the accused and appearing at first examination as well as appearing at any further examination.

At first examination the accused is entitled to make a 'declaration' if he wishes, but he is not obliged to do so[7]. A declaration is a statement by the accused, saying anything which he may wish to say about the crime with which he is charged. It must be in the accused's own words and not prepared for him by his solicitor, although the accused may read from a statement prepared by himself[8]. In practice it is rare for an accused to make a declaration, but there are advantages in his doing so if he wishes to put forward a particular line of defence and the procurator fiscal does not wish to ask him questions in terms of section 36 of the 1995 Act[9]. An accused may make a declaration at a later stage if he wishes[10]. The procurator fiscal

---

1  See the case of *David Balfour* at pp 11, 12. A petition is not strictly necessary (*O'Reilly v HMA* 1984 SCCR 352, 1985 SLT 99), but it is very rare for an accused who is a natural person to be indicted without having first appeared in court on petition.

2  In this case it may be only when he is served with a petition that he is made aware that he is to be subject to solemn rather than summary proceedings. It is for the procurator fiscal to decide which is the appropriate form of proceedings.

3  *Hamilton v HMA* 1996 SCCR 744. The statute in question here was the Trade Descriptions Act 1968, s 19 of which provides that proceedings have to commence within one year of the offence being discovered by the prosecutor.

4  1995 Act, s 35(7).

5  Legal Aid (Scotland) Act 1986, s 22(1)(b).

6  See below at pp 106, 107.

7  1995 Act, s 35(3).

8  *Carmichael v Armitage* 1983 JC 8; 1982 SCCR 475; 1983 SLT 216.

9  See below at pp 108–111.

10  1995 Act, s 35(4).

must provide for a *verbatim* record to be made of any declaration made by the accused[1]. However, a failure to do so will not nullify any future proceedings[2].

In the great majority of cases the first examination is formal and brief. The accused's solicitor intimates that the accused does not wish to make any plea or declaration, and the fiscal moves that he be committed for further examination or, less commonly, for trial.

Committal for trial, which is properly called committal 'until liberated in due course of law', is also known as 'full committal'. It means that the accused (unless released on bail) is committed to prison until either released as a result of some legal process, or acquitted or sentenced. The accused must receive a copy of the warrant committing him to prison after full committal[3].

If the accused is committed for further examination and is not released on bail, he must be brought before the court again for full committal. This should probably be within eight days, excluding both the day of committal for further examination and the day of full committal. Very surprisingly this time limit has never been authoritatively determined[4]. In practice the appearance for full committal is usually within one week of first examination.

It is competent to challenge the relevancy of a petition by seeking to suspend the warrant of committal for trial[5].

## BAIL

The sheriff may not competently grant bail to persons accused of murder and treason[6]. The sheriff is also not entitled to grant bail in the case of a person charged with attempted murder, culpable homicide, rape or attempted rape if that person has previously been convicted by a court in any part of the United Kingdom of any of these offences or of murder or manslaughter[7]. The only exception is if the conviction for culpable homicide or manslaughter did not result in a custodial sentence or, in the case of a child or a person suffering from mental disorder, an equivalent disposal[8]. 'Conviction' in this context is widely defined[9], and a conviction counts even though it is under appeal[10]. A person serving a prison sentence may not be granted bail, even if just about to be released[11].

Even in the case of crimes for which the sheriff may not competently grant bail the Lord Advocate or the High Court may release a person on bail[12].

An application for bail may be made immediately after an accused has been brought before a sheriff for examination[13]. If the accused is released on bail prior to full committal (ie when only committed for further examination), he does not

---

1  1995 Act, s 37(1), and see also the 1996 Rules, rr 5.3 and 5.4.
2  *Robertson v HMA* 1995 SCCR 152.
3  1995 Act, s 40(3).
4  *Dunbar, Petr* 1986 SCCR 602.
5  *Mellors v Normand* 1996 SCCR 500, 1996 SLT 704.
6  1995 Act, ss 23(1), 24(1).
7  1995 Act, s 26(1), (2).
8  1995 Act, s 26(2)(b).
9  1995 Act, s 26(4).
10  1995 Act, s 26(3).
11  *Currie v HMA* (1980) SCCR Supp 248.
12  1995 Act, s 24(2). For modern examples of an application for bail in a charge of murder see *Welsh, Petr* 1990 SCCR 763, 1992 SLT 903; *Boyle, Petr* 1993 SCCR 251.
13  1995 Act, s 23(1).

require to be fully committed before an indictment may be served on him[1]. If bail is refused at the stage of first examination, the accused may again apply when brought before the court for full committal[2]. An application for bail at the stage of full committal must be disposed of within 24 hours of its first being placed before the sheriff, failing which the accused must be released[3]. This does not of course mean that the accused cannot thereafter be indicted, simply that he may no longer be detained. If, for whatever reason, an accused person does not apply for bail before he is fully committed, he may still do so at a later stage[4].

An application for bail is normally made by petition for which there is no statutory form, although a standard form has been developed. This narrates inter alia that the accused is innocent of the crime charged[5]. Bail application forms are usually available from the sheriff clerk's office. An application for bail may also be made orally.

The prosecutor must be given an opportunity to be heard on an application for bail, whether before or after full committal[6]. If the prosecutor does not oppose bail, the sheriff should grant it[7].

Before full committal an accused has no right of appeal against a sheriff's refusal to grant bail[8]. However, at that stage as well as after full committal, the Crown has a right to appeal against a grant of bail[9]. After full committal the accused has a right of appeal against refusal of bail or a condition of bail[8].

There is a presumption in favour of granting bail[10].

In *Smith v M*[11] Lord Justice-Clerk Wheatley laid down guidelines about the criteria to be applied by a sheriff when deciding whether or not to grant bail. For the pre-trial stage these were: (1) bail may be refused if the accused has a significant record for crimes analogous to the offence charged, especially if the accused has recently been released from prison; (2) unless there is a cogent reason to the contrary, bail should be refused when the accused is alleged to have committed the offence charged while in a position of trust, eg awaiting trial (whether on bail or not), on licence or parole, on probation or deferred sentence, or performing a community service order; (3) bail may be refused when possible intimidation of witnesses is alleged, when the accused is of no fixed abode, when there are reasonable grounds for expecting that he will not attend for trial, or, in very special circumstances, because of the nature of the offence.

*Smith* still offers a reasonable guide to the sort of reasons why a sheriff may, if so moved by the fiscal, refuse bail. Another reason for refusal which is put forward by the Crown fairly frequently is that there are further inquiries to be made which

1  1995 Act, s 23(3). An accused released on bail prior to full committal, who thereafter fails to attend court to answer an indictment properly served on him, has no statutory right to apply for bail as s 23(5) (see note 4 below) applies only to a person who has been fully committed. However, he may apply for bail to the *nobile officium* of the High Court: *Campbell, Petr* 1989 SCCR 722, 1990 SLT 875.
2  1995 Act, s 23(4).
3  1995 Act, s 23(7). The 24 hour period is mandatory: *Gibbons, Petr* 1988 SCCR 270, 1988 SLT 657.
4  1995 Act, s 23(5).
5  For the form of bail application see the case of *David Balfour* at p 16 above.
6  1995 Act, s 23(1), (5).
7  *G v Spiers* 1988 SCCR 517; *Maxwell v McGlennan* 1989 SCCR 117, 1989 SLT 282 sub nom *Spiers v Maxwell*.
8  1995 Act, s 32(1)(a), which confers a right of appeal *after* full committal.
9  1995 Act, s 32(2)(a).
10  *G v Spiers* 1988 SCCR 517.
11  *Smith v M* 1982 JC 67, 1982 SCCR 517, 1982 SLT 421.

would be likely to be impeded if the accused were released. The High Court has held that where such a reason is put forward, the sheriff should not seek to go behind the statement made by the Crown[1]. As in so many situations in the field of the criminal law, it is a question of balancing the public interest against the interests of the individual accused.

Money bail has been virtually abolished in Scotland. Bail may now be granted only on conditions, and these should not include a pledge or deposit of money except in special circumstances[2].

The conditions which may be imposed are divided into two categories. First there are the 'standard conditions'[3].These are[4] that the accused:

'(a) appears at the appointed time at every diet relating to the offence with which he is charged of which he is given due notice;
(b) does not commit an offence while on bail;
(c) does not interfere with witnesses or otherwise obstruct the course of justice whether in relation to himself or any other person; and
(d) makes himself available for the purposes of enabling inquiries or a report to be made to assist the court in dealing with him for the offence with which he is charged.'

Secondly, there are such other conditions[5] as are necessary to secure:

'(i) that the standard conditions are observed; and
(ii) that the accused makes himself available for the purpose of participating in an identification parade or enabling any print, impression or sample to be taken from him.'

Examples of other conditions which might be added in terms of section 24(4)(b), as securing that the standard conditions are observed, could be that the accused surrenders his passport, that he stays away from a particular person or place, or, as in the case of *David Balfour*, the imposition of a curfew. The accused will not be released on bail until he has accepted the conditions[6]. It is not unknown for a person to refuse to accept bail conditions. In that event he must either be remanded in custody or released without conditions and simply ordained to appear.

The bail order must specify 'an address within the United Kingdom (being the accused's normal place of residence or such other place as the court may, on cause shown, direct) which ... shall be his proper domicile of citation'[7]. It is not strictly speaking a condition of bail that the accused should remain at that address but it is only at that address that the indictment and any other documents in connection with his case will be served[8]. An accused may apply to the court to change his domicile of citation[9].

Breach of a bail condition (other than the condition that an accused does not commit an offence while on bail) is an offence[10], normally punishable by imprisonment for not more than three months and/or a fine not exceeding £1,000[11].

1  *Normand v B* 1995 SCCR 128. Cf *Normand v L* 1995 SCCR 130.
2  1995 Act, s 24(3)(a), (6).
3  1995 Act, s 24(4)(a).
4  1995 Act, s 24(5).
5  1995 Act, s 24(4)(b).
6  1995 Act, s 24(7)(c).
7  1995 Act, s 25(1).
8  1995 Act, s 25(3).
9  1995 Act, s 25(2).
10 1995 Act, s 27(1).
11 1995 Act, s 27(2). The fine is expressed as level 3 on the standard scale which is presently £1,000. If the conviction for breach of the bail condition is in the district court, the maximum period of imprisonment is 60 days (s 27(2)(b)(i)).

Failure to appear at a diet in respect of solemn proceedings is an offence carrying a particularly heavy maximum penalty[1]. A charge alleging breach of a bail condition may be added to an indictment at any time before trial[2]. A sentence imposed for a breach of a bail condition may be imposed in addition to any other penalty competent to the court, notwithstanding that the total penalty may exceed what would normally be the maximum for the court concerned[3].

Up until the coming into effect of Part III of the 1995 Act (on 1 April 1996) an allegation that an accused had committed an offence while on bail could be libelled as a separate offence[4]. That, however, is no longer the case except where the bail order, a condition of which the accused is alleged to have breached by committing the new offence, was made prior to 1 April 1996[5]. The normal rule is now that the fact that an offence was committed while an accused was on bail must be libelled as an aggravation of that offence and not as a separate charge[6]. When the court comes to sentence for the offence committed while on bail (in the Act referred to as 'the subsequent offence')[7], provided that the aggravation has been libelled[8], the court

*SEN-WHEN on BAIL.*

'shall, in determining the appropriate sentence or disposal for [the subsequent] offence, have regard to
(a) the fact that the offence was committed by [the accused] while on bail and the number of bail orders to which he was subject when the offence was committed;
(b) any previous convictions of the accused for an offence [of failing without reasonable excuse to comply with a condition of a bail order other than a failure to appear]; and
(c) the extent to which the sentence or disposal in respect of any previous conviction of the accused differed, by virtue of this subsection, from that which the court would have imposed but for this subsection'[9].

The intention of this provision is clearly to make life unpleasant for the person who habitually breaches a condition of bail, whether by committing further offences or in some other way. The court's power of sentencing for the subsequent offence, if the aggravation is libelled, is increased beyond what would normally be its maximum power, in the case of a fine by £1,000[10] and, in the case of imprisonment by six months in the case of the High Court or sheriff court[11] and 60 days if the conviction is in the district court[12]. Unless an accused gives notice of an objection to

---

1  1995 Act, s 27(7): imprisonment for two years and/or an unlimited fine.
2  1995 Act, s 27(8).
3  1995 Act, s 27(9).
4  Bail etc (Scotland) Act 1980, s 3(1)(b).
5  *Hamilton v Robertson* 1996 SCCR 539, 1996 SLT 1216, in which it was held that in such circumstances a charge under s 27(2)(b) of the 1995 Act was not competent. The opinion was expressed that if an accused who has been granted bail on or before 31 March 1996 is alleged to have committed at any time a further offence while subject to that bail order, the appropriate charge is one under s 3(1)(b) of the 1980 Act. The situation created by the new bail provisions was described by the Lord Justice-General (at p 549D, 1222I) as 'highly confusing and unsatisfactory'.
6  1995 Act, s 27(3), (4). See the indictment in the case of *David Balfour*.
7  1995 Act, s 27(3).
8  1995 Act, s 27(3), (4).
9  1995 Act, s 27(3). See *Hill v HMA* 1997 SCCR 376.
10  1995 Act, s 27(5)(a), which provides that the increase shall be level 3 on the standard scale, this presently being £1,000.
11  1995 Act, s 27(5)(b)(i). In *Connal v Crowe* 1996 SCCR 716 it was suggested by the court that no matter how many aggravated charges there were against an accused in an indictment or complaint, the sheriff could impose no more than a total of six months in respect of the aggravation of being on bail. This, however, may not be correct: see the commentary by Sheriff G H Gordon (editor of SCCR) at 1996 SCCR 718D.
12  1995 Act, s 27(5)(b)(ii).

the allegation that he was on bail at the time of the subsequent offence, he is held to have admitted that fact[1].

An accused may apply to the sheriff for a review of his decision to refuse bail or to grant bail subject to conditions[2]. An application for review may also be made by an accused who wishes to have a condition deleted from a bail order[3]. An application for review (which is to be distinguished from an appeal) may be made not earlier than the fifth day after the original decision and thereafter not earlier than the fifteenth day after any subsequent decision[4].

The prosecutor may also apply to a sheriff for a review of his decision to grant bail where the prosecutor 'puts before the court material information which was not available to it when it granted bail'[5].

As has already been noted[6], both the accused and the Crown have a right of appeal against a sheriff's decision on bail. Written notice of appeal must be given to the other party[7]. If the appeal is by the Crown against a grant of bail, the accused is not released until the appeal has been disposed of[8], provided that the appeal is heard within 72 hours (unless the High Court grants an order for the further detention of the accused)[9]. A bail appeal is usually heard in chambers by a single judge of the High Court, although it may be heard in open court by more than one judge[10]. The accused is not normally present at a bail appeal.

A bail order continues in force until the case for which it was granted has been disposed of. Thus, even though an accused fails to attend a trial diet and a warrant for his arrest is granted, the bail order continues in force until he is taken into custody[11]. A case is not disposed of so long as the accused remains at liberty, even if he is on bail pending an appeal and abandons his appeal[12]. A constable may arrest without warrant an accused who has been released on bail where the constable has reasonable grounds for suspecting that the accused has broken, is breaking or is likely to break any bail condition[13].


# LEGAL AID[14]


Whether or not an accused has been represented by the duty solicitor at examination before the sheriff, he may apply to the sheriff for legal aid[15]. Such an application is usually made at first examination. It must be in writing and 'in such form as

---

1   1995 Act, s 27(4A). The objection is to be treated as if it were an objection to an allegation that the accused was acting in a special capacity and notice is to be given in terms of the 1995 Act, s 72(1)(b) (in the case of a sheriff court indictment, as applied by s 71(2)). See below at pp 133–135.
2   1995 Act, s 30(1), (2).
3   *Gilchrist, Petr* 1991 SCCR 699, 1991 SLT 919.
4   1995 Act, s 30(3).
5   1995 Act, s 31(1).
6   See above at p 103.
7   1995 Act, s 32(3).
8   1995 Act, s 32(2).
9   1995 Act, s 32(7).
10  1995 Act, s 32(4).
11  *Walker v Lockhart* 1993 SCCR 148, 1994 SLT 209.
12  *Mayo v Neizer* 1994 SCCR 126, 1994 SLT 931. See also *Fitzpatrick v Normand* 1994 SCCR 272, 1994 SLT 1263.
13  1995 Act, s 28(1).
14  The statutory provisions for criminal legal aid will be substantially amended if the 1997 Act, Part V comes into force. See the Appendix at p 319 below.
15  Legal Aid (Scotland) Act 1986, s 23.

the court may require'¹. In practice a standard form has been devised, and it is in common use². This provides for the accused to give details of his financial situation (income, capital, outlays) and of his dependants, together with the category of crime with which he is charged.

In solemn proceedings legal aid may be refused only on financial grounds. The sheriff must grant the application if he is satisfied, after consideration of the accused's financial circumstances, that the expenses of the case cannot be met by the accused himself without undue hardship to him or his dependants³. This is subject to the proviso that legal aid will be available only on special cause shown if the accused has available rights and facilities making it unnecessary for him to obtain legal aid, or has a reasonable expectation of receiving financial or other help from a body of which he is a member⁴. This is intended to meet the situation if the accused is a member of a trade union, motoring organisation or the like, which might pay for legal representation.

An accused may be required to make a statement on oath in connection with his application for legal aid⁵.

When assessing whether the accused could meet the expenses of the case without undue hardship the sheriff may take account of whether or not it is likely to go to trial. If an accused is fully committed in custody, it is unlikely that legal aid would be refused unless he has a reasonable amount of capital.

There is no right of appeal against a refusal of legal aid⁶, but it may be that an application could be made to the *nobile officium* of the High Court if a sheriff could be shown to have failed completely to apply his mind to the issue of undue hardship⁷. It is probably not competent to apply to the Court of Session for judicial review of a sheriff's decision on a legal aid application⁸. If a legal aid application is refused, the accused may reapply if there has been a change of circumstances, or if it becomes apparent that the trial is likely to be of exceptional length or complexity.

Legal aid, once granted, continues until the accused is acquitted or sentenced (including a remit to the High Court for sentence)⁹. However, it may be discontinued by the court on the ground of the accused's misconduct¹⁰.

As we have seen, it is usually the sheriff who considers a legal aid application. However, if an accused who is being tried before the High Court has not previously received legal aid, he may apply for it to the High Court, which may grant it¹¹ or remit to the sheriff for him to consider the application¹².

1 Criminal Legal Aid (Scotland) Regulations 1987, SI 1987/307, reg 6.
2 See the case of *David Balfour* at pp 14, 15.
3 Legal Aid (Scotland) Act 1986, s 23(1).
4 Criminal Legal Aid (Scotland) Regulations 1987, SI 1987/307, reg 7.
5 1996 Rules, r 33.4.
6 This is not stated in terms in the current legislation as it was under earlier legal aid legislation in the Act of Adjournal (Rules for Legal Aid in Criminal Proceedings) 1964, SI 1964/1409, para 9. There are, however, no provisions for appeal in the 1986 Act, the 1987 Regulations (SI 1987/307) or the 1996 Act of Adjournal (SI 1996/513).
7 By analogy with *Rae, Petr* 1981 SCCR 356, 1982 SLT 233; but see also *McLachlan, Petr* 1987 SCCR 195.
8 *Reynolds v Christie* 1988 SLT 68 (an Outer House decision).
9 Criminal Legal Aid (Scotland) Regulations 1987, SI 1987/307, reg 4(1)(c), (2)(b).
10 1996 Rules, r 33.3.
11 Legal Aid (Scotland) Act 1986, s 23(2)(a)(ii).
12 1996 Rules, r 33.2.

# JUDICIAL EXAMINATION

Strictly speaking 'judicial examination' includes any appearance on petition before a sheriff, whether for first or further examination. If an accused emits a declaration, that too is part of his judicial examination[1]. However, since 1980, the term has been commonly used to describe the form of questioning introduced by section 6(2) of the Criminal Justice (Scotland) Act 1980 and repeated with certain modifications in the 1995 Act. In this section of the chapter 'judicial examination' will be used in this restricted sense.

The present procedure provides that, when an accused is brought before a sheriff for examination (first or further), he may be questioned by the prosecutor (ie the procurator fiscal or one of his deputes) 'in so far as such questioning is directed towards eliciting any admission, denial, explanation, justification or comment which the accused may have as regards anything to which [the three following subsections] apply'[2].

The next subsection[3] applies to

'matters averred in the charge, and the particular aims of a line of questions under this subsection shall be to determine –
(a) whether any account which the accused can give ostensibly discloses a defence; and
(b) the nature and particulars of that defence.'

The second of the three subsections[4] applies to

'the alleged making by the accused, to or in the hearing of a constable, of an extra-judicial confession (whether or not a full admission)[5] relevant to the charge, and questions under this subsection may only be put if the accused has, before the examination, received from the prosecutor or from a constable a written record of the confession allegedly made.'

The prosecutor must provide to the sheriff who presides at the judicial examination a copy of a written record of the alleged confession[6]. If such a copy is not provided to the sheriff the prosecutor is not permitted to ask the accused any questions about the alleged confession[7].

The last of the three subsections[8] applies to

'what is said in any declaration emitted in regard to the charge by the accused at the examination.'

---

1   Although a declaration, if made at all, is usually made at first examination, an accused may make one at any time on intimating to the fiscal his desire to do so: 1995 Act, s 35(4).
2   1995 Act, s 36(1).
3   1995 Act, s 36(2).
4   1995 Act, s 36(3).
5   'Confession' means any statement clearly susceptible of being regarded as incriminating: *McKenzie v HMA* 1983 JC 13, 1982 SCCR 545, 1983 SLT 304. The statement in that case which was held to be susceptible of being so regarded was: 'Just my luck, I knew I'd be picked out'. It should be noted that the fiscal may seek a judicial examination on the basis of an alleged confession even after an accused has been fully committed, provided that he has not previously been examined about that confession: 1995 Act, s 35(5).
6   1996 Rules, r 5.5(1).
7   1996 Rules, r 5.5(2).
8   1995 Act, s 36(4).

There are certain principles[1] to which the fiscal must have regard in framing questions. These are:

'(a) the question should not be designed to challenge the truth of anything said by the accused;
(b) there should be no reiteration of a question which the accused has refused to answer at the examination; and
(c) there should be no leading questions'.

The sheriff must ensure that the questions are fairly put to and understood by the accused[1]. The accused is not put on oath[2].

The accused must be told by the sheriff that if in answering the fiscal's questions he discloses an ostensible defence, the prosecutor will be under a duty to secure 'to such an extent as is reasonably practicable', the investigation of that defence[3].

If the accused is represented by a solicitor (as he almost invariably is), he is entitled to confer with his solicitor before answering any question, and the sheriff must inform him of this entitlement[4]. Such consultation usually takes place in the room where the judicial examination is being held, and is in the form of a whispered conversation between the solicitor and his client. There is no reason why, if the accused or his solicitor requests it, they should not be permitted to consult in private, although there would be obvious disadvantages if this happened every time the fiscal asked a question.

An accused and his solicitor will, of course, have had an opportunity to consult together prior to the judicial examination. The solicitor will have received a copy of the petition and the written record of any alleged extrajudicial confession. The solicitor should advise the accused of the purpose of the judicial examination. He should advise him that, if there is any particular line of defence upon which the accused is founding (eg self-defence or alibi), he should describe that clearly at the judicial examination. The solicitor should go through any alleged extrajudicial confession in detail with the accused and should question him about the circumstances in which it was made. If there is anything untoward about these circumstances, the solicitor should advise the accused to mention this at the judicial examination.

The solicitor should write nothing on the accused's own copy of the petition and other documents as this might be misinterpreted as 'coaching'.

An accused at judicial examination is not obliged to answer any question asked by the fiscal[5]. However, if he declines to answer a question, the fact of his so declining may be commented upon at his trial by the prosecutor, the judge or a co-accused, where, in giving evidence at the trial, the accused says something which he could appropriately have said in answer to that question[5]. If an accused does decline to answer a question the trial judge may have regard to the terms of the charge to which the question related in determining whether to comment himself or permit comment by others on the failure to answer[6].

1 1995 Act, s 36(5).
2 1996 Rules, r 5.5(3).
3 1995 Act, s 36(6)(b), (10).
4 1995 Act, s 36(6)(a).
5 1995 Act, s 36(8).
6 1996 Rules, r 5.5(4). The way in which the record of proceedings at a judicial examination is introduced in evidence at a trial is discussed below at pp 169–170.

Some solicitors invariably advise the accused not to answer any questions at judicial examination. The accused then tells the sheriff that, acting on legal advice, he is not going to answer any question. This may be sound advice in some cases, but not if there is a definite line of defence which should be put forward as soon as possible[1].

The accused's solicitor has a very limited right to ask questions at the judicial examination. He requires the permission of the sheriff, and the purpose of his question must be confined to clarifying any ambiguity in an answer given by the accused to the fiscal, or to give the accused an opportunity to answer any question which he has previously refused to answer[2]. The solicitor is given no specific right to object to any question asked by the fiscal, but it is suggested that he is entitled to and should object if the fiscal clearly goes beyond the bounds of what is permitted by the statute, and the sheriff himself has not stepped in.

There are very detailed rules laid down for the recording of what happens at a judicial examination[3]. The fiscal must provide for a *verbatim* record of the whole proceedings, including any declaration made by the accused, to be made either by a shorthand writer or by mechanical means (ie tape-recording)[4]. If the shorthand writer is of a standard such that he or she would be acceptable to a court to note evidence at a trial or proof, then it is not necessary that the proceedings should be tape-recorded[5]. If the shorthand writer is not of such a standard, then a tape recording of the proceedings must also be made[6]. In practice nowadays usually only a tape recording of the proceedings is made and there is no shorthand writer, this having been made competent in 1993[7].

If a tape-recorder is used, it must record on two tapes simultaneously[8]. One of the tapes is given to the fiscal[9], and the other is sealed in an envelope and retained by the sheriff clerk until the fiscal informs him in writing that the proceedings against the accused have come to an end[10]. The sheriff clerk must then return the tape to the fiscal[11]. The prosecutor is responsible for the making of a transcript of the record of the judicial examination, whether that record is contained in a shorthand note or on tape[12].

Within fourteen days of the date of the examination the fiscal must serve a copy of the transcript on both the accused and his solicitor (if he has one)[13]. The 1995 Act and the 1996 Rules make provision for rectification of errors in the transcript[14]. The ultimate decision on whether there has been an error and what rectification of it should be made is for the sheriff[15].

If the case proceeds to trial, the list of productions appended to the indictment must include the record of any judicial examination[16]. The execution of service of

1  See eg *McEwan v HMA* 1990 SCCR 401.
2  1995 Act, s 36(7).
3  1995 Act, s 37 and 1996 Rules, rr 5.3 and 5.4.
4  1995 Act, s 37(1).
5  1996 Rules, r 5.3(1)(a).
6  1996 Rules, r 5.3(1)(b), (2).
7  Prisoners and Criminal Proceedings (Scotland) Act 1993, Sch 5, para 1(2) amending the 1975 Act, s 20B.
8  1996 Rules, r 5.4(1).
9  1996 Rules, r 5.4(4).
10  1996 Rules, r 5.4(5).
11  1996 Rules, r 5.4(8).
12  1995 Act, s 37(4).
13  1995 Act, s 37(6).
14  1995 Act, s 38 and 1996 Rules, r 5.6.
15  1995 Act, s 38(4).
16  1995 Act, s 68(1).

the transcript on the accused[1] is also invariably a production for the Crown, and, where the proceedings at judicial examination have been tape-recorded, the tape itself is usually one of the labels.

## PRECOGNITION

Once an accused has been fully committed or committed for further examination and released on bail the procurator fiscal must have the case against him precognosced in order that Crown counsel may consider what, if any, proceedings are appropriate.

A witness's precognition is a statement taken from him (in the case of the Crown) by the fiscal, one of his deputes or, more usually, a precognition clerk in the fiscal's office. A precognition should, so far as possible, use the witness's own words. It may include evidence whose admissibility at a trial would be at least doubtful, eg the finding of drugs following upon an unlawful search, as one of the purposes of the precognition is to give Crown counsel as full a picture as possible of the evidence in the case. The precognoscer may append to the precognition a comment on the impression which the witness is likely to make in court. If the witness has some physical or mental disability (for example is of low intelligence, deaf or blind), this should be indicated in the precognition.

Most witnesses attend for precognition as a result of a request from the fiscal. However, if a witness is reluctant to attend, he may be compelled to do so by means of citation. The usual warrant granted in the original petition includes a warrant to cite witnesses for precognition[2], but if, for some reason, this has not been granted, the fiscal may make a separate application to the sheriff for a warrant[3].

The fiscal sometimes considers it appropriate that a witness should give his precognition on oath. This might, for example, occur if it were expected that the witness was likely to renege on his precognition when he came to give evidence at the trial or if the witness had given a precognition in ordinary course which contradicted his statement to the police[4]. A precognition on oath is taken before a sheriff. The witness is not normally entitled to have a solicitor present on his behalf[5]. The witness, having taken the oath, is questioned by the fiscal. The questions and the witness's answers are recorded by a shorthand writer. The precognition is then transcribed, and the witness must appear before the sheriff again in order to sign the transcript.

It is not competent to put to a witness the terms of an unsworn precognition made by him, notwithstanding the terms of section 263(4) of the 1995 Act (which permits a witness at a trial to be asked about a statement previously made by him which differs from the evidence which he is giving). This is because the precognition is considered to be the words of the precognoscer rather than those of the witness[6]. However, a precognition on oath (where the words are indisputably those of

---

1 In conformity with the 1995 Act, s 37(6).
2 See the case of *David Balfour* at p 11.
3 This is no longer necessary: 1997 Act, s 57. See the Appendix at p 321 below.
4 *Carmichael, Petr* 1992 JC 165, 1992 SCCR 553, 1993 SLT 305 sub nom *Carmichael, Complainer*.
5 *Carmichael v B* 1991 JC 177, 1991 SCCR 715, 1992 SLT 101.
6 *Kerr v HMA* 1958 JC 14 at 19, 1958 SLT 82 at 84, per Lord Justice-Clerk Thomson.

the witness) may be put to a witness[1]. A precognition on oath may even be admissible as *evidence* under the statutory provisions governing hearsay evidence contained in section 259 of the 1995 Act[2].

Once the precognoscing of the witnesses is complete, the full precognition, together with documentary productions, is sent to the Crown Office in Edinburgh. There it is read by Crown Counsel (usually one of the advocates-depute, but, if the case is one of great importance or difficulty, possibly one of the Law Officers) who will direct whether proceedings are to be taken and, if so, of what sort. The nature of the proceedings and the court in which they take place usually depend on the gravity of the charge. The criminal record of the accused may also be a factor. Crown Counsel will have in mind the maximum powers of sentencing possessed by a sheriff. The Lord Advocate may have issued directions that certain types of case are to be prosecuted in a particular forum.

If the decision is that no proceedings are to be taken, the accused must be liberated forthwith if he is in custody. If he is on bail, he must be informed. For a case to be marked 'no pro' does not necessarily preclude proceedings at a later date if new evidence emerges. However, further proceedings will be incompetent if the Crown is, by its actings, personally barred from taking further action against an accused, for example by informing him that no further steps will be taken in the matter[3], or by issuing a general statement of policy[4].

If it is decided to indict the case in the High Court, the indictment will be prepared in the Crown Office, and it will be signed by an advocate-depute[5]. If it is decided to indict in the sheriff court, the precognition is returned to the fiscal with instructions to him to prepare an indictment. The indictment is then signed by the fiscal or one of his deputes 'by authority of Her Majesty's Advocate'[6].

If the decision is that summary prosecution rather than solemn proceedings is appropriate, the precognition is returned to the fiscal with instructions to him to prepare the appropriate summary complaint. In that event the case proceeds as a normal summary prosecution[7] with the accused (who will almost certainly be on bail) being told when he is to appear in court. As a matter of courtesy the procurator fiscal usually informs the defence solicitor that the case has been reduced to summary level.

# THE INDICTMENT

## General

The indictment is the document which contains the charge(s) against an accused who is to be tried before a jury. The accused is indicted 'at the instance of' the Lord Advocate, although, if there is no Lord Advocate at the time, the indictment may proceed in the name of the Solicitor General[8].

1  *Coll, Petr* 1977 JC 29.
2  See below at pp 154–156.
3  *Thom v HMA* 1976 JC 48, 1976 SLT 23; *HMA v Stewart* 1980 JC 84.
4  Such a statement is, however, given a restricted interpretation: *Lockhart v Deighan* 1985 SCCR 204, 1985 SLT 549.
5  1995 Act, s 64(3). The subsection actually says that the indictment is to be 'signed by the Lord Advocate or one of his deputes', but in practice it is invariably signed by an advocate-depute.
6  1995 Act, s 64(4).
7  See ch 6 below.
8  1995 Act, s 287(2).

The essentials of an indictment are that it should name the accused, it should state the time when and the place where the crime was committed, and it should set forth the way in which the crime was committed. Styles for the more usual common law crimes are set forth in Schedule 2 of the 1995 Act (which is applied by sections 34 and 64(2)). The terms of the Schedule are taken without any substantial alteration from Schedule A of the Criminal Procedure (Scotland) Act 1887 and include such delightful archaisms as stealing 'a shawl and a boa' and robbing 'Charles Doyle, a cattle dealer, of Biggar, Lanarkshire, of a watch and chain'. The general form of these styles should, however, be adhered to unless there is good reason to the contrary.

An indictment may be written or printed or a combination of both[1]. In practice most indictments in both the High Court and the sheriff court are produced by computer.

Schedule 3 of the 1995 Act as applied by section 64(6) contains detailed provisions (originating in the 1887 Act) intended to simplify the form of indictment as compared with the pre-1887 form. Some of these are now discussed.

## The accused

An accused may be named and designed according to the name and designation (ie address) which he gave at examination or full committal[2], and it is not necessary to set forth any other name or designation by which he may be known[2]. In practice, however, if an accused has an alias, it is common to state it in the indictment. Thus the libel might be against 'David Balfour also known as John Smith'. The designation of an accused is usually 'prisoner in the prison of X' if he is in custody, or 'whose domicile of citation has been specified as 1 Y Street, X' if he is on bail. The domicile of citation is the address at which an accused who is on bail will be cited[3].

## Naming the crime

It is not necessary to specify the crime charged in an indictment by any particular legal name. It is enough that the indictment sets forth facts relevant and sufficient to constitute an indictable crime[4].

## Multiple accused

If two or more persons are charged together with committing a crime, it is implied that they acted jointly and/or severally[5]. If it is alleged that the accused acted with

---

1 1995 Act, s 64(5).
2 1995 Act, Sch 3, para 1. This also provides that an accused may be named and designed 'according to the existing practice'. The Criminal Procedure (Consequential Provisions) (Scotland) Act 1995, s 6(2) provides that the repeal of certain sections of the Criminal Procedure (Scotland) Act 1975 which are listed in Sch 6 'shall not revive any rule of law or practice having effect before the coming into force of the Criminal Procedure (Scotland) Act 1887'. The practical effect of that provision is that the provisions contained in the sections listed in Sch 6 continue to have the force of law.
3 1995 Act, s 25(1)(b); 1996 Rules, r 2.2(3). See below at p 121.
4 1995 Act, Sch 3, para 2.
5 There was a specific provision to this effect in the 1975 Act, s 45. For a reason which is obscure this provision was not repeated in the 1995 Act, although for practical purposes it continues in effect.

another or others who are not charged in the same indictment, it is desirable that this should be set out in the libel[1].

## Accession

It is implied that a person charged is guilty actor (ie as principal) or art and part (ie as accessory)[2]. However, there are occasions when greater specification is required. For example, a woman might be charged with rape, a crime in which she clearly could not be the principal. However, she could be guilty as an accessory because she assisted in overcoming the victim's resistance while her male co-accused had intercourse. In such a situation it would be necessary as a matter of fair notice to specify what part each accused played in the commission of the crime.

## Time

The indictment must specify the time when the crime was alleged to have been committed. Usually it is only the date which is given, but there are certain crimes where the exact time of day may be crucial to the charge, in which case it too must be set forth[3]. If a single date is stated and the exact time is not of the essence, there is an implied latitude of three months, ie covering the month libelled, the previous month and the month after[4]. If the crime is charged as having been committed between two specified dates, the prosecutor is confined to the period between these dates, and there is no further latitude[5].

If the period of time libelled is greater than three months, the exceptional latitude must be justified by the prosecutor[6]. In many cases an exceptional latitude has been allowed, and it is difficult to generalise about the circumstances which have justified it. Sexual offences against children are one field where a wide latitude is commonly permitted[7]. That the crime was committed at some time during a period when the accused was in a particular occupation, or that, because of the lapse of time since it was committed, witnesses cannot be expected to remember exact dates, are reasons why the latitude may be extended.

It is unnecessary to set forth in the indictment the circumstances which justify an exceptional latitude[8], but evidence must be led at the trial to show that it is not unfair to the accused[9].

An exceptional latitude of time may, of course, prejudice an accused if he is seeking to put forward a defence of alibi. However, this is not a reason for dismissing an indictment, provided that the Crown has exercised due diligence. The appropriate remedy for the accused is to seek an adjournment during the course of the trial as the evidence emerges[10].

1  *HMA v McWilliam* 1994 SCCR 152; *Mitchell v HMA* 1994 SCCR 440 at 449B, 1995 SLT 1168 at 1174D, per Lord Clyde.
2  This was provided in s 46 of the Criminal Procedure (Scotland) Act 1887.
3  Eg night poaching, which is committed between 'the expiration of the first hour after sunset' and 'the beginning of the last hour before sunrise' (Night Poaching Act 1828, s 12).
4  *Hume* II, 221; Alison *Practice* p 251; 1995 Act, Sch 3, para 4(1).
5  *Creighton v HMA* (1904) 4 Adam 356, 6 F (J) 72, 12 SLT 36; *Andrew v HMA* 1982 SCCR 539.
6  Alison *Practice* p 256, quoted with approval by Lord Russell in *Ogg v HMA* 1938 JC 152 at 154.
7  Eg *HMA v AE* 1937 JC 96, 1938 SLT 70; *HMA v Hastings* 1985 SCCR 128, 1985 SLT 446.
8  1995 Act, Sch 3, para 4(3). See *Hunter v Guild* 1989 SCCR 717.
9  *HMA v Mackenzie* (1913) 7 Adam 189, 1913 SC (J) 107, 1913 SLT 48.
10  1995 Act, Sch 3, para 4(4). See also *Murray v HMA* 1987 SCCR 249.

# Place

Specification of the place where the crime was committed is essential as it is that which usually determines the jurisdiction of the court[1]. The words 'or near' or 'in the near neighbourhood of' are implied in all descriptions of the locus unless the actual place is of the essence of the charge[2]. The libel of place should be as specific as possible in order to give the accused fair notice. However, there are cases where, because of the nature of the charge, the prosecutor cannot be more specific than to say something along the lines of 'or elsewhere in Glasgow to the prosecutor unknown'[3].

# The facts of the crime

The indictment must libel facts and circumstances which constitute a crime known to the law of Scotland. Thus, to charge that an accused attempted to cause a woman to abort, libelling only a belief that she was pregnant and not that she actually *was* pregnant, was held to be irrelevant, as the crime of attempted abortion requires a foetus *in utero*[4].

# Qualifying words

Certain words from which wicked intention or guilty knowledge could be inferred and which previously had to be inserted in a charge, are now implied where necessary[5]. However, it should be noted that, in the case of fire raising, it is still necessary to specify whether the crime was committed 'wilfully' or 'culpably and recklessly' as these are two different crimes.

# Statutory charges

If the crime charged is a statutory contravention, it is not necessary to quote the words of the statute. It is sufficient to libel that the crime was committed contrary to the Act of Parliament, referring to the appropriate section of the Act[6].

# Descriptions

Words such as 'or thereby' in relation to quantities[7] or 'to the prosecutor unknown' in relation to the 'perpetration of any act regarding persons, things or modes'[8] are now implied where appropriate in every case. That property (heritable

---

1 See above at p 99.
2 1995 Act, Sch 3, para 4(2).
3 *Gold v Neilson* (1907) 5 Adam 423, 1908 SC (J) 5, 15 SLT 458, which is a summary case, but the principle is the same. The charge was reset of 44 different articles.
4 *HMA v Anderson* 1928 JC 1, 1927 SLT 651. Note that the actual ratio of this case (namely the fact that it is impossible to commit the completed crime precludes charging an attempt) has now been disapproved: *Docherty v Brown* 1996 SCCR 136, 1996 SLT 325.
5 1995 Act, Sch 3, para 3.
6 1995 Act, Sch 3, para 13.
7 1995 Act, Sch 3, para 4(6).
8 1995 Act, Sch 3, para 4(7).

or moveable) is not the property of the accused is to be implied where that is essential to the criminality of the charge[1]. In the case of persons, the words 'now or lately' residing at a particular address are to be implied[2]. It is not necessary to specify the material of which an article is made[2]. Nor is it necessary to specify the form of a sum of money; all that requires to be libelled is the amount and that it consists of money[3]. The contents of a document need not be narrated at length. It is sufficient to describe the document and, where it is a production, to refer to the number given to it in the list of productions[4].

## LISTS OF PRODUCTIONS AND WITNESSES

There are appended to the indictment a list of the productions upon which the Crown intends to found and a list of the witnesses whom the Crown intends to lead in support of the charge(s) against the accused[5].

The list of productions is divided into two parts, the first being documentary productions (referred to as 'productions'), and the second being other articles (referred to as 'labels' because an article normally has a label attached to it for identification purposes).

The list of witnesses should give the name of each witness together with an address at which he can be contacted for the purpose of precognition[6]. In recent years there has grown up a practice of giving the address of some witnesses (especially the victims of crime) as 'care of' the local police force. This is no doubt intended for the protection from intimidation of such witnesses. In the case of many witnesses it is their professional or business address, rather than that of their residence which is given. Police witnesses are usually described by their rank, the force to which they belong and the place where they are stationed.

Any objection in respect of misnomer or misdescription of any witness in the list of witnesses must be intimated in writing to the trial court, the prosecutor and any other accused[7]. If the trial court is the sheriff court this must be done at or before the first diet[8]. If the trial court is the High Court intimation must be made not less than ten clear days before the trial diet[7]. If the court is satisfied that the accused has not been given sufficient information to enable him to find such a witness in time to precognosce him before the trial, the court may grant whatever remedy it considers appropriate[9].

1  Criminal Procedure (Consequential Provisions) (Scotland) Act 1995, Sch 6 referring to the 1975 Act, s 52.
2  Criminal Procedure (Consequential Provisions) (Scotland) Act 1995, Sch 6 referring to the 1975 Act, s 53.
3  Criminal Procedure (Consequential Provisions) (Scotland) Act 1995, Sch 6 referring to the 1975 Act, s 54.
4  Criminal Procedure (Consequential Provisions) (Scotland) Act 1995, Sch 6 referring to the 1975 Act, s 55.
5  In practice, as a matter of courtesy the defence solicitor usually receives from the procurator fiscal a copy of the indictment together with the lists of witnesses and productions and the notice of previous convictions, if any. The defence may also be provided with copies of the documentary productions.
6  1995 Act, s 67(1).
7  1995 Act, s 67(3).
8  1995 Act, s 67(3). For 'first diet' see below at pp 132–134.
9  1995 Act, s 67(4).

# TIME LIMITS

For many years the prosecution of crime in Scotland under solemn procedure has been governed by strict time limits. These are intended, primarily, to prevent an accused being detained for unnecessarily long periods without receiving an indictment or being brought to trial. They are now contained in section 65 of the 1995 Act, which also includes a general time limit on the prosecution of cases on indictment even if the accused has not been detained in custody. It is this latter time limit which will be considered first.

## The twelve-month rule

A jury trial of an accused must be commenced[1] within twelve months of the accused's first appearance on petition[2]. If the trial does not begin within that period, the accused 'shall be discharged forthwith from any indictment as respects the offence and shall not at any time be proceeded against on indictment as respects the offence'. The time limit does not apply to an accused for whose arrest a warrant has been granted in respect of his failure to appear at a diet of the case[3] The circumstances leading to the granting of the warrant are irrelevant[4].

The court has power 'on cause shown' to extend the twelve-month period[5]. An application for extension is normally made to the sheriff, but, if the accused has already been served with a High Court indictment, the application must be made to a High Court judge[5]. The application need not be in writing[6].

The leading case on extension of the twelve-month limit is *Her Majesty's Advocate v Swift*[7]. In that case the High Court, on appeal, refused to grant an extension and laid down the following principles: (1) an extension is to be granted only if sufficient reason for it is shown and the judge is prepared to exercise his discretion in favour of the Crown; (2) fault on the part of the Crown is not an absolute bar to the extension being granted, but the nature and degree of that fault are relevant factors in assessing sufficient reason and in the exercise of discretion under principle (1); (3) the gravity of the charge(s) is not in itself a sufficient reason for granting an extension; (4) the shortness of the extension sought and the fact that the accused is not prejudiced are not relevant in assessing the sufficiency of the reason for granting the extension, but they may be relevant factors in the question of exercising discretion when sufficient reason has been demonstrated.

It has been emphasised that mere pressure of business is not enough to justify an extension[8], but pressure of business has been somewhat narrowly interpreted in

---

1 A trial commences, for the purposes of this section, when the jury is sworn: 1995 Act, s 65(9).
2 1995 Act, s 65(1) (as amended by the Criminal Procedure and Investigation Act 1996, s 73). If the charge is reduced to summary proceedings, the twelve-month limit does not then apply. The 1996 amendment has the effect of negativing the decision in *Gardner v Lees* 1996 SCCR 168, 1996 SLT 342.
3 1995 Act, s 65(2).
4 *HMA v Taylor* 1996 SCCR 510, 1996 SLT 836, a case in which a warrant was granted even though the accused was in the court building but not in the actual courtroom when the case was called.
5 1995 Act, s 65(3).
6 *Ferguson v HMA* 1992 JC 133, 1992 SCCR 480.
7 *HMA v Swift* 1984 JC 83, 1984 SCCR 216, 1985 SLT 26. See also *Lyle v HMA* 1991 SCCR 599, 1992 SLT 467; *HMA v Davies* 1993 SCCR 645, 1994 SLT 296; *Forrester v HMA* 1997 SCCR 9.
8 *McGinty v HMA* 1984 SCCR 176, 1985 SLT 25.

later cases[1]. If the prosecutor has excused attendance of a witness whose evidence is essential to the Crown case, that is not a good reason for extending the twelve-month period[2]. The administrative convenience of trying two accused together is also an inadequate reason for granting an extension[3].

An extension of the twelve-month limit may be applied for and granted even after the period has already expired[4].

An application for an extension is an independent proceeding and is not affected by any question of the competency of an indictment which is called on the same day, as it is always open to the Crown to serve a fresh indictment if the extension is granted[5].

An extension may be applied for where the accused has disappeared[6]. If the application cannot be served on the accused himself because he cannot be traced, it should be intimated to his solicitor, if known[7].

Both the accused and the Crown have a right of appeal to the High Court against the sheriff's or judge's decision on an application for an extension of the twelve-month limit[8].

## The 80-day rule

An accused who has been committed for trial in custody may not be detained for a total period of more than 80 days from full committal without having been served with an indictment[9]. If no indictment has been served within that period, the accused must be liberated forthwith[9]. This does not mean that he cannot thereafter be served with an indictment, but simply that he may no longer be detained in custody pending his trial.

If an indictment is served within the 80 days but then falls because the accused is not called to answer it in court on the specified date, he should be released unless a new indictment is served before the 80-day period has expired[10]. However, if he *is* detained beyond the 80-day period that does not render incompetent any indictment then served on him[11].

The Crown may apply to a single judge of the High Court for an extension of the 80-day limit, and the judge may extend it 'for any sufficient cause'[12] but should

---

1 *Dobbie v HMA* 1986 SCCR 72, 1986 SLT 648; *Rudge v HMA* 1989 SCCR 105, 1989 SLT 591 (note the critical comment by Sheriff G H Gordon (editor of SCCR) at 1989 SCCR 108); *Fleming v HMA* 1992 SCCR 575.
2 *Ferguson v HMA* 1992 SCCR 480.
3 *Mejka v HMA* 1993 SCCR 978, 1993 SLT 1321. See also *Ashcroft v HMA* 1996 SCCR 608, 1997 SLT 60.
4 *HMA v M* 1987 JC 1, 1986 SCCR 624, 1986 SLT 475 sub nom *HMA v Mullen*, a rather unusual case where an appeal from a preliminary diet caused the trial, which had been fixed just within the twelve months, to be discharged. The decision in this case was approved by a bench of five judges in *McDowall v Lees* 1996 SCCR 719, 1996 SLT 871.
5 *McDonald v HMA* 1988 SCCR 298, 1988 SLT 693.
6 *Watson v HMA* 1983 SCCR 115, 1983 SLT 471.
7 *Campbell v HMA* 1986 SCCR 573, 1987 SLT 399.
8 1995 Act, s 65(8). Procedures are provided for by the 1996 Rules, r 8.1 which specifies that Form 8.1A should be used in an appeal. The ground of appeal *must* be set out in the application: *Johnston v HMA* 1993 JC 187, 1993 SCCR 295.
9 1995 Act, s 65(4)(a).
10 *HMA v Walker* 1981 JC 102, 1981 SCCR 154, 1981 SLT (Notes) 3.
11 *McCluskey v HMA* 1992 SCCR 920, 1993 SLT 897. The court expressed the opinion that the accused's remedy for illegal detention lay with the civil courts.
12 1995 Act, s 65(5).

not do so if he is satisfied that, 'but for some fault on the part of the prosecutor', the indictment could have been served within the period[1]. The power to extend may be exercised even after the period has actually expired[2].

Both the accused and the Crown have a right of appeal to the High Court against the decision of the single judge[3].

## The 110-day rule

An accused who has been committed for trial in custody must be brought to trial and the trial commenced[4] within 110 days from full committal[5]. If the trial is not begun within that period, then the accused must be liberated forthwith, and he is thereafter 'for ever free from all question or process for that offence'[5]. The time limit applies equally where an accused is granted bail with a condition of residence which is tantamount to his being in custody[6]. Bail with a condition of remaining at home except for necessary court appearances does not have the same effect; the test is whether there is intervention by a custodial agency[7].

The Crown may apply to a single judge of the High Court to extend the period on the following grounds: (a) the illness of the accused or of a judge; (b) the absence or illness of any necessary witness; (c) any other sufficient cause which is not attributable to any fault on the part of the prosecutor[8]. Clearly this last ground leaves a great deal to the discretion of the judge. In *Her Majesty's Advocate v McTavish*[9] an extension was refused when the reason advanced by the Crown for seeking it was to enable the carrying out of tests which might have resulted in different, more serious charges. In *Gildea v Her Majesty's Advocate*[10] an extension was allowed when the reason for seeking it was that a previous trial in the circuit had lasted longer than had been foreseen. The court is required to adopt a more exacting test in deciding whether to grant an extension to the 110 days than the test which it should apply in deciding whether to extend the twelve-month period[11].

Both the accused and the Crown have a right of appeal to the High Court against the decision of the single judge[12].

---

1   1995 Act, s 65(6).
2   *Farrell v HMA* 1984 JC 1, 1984 SCCR 301, 1985 SLT 58.
3   1995 Act, s 65(8). Procedures are provided for by the 1996 Rules, r 8.1 which specifies that Form 8.1B should be used in an appeal. The ground of appeal *must* be set out in the application: *Johnston v HMA* 1993 JC 187, 1993 SCCR 295.
4   A trial commences, for the purposes of this section, when the jury is sworn: 1995 Act, s 65(9).
5   1995 Act, s 65(4)(b).
6   *K v HMA* 1991 SCCR 343, 1993 SLT 77 (condition of residence in List D school). However, see also *X, Petr* 1995 SCCR 407, where bail with a condition that the accused reside in a List D school but not in secure accommodation therein was held not to amount to custody (and see also the sequel, *X, Petr* 1996 SCCR 436).
7   *Brawls v Walkingshaw* 1994 SCCR 7.
8   1995 Act, s 65(7). For an exceptional case where two extensions were granted (making the total period 186 days), see *Young v HMA* 1990 SCCR 315.
9   *HMA v McTavish* 1974 JC 19, 1974 SLT 246.
10  *Gildea v HMA* 1983 SCCR 144, 1983 SLT 458 (note the critical comment by Sheriff G H Gordon (editor of SCCR) at 1983 SCCR 148).
11  *Beattie v HMA* 1995 SCCR 606, 1995 SLT 946.
12  1995 Act, s 65(8). Procedures are provided for by the 1996 Rules, r 8.1 which specifies that Form 8.1B should be used in an appeal. The ground of appeal *must* be set out in the application: *Johnston v HMA* 1993 JC 187, 1993 SCCR 295.

**Computation of time limits under the 80-day and 110-day rules**

The time limits apply only to periods spent in custody as a result of the committal warrant. A sentence imposed on a different charge interrupts the running of the period[1]. This is the case even if the sentence is subsequently quashed as incompetent; the court must look to see what warrant for detention was actually in existence at the relevant time[2]. If the accused, having been fully committed, is liberated after having been detained for a period and is then fully committed on a second warrant on different charges, any time in custody following thereon will be attributed to the second warrant and not to the earlier one[3]. However, if the accused is fully committed on a second warrant *without* having been liberated, the time spent in custody is still computed from the date of the first warrant so far as the charges covered by that warrant are concerned[4].

# CITATION OF THE ACCUSED

When any sitting of a court has been appointed to be held for a jury trial or trials, the sheriff clerk (in the case of sheriff court trials) or the Clerk of Justiciary (in the case of High Court trials) issues a warrant to cite accused persons, witnesses and jurors[5]. The warrant is authority to cite for the first day of the sitting 'with continuation of days'[5].

The record copy of the indictment (ie the copy which will form part of the official record of the court) together with copies of the lists of witnesses and productions must be lodged with the clerk of the appropriate court on or before the date of service of the indictment[6].

**Service of the indictment on the accused**

The accused must be served with an indictment[7]. If he is not so served, the proceedings are incompetent[8].

Service of an indictment may be effected by any officer of law[9], which includes any macer, messenger-at-arms, sheriff officer or other person having authority to execute a warrant of the court; any constable within the meaning of the Police

---

1  *Wallace v HMA* 1959 JC 71, 1959 SLT 320. See also *Brown v HMA* 1988 SCCR 577, in which it was held that the prison practice of releasing on Friday a prisoner whose release date should truly have been the following Sunday, should be ignored in computing a period of imprisonment which interrupts the 110 days.
2  *Thomson v HMA* 1996 SCCR 671, 1996 SLT 1257.
3  *HMA v Boyle* 1972 SLT (Notes) 16.
4  *Ross v HMA* 1990 SCCR 182.
5  1995 Act, s 66(1); 1996 Rules, r 8.2.
6  1995 Act, s 66(5). Failure to lodge the record copy timeously does not, however, amount to a fundamental nullity: *HMA v Graham* 1985 SCCR 169, 1985 SLT 498.
7  1995 Act, s 66(4).
8  *McAllister v HMA* 1985 SCCR 36, 1985 SLT 399, in which it was held that there had been no service, although an execution of service bearing that the accused had been personally served at his domicile of citation was produced. This was conceded by the Crown to be inaccurate as there had in fact been no personal service.
9  1995 Act, s 66(7).

(Scotland) Act 1967; any civilian employee of a police force under section 9 of the Police (Scotland) Act 1967 who is authorised by the chief constable in relation to service and execution of documents; (only in the case of an accused who is in prison) a prison officer; and any other person or class of persons authorised for the time being by the Lord Advocate or Secretary of State to effect service and execution[1].

Service may be effected in four separate ways[2]:

(a) delivering the document to the accused personally;
(b) leaving the document in the hands of a member of the family of the accused or other occupier or employee at the proper domicile of citation of the accused[3];
(c) affixing the document to the door of, or depositing it in, the proper domicile of citation of the accused;
(d) where the officer of law serving the document has reasonable grounds for believing that an accused, for whom no proper domicile of citation has been specified, is residing at a particular place but is unavailable –
  (i) leaving the document in the hands of a member of the family of the accused or other occupier or employee at that place; or
  (ii) affixing the document to the door of, or depositing it in, that place.

Note that paragraph (d) applies only in the rare case where no proper domicile of citation has been specified. This would be only when the accused has neither been remanded in custody nor been released on bail.

Where the accused is in custody service should be made personally. If the accused is on bail, the indictment should be served at his proper domicile of citation[3], by an officer of law[4] using one of the methods specified in paragraphs (b) and (c) above. Citation of the accused at that address by one of these methods will be presumed to have been duly carried out[5]. In a case decided under earlier bail legislation[6] the High Court held that, even if an accused had been detained on another charge following his release on bail and was actually in prison, service by leaving the indictment at his domicile of citation was good. This was at a time when it was common to specify the sheriff clerk's office as the domicile of citation (as was done in this case), which meant at least that the accused's solicitor could receive the service copy indictment from the sheriff clerk. It might have been hoped that the court would not take an equally strict view under the modern bail legislation where the domicile of citation is normally the accused's residence. This would, however, have been too optimistic a view[7].

---

1  1995 Act, s 307(1).
2  1996 Rules, r 2.2(2).
3  The 1995 Act, s 25(3) and the 1996 Rules, r 2.2(3) provide that 'proper domicile of citation' means 'the address at which the accused may be cited to appear at any diet relating to the offence with which he is charged or any offence charged in the same proceedings as that offence or to which any other intimation or document may be sent'. An accused may apply to the court in writing to have his domicile of citation changed (1995 Act, s 24(2); 1996 Rules, r 4.1). The application must be served on the procurator fiscal (r 4.1(1)(b)). The result of the application must be notified by the clerk of court to the fiscal and to any co-accused (r 4.1(5)). If the fiscal is not notified of the result the Crown may be entitled to an extension of the twelve-month limit: *Black v HMA* 1990 SCCR 609.
4  See above at p 120.
5  1995 Act, s 25(3).
6  *Bryson v HMA* 1961 JC 57, 1961 SLT 289.
7  In *Jamieson v HMA* 1990 SCCR 137, 1990 SLT 845, another case where the accused was in prison at the time of service at his domicile of citation, *Bryson v HMA* (above) was approved and followed. In *Welsh v HMA* 1986 SCCR 233, 1986 SLT 664, the address specified as the proper domicile of citation was a house which had been demolished, but sticking the indictment on a remaining main door was held to be a good service. See also *McAllister v HMA* 1985 SCCR 36, 1985 SLT 399.

## Documents served with indictment

Along with the indictment are served the lists of productions[1] and witnesses[2].

There must also be served at the same time any notice of previous convictions which the prosecutor intends to place before the court in the event of conviction[3]. Convictions contained in such a notice, duly served, are held to apply to the accused unless he gives written notice of objection at least five clear days before the trial diet[4]. If the accused intends to plead guilty under the procedure provided for by section 76 of the 1995 Act different procedures apply. These will be discussed below[5].

With the indictment the accused must also receive a notice calling upon him to appear for the appropriate diet[6]. This stipulates the court, the date and the time of his appearance. It is here that, for the first time, the procedure in the High Court and that in the sheriff court diverge. In the case of a High Court indictment the notice served on the accused simply calls upon him to appear for trial in the High Court on a date which must not be less than 29 clear days after service of the indictment[7]. If the trial is to be in the sheriff court the notice calls on the accused to appear (i) at a first diet[8] on a date which must be not less than fifteen clear days before the trial diet[9]; and (ii) at a trial diet on a date which must not be less than 29 clear days after service of the indictment[7]. Under the 1975 Act procedure it was held that service on a date less than 29 clear days from the trial diet did not amount to a fundamental nullity[10]. That was in a High Court case where the procedure has effectively not changed. It is perhaps open to question whether the ratio of the case would apply now to a sheriff court case where there has to be a first diet.

## Body corporate

If an accused is a body corporate, service is effected by delivering a copy of the indictment together with a notice to appear to its registered office or (if there is no registered office in the United Kingdom) to its principal place of business in the United Kingdom[11]. This delivery may be made by registered post or recorded delivery[11].

## Correction of errors prior to service

Prior to service any error in the indictment may be corrected by deletion or alteration on the record copy and service copies, and such a deletion or alteration is sufficiently authenticated by the initials of any person authorised to sign the

---

1  This must include the record of the transcript of the judicial examination: 1995 Act, s 68(1).
2  1995 Act, s 66(4).
3  1995 Act, s 69(2).
4  1995 Act, s 69(3). The notice must be given to the Crown Agent in the case of a High Court trial, and to the procurator fiscal in the case of a trial in the sheriff court.
5  For s 76 procedure see below at pp 141–143.
6  1995 Act, s 66(6).
7  1995 Act, s 66(6)(b).
8  See below at pp 132–134.
9  1995 Act, s 66(6)(a).
10  *HMA v McDonald* 1984 JC 94, 1984 SCCR 229, 1984 SLT 426.
11  1995 Act, s 70(2).

indictment[1]. In the case of the service copy any correction is also sufficiently authenticated by the initials of the person serving it, and this applies also to any notice served on an accused[2].

## Lodging of Crown productions

There is no statutory provision about the lodging of Crown productions, although it is clear that productions for a sheriff court trial should be lodged with the sheriff clerk and that those for a High Court trial should be lodged with the Clerk of Justiciary[3]. The productions should be lodged at a time which provides the accused (or more probably his solicitor) with sufficient opportunity to examine them before the start of the trial[4]. If productions are lodged late, they may still be admissible in evidence. The accused's remedy is to seek an adjournment of the trial in order to examine them if he so wishes[5]. The proper time for the accused to take objection to the late lodging (or a complete failure to lodge) is before the jury is sworn[5]. In practice documentary productions are usually lodged along with the record copy of the indictment[6].

# CROWN WITNESSES

All the witnesses on the list appended to the indictment should be cited by the Crown. The 1995 Act provides that a witness may be cited by any officer of law[7]. The officer's evidence is sufficient to prove citation[7]. The situation is, however, not entirely straightforward as the 1996 Rules provide that 'in *any* proceedings' (emphasis added) a witness may be cited (whether by the prosecution or the defence) in the first instance by post[8]. The rule for postal citation of a witness provides that the witness should within 14 days return a form sent with the citation whereby he acknowledges receipt of the citation[9]. It is only if postal citation has been attempted and has been unsuccessful or the witness has failed to return the appropriate form that citation is then to be carried out by an officer of law 'delivering the document to the witness personally'[10]. I understand that, at least in solemn cases, procurators fiscal do not intend to make use of postal citation of witnesses but will continue to rely on the time-tested method of citation by officer of law.

Although the Crown must append a list of witnesses to the indictment, it is not limited to leading evidence only from the witnesses named in that list. Additional witnesses may, with the leave of the court, be examined provided that written notice has been given to the accused not less than two clear days before the date on

---

1  1995 Act, s 66(12).
2  1995 Act, s 66(13).
3  This is implicit in the terms of the 1995 Act, s 68(2).
4  *Hume* II, 388; Alison *Practice* p 594; *Renton and Brown*, para 14–24.
5  *MacNeil v HMA* 1986 SCCR 288.
6  *Renton and Brown*, para 14–24.
7  1995 Act, s 66(9). For the definition of 'officer of law', see above at pp 120, 121.
8  1996 Rules, r 2.4(1).
9  1996 Rules, r 8.2(3).
10  1996 Rules, r 2.4(2).

which the jury is sworn to try the case[1]. The notice should contain the name and address of each witness[1]. A similar provision applies to productions which are not on the Crown list[1]. Copies of such notices are usually sent also to the accused's solicitor.

The Crown may also call a witness or put in evidence a production included in any list or notice lodged by the accused[2].

There are various circumstances in which witnesses and productions not contained in lists or notices for either party may nevertheless be put in evidence. These will be noted at the appropriate places in the text.

# DUTY OF CROWN TO DISCLOSE EVIDENCE FAVOURABLE TO DEFENCE

The duty of the Crown to produce evidence which is favourable to the accused is, surprisingly, not entirely clear. In a brief opinion delivered without reference to authority the High Court in 1990 stated that 'there is no obligation on the Crown to disclose any information in their possession which would tend to exculpate the accused'[3]. It is doubtful if this dictum would be founded on by the Crown today as in a more recent case[4] the advocate depute specifically dissociated the Crown from it.

# PREPARATION BY THE DEFENCE

It is only with service of the indictment (a copy of which is also usually sent to the accused's solicitor) that the accused is officially informed of the exact charge against him and of the witnesses and productions. In practice, however, it is probable that the defence solicitor has already had informal discussions with the fiscal and has been given some information about these matters. The solicitor will almost certainly also have had at least one consultation with his client since full committal.

It is strongly recommended that a solicitor should begin preparing for a trial, insofar as he is able, prior to service of the indictment, but, for the purposes of this section only, we shall assume that the solicitor has had no contact with either the fiscal or his client between full committal and service. This means that the defence must move very fast, especially in a sheriff court case, as the first diet may be as early as fifteen days after service of the indictment[5]. In a High Court case, the trial may be as early as 29 days after service[5].

### Precognition of crown witnesses by the defence

The first thing which the defence solicitor should do is to have precognitions taken from the Crown witnesses. It may not be necessary to precognosce all the witnesses

1  1995 Act, s 67(5).
2  1995 Act, s 67(6).
3  *Higgins v HMA* 1990 SCCR 268 at 269B, per Lord Cowie giving the opinion of the court.
4  *HMA v Ward* 1993 SCCR 595, 1993 SLT 1202.
5  See above at p 122.

on the Crown list. In some cases it will be obvious that precognition is unnecessary, eg witnesses speaking to the contents of uncontroversial reports. If the solicitor has had a preliminary discussion with the fiscal, that may have given him some indication of which witnesses need not be precognosced.

A solicitor may take precognitions himself, and it is advisable in the case of a particularly sensitive witness, such as the alleged victim in a rape case, that he should. However, the more common practice nowadays is to use a private inquiry agency. The employees of such agencies are very often former police officers and should therefore be familiar with the technique of taking statements from witnesses. Precognoscers should be informed of what the line of defence is and whether there are any particular points to be put to witnesses.

There is no legal obligation on a Crown witness to give a precognition to the defence, although there is judicial authority for the proposition that it is his civic duty to do so[1]. Crown witnesses are notoriously reluctant to give statements to the defence. It may sometimes prove beneficial to remind a witness that it is only by precognition that an accused may be made fully aware of the strength of the case against him, and that this might result in a plea of guilty.

The defence is entitled to apply to have a witness cited for precognition on oath[2]. There has been a difference of shrieval opinion on the scope of this entitlement. On the one hand the opinion has been expressed that an accused should be allowed to precognosce a witness on oath only in the same exceptional circumstances as those in which the Crown would do so, and not just where it is desired to obtain a precognition from a witness who is being unco-operative[3]. On the other hand it has been held that the object of the statutory provision is to place the defence on equal terms with the Crown in preparation of the case, and that the words 'on oath' do not restrict such precognition by the defence to exceptional circumstances[4]. It is submitted that the latter view is to be preferred and that the true purpose of the provision is to enable the defence to obtain a precognition from a reluctant or recalcitrant witness. The fact that the precognition is on oath is, as the sheriff in *Brady* put it, 'so that the exercise can be a meaningful one, and of some value to the defence'[5].

If the defence solicitor suspects that a Crown witness has a criminal record, there seems to be no way in which he may obtain official confirmation of his suspicion. As a matter of practice procurators fiscal will not usually make copies of the record available to the defence. The High Court will not grant a commission and diligence for the recovery of the record[6]. The best that the defence solicitor can do is to inform the prosecutor that he thinks that the witness has a record and ask that the prosecutor have the record, if any, available in court. If the witness then denies in evidence that he has convictions when in fact he has, the prosecutor, as an officer of court, should put his record to him[6].

1 *HMA v Monson* (1893) 1 Adam 114 at 135, 21 R (J) 5 at 11, per Lord Justice-Clerk Macdonald.
2 1995 Act, s 291. This power has been held not to apply to a convicted person who is applying to the Secretary of State to have his case referred to the High Court (now under the 1995 Act, s 124): *Gilmour, Petr* 1994 SCCR 872 (Sh Ct).
3 *Low v Macneill* 1981 SCCR 243 (Sh Ct); *Cirignaco v Lockhart* 1985 SCCR 157 (Sh Ct), 1985 SLT (Sh Ct) 11.
4 *Brady v Lockhart* 1985 SCCR 349 (Sh Ct).
5 *Brady v Lockhart* 1985 SCCR 349 at 351, per Sheriff Lunny.
6 *HMA v Ashrif* 1988 SCCR 197, 1988 SLT 567.

## Identification parade

As has already been noted[1], the accused is in certain circumstances entitled to apply to the sheriff to have the fiscal ordered to hold an identification parade with the accused in it[2].

## Examination of Crown productions

The defence solicitor will normally receive copies of the documentary productions for the Crown, such as forensic science reports and transcripts of tape recorded interviews. The 1995 Act provides that, in the case of several categories of documentary evidence, oral evidence to prove the documents at a trial is unnecessary provided that due notice has been given and no party objects[3]. These provisions will be discussed below[4]. When the Crown seeks to make use of these provisions copies of the documentary productions concerned are served on the accused and so are available to the defence solicitor.

The accused (or his solicitor) is entitled to examine and inspect the productions which have been lodged by the Crown[5] and should do so. If the accused has difficulty in obtaining access to any production, he may apply to the court in which his trial is to take place for a warrant, and this may include an application to submit the production to tests[6]. However, the accused's entitlement to examine a production probably extends only to those listed in the indictment. If, as not infrequently happens, what appears in the list is a label 'in lieu' of an article which has been returned to its owner or otherwise disposed of, the accused is probably entitled to see only the label[7].

## Defence witnesses and productions

The accused is entitled to lead evidence from any witness on the Crown list and also to put in evidence any production on the Crown list[8]. However, if the defence wishes to lead evidence from any other witness (apart from the accused himself who is entitled to give evidence without notice), or to found on any other production, written notice of these must be given, in the case of a sheriff court trial to the procurator fiscal at or before the first diet, and in the case of a High Court trial, to the Crown Agent at least ten clear days before the day on which the jury is sworn to try the case[9]. Notice must also be served on any co-accused or his solicitor[10]. The court has a discretion to allow late notice to be given on cause shown[11]. In practice the Crown very often consents to late notice being given by an accused provided that the Crown is not prejudiced thereby. A copy of the note of defence

1  See above at p 95.
2  1995 Act, s 290.
3  1995 Act, ss 258, 280, 282, 283, 284.
4  See below at pp 171–172.
5  1995 Act, s 68(2).
6  *Davies, Petr* 1973 SLT (Notes) 36.
7  *Houston v HMA* 1990 SCCR 4, 1990 SLT 514.
8  1995 Act, s 67(6).
9  1995 Act, s 78(4)(a).
10  1996 Rules, r 11.2.
11  1995 Act, s 78(4)(b).

witnesses and productions must be lodged, at or before the trial diet, with the sheriff clerk or the Clerk of Justiciary, as the case may be[1]. Any defence productions
should, of course, themselves be lodged.

The provisions about citation of witnesses for the Crown apply equally to citation of defence witnesses[2].

It is competent for the accused to apply to the High Court for commission and
diligence for the recovery of documents. As in a civil case, a specification of documents is lodged. The accused must satisfy the court that there is a connection
between the document sought to be recovered and the defence which is to be put
forward[3]. If calls are so wide as to amount to a 'fishing diligence' they will be
refused[4]. If commission and diligence is granted, it is executed in exactly the same
way as in a civil case. Only the High Court has the power to grant commission and
diligence, even though the trial may be in the sheriff court[5]. If an accused is unsuccessful in his application for commission and diligence the haver who opposed it is
entitled to expenses[6].

## Consultation

When the defence solicitor has obtained precognitions of all the witnesses who he
considers require to be precognosced and has examined the productions, he should
arrange a consultation with his client, in order to discuss the case. The solicitor
should advise the accused of the strength of the Crown case, and it may be that,
being confronted with this, the accused will decide to plead guilty to all or part of
the indictment. In practice the solicitor is likely to have more than one consultation with his client. The solicitor should take the opportunity to explain the court
procedure to the accused - assuming, of course, that the latter is not already well
versed in it!

## Counsel

If the trial is to be in the High Court, the defence solicitor (unless he is a solicitor
advocate[7] who intends himself to represent the accused at the trial) must take steps
to instruct counsel. This should be done as early as possible. Counsel should have
at least one consultation with his client, even though the solicitor may already have
seen the accused several times. For a High Court case the granting of legal aid automatically covers the employment of one junior counsel, but the employment of
more than one junior or of senior counsel (whether with or without a junior)
requires the approval of the Scottish Legal Aid Board except in cases of murder[8].
Even if the trial is to be in the sheriff court, the solicitor may consider that counsel
should represent the accused. If the accused is on legal aid, an application must be

1 1995 Act, s 78(5).
2 1995 Act, s 66(9), 1996 Rules, rr 2.4, 8.2(3). See above at p 123.
3 *Hasson v HMA* 1971 JC 35, 1971 SLT 199. See also *Hemming v HMA* 1997 SCCR 257.
4 *HMA v Ward* 1993 SCCR 595, 1993 SLT 1202.
5 *HMA v Ashrif* 1988 SCCR 197, 1988 SLT 567.
6 *Gallacher, Petr* 1990 JC 345, 1990 SCCR 492, 1991 SLT 371.
7 See above at p 97.
8 Criminal Legal Aid (Scotland) Regulations 1987, SI 1987/307, reg 14(1)(a).

made to the Scottish Legal Aid Board for approval of the employment of counsel in the sheriff court[1].

The defence solicitor may instruct the advocate of his choice directly. Alternatively, he may make contact with one of the advocates' clerks employed by Faculty Services Ltd at Parliament House in Edinburgh. The clerk will advise on the availability of counsel. When it has been decided which advocate is to be employed, the solicitor sends him a full set of instructions, including the indictment, precognitions and copies of productions.

### Discussion with the prosecution

Following the consultation, if the trial is to be in the sheriff court, the solicitor should ideally make contact with the procurator fiscal depute who is to conduct the trial. This may, however, not be feasible as, at least in the larger courts, it may not be known very far in advance of the trial which particular depute fiscal is to conduct it. There is also the possibility that the trial may be conducted by a temporary procurator fiscal depute, who will not be available for discussion until the actual day of the trial. The defence solicitor should, in any event, make every effort to discuss the case with a depute fiscal who is in a position to take a decision about any matters of importance. If the accused has decided to offer a partial plea, the fiscal's view on the acceptability of this must obviously be sought. If there are real possibilities of negotiating a plea, there may be several meetings between the fiscal and the defence solicitor.

It is clearly advantageous to agree a plea as far in advance as possible, in order that witnesses and potential jurors may be informed that they need not attend court. An early plea also enables the accused to take advantage of the statutory provision that a court may take into account the stage in the proceedings at which and the circumstances in which a plea of guilty has been tendered[2]. If an accused does instruct his solicitor to tender a plea of guilty, the solicitor is usually well advised to obtain written confirmation of the plea from his client. If the accused, having instructed a plea of guilty, then reneges, the solicitor can no longer represent him.

If the trial is to be in the High Court, defence counsel should speak to the advocate depute on the same basis as suggested above, although there is likely to be less in the way of negotiation in this situation.

### Uncontroversial evidence: agreement of evidence

In many cases there will be facts which are important but of which the evidence is nevertheless uncontroversial and unlikely to be disputed. The 1995 Act makes provision[3] for any party (in practice usually the Crown) to give notice to all other parties of facts which it is thought fall into that category. The facts are put into or annexed to a statement which must be served on all other parties not later than fourteen days before the trial diet[4]. Unless any party receiving such a statement serves notice on the

---

1 Criminal Legal Aid (Scotland) Regulations 1987, SI 1987/307, reg 14(1)(b). For the form of application, see the case of *David Balfour* at pp 31–32.
2 1995 Act, s 196. See below at p 224
3 1995 Act, s 258.
4 1995 Act, s 258(2); 1996 Rules, r 21.1; Forms 21.1A and 21.1B. In practice the notice is usually served at the same time as the indictment. The defence solicitor may receive a copy along with his courtesy copy of the indictment (see above at p 124).

first party (ie the party who served the statement) not more than seven days after service of the statement that he is challenging any fact specified or referred to in the statement, the facts so specified or referred to are deemed to have been conclusively proved[1]. The period for challenge may be extended by the court 'in special circumstances'[1]. If only some of the facts in the original statement are challenged the remaining facts are deemed to be conclusively proved[2]. Service of a statement does not preclude the first party from leading evidence of the facts specified therein[3]. It is open to the court on the application of any party to waive the deeming provisions of the section where the court is satisfied that there are special circumstances[4]. If all parties agree that the provisions should be waived the court is bound to accede[5]. An application to waive may be made at any time from the commencement of the trial until the prosecutor begins to address the jury[6]. If the application is granted the court should, unless all parties agree otherwise, adjourn the trial[7]. Thereafter evidence of the fact concerned may be led, even though a witness speaking to it or the production related to it is not on a list lodged by any party or contained in any notice under section 67(5) or section 78(4) of the 1995 Act[7].

There is an obligation on each party to identify any facts which he considers unlikely to be disputed and of which he does not wish to lead proof by oral evidence[8]. Having identified such facts the party 'shall, without prejudice to section 258 of this Act, take all reasonable steps to secure the agreement of the other party (or each of the other parties) to them; and the other party (or each of the other parties) shall take all reasonable steps to reach such agreement'[8]. The duty laid on the parties applies, in the case of solemn proceedings which are to proceed to trial, from the date of service of the indictment until the swearing of the jury[9]. The provision does not apply to proceedings in which any of the accused is not legally represented[10]. There is no sanction against any party who fails to comply with the duty set out above, and it is perhaps open to question whether the provision is more than a pious hope that something will be done.

Quite apart from these statutory provisions it is, of course, entirely proper that parties should seek either to admit or reach agreement on any matter which is not in dispute. The 1995 Act provides[11] that it is not necessary for any party to prove any fact which is admitted by the other or to prove any document the terms of which are not in dispute[12]. It is also provided that parties may agree that a copy document may be accepted as the equivalent of the original[12]. Any admission or agreement should be incorporated in a minute which should be lodged with the clerk of court[13]. If such a minute is lodged any fact or document admitted or agreed therein is deemed to have been duly proved[14].

1  1995 Act, s 258(3); 1996 Rules, r 21.2; Form 21.2. Because the time limits are very tight, the defence solicitor may well lodge a blanket counter-notice in order to preserve his client's position. If he does so, he should clarify the position with the prosecutor as soon as he has full instructions.
2  1995 Act, s 258(4).
3  1995 Act, s 258(5).
4  1995 Act, s 258(6)(a).
5  1995 Act, s 258(6)(b).
6  1995 Act, s 258(7).
7  1995 Act, s 258(8).
8  1995 Act, s 257(1).
9  1995 Act, s 257(3).
10  1995 Act, s 257(2).
11  1995 Act, s 256.
12  1995 Act, s 256(1).
13  1995 Act, s 256(2). The subsection refers both to minutes signed by only one party and to joint minutes signed by all parties. In practice the latter is almost always what is used.
14  1995 Act, s 256(3).

## Special defences

There are certain defences of which the accused must give advance notice to the Crown. These are known as 'special defences'. It was for long accepted that there were only four special defences: alibi; incrimination; self-defence; and insanity[1]. Indeed this is strictly speaking still the case. However, it is now provided that the defences of automatism and coercion are to be treated 'as if' they were special defences[2], so for all practical purposes it can now be said that there are six special defences.

Alibi means that the accused maintains that, at the time when the crime was committed, he was not at the locus libelled, but at some other specified place. The notice of special defence should give the exact times between which an accused maintains he was at the specified place. It should not just say 'at the time when the crime was committed', as this effectively begs the question. It is a matter of degree whether a special defence of alibi requires to be lodged by an accused who admits that he was near but not at the place libelled in the charge at the relevant time[3].

Incrimination (sometimes rather dubiously called 'impeachment') means that the accused maintains that the crime was committed not by him but by some other named person. It may be noted that the practice of citing the incriminee as a witness and having him brought into court for the prosecution witnesses to see has the approval of the High Court[4]. If the accused alleges that the crime was committed not by him but by a co-accused, this is not a special defence, but the accused must still lodge a notice of intention to lead evidence incriminating the co-accused[5]. A notice is necessary only if the evidence incriminating the co-accused is intended completely to exculpate the accused[6].

Self-defence means that the accused maintains that he was defending himself or a third party against an attack, or what he reasonably perceived to be an attack, by the alleged victim of the crime. It is a complete defence to a charge of assault or homicide. It is to be distinguished from provocation, which is not a complete defence, which (except in the case of murder, where it reduces the crime to culpable homicide) goes only towards mitigation and of which no advance notice need be given.

Insanity means that the accused's reason was impaired by some mental disorder and that he was thereby rendered incapable of exerting his reason to control his conduct and reactions. If proved, the defence results in a verdict of not guilty by reason of insanity. It is to be distinguished from diminished responsibility, which is not a special defence, of which no advance notice is required and which, if proved, has the effect of reducing a charge of murder to one of culpable homicide[7].

Automatism means that the accused is unable to form the necessary *mens rea* for the crime because of some external factor which was not self-induced, which was outwith the accused's control, which was a situation which the accused was not bound to foresee and which has resulted in a total alienation of reason amounting to a complete absence of self-control[8].

1  *Macdonald*, p 265.
2  1995 Act, s 78(2).
3  *Balsillie v HMA* 1993 JC 233, 1993 SCCR 760, 1994 SLT 1116.
4  *Scougall v Lees* 1994 SCCR 815, 1995 SLT 1008.
5  1995 Act, s 78(1), which also applies to special defences.
6  *McQuade v HMA* 1996 SCCR 347, 1996 SLT 1129.
7  The onus of proving diminished responsibility is on the defence: *Lindsay v HMA* 1996 SCCR 870, 1997 SLT 67.
8  *Ross v HMA* 1991 JC 210, 1991 SCCR 823, 1991 SLT 564.

Coercion means that the accused has been compelled to commit the crime by threats which were immediate and which could not be resisted or avoided[1].

There is no onus of proof on an accused in respect of a special defence other than insanity[2]. In the case of insanity there is an onus on the accused to prove, on balance of probabilities, that he was insane at the time the crime was committed[3].

Where the trial is in the High Court a special defence or a notice of incrimination of a co-accused must be lodged not less than ten clear days before the trial diet[4]. When the trial is in the sheriff court the special defence or notice must be lodged at or before the first diet[5]. If the special defence or notice of incrimination is not lodged timeously, it may be lodged late on cause shown[6]. The written notice of special defence or of incrimination must be lodged with the clerk of the court in which the trial is to take place and, at the same time, a copy of the notice must be sent to the Crown (Crown Agent if the trial is in the High Court, procurator fiscal if it is in the sheriff court) and to any co-accused or his solicitor[7].

The usual form of a special defence of self-defence is: 'McKenzie for the panel[8] [*or* accused] David Balfour pleads not guilty and, specially and without prejudice to said plea, states that, on the occasion libelled in the indictment, he was acting in self-defence, he having been assaulted by the said John Henry Starr'. The other special defences run in a similar vein. The special defence is signed by the accused's solicitor or, in the High Court, by his counsel or his solicitor.

## Attack on character

If the accused intends to attack the character of his alleged victim, he must give notice of this intention to the Crown and to the court[9]. There is no statutory provision for this. It is suggested that the notice should be in writing and should be along the same lines as a notice under section 78 of the 1995 Act (notice of special defence, incrimination of co-accused, defence witnesses or productions)[10].

## Objection to witness

An accused is entitled to object to any misnomer or misdescription of any person named in the indictment or of any witness in the list of Crown witnesses[11]. The objection must be in writing and should be intimated to the court, the prosecutor and to any co-accused not less than ten clear days before the trial diet if the trial is in the High Court or at or before the first diet if the trial is in the sheriff court[11]. If no such intimation is made an objection will be allowed only on cause shown[11]. If

---

1  *Thomson v HMA* 1983 JC 69, 1983 SCCR 368, 1983 SLT 682.
2  *Lambie v HMA* 1973 JC 53, 1973 SLT 219; *Ross v HMA* 1991 JC 210, 1991 SCCR 823, 1991 SLT 564.
3  See *Jessop v Robertson* 1989 SCCR 600 (Sh Ct), for a rare example of a case where the question of onus was raised.
4  1995 Act, s 78(1)(a), (3)(a).
5  1995 Act, s 78(1)(a), (3)(b). For 'first diet' see below at pp 132–134.
6  1995 Act, s 78(1)(b).
7  1996 Rules, r 11.1.
8  'Panel', sometimes spelt 'pannel', is the old Scots word for an accused person in a jury trial. It is still in fairly common use.
9  Alison *Practice* p 533; *Macdonald* p 304; *Renton and Brown*, para 14–28.
10  *Renton and Brown*, para 14–28, note 1.
11  1995 Act, s 67(3).

the court considers the objection to be well founded, it may grant 'such remedy by postponement, adjournment or otherwise' as it considers appropriate[1].

## POSTPONEMENT OF TRIAL

On occasions either the defence or the Crown may wish to have the trial postponed until a later date. It is also possible that the Crown and the defence are both agreed that there should be a postponement. An application for postponement of a trial diet may be made to the court before which the trial is to take place at any time prior to the trial diet[2].

The application is made by way of a minute lodged with the sheriff clerk or the Clerk of Justiciary, as the case may be[3].

If the application is by only the one party, the court fixes a date for the hearing of it and appoints intimation to all the other parties[4]. Having heard the parties in open court, the court may refuse the application or, if it grants it, fix a new trial diet or give leave to the prosecutor to serve a notice fixing a new trial diet[5]. The accused should be present at the hearing unless the court permits it to proceed in his absence[6].

If all parties make a joint application[7], the court may dispose of it without hearing parties. In that event it is dealt with by a judge or sheriff in chambers[8].

## FIRST DIET

In any solemn case in the sheriff court there must be a first diet[9]. This was introduced by the 1995 Act as part of a general policy to enable the court to exercise greater control over the progress of a case. The intermediate diet in summary procedure[10] which was introduced in 1980[11] was an earlier example of the same policy and there are strong similarities between the two diets. In the context of civil procedure in the sheriff court the options hearing[12] was intended to achieve the same objective - that the court rather than the parties should decide how a case should proceed. The success of intermediate diets and options hearings in achieving this objective has not been universal, and it remains to be seen whether first diets will be effective.

1  1995 Act, s 67(4).
2  1995 Act, s 80(2).
3  1996 Rules, r 12.2. An application by one party is in Form 12.2A. A joint application is in Form 12.2B.
4  1996 Rules, r 12.3.
5  1995 Act, s 80(3). Detailed rules are contained in the 1996 Rules, rr 12.4–12.7. Even if the court gives leave to the prosecutor to serve a notice fixing a new trial in terms of s 80(3), it is still open to the Crown to serve a new indictment containing the same charges: *HMA v Dow* 1992 SCCR 421, 1992 SLT 577.
6  1995 Act, s 80(5).
7  1996 Rules, r 12.2(2); Form 12.2B.
8  1995 Act, s 80(4); 1996 Rules, r 12.8.
9  1995 Act, s 66(6)(a).
10  See below at pp 201–202.
11  1975 Act, s 337A, inserted by the Criminal Justice (Scotland) Act 1980, s 15.
12  1993 Ordinary Cause Rules, r 9.12.

At a first diet the court must[1]:

'so far as reasonably practicable, ascertain whether the case is likely to proceed to trial on the date assigned as the trial diet and, in particular –

(a) the state of preparation of the prosecutor and the accused with respect to their cases; and

(b) the extent to which the prosecutor and the accused have complied with the duty under section 257(1)[2] of this Act'.

The court must also consider certain matters of which notice has been given[3]. These matters are detailed in the following section of the Act which deals with preliminary diets in the High Court[4] but it is appropriate to discuss them here. They are:

'(a) that [a party] intends to raise –

(i) a matter relating to the competency or relevancy of the indictment; or

(ii) an objection to the validity of the citation against him, on the ground of any discrepancy between the record copy of the indictment and the copy served on him, or on account of any error or deficiency in such service copy or in the notice of citation[5];

(b) that he intends –

(i) to submit a plea in bar of trial;

(ii) to apply for separation or conjunction of charges or trials;

(iii) to raise a preliminary objection under section 255 of this Act [challenge to special capacity]; or

(iv) to make an application under section 278(2) of this Act [application to dispense with reading of record of judicial examination[6]];

(c) that there are documents the truth of the contents of which ought to be admitted, or that there is any other matter which in his view ought to be agreed;

(d) that there is some point, as regards any matter not mentioned in paragraph (a) to (c) above, which could in his opinion be resolved with advantage before the trial ...'.

A party wishing the court to consider any of these matters must give notice to the court and all other parties at least two clear days before the first diet[7]. Notice is given in the form of a minute which should set out the matter which it is intended to raise at the first diet[8]. It is open to a party with the leave of the court and on cause shown to apply later for these matters to be dealt with[9].

The legislation makes it clear that the sheriff is expected to take a proactive role as it provides that he 'may ask the prosecutor and the accused any question in connection with any matter which [he] is required to ascertain or consider under subsection (1) or (2) above'[10].

---

1 1995 Act, s 71(1).
2 See p 129 above.
3 1995 Act, s 71(2).
4 1995 Act, s 72(1).
5 An accused is not entitled to object to tendering a plea to the charge against him on the ground of such discrepancy, error or deficiency unless the court is satisfied that it tends substantially to mislead and prejudice him: 1995 Act, s 79(2).
6 See pp 108–111 above.
7 1995 Act, s 71(2).
8 1996 Rules, r 9.1; Form 9.1. See also rr 9.2, 9.3.
9 1995 Act, s 79(1).
10 1995 Act, s 71(3).

The accused must attend the first diet[1] and if he fails to do so a warrant for his arrest may be granted[1]. However, a first diet *may* proceed in his absence[2].

The accused (or more probably his solicitor) must state how he pleads to the indictment[3]. If he pleads not guilty or if his plea of guilty is not accepted by the Crown, the case will usually be continued to the trial diet, the date of which is, of course, already known, although no formal order to that effect is required[4]. If, however, the court considers that the case is unlikely to proceed to trial on that date it should 'unless having regard to previous proceedings in the case it considers it inappropriate to do so', postpone the trial diet[5] and may also fix a further first diet[6]. In any case it is open to the court to adjourn a first diet[7].

Proceedings at a first diet must be recorded in the same way as proceedings at a trial[8]. This means that they must be recorded by a shorthand writer or by a tape recorder[9].

## APPEAL FROM FIRST DIET

There is a limited right of appeal against a sheriff's decision at a first diet[10]. An appeal requires the leave of the court either on the motion of a party or granted by the court on its own motion[10]. Leave should be asked for immediately the decision sought to be appealed against has been given[11]. If he grants leave to appeal the sheriff may discharge the trial diet and fix a new diet[12]. This right of appeal is stated to be without prejudice to any right of appeal under section 106 (appeal against conviction and/or sentence), section 108 (Lord Advocate's appeal against sentence) or section 131 (right of prosecutor to appeal by advocation)[13]. No appeal under this section is competent against a decision to adjourn the first diet or to postpone the trial diet[14] Any appeal under the section must be taken not later than two days after the decision appealed against[15]. A note of appeal is lodged with the sheriff clerk[16]. The sheriff clerk asks the sheriff to provide a report[17] and the sheriff must 'as soon as possible' provide his report which is sent to the Clerk of Justiciary[18]. Copies of the sheriff's report are made available to all the parties[19].

The High Court, in considering the appeal, may postpone the trial and direct that the period of postponement or part thereof should not count towards any time

1   1995 Act, s 71(4).
2   1995 Act, s 71(5).
3   1995 Act, s 71(6). Procedure on a plea of guilty is governed by s 77: see below at pp 142–143.
4   1996 Rules, r 9.10(4).
5   1995 Act, s 71(7)(a).
6   1995 Act, s 71(7)(b).
7   1995 Act, s 71(8).
8   1996 Rules, r 9.10(2).
9   1995 Act, s 93(1). See below at p 144.
10  1995 Act, s 74(1).
11  1996 Rules, r 9.11(1).
12  1996 Rules, r 9.11(2).
13  1995 Act, s 74(1). See *HMA v Shepherd* 1997 SCCR 246.
14  1995 Act, s 74(2)(b).
15  1995 Act, s 74(2)(b).
16  1996 Rules, r 9.12(1)(b).
17  1996 Rules, r 9.13(2)(b).
18  1996 Rules, r 9.14(1).
19  1996 Rules, r 9.14(2).

limit applicable to the case[1]. The court may dispose of an appeal by affirming the sheriff's decision or by remitting the case to him with such directions as it thinks fit[2]. If the sheriff has dismissed the indictment or any part of it the High Court may reverse his decision and direct that he fixes a trial diet if one has not already been fixed[3].

# PRELIMINARY DIET

In cases indicted for trial in the High Court there is no first diet. This is because of the practical difficulties which would arise in holding such a diet given that the High Court sits in many different parts of Scotland. In High Court cases, however, a preliminary diet may be held in certain circumstances if requested by either the Crown or the defence.

If an accused wishes to take a plea to the competency or relevancy of the indictment or any part of it, he must apply for a preliminary diet[4]. A similar rule applies if an accused wishes to take objection to the validity of the citation against him on the ground of any discrepancy between the record copy of the indictment and the copy served on him, or on account of any error or deficiency in the service copy or in the notice of citation[5]. An accused must make an application for a preliminary diet to consider these matters within fifteen clear days after service of the indictment[6]. On receipt of such an application the court *must* order that a preliminary diet be held[7]. Even though no timeous application for a preliminary diet to deal with these matters has been made, the plea or objection may be taken later by leave of the court and on cause shown[8].

If an accused wishes to submit a plea in bar of trial, apply for separation or conjunction of charges or trials, raise a preliminary objection under section 255 of the 1995 Act (challenge to special capacity) or to make an application under section 278(2) (application to dispense with reading of record of judicial examination)[9], he must apply for a preliminary diet[10], and must do so no later than ten clear days before the trial diet[11]. On receipt of such an application the court *may* order that a preliminary diet be held but is not obliged to do so[12]. Again, if no application for a preliminary diet has been made timeously, the plea or application may be entertained later by leave of the court and on cause shown[13].

1  1995 Act, s 74(3).
2  1995 Act, s 74(4)(a).
3  1995 Act, s 74(4)(b).
4  1995 Act, s 72(1)(a)(i).
5  1995 Act, s 72(1)(a)(ii). An accused is not entitled to object to pleading on the ground of such discrepancy, error or deficiency unless the court is satisfied that it tends substantially to mislead and prejudice him: s 79(2).
6  1995 Act, s 72(6)(a).
7  1995 Act, s 72(1).
8  1995 Act, s 79(1).
9  See pp 108–111 above.
10  1995 Act, s 72(1)(b).
11  1995 Act, s 72(6)(b).
12  1995 Act, s 72(1).
13  1995 Act, s 79(1).

If a party considers that there are documents the truth of the contents of which ought to be admitted he may apply for a preliminary diet[1] and may do so any time between service of the indictment and the trial diet[2]. Again the court has a discretion whether or not to order that a preliminary diet should take place.

If either the Crown or the defence considers that there is some matter, other than those mentioned in the three preceding paragraphs, which could with advantage be resolved before the trial diet, they may apply to the court to hold a preliminary diet[3]. The application may be made at any time between service of the indictment and the trial diet[4]. The court *may* grant such an application[5].

All applications for a preliminary diet must be made by written notice to the Clerk of Justiciary and the application must be intimated to all other parties in the case[5]. There are detailed rules for the procedure following the lodging of such a notice[6].

When it orders that a preliminary diet is to take place, the court may postpone the trial diet, initially for a period not longer than 21 days[7], but this period may be extended by the court[8]. Any postponement, whether of 21 days or more, does not count towards any time limit in respect of the case[9].

The accused should attend a preliminary diet[10], but the diet may proceed in his absence if the court permits[11].

In any case in which a preliminary diet is held the High Court should carry out the same exercise relating to the state of preparedness of the parties and the likelihood of the case proceeding to trial as that to be carried out by the sheriff at a first diet[12]. The court has the same powers of questioning as has a sheriff at a first diet[13]. The court may also, as at a first diet, postpone the trial diet and fix a further preliminary diet[14]. A preliminary diet may be adjourned[15]. At the conclusion of a preliminary diet the accused, if present, must state how he pleads to the indictment[16].

Proceedings at a preliminary diet must be recorded in the same way as proceedings at a trial[17]. This means that they must be recorded by a shorthand writer or by a tape recorder[18].

Any matter which could have been the subject of a preliminary diet, notice of which was not timeously given, may still be considered by the court at a preliminary diet (fixed to deal with another matter) provided that notice has been intimated to the court and to the other parties at least 24 hours prior to the preliminary diet[19].

1  1995 Act, s 72(1)(c).
2  1995 Act, s 72(6)(c).
3  1995 Act, s 72(1)(d).
4  1995 Act, s 72(6)(c).
5  1995 Act, s 72(1).
6  1996 Rules, rr 9.1–9.6.
7  1995 Act, s 72(4).
8  1995 Act, s 72(5).
9  1995 Act, s 72(4).
10  1995 Act, s 73(1).
11  1995 Act, s 73(2).
12  1995 Act, s 73(3). For the duties of the sheriff at a first diet see pp 132–134 above.
13  1995 Act, s 73(4).
14  1995 Act, s 73(5).
15  1995 Act, s 73(6).
16  1995 Act, s 73(1).
17  1996 Rules, r 9.10(2).
18  1995 Act, s 93(1). See below at p 144.
19  1995 Act, s 72(3).

It is open to the Crown to indicate expressly or implicitly that it no longer intends to proceed with an indictment which has been called to a preliminary diet[1].

# APPEAL FROM PRELIMINARY DIET

Either party may appeal to the High Court sitting in its appellate capacity against a court's decision at a preliminary diet in exactly the same way *mutatis mutandis* as in an appeal against a decision at a first diet in the sheriff court. The statutory provisions are exactly the same[2] and it is not intended to repeat them here. The only major difference is that there is no provision for the making of a report by the High Court judge who presided at the preliminary diet, although no doubt the appeal court could call for a report if it considered it to be necessary.

# MATTERS TO BE RAISED AT A FIRST OR PRELIMINARY DIET

We shall now briefly consider the various matters which may be raised at a first or preliminary diet other than the actual progress of the case.

### Competency and relevancy

The same principles governing competency and relevancy apply in criminal as in civil cases.

A case is incompetent if it cannot be tried by the court before which it is brought. Examples of incompetency are: lack of jurisdiction (whether because of the territorial limitations of the court or because it is a crime which cannot be tried in that court, for example rape in the sheriff court); that the prosecutor has no title to prosecute; that the charge is time barred; that the 110-day rule has been broken. If the case is held to be incompetent, that is usually an end of the matter as incompetency cannot be cured by amendment.

A charge is irrelevant if what is libelled does not correspond with the requirements of the law relating to such a charge. A libel that set forth facts not amounting to a crime, for example, would be irrelevant. Irrelevancy may very often be cured by amendment, and, if the amendment is allowed, the case may proceed to trial[3].

### Plea in bar of trial

A plea in bar of trial is a plea to the effect that the trial should not take place at that particular time and place (or perhaps not at all, in which case the plea is indistinguishable from a plea to the competency although a plea in bar of trial is the

---

1  *Smith v HMA* 1996 SCCR 664, a case in which the Crown had served a second indictment relating to the same charge as the first.
2  1995 Act, s 74; 1996 Rules, rr 9.11–9.13. See pp 134–135 above.
3  For amendment see pp 177–178 below.

appropriate course to take[1]). The following are examples of circumstances in which a plea in bar of trial may be taken: (1) the accused is insane and unable to plead or to give instructions for his defence; (2) the accused has 'tholed his assize', ie has already been tried for the crime concerned. In this connection it may be noted that a person who has been convicted of assault may thereafter be tried on a charge of homicide if his victim subsequently dies[2]; (3) the accused has been a witness for the Crown in the trial of another person on the same charge[3]; (4) the prosecutor is personally barred from proceeding[4]. It may be noted that a statement from the *police* (as opposed to the prosecutor) to the effect that they are taking no further action does not bar the Crown from proceeding[5]; (5) there has been undue delay amounting to oppression in bringing the accused to trial[6]. The test is whether there is a risk of prejudice to the accused so grave that no direction by the trial judge could be expected to remove it[7]; (6) the accused has been interviewed by the procurator fiscal about a matter arising out of the same circumstances as those relating to the subject matter of the trial[8]; (7) the accused cannot have a fair trial because of pre-trial publicity[9].

## Separation of charges

If there is more than one charge on an indictment, the accused may move the court to have the charges separated so that each would be tried before a different jury. Although the test has been said to be one of fairness to the accused[10], the modern law is that separation of charges will not be granted unless there is a material risk of real prejudice, which does not arise merely because the charges are of different kinds of crime committed at different times in different places and circumstances[11] or because the defence to one charge would involve attacking the character of Crown witnesses[12]. A motion for separation of charges is relatively rarely granted[13]. The decision whether to grant such a motion is essentially one for the discretion of the judge of first instance, and leave to appeal against such a decision should be granted only if the matter is finely balanced[14].

1   *McFadyen v Annan* 1992 JC 53, 1992 SCCR 186, 1992 SLT 163.
2   *Tees v HMA* 1994 SCCR 451, 1994 SLT 701.
3   For the limitations of this plea see *O'Neill v Wilson* 1983 JC 42, 1983 SCCR 265, 1983 SLT 573.
4   See eg *Thom v HMA* 1976 JC 48, 1976 SLT 23; *HMA v Stewart* 1980 JC 84.
5   *Huston v Buchanan* 1994 SCCR 512, 1995 SLT 86; *McGhee v Maguire* 1996 SLT 1012.
6   See eg *McGeown v HMA* 1989 SCCR 95, 1989 SLT 625; *McGill v HMA* 1997 SCCR 230.
7   *McGeown v HMA* 1989 SCCR 95, 1989 SLT 625; *Campbell v HMA* 1993 SCCR 1034.
8   *McLeod v Tiffney* 1994 JC 77, 1994 SCCR 169, 1994 SLT 531. This case contains a useful discussion about how the procurator fiscal should act in such circumstances.
9   For a full discussion of this see *X v Sweeney* 1982 JC 70, 1982 SCCR 161, 1983 SLT 48 sub nom *H v Sweeney*. *Kilbane v HMA* 1989 SCCR 313, 1990 SLT 108, is a recent example of a case in which the plea was taken and was unsuccessful. See also *Johnston v HMA, HMA v Johnston* 1996 SCCR 808, 1997 SLT 64 sub nom *HMA v Johnston*. In *HMA v Mitchell* 1993 SCCR 793, 1994 SLT 144, the sheriff's decision to desert the diet *pro loco et tempore* to enable the trial to take place in a different court was upheld on appeal.
10  *HMA v McGuiness* 1937 JC 37, 1937 SLT 274.
11  *Reid v HMA* 1984 SCCR 153, 1984 SLT 391; *HMA v Johnstone* 1991 SCCR 96, 1992 SLT 905.
12  *Brown v HMA* 1992 SCCR 59, 1992 SLT 272; *Toner v HMA* 1995 SCCR 697, 1996 SLT 24.
13  *HMA v Maitland* 1985 SCCR 166, 1985 SLT 425, is a rare modern example of the granting of a motion to separate charges.
14  *Reid v HMA* 1984 SCCR 153, 1984 SLT 391.

## Separation of trials

The Crown has a wide discretion to place more than one accused together in an indictment, provided that there is some connection between the accused and/or the crimes[1]. If two or more persons are charged on the one indictment, each may move the court to separate the trials so that he is tried before a different jury from that which tries the other(s). As with separation of charges the test is fairness, but a motion to separate trials is seldom granted[2]. The decision is very much one for the judge of first instance. 'A decision to separate trials is one peculiarly within the discretion of the trial judge ... It has been said that an appeal court will interfere only if oppression is demonstrated. It is perhaps more accurate to say that an appeal court will not interfere unless there is shown to have taken place a palpable failure of justice'[3].

## Conjunction of trials

If several accused are charged on separate indictments, they may move the court to be tried together. Such a motion is relatively rare, but will be granted if the court considers that the defence of the accused would be so prejudiced by separate trials that a miscarriage of justice might result[4]. It should be noted, however, that the practice of charging all participants in a crime in one indictment is only a practice and not a rule of law[5].

## Other matters which may be raised at a first or preliminary diet

There is no limit to the matters which may be raised at a first diet or a preliminary diet in terms of section 72(1)(d) of the 1995 Act[6], but most applications under the equivalent provision of the Criminal Procedure (Scotland) Act 1975[7] (which was in force until 31 March 1996) concerned the admissibility of evidence[8]. Evidence may be led at a first or preliminary diet[9].

# JURORS

Every person up to the age of 65 who is registered as a parliamentary or local government elector is eligible for jury service, provided that he has been ordinarily resident

1 *Hume* II, 177. *HMA v Granger* 1985 SCCR 4, 1985 SLT 496, is perhaps a fairly extreme example. Two accused were charged on the same indictment with perjury, and there was no suggestion of concert. It was held that, as the purpose of each accused's perjury was the same, ie to defeat the ends of justice, their trials should not be separated.
2 *Sangster v HMA* (1896) 2 Adam 182 at 189, 24 R (J) 3 at 7, 4 SLT 135 at 136, per Lord Moncrieff.
3 *Davidson v HMA* 1981 SCCR 371 at 376, per Lord Justice-General Emslie.
4 *HMA v Clark* 1935 JC 51, 1935 SLT 143; *HMA v McWilliam* 1994 SCCR 152.
5 *HMA v O'Neill* 1992 SCCR 130, 1992 SLT 303 (which was distinguished in *HMA v McWilliam* 1994 SCCR 152). See also *Elder v HMA* 1995 SCCR 84, 1995 SLT 579.
6 This provides: 'that there is some point, as regards any matter not mentioned in paragraph (a) to (c) above, which could in [a party's] opinion be resolved with advantage before the trial ...'.
7 1975 Act, s 76(1)(c).
8 See eg *HMA v Cumming* 1983 SCCR 15 (Sh Ct), *McDonald v HMA* 1989 SCCR 165, 1989 SLT 627 (a case where the Crown challenged the competency of witnesses cited for the defence).
9 *HMA v Bell* 1984 SCCR 430, 1984 SLT 349.

in the United Kingdom, Channel Islands or Isle of Man for at least five years since attaining the age of thirteen, and provided that he is not disqualified or ineligible[1].

A person who has served a prison sentence (or the equivalent for a young offender) of three months or more is disqualified for jury service unless rehabilitated under the Rehabilitation of Offenders Act 1974[2]. A person who has been sentenced to imprisonment (or the equivalent for a young offender) for five years or more is permanently disqualified for jury service[2]. A person who is on bail in or in connection with criminal proceedings anywhere in the United Kingdom is disqualified from jury service[3].

The list of those who are ineligible for jury service is long[4]. It consists mainly of those concerned in the administration of justice. Certain other categories, such as members of either House of Parliament, servicemen and members of the medical and allied professions, are eligible for jury service, but are entitled as of right to be excused[5].

The sheriff principal of each sheriffdom is responsible for preparing the list of assize, that is the list of potential jurors who will be cited to attend court for a trial and from whom the jury will be selected[6]. The names are taken in rotation from the list of those eligible for jury service within the sheriffdom[7]. If the trial is in the sheriff court, the potential jurors are taken from the list for the sheriff court district concerned[8]. The Lord Justice-General, whom failing the Lord Justice-Clerk, may give directions as to the areas from which and the proportions in which jurors are to be summoned for High Court trials, and the sheriff principal must requisition jurors from those areas and in these proportions[9]. If a sitting of the High Court is held in a town where the High Court does not usually sit, jurors will be summoned only from the sheriff court district in which that town is situated[10].

It should be noted that, although throughout this section reference has been made to trial in the singular, it is more likely that jurors will be summoned to attend at a sitting of the court where several trials may take place.

Jurors are usually cited by recorded delivery or registered post[11], but may be cited by officer of law[11].

Any person cited for jury service may be excused for a good reason by the clerk of court[12] or the judge[13].

Any person who is cited as a juror and who fails to respond to the citation is guilty of an offence and may be fined up to £1,000[14], but this fine may be remitted by a High Court judge or a sheriff according to whether the juror was cited to attend the High Court or the sheriff court[15].

1  Law Reform (Miscellaneous Provisions) (Scotland) Act 1980, s 1(1).
2  1980 Act, Sch 1, Pt II.
3  1980 Act, Sch 1, Pt II as amended by the Criminal Procedure (Consequential Provisions) (Scotland) Act 1995, Sch 4, para 32(4).
4  1980 Act, Sch 1, Pt I. For an accessible summary see *Renton and Brown*, para 15–03.
5  1980 Act, Sch 1, Pt III; *Renton and Brown*, para 15–04.
6  1995 Act, s 84(1).
7  1995 Act, s 84(5).
8  1995 Act, s 84(4).
9  1995 Act, s 84(2).
10  1995 Act, s 84(3).
11  1995 Act, s 85(4). For the definition of 'officer of law' see above at pp 120, 121.
12  Law Reform (Miscellaneous Provisions) (Scotland) Act 1980, s 1(5).
13  1980 Act, s 1(6); 1995 Act, s 88(7). Under the latter provision the juror seeking to be excused must state his ground for doing so in open court, but this may be done in general terms: *Hughes, Petr* 1989 SCCR 490, 1990 SLT 142.
14  1995 Act, s 85(6). The fine is expressed as level 3 on the standard scale which is presently £1,000.
15  1995 Act, s 85(7).

# CHAPTER 5

# SOLEMN PROCEDURE: THE TRIAL

## PROCEDURE WHERE ACCUSED DESIRES TO PLEAD GUILTY UNDER SECTION 76 OF THE 1995 ACT

Very many cases do not in fact proceed to trial at all as the accused is prepared to plead guilty[1]. It is therefore convenient before discussing the procedure at a trial to take notice of what happens when an accused wishes to have a case disposed of on a plea of guilty without going to trial.

Section 76 of the 1995 Act provides that an accused may intimate in writing[2] to the Crown Agent an intention to plead guilty, in which case an accelerated procedure is followed. The section does not specify when 'a section 76 letter' (as the intimation is usually called) may be submitted. One of the prescribed forms of notice[3] implies that it may be at any time after full committal. However, looking to the actual terms of the section, there seems to be no reason in principle why the procedure should not be invoked before full committal. Indeed, there is nothing to prevent a section 76 letter being submitted even before service of a petition, although this would obviously present practical difficulties as to what charges the offer to plead guilty should be directed at. The section states that intimation is to be made to the Crown Agent, but in practice the section 76 letter is usually delivered to the fiscal, who forwards it to Crown Office. It is then for Crown Counsel to instruct whether the section 76 procedure should be followed.

The actual plea offered in a section 76 letter may be the result of negotiation between the defence and the Crown, and it may well not completely reflect the charges in the petition. It is in the interests of the accused that a plea be negotiated as early as possible. The court may take into account when deciding what sentence to impose on an accused who has pleaded guilty 'the stage in the proceedings ... at which the offender indicated his intention to plead guilty, and the circumstances in which that indication was given'[4].

A section 76 letter may be submitted by an accused even if he has already been served with an indictment for trial in normal course. The advantage of having the case brought forward in such a situation is unlikely to be very great unless the indictment has been served a long time prior to the trial diet. Of course it is always beneficial to give advance information of a plea of guilty in order that witnesses and prospective jurors may be told that they need not attend court. This can, however, be done simply by the defence informing the prosecutor without going through

---

1  See Robin M White 'What happens after a guilty plea?' 1995 JR 465.
2  The letter should be signed by the accused himself and not by his solicitor.
3  1996 Rules, r 10.1; Form 10.1A.
4  1995 Act, s 196.

the formality of section 76 procedure. In practice most section 76 letters come before any indictment has been served.

If the Crown agrees to accept the section 76 letter, and an indictment has not already been served, a special section 76 indictment is served on the accused. This does not have any list of witnesses or productions appended[1]. With the indictment is served a notice telling the accused where and when to appear, which must be not less than four clear days after the date of the notice[1], although the period of notice may probably be waived by the accused[2]. If the accused has already received an indictment, only a notice is served on him. The form of notice will depend on whether the accused has already been served with an indictment[3]. A copy of the section 76 indictment with intimation of the date of calling is usually sent by the fiscal to the defence solicitor as a matter of courtesy.

If the accused has previous convictions which the prosecutor intends to place before the court, the section 76 indictment should be accompanied by a list of these convictions[4]. Any objection to a conviction on that list must be intimated in writing to the fiscal within two days after service of the indictment[5].

If the accused submits his section 76 letter prior to service of an indictment, the Crown may indict him in either the sheriff court or the High Court[6]. If he has already been served with a sheriff court indictment, then the section 76 diet will be held in the court specified in the notice served with that indictment[7]. However, if the accused has already been indicted in the High Court, the section 76 diet may take place in Edinburgh, notwithstanding that the notice served with the indictment indicates a different venue[8].

When the section 76 diet calls, the accused usually pleads guilty as he has intimated in his letter. However, sometimes he has changed his mind and pleads not guilty or tenders a plea of guilty to only part of the indictment. In that event, unless the prosecutor is prepared to accept the plea tendered, the diet is deserted *pro loco et tempore* (ie for that particular time and place), and the case proceeds as if there had been no section 76 letter[9]. If the accused has already been served with an indictment prior to the section 76 letter, and a trial has therefore been fixed, the court may postpone that trial diet, and the period of postponement will not count towards any time limit which would otherwise apply to the case[10]. If the Crown receives advance warning that the accused has changed his mind, the section 76 indictment may simply not be called in court. Matters will then proceed as if no section 76 letter had been submitted.

If the accused does plead guilty at the section 76 diet, he must sign the plea, and the judge countersigns it[11]. The prosecutor then moves for sentence and produces

1   1995 Act, s 76(1).
2   *McKnight v HMA* 1991 SCCR 751.
3   1996 Rules, r 10.1; Forms 10.1A, 10.1B.
4   1995 Act, s 69(4).
5   1995 Act, s 69(5). The section specifically states 'procurator fiscal' and does not indicate that, if the case is being indicted in the High Court, the intimation should be sent to the Crown Agent, although the 1996 Rules, r 2.1(a) would normally imply this.
6   1995 Act, s 76(1), (2)(a). If in the High Court, the diet will usually be in Edinburgh, but could be at any other place where the High Court is sitting.
7   1995 Act, s 76(1), (2)(b).
8   1996 Rules, r 10.1(2).
9   1995 Act, s 76(3).
10  1995 Act, s 76(3); 1996 Rules, r 10.1(3), (4).
11  1995 Act, s 77(1). This rule applies even when the accused tenders a plea of guilty to only part of the indictment and the prosecutor is not prepared to accept the restricted plea. If the prosecutor does not accept the restricted plea, this fact must be recorded (s 77(2)).

any notice of previous convictions served on the accused. Any error in the notice of previous convictions may be cured by amendment[1] but such amendment must not be to the prejudice of the accused[2]. He gives a summary of the facts of the case and informs the court of the period, if any, during which the accused has been in custody. Counsel or the solicitor for the accused makes a plea in mitigation, and the judge either proceeds to sentence or adjourns in order to obtain reports. If the version of the facts given by the Crown is disputed by the defence, the court should ascertain whether there is any possibility of reconciling the discrepancies. If this is not possible, either the disputed facts should be ignored[3] or a proof in miti-gation may take place[4]. In the latter case evidence is led by the defence, and the Crown may then lead evidence to refute the defence case. The judge decides which version of the facts he prefers, and he sentences on the basis of that version. Alternatively, in the event of the discrepancies between Crown and defence not being reconciled, the court may permit the accused to withdraw his plea of guilty, and the case can then proceed to trial in due course as if a plea of not guilty had originally been tendered[5].

If it is apparent that reports will be required before sentence can be passed, the court may very well adjourn the case for reports without having heard the facts. In that event the case may be dealt with by a different judge when it next calls – at least in the sheriff court. In the High Court the practice is that the same judge deals with a case from beginning to end.

Even though the case has been brought in the sheriff court, it may be remitted to the High Court for sentence if the sheriff considers his powers to be inadequate[6].

A plea of guilty, whether tendered at a section 76 diet or at a diet of trial in nor-mal course, may be withdrawn in certain very limited circumstances, eg if the plea was tendered under a substantial error or misconception, or if it was a plea to an incompetent or irrelevant charge[7].

## JURY TRIAL

The procedure at a jury trial will now be discussed so far as possible in chronolog-ical order of events.

## PRELIMINARY MATTERS

### Clerk to speak to prospective jurors

The clerk of court should speak to the unempanelled jurors, tell them the names of the accused, the complainer and any other person named in the indictment, and ask them to tell him if they know any of these persons[8].

1 1995 Act, s 101(4).
2 1995 Act, s 101(5). This provision ceased to apply on 1 August 1997: 1997 Act, s 31. See the Appendix at p 320 below.
3 *Barn v Smith* 1978 JC 17, 1978 SLT (Notes) 3.
4 *HMA v Bennett* 1996 SCCR 331, 1996 SLT 662.
5 See *Nicholson* para 7–03.
6 1995 Act, s 195. See below at p 222.
7 *HMA v Black* (1894) 1 Adam 312; *HMA v Robertson* (1899) 3 Adam 1, 1 F (J) 74, 7 SLT 10. It is com-petent to allow the plea to be withdrawn in the sheriff court as well as in the High Court: *Healy v HMA* 1990 SCCR 110.
8 *Pullar v HMA* 1993 JC 126, 1993 SCCR 514.

## Recording of proceedings

The whole proceedings at the trial must be recorded either mechanically (ie by tape recorder) or by a shorthand writer[1]. If any part of the proceedings is not recorded, this may result in a successful appeal against conviction[2]. In practice in both the High Court and the sheriff court the proceedings are now usually tape-recorded.

## Calling of the diet

The first thing which happens at a trial diet is that the clerk of court calls the diet[3] and asks the accused to confirm his identity.

It is essential that the accused be present at the trial diet[4], as well as the prosecutor[5]. If the accused is not present, the court usually grants a warrant for his arrest, if satisfied that he has been properly cited to attend the diet. Alternatively, if a warrant for a subsequent sitting of the court within two months has been issued (under section 66(1) of the 1995 Act) the diet may be adjourned under section 80(1) of the Act to that sitting. Another possibility is that the accused may be cited to a fresh diet under section 81(1) of the same Act[6]. The procedure under sections 80(1) or 81(1) may also be used when, for whatever reason, a case is not called for trial.

A body corporate, being an artificial person, cannot physically appear at a trial diet. If the case is actually proceeding to trial the body corporate must be represented by counsel or a solicitor, but, if the case is not going to trial, it may appear by a 'representative'[7]. The representative may appear to state objection to the competency or relevancy of the indictment, to tender a plea of guilty or not guilty, or to make a plea in mitigation[7]. If, at a trial diet, a body corporate is not represented by anyone, the court may hear and dispose of the case in its absence, provided that it is satisfied that the body corporate has been properly cited[8].

## Pleading

The accused in a sheriff court case will, of course, already have tendered a plea at the first diet[9] and, even in the High Court, may have done so if a preliminary diet was held[10]. It is still, however, appropriate for counsel or the solicitor for the

1   1995 Act, s 93.
2   *McLaughlan v HMA* 1996 SLT 304.
3   See the case of *David Balfour* at p 38 above.
4   1995 Act, s 92(1). Section 92(2) provides: 'If during the course of his trial an accused so misconducts himself that in the view of the court a proper trial cannot take place unless he is removed, the court may order — (a) that he is removed from the court for so long as his conduct makes it necessary; and (b) that the trial proceeds in his absence, but if he is not legally represented the court shall appoint counsel or a solicitor to represent his interests during such absence'.
5   *Walker v Emslie* (1899) 3 Adam 102, 2 F (J) 18, 7 SLT 281.
6   1995 Act, s 81(1) provides for the accused being served with another copy of the indictment within nine clear days of the abortive trial diet, along with a notice to appear to answer the indictment at another diet (which may be in the same court or a different court). That diet must be not less than nine clear days after the date when notice was given (s 81(5)).
7   1995 Act, s 70(4). 'Representative' is defined as 'an officer or employee of the body corporate duly appointed by it for the purpose of those proceedings' (s 70(8)).
8   1995 Act, s 70(5).
9   See above at p 134.
10  See above at p 136.

accused to intimate how the accused is pleading. If the accused is unrepresented, the clerk or the judge will ask him how he pleads. If the plea is one of guilty (whether to all or part of the indictment), it must be signed by the accused himself and countersigned by the judge[1]. If the plea is guilty to the whole indictment, or if the prosecutor accepts a restricted plea, there is no need to empanel a jury, and the court may proceed to deal with the case as if the accused had been found guilty after trial. The procedure is then the same as that described for a plea of guilty under the section 76 procedure[2].

A restricted plea of guilty, which it is known the Crown will not accept, should normally be tendered outwith the presence of potential jurors if at all possible. This is so that the jurors will be unaware of the fact that the accused is guilty of any offence. However, in certain circumstances it may be to the advantage of the defence that the prospective jurors know that the accused has been prepared to plead guilty to some extent. In that event there is no reason why the plea should not be tendered in the presence of the jury panel.

If the accused pleads guilty to part of the indictment and this plea is accepted but other charges on the indictment are to proceed to trial, sentence on the charges to which the guilty pleas have been tendered should be deferred until the end of the trial[3].

If the plea is one of not guilty, the accused may seek to give late intimation of a special defence or of the incrimination of a co-accused, or to be allowed to lodge a list of witnesses or productions[4].

## The jury

If the accused has pleaded not guilty or has tendered a restricted plea of guilty which the prosecutor has not accepted, the case will go to trial. Accordingly a jury must be empanelled. The name of each person summoned to the diet as a potential juror will have already been written on a piece of paper together with his or her number on the list of assize. The folded papers will have been put into a box or jar, from which fifteen are now drawn by the clerk of court[5].

Jury vetting does not exist in Scotland[6].

The prosecutor and the defence solicitor or counsel (or the accused himself if unrepresented) will have been furnished with a copy of the list of assize, which gives the name and address of each potential juror[7]. It used to be the case that the occupation of the potential juror was also given but this is no longer the case. It is arguable that the absence of the occupation may be prejudicial to the accused in certain cases. If, for example, the charge is an assault on a taxi-driver it would be undesirable that a taxi-driver should be selected to sit on the jury. The accused should be told by his legal representative to indicate if there is any person called to serve on the jury to whom he may take exception for good reason, perhaps, for example, because he knows him.

---

1 1995 Act, s 77(1). Refusal by a prosecutor to accept a restricted plea must be recorded: s 77(2).
2 See above at pp 142, 143.
3 *Cogan v Carmichael* 1993 SCCR 628, 1994 SLT 851.
4 See above at pp 126, 127 and 130, 131.
5 1995 Act, s 88(2).
6 *McCadden v HMA* 1985 SCCR 282 at 286, 1986 SLT 138 at 141, per Lord Justice-Clerk Wheatley.
7 The statutory provisions governing the provision of lists of assize changed with effect from 1 August 1997: 1997 Act, s 58. See the Appendix at p 319 below.

Up until the coming into force of the 1995 Act each party in a jury trial had a right to object to three jurors without stating any reason for doing so. These were known as 'peremptory challenges'. They have now been abolished although it is still possible for a juror to be objected to without any reason being stated provided that all parties agree[1].

Any party may, however, object to any number of jurors 'on cause shown'[2]. 'Cause shown' is interpreted fairly narrowly.

'It is not a sufficient cause for a juror to be excused that he is of a particular race, religion or political belief or occupation, or indeed that the juror might or might not feel prejudice one way or the other towards the crime itself or to the background against which the crime has been committed. A juror can, of course, be excused on limited personal grounds. If he is personally concerned in the facts of the particular case, or closely connected with a party to the proceedings or with a witness, or if he suffers from some physical disability such as deafness or blindness, there would be special cause for excluding him. Personal hardship or conscientious objection to jury service by itself may also be a ground for excusing a juror, at the discretion of the trial judge. The essence of the system of trial by jury is that it consists of fifteen individuals chosen at random from amongst those who are cited for possible service'[3].

General questioning of potential jurors in advance of balloting is not appropriate[3], although it may be appropriate to ask jurors, after they have been balloted, whether there are any reasons known to them which make it desirable that they should not take part in that particular trial, and, indeed, this may be done by the presiding judge after the indictment has been read out to the jurors and before they are sworn[4].

After the jury has been sworn to try the case no objection to a juror is competent[5]. However, a juror, even though sworn, may be excused by the judge for good reason (for example familiarity with the case), provided that the juror has stated in open court his reason for wishing to be excused[6]. In that event another person is balloted to take his place. The unempanelled jurors should not be released so long as there is a possibility that an empanelled juror may have to be excused[7]. In practice this means that the unempanelled jurors are usually asked to remain until the court reconvenes following the usual brief adjournment for the empanelled jurors 'to make themselves comfortable'[8].

Once the jury has been selected (subject to the possibility of a juror's being replaced as just described), the clerk usually reads over the whole indictment to the jurors, substituting the third person for the second person throughout[9]. If the indictment is long or complex, the clerk may read a summary approved by the judge[9]. Jurors should be provided with copies of the indictment excluding the lists of witnesses and productions[9]. It is suggested that unless the indictment is very short and simple the jury should be provided with their copies before it is read to them and asked to follow its terms in their copies as it is read out. Copies of the indictment given to the jury should not include any charge to which the accused

1   1995 Act, s 86(1).
2   1995 Act, s 86(2).
3   M v HMA 1974 SLT (Notes) 25, per Lord Justice-General Emslie.
4   Spink v HMA 1989 SCCR 413; Pullar v HMA 1993 JC 126, 1993 SCCR 514.
5   1995 Act, s 86(4).
6   1995 Act, s 88(7). All fifteen jurors may be excused and a completely new jury empanelled in terms of this provision: Hughes, Petr 1989 SCCR 490, 1990 SLT 142.
7   Pullar v HMA 1993 JC 126, 1993 SCCR 514.
8   See below at p 148.
9   1995 Act, s 88(5).

has pleaded guilty and which is therefore not proceeding to trial before the jury. This may mean that the copy of the indictment given to the jury has to be specially typed.

If the accused has lodged a special defence it should normally be read out to the jury after the indictment[1]. However, the judge may, on cause shown, direct that the special defence should not be read in full, in which case he must inform the jury of its general character[2]. Copies of the special defence should be provided to the jury[3]. On the face of it this last provision is mandatory, even if the judge has directed that the full terms of the special defence should not be read out, but it may be that, in that event, no copies would be given to the jury. A notice incriminating a co-accused is not a special defence and does not require to be read out to the jury[4].

After the charges (and the special defence, if any) have been read to the jurors they take the oath (or affirmation) that they will 'well and truly try the accused and give a true verdict according to the evidence'[5]. If a juror is replaced after the jury has been sworn (as described in the previous paragraph), the indictment and special defence, if any, are read out to the new juror and he or she takes the oath or affirms as an individual.

If a juror dies or becomes ill in the course of the trial or is 'for any other reason unfit to continue to serve as a juror', the court may, in its discretion, on the application of either the Crown or the defence, direct that the trial continue with the remaining jurors, provided that their number is not less than twelve[6]. If the number of jurors is thus reduced below fifteen, at least eight are still required for a majority verdict of guilty[7]. 'Any other reason' leaves much scope for the discretion of the trial judge, although a sheriff has held that the need to cancel a holiday because of the length of the trial did not fall into that category[8].

In exceptional circumstances something (such as an impropriety involving a juror) may occur which requires the whole jury to be discharged and the diet deserted *pro loco et tempore*, but this is a last resort. Usually any impropriety should be dealt with by discharge of the juror concerned and appropriate directions to the remaining jurors[9].

## Introduction by the judge

There are no opening speeches by either the Crown or the defence in a criminal jury trial in Scotland. It used to be the case that, the jury having been sworn, the prosecution evidence was led without any more ado. Since about the 1970s, however, the practice has grown up among the majority of judges in both the High Court and the sheriff court of making some brief introductory remarks to the jury, partly in order to give them some idea of what is going to happen, and also partly to provide them with an opportunity to settle down.

1   1995 Act, s 89(1).
2   1995 Act, s 89(2).
3   1995 Act, s 89(3).
4   *McShane v HMA* 1989 SCCR 687.
5   1995 Act, s 88(6); 1996 Rules, r 14.3; Forms 14.3A, 14.3B.
6   1995 Act, s 90(1).
7   1995 Act, s 90(2).
8   *Farrell v HMA* 1985 SCCR 23, 1985 SLT 324.
9   *Stewart v HMA* 1980 JC 103, 1980 SLT 245; *McCadden v HMA* 1985 SCCR 282, 1986 SLT 138; *Hamilton v HMA* 1986 SCCR 227, 1986 SLT 663. See also *Russell v HMA* 1991 JC 194, 1991 SCCR 790, 1992 SLT 25; *Gray v HMA* 1994 SCCR 225, 1994 SLT 1237.

The usual procedure is thus as follows: the clerk of court speaks to those summoned for jury service and tells them the names of those involved in the case; the jury is empanelled and sworn; the court adjourns for a few minutes so that the jurors may make themselves comfortable; after the adjournment the judge confirms with the jurors that there is no reason why they should not serve on the jury; the unempanelled jurors are released; the judge makes his introductory remarks; the evidence begins with the first Crown witness being sworn.

In his remarks the judge usually introduces those appearing in the case and describes the procedure in outline[1]. It must be emphasised that the practice of giving an introduction has no statutory authority, and there is no obligation on a judge to follow it. However, it is submitted that in most cases it makes good sense.


# THE EVIDENCE

Evidence for the Crown is led first. There is no obligation on the defence to lead evidence, but defence evidence is frequently led. This section will deal with various aspects of evidence. Much of what will be said applies equally to both the Crown and the defence.


## Oath or affirmation

Each witness must give his evidence after taking an oath or, if he objects to being sworn, making a solemn affirmation[2]. If practical, a witness is entitled to take an oath according to the forms of his own religion. Thus a Jew takes the oath with his head covered and a Muslim swears on the Koran, a copy of which is kept in many courts. If it is impractical for a witness to take a particular form of oath, he must affirm[3].


## Child witnesses: special statutory provisions

In recent years the law relating to child witnesses has undergone radical changes. There is much more emphasis than there used to be on ensuring that a child witness will not be distressed by having to give evidence. While there is no doubt that many children do find giving evidence to be an ordeal, the same comment might be made about other categories of witnesses, the elderly and complainers in cases of sexual assault, for example. It is arguable that there is no reason in principle why the provisions for child witnesses should not be extended to other categories of 'vulnerable' witnesses as has in fact now happened[4], although it may be thought that great care should be taken before eroding in any further way the principle that an accused is entitled to be confronted by his alleged victim in court before a jury.

---

1   See the case of *David Balfour* at p 39 above.
2   Oaths Act 1978, s 5(1). The forms of oath and affirmation are set out in 1996 Rules, r 14.5, Forms 14.5A (oath) and 14.5B (affirmation). These forms are directory and not mandatory: *McAvoy v HMA* 1991 JC 16, 1991 SCCR 123, 1992 SLT 46.
3   Oaths Act 1978, s 5(2).
4   1997 Act, s 29 which came into force on 1 August 1997. See the Appendix at p 320 below.

The special provisions relating to child[1] witnesses are now contained in section 271 of the 1995 Act. There are three possible ways in which a child may give evidence other than in the normal way in court: on commission[2]; by live television link[3]; in court but from behind a screen which conceals the accused from the child's sight[4].

In order for any of these provisions to be put into effect application must be made to the court. The court may grant such an application only on cause shown having regard to (a) the possible effect on the child if he or she is required to give evidence in the normal way, and (b) whether it is likely that the child would be better able to give evidence if the application were to be granted[5]. The court, when considering whether to grant an application, may take into account, where appropriate, the age and maturity of the child, the nature of the alleged offence, the nature of the evidence which the child is likely to be called on to give, and the relationship, if any, between the child and the accused[6]. If an application is made in a sheriff court which does not have the necessary equipment for implementing the application, the sheriff, if he would otherwise have granted it, may transfer the case to a court which has the necessary equipment[7], and that court is deemed to have granted the application[8].

Clearly there may be difficulties about identification of the accused if the child witness does not see him in court. This contingency is taken account of by providing that when 'the child gives evidence that he recalls having identified, prior to the trial, a person alleged to have committed an offence, the evidence of a third party as to the identification of that person by the child prior to the trial shall be admissible as evidence as to such identification'[9].

In the case of an application to take a child's evidence on commission application may be made to the trial court at any time before the oath is administered to the jury[10] or, in exceptional circumstances, during the course of the trial[11]. The commissioner appointed must have been qualified as an advocate or solicitor for not less than five years[12]. Proceedings before the commissioner are recorded by video recorder[13] – hence the need for the court to be appropriately equipped to play the recording. The accused is entitled to watch and hear the proceedings before the commissioner but is not entitled to be in the same room as the child and commissioner unless the commissioner grants leave to that effect[14]. In practice this means that the accused would watch the proceedings by a live television link. The general provisions which apply to evidence on commission in criminal cases apply also to the application for and the taking of evidence from a child witness on commission[15]. These include: (1) that an application to take evidence on commission

1  'Child' means a person under 16 years of age: 1995 Act, s 271(12).
2  1995 Act, s 271(1).
3  1995 Act, s 271(5).
4  1995 Act, s 271(6).
5  1995 Act, s 271(7).
6  1995 Act, s 271(8).
7  1995 Act, s 271(9).
8  1995 Act, s 271(10).
9  1995 Act, s 271(11).
10  1995 Act, s 271(1)(a).
11  1995 Act, s 271(1)(c).
12  1995 Act, s 271(1).
13  1995 Act, s 271(2).
14  1995 Act, s 271(3).
15  1995 Act, s 271(4) applying the provisions of s 272(2)–(6), (8), (9).

must be considered in chambers but may be disposed of without a hearing if the application is unopposed[1]; (2) that an application may be granted only if the judge is satisfied that the witness's evidence is 'necessary for the proper adjudication of the trial'[2] and that there would be no unfairness to the other party if the evidence were to be taken on commission[3]; (3) that the record of the proceedings on commission (in the case of a child's evidence, a video recording) must be accompanied by a transcript of its contents[4].

An application to take the evidence of a child by live television link must be made by petition not later than 14 days before the trial diet 'except on special cause shown'[5]. If the trial is in the High Court the petition is lodged with the Clerk of Justiciary or, if in the sheriff court, with the sheriff clerk[5]. The petition should give as full reasons as possible for the granting of the application[6]. The court must order intimation of the petition to all other parties and fix a hearing[7]. At the hearing the court may grant or refuse the application[8]. In the case of a sheriff court which does not have the appropriate equipment the sheriff may make an order transferring the case to a suitably equipped court in terms of section 271(9) of the Act[9]. It is competent for a judge to refuse an application *in hoc statu* (ie in that particular situation), implicitly reserving the right for the application to be renewed, even during the trial[10].

If the application to take a child's evidence by live television link is granted the child gives his or her evidence in a room in which there is a television camera. It is usual for the child to be accompanied in the room by a supporting adult but that adult must not communicate in any way with the child while he or she is giving evidence. There are monitors in the courtroom through which the judge, the jury, the accused and counsel and/or solicitors can view the child. The leading case on evidence by live television link is *Brotherston v Her Majesty's Advocate*[11]. It established the following principles: (1) there is no reason why the child should not be able to see a television picture of what is in the courtroom; (2) this extends to allowing a camera in the courtroom to pan across the court in order that the child may see all persons in court with a view to identifying the accused notwithstanding the statutory provision for identification through a third party[12]; (3) the fact that authority has been given for evidence by live television link does not make it incompetent for the child to give evidence from the witness box, but once a child has begun to give evidence by television link, fairness requires that the whole of his or her evidence is given by that means; (4) if a child is likely to be distressed by being shown the accused on a television link, identification should be by some other means; (5) a jury is entitled to attach the same value to evidence given by live television link as to evidence given in court.

An application for a child witness to give evidence in court but from behind a screen so that the child cannot see the accused may be made at any time before the

1  1995 Act, s 272(2).
2  1995 Act, s 272(3)(a).
3  1995 Act, s 272(3)(b).
4  1995 Act, s 272(5).
5  1996 Rules, r 22.1(2).
6  *HMA v Birkett* 1992 SCCR 850, 1993 SLT 395.
7  1996 Rules, r 22.1(3).
8  1996 Rules, r 22.2(1)(a).
9  1996 Rules, r 22.2(1)(b). See above at p 149.
10  *HMA v Birkett* 1992 SCCR 850, 1993 SLT 395.
11  *Brotherston v HMA* 1995 SCCR 613, 1996 SLT 1154.
12  1995 Act, s 271(11). See above at p 149.

child commences his or her evidence[1]. The screen must be so arranged that even though the child cannot see the accused, the accused is able to see and hear the child while he or she gives evidence[1]. A television camera may be used for this purpose.

## Child witnesses: general

If a witness is a child of twelve or under, he will not be asked to take the oath. The judge must ascertain by questioning the child and possibly by hearing evidence from other persons whether he understands the difference between truth and untruth[2]. If the judge is satisfied that the child does understand the difference, the judge should tell him that he must tell the truth[2]. If the child does not understand the difference, he is not a competent witness.

A child between twelve and fourteen may be put on oath if the judge is satisfied that he understands the meaning of the oath[3]. A cynic might wonder how many adult witnesses would be able to satisfy a judge that *they* understood the meaning of the oath, if they were asked.

If a child gives evidence in court in the normal way and not in terms of the special provisions discussed above, the court usually adopts a degree of informality in order to put the witness at his ease[4]. The judge may remove his wig and gown and either have the child beside him on the bench or sit at the clerk's table with the child. Counsel and solicitors very often also abandon their wigs and gowns. Both the examiner and the witness may remain seated during the taking of evidence. The public may be excluded while a child witness is giving evidence in a case with sexual connotations[5].

## Witnesses requiring interpretation

If a witness does not speak or understand English, or is deaf and unable to speak, an interpreter will be required. It is the responsibility of the fiscal to provide an interpreter. The interpreter takes an oath that he will faithfully perform his duties as interpreter (the oath *de fideli administratione officii*). He must translate every word of the witness's evidence.

If an accused does not speak or understand English or is deaf and mute, the whole proceedings must be translated for his benefit. This applies not only to the trial but to all preliminary proceedings[6].

## Presentation of evidence

In many cases insufficient thought is given in advance as to how evidence should be presented. It must be borne in mind that the jury knows nothing about the case

---

1  1995 Act, s 271(6).
2  *Rees v Lowe* 1989 SCCR 664, 1990 SLT 507; *Kelly v Docherty* 1991 SCCR 312, 1991 SLT 419.
3  *Quinn v Lees* 1994 SCCR 159. If the judge fails to make the necessary inquiry, the child's evidence is still admissible unless objected to: *Jardine v Howdle* 1997 SCCR 294.
4  See Memorandum by Lord Justice-General Hope, 26 July 1990. This is conveniently available in *Renton and Brown* Appendix D.
5  1995 Act, s 50(3).
6  *Mikhailitchenko v Normand* 1993 SCCR 56, 1993 SLT 1138.

other than what is contained in the indictment and what has been disclosed by evidence already led. The same also applies to the judge (unless he was the sheriff who presided at the first diet[1]), except that he will probably have seen and read copies of the productions prior to the commencement of the trial. Accordingly, evidence should be presented in a way which makes it easy for the jury to understand and follow. Careful thought must be given to the order in which witnesses should be called and about the order in which questions should be asked of each witness. Before any question is asked of a witness the examiner should reflect on exactly what evidence he hopes to obtain from the witness and frame his questions accordingly. This will inevitably involve a good deal of time being devoted to preparation of the case, but it will be time well spent.

The actual technique of asking questions will of course vary from case to case and from witness to witness, but there are certain principles which apply to all cases and every witness.

First and most importantly, the examiner must ensure that the witness's evidence is audible to the jury and the judge. A convenient way of achieving this is usually for the examiner to stand beside the jury rather than next to the witness box. The witness is then encouraged to project his voice towards the jury. The examiner should observe the jurors in order to see whether any of them has apparent difficulty in hearing the witness. If the judge has difficulty in hearing, he is unlikely to keep quiet about it.

Questions should be as brief as possible. Only one question should be asked at a time. There is a great temptation, especially in cross-examination, to ask a series of questions together. This is usually a waste of time.

So far as possible, technical language should be avoided in asking questions. If the witness is giving evidence about technical matters, he should always be asked to explain the technicalities in everyday language. These comments apply equally to legal technicalities. The use of legal jargon should, in any event, be avoided if at all possible.

### Leading questions

A leading question is one which suggests its own answer. Such questions often begin with such words as 'Isn't it the case that' or 'Do you agree that'. The general rule is that leading questions are not permitted in examination-in-chief (ie when a witness is being examined on behalf of the party calling him)[2], but are permissible in cross-examination (ie examination on behalf of the other party or parties in the case). However, this rule is subject to certain exceptions.

Preliminary matters, such as a witness's name and designation, may be the subject of leading questions in chief. If it is clear that part of a witness's evidence is not in dispute, that may be led on. It is good manners for an advocate (using the word here to mean any lawyer presenting a case in court) to indicate to his opponent if there is an area of evidence on which he has no objection to leading questions being asked in chief.

If a witness appears to be 'hostile' (a term which has no technical meaning in Scotland), by going back on his precognition or prevaricating, it is generally

---

1 For first diet see above at pp 132–134.
2 The reason for this rule is fairly obvious. It is the witness's evidence and not that of the examiner, which the jury is entitled to hear.

accepted that leading questions may be asked of him, although the authority for this proposition is somewhat sparse[1].

## Prior statements

A particular example of a competent leading question is that a witness may be asked if he has, on a previous occasion, made a statement about a matter which is different from the evidence which he has given about it at the trial. If he denies having made such a statement or its terms, the making of it and its contents may be proved[2]. If the prior statement, the making or accuracy of which is denied, is not contained in a document then it cannot replace the evidence given by the witness in court and that evidence remains the witness's evidence although his credibility may be put in question. If, however, the witness does not deny making the prior non-documentary statement but says that he has no recollection of making it or of the events to which it relates, the statement may be proved and count as the witness's evidence[3].

If the prior statement *is* contained in a document then it may be admissible even though its accuracy is denied by the witness when giving evidence. This is the case if the prior statement is contained in a precognition on oath[4] or was made in other legal proceedings, whether civil or criminal, anywhere in the world[5], provided in both cases that the statement is sufficiently authenticated[6]. Other documentary statements (eg in a policeman's notebook) may also be admissible as the witness's evidence in certain circumstances[7]. First, the witness must in the course of giving evidence have indicated that the statement in question was made by him and that he adopts it as his evidence[8]. Secondly, the witness must, at the time when the statement was made, have been a competent witness in the proceedings[9]. It should be noted that these statutory provisions do not replace the common law concerning prior statements[10] which may, in some cases, be admissible even if not contained in a document[11].

## Hearsay: common law

Hearsay evidence is evidence of what a person has said. It is sometimes asserted that, at common law, such evidence is inadmissible in a criminal trial, but that is not completely accurate. Hearsay evidence is generally inadmissible at common law in so far as it is relied upon to prove the accuracy of the statement spoken to.

---

1 *Frank v HMA* 1938 JC 17 at 22, 1938 SLT 109 at 110, per Lord Justice-Clerk Aitchison; A G Walker and N M L Walker *The Law of Evidence in Scotland* pp 364–5; *Renton and Brown* para 18–54.
2 1995 Act, s 263(4). This applies only if the previous statement is admissible in evidence. For example, a precognition (other than a precognition on oath), is not admissible. For the purpose of this section the defence may be able to recover statements made by witnesses to the police: *Hemming v HMA* 1997 SCCR 257.
3 *Jamieson v HMA (No 2)* 1994 SCCR 610, 1995 SLT 666.
4 1995 Act, s 260(1), (4)(a).
5 1995 Act, s 260(1), (4)(b).
6 1995 Act, s 260(4). Authentication is by a certificate indorsed on or attached to the first page of the statement: 1996 Rules, r 21.4; Form 21.4.
7 1995 Act, s 260(1), (2)(a).
8 1995 Act, s 260(2)(b).
9 1995 Act, s 260(2)(c).
10 1995 Act, s 260(3).
11 Eg *Jamieson v HMA (No 2)* 1994 SCCR 610, 1995 SLT 666.

For example, if a witness says, 'John Smith told me that he had been threatened by the accused', this is not admissible evidence of the fact that John Smith was threatened. However, it is perfectly good evidence of the fact that John Smith made the statement that he had been threatened, and may be admissible for that purpose.

Recently introduced statutory exceptions to the common law rule against hearsay will be discussed in the next section, but there are many circumstances even at common law in which hearsay evidence may in fact be admissible, and some of the most important are noted here.

Evidence of a statement made by an accused is admissible subject to the general rules of admissibility of incriminating statements[1]. However, a statement by one accused is not evidence against another accused, unless made in the presence of the latter[2]. An alleged admission by a person who is incriminated by an accused is not admissible[3]. If the incriminee is a co-accused the statement by him is admissible as evidence against the incriminee himself, but not as evidence for or against the first accused[4].

A statement which is part of the *res gestae* (ie part of what actually happened at the time the crime was committed) is normally admissible. For example, if a witness depones that he heard someone at the scene of the crime cry out, 'My God, Jim's got a knife', and this was immediately followed by a stabbing, this would be admissible. The person who shouted out the remark should be led as a witness if he can be found.

Evidence of what the victim of a crime said shortly after the commission of the crime may be admissible. This is known as 'a *de recenti* statement'. It is admissible only as fortifying the credibility of the victim's evidence.

Evidence of a previous identification of the accused by a witness who, in court, cannot or will not identify him is admissible[5]. This is the case even if the witness cannot remember what happened at the time of the incident or what he said to the police[6].

## Hearsay: statutory provisions

Section 259 of the 1995 Act contains important provisions relating to the admissibility of hearsay evidence which would be inadmissible at common law. These will now be considered.

The hearsay evidence will be admissible only if direct oral evidence of the matter with which it deals would have been admissible[7] and the person who made the statement, hearsay evidence of which it is sought to lead, would have been a competent witness[8]. In addition there must be evidence which would entitle the jury, properly directed, to find that the statement founded on was made and that either it is contained in a document or the person who gives oral evidence about it at the trial has direct personal knowledge of its making[9].

---

1  See above at pp 81, 82.
2  See eg *McIntosh v HMA* 1986 SCCR 496, 1987 SLT 296.
3  *Perrie v HMA* 1991 JC 27, 1991 SCCR 255, 1991 SLT 651.
4  *McLay v HMA* 1991 SCCR 397, 1994 SLT 873.
5  *Muldoon v Herron* 1970 JC 30, 1970 SLT 228; *Smith v HMA* 1986 SCCR 135; *Maxwell v HMA* 1990 JC 340, 1990 SCCR 363, 1991 SLT 63.
6  *Jamieson v HMA (No 2)* 1994 SCCR 610, 1995 SLT 666.
7  1995 Act, s 259(1)(b).
8  1995 Act, s 259(1)(c).
9  1995 Act, s 259(1)(d).

The person who made the statement, hearsay evidence of which it is sought to lead, must be unavailable to give evidence at the trial for one of a number of possible reasons[1]. These reasons[2] are that the person who made the statement:

'(a) is dead or is, by reason of his bodily or mental condition, unfit or unable to give evidence in any competent manner;

(b) is named and otherwise sufficiently identified, but is outwith the United Kingdom and it is not reasonably practicable to secure his attendance at the trial or to obtain his evidence in any other competent manner;

(c) is named and otherwise sufficiently identified, but cannot be found and all reasonable steps which, in the circumstances, could have been taken to find him have been so taken;

(d) having been authorised to do so by virtue of a ruling of the court in the proceedings that he is entitled to refuse to give evidence in connection with the subject matter of the statement on the grounds that such evidence might incriminate him, refuses to give such evidence; or

(e) is called as a witness and either –

   (i) refuses to take the oath or affirmation; or

   (ii) having been sworn as a witness and directed by the judge to give evidence in connection with the subject matter of the statement refuses to do so and in the application of this paragraph to a child, the reference to a witness refusing to take the oath or affirmation or, as the case may be, to having been sworn shall be construed as a reference to a child who has refused to accept an admonition to tell the truth or, having been so admonished, refuses to give evidence as mentioned above.'

The hearsay statement will not be admissible if the judge is satisfied 'that the occurrence of any of the circumstances mentioned in paragraphs (a) to (e) is caused by either the person in support of whose case the evidence would be given or any other person acting on his behalf for the purpose of securing that the person who made the statement does not give evidence for the purposes of the proceedings either at all or in connection with the subject matter of the statement'[3].

In the case of statements by persons falling within categories (a) to (c) and (e)(i) there are certain provisions which enable the credibility of the hearsay evidence to be tested[4]. These are:

'(a) any evidence which, if that person had given evidence in connection with the subject matter of the statement, would have been admissible as relevant to his credibility as a witness shall be admissible for that purpose [at the trial];

(b) evidence may be given of any matter which, if that person had given evidence in connection with the subject matter of the statement, could have been put to him in cross-examination as relevant to his credibility as a witness but of which evidence could not have been adduced by the cross-examining party; and

(c) evidence tending to prove that the person, whether before or after making the statement, made in whatever manner some other statement which is inconsistent with it shall be admissible for the purpose of showing that he has contradicted himself.'

In the case of hearsay evidence falling into categories (a), (b) or (c) of section 259(2) (maker of statement dead or unfit, outwith the United Kingdom or cannot be found) the party seeking to apply to have the hearsay statement admitted as evidence must give notice in writing of that fact and of the witnesses and productions

---

1  1995 Act, s 259(1)(a).
2  1995 Act, s 259(2).
3  1995 Act, s 259(3).
4  1995 Act, s 259(4).

to be adduced in connection therewith to every other party[1]. The witnesses and productions need not be included in the list attached to the indictment or in any other list of witnesses or productions to be lodged in terms of sections 67(5) or 78(4) of the Act[2]. Notice need not be given if the need to lead hearsay evidence emerges only in the course of the trial (categories (d) and (e) of section 259(2))[3] or if the party seeking to lead the evidence satisfies the judge that there is good reason for not giving such notice[4].

Hearsay evidence may be admitted with the consent of all parties[5].

A statement made by a party seeking to introduce hearsay evidence as to the circumstances supporting the introduction of the hearsay evidence is presumed to be correct unless challenged by another party[6]. If such a challenge is persisted in the judge will determine the issue on balance of probabilities[7].

If hearsay evidence is admitted under this section on application of one party the judge may permit any other party to lead additional evidence even though a witness or production concerned is not on any list lodged by that party[8].

At the time of writing, these provisions are relatively new and untried. It remains to be seen whether the High Court will give them a narrow or a liberal interpretation.

## Examination-in-chief

The purpose of examination-in-chief is to lead evidence of facts favourable to the examiner's side. The limitation on leading questions has already been noted[9].

## Cross-examination[10]

After the party leading a witness has finished his examination-in-chief, the other parties have the right to cross-examine. If there are several accused, they usually cross-examine in the order in which they appear on the indictment, although the judge may permit a different order, if he considers that any accused might be prejudiced by following the normal practice. If an accused or other defence witness gives evidence, the prosecutor always cross-examines last, ie after cross-examination for any other accused has been completed.

There are two main purposes of cross-examination: (1) to cast doubt on the credibility or reliability of the witness; and (2) to elicit evidence of facts favourable

---

1  1995 Act, s 259(5)(a), (b), (6). The form of notice is specified in 1996 Rules, r 21.3; Form 21.3.
2  1995 Act, s 259(5). For ss 67(5) and 78(4) see above at pp 123, 124, 126, 127.
3  1995 Act, s 259(6)(a).
4  1995 Act, s 259(5)(b).
5  1995 Act, s 259(7).
6  1995 Act, s 259(8)(a).
7  1995 Act, s 259(8)(b).
8  1995 Act, s 259(9).
9  See above at pp 152, 153.
10  For a specialised examination of cross-examination in relation to criminal cases see Stone *Cross Examination in Criminal Trials* (1988). For a rather old-fashioned but nonetheless valuable and reasonably concise discussion on the technique of cross-examination in general see Lees *A Handbook of Written and Oral Pleading* (2nd edn of 1920 reprinted in 1988 by Caledonian Books) pp 91–102. Although dealing mainly with civil cases, the comments made there apply, on the whole, equally to criminal trials.

to the cross-examiner's side. In the case of some witnesses only one of these purposes will be relevant. If it is not necessary to achieve either of these purposes with the witness, then he should not be cross-examined at all.

As has already been noted[1], leading questions are permitted in cross-examination.

In civil cases failure to cross-examine a witness on a particular matter may entitle the court to draw the inference that the witness's evidence on that matter is accepted by the cross-examiner as true. No such inference may be drawn from failure to cross-examine in a criminal trial[2].

> 'Ordinarily, there is no burden on the accused and he is entitled to sit back and leave the Crown to it. Of course, if he sits back too far and too long, he may come to grief, but that is his own affair. He may leave the Crown evidence severely alone, in the hope that it does not reach the standard of reasonable certainty, or he may intervene at points where he is hopeful of raising a reasonable doubt. It follows that the procurator for the accused may be as selective as he chooses in cross-examination. The worst that can happen to him is that his selection may be criticised and his omissions commented on'[3].

Although there is no doubt that this is the law, it is generally rash, if not foolish, for the defence agent or counsel to fail to cross-examine a witness who has given strong evidence against his client – especially before a jury.

> 'I am not, of course, suggesting that any fact in a criminal prosecution can be established merely by failure to cross-examine, and there are many cases where wise defending counsel asks as few questions in cross as possible. On the other hand, the silent defender does take a risk, and if he fails to challenge evidence given by witnesses for the Crown by cross-examination or, in addition, by leading substantive evidence in support of his challenge, he cannot complain if the court not merely accept that unchallenged evidence but also, in the light of all the circumstances, draw from it the most unfavourable and adverse inference to the defence that it is capable of supporting'[4].

If the defence intends to lead evidence of a particular fact, then, notwithstanding what was said in *McPherson*, it is advisable, and probably necessary, to put that fact to the Crown witnesses in cross-examination, if they have given evidence which is incompatible with it. As was said in a recent High Court case[5]:

> 'By not cross-examining Crown witnesses on points to be taken later from witnesses in the defence case, the accused's procurator will run the risk that this will be a matter of comment especially when the jury are addressed on the evidence on behalf of the Crown. It will also be open to the presiding judge to remind the jury that points which were made in the course of the defence case were not put to the Crown witnesses and that they are entitled to take this into account in their consideration of the evidence.'

This procedure of putting the defence case to Crown witnesses is known as 'laying a foundation in cross'. The first reason for the rule is to give the Crown witness an opportunity to comment on the defence version of the facts – it is not

---

1  See above at p 52.
2  *McPherson v Copeland* 1961 JC 74, 1961 SLT 373 (a summary case, but the principle is the same in both solemn and summary cases).
3  *McPherson v Copeland* 1961 JC 74 at 78, 1961 SLT 373 at 375, per Lord Justice-Clerk Thomson.
4  *McIlhargey v Herron* 1972 JC 38 at 42, 1972 SLT 185 at 188, per Lord Justice-Clerk Grant.
5  *Mailley v HMA* 1993 JC 138 at 143E, 1993 SCCR 535 at 540C, 1993 SLT 959 at 962E, per Lord Justice-General Hope giving the opinion of the court. See also *Lindsay v Smith* 1990 SCCR 581; *Rauf v HMA* 1997 SCCR 41.

impossible that he may agree with it! Secondly, if the matter has been put in cross-examination, it cannot be suggested by the Crown that the accused has only just thought it up when he himself gives evidence about it. If, of course, the accused has not informed his solicitor of something and then comes out with it for the first time in his own evidence, there is not much that can be done about it.

It has been held by the High Court in an appeal in a summary case that failure on the part of a prosecutor to cross-examine an accused did not bar the prosecutor from seeking a conviction[1]. In a jury trial a prosecutor who did not cross-examine an accused but nevertheless asked the jury to convict would almost certainly occasion remarks of disapproval from the bench.

The likely scope of cross-examination should be apparent if the case has been properly prepared by the defence. In cross-examination, as in so much else, moderation is advisable. Hectoring and bullying are seldom productive and may antagonise the jury. If the cross-examiner obtains the answer he wants, he should stop there and not ask further questions which may result in answers which undermine any good already done.

### Re-examination

After all the parties have cross-examined, the party calling the witness has a limited right to ask questions in what is called re-examination. The right to ask questions is limited to dealing with new matters raised in cross-examination or to clarifying any ambiguities arising from cross-examination. It is not a proper use of re-examination to introduce new matters which could properly have been raised in examination-in-chief. However, such questions may be permitted subject to the right of other parties to ask further questions in cross-examination relating to these matters only. As the sheriff reminded the depute fiscal in the case of *David Balfour*[2], leading questions should not be asked in re-examination[3].

### Questions by the judge

The judge may ask questions of any witness. According to the strict procedural rule, after re-examination *only* the judge may ask questions; any party who wishes to have further questions put must do so through the judge. However, this rule has been relaxed to some extent in recent years so that judges sometimes permit further questions with a limited right of further cross-examination as described in the previous paragraph.

If the judge does ask questions, he must do so circumspectly and ensure that he is not usurping the function of the advocate.

'I must deprecate the practice of ... constant interruptions by a presiding judge. Basically his function is to clear up any ambiguities that are not being cleared up either by the examiner or the cross-examiner. He is also entitled to ask such questions as he might regard relevant and important for the proper determination of the case by the jury, but that right must be exercised with discretion, and only exercised when the occasion requires it. It should not result in the presiding judge taking over the

1   *Young v Guild* 1984 SCCR 477.
2   See above at p 42.
3   I D Macphail *A Revised Version of a Research Paper on the Law of Evidence in Scotland* (1987) para 8.33.

role of examiner or cross-examiner. Normally the appropriate time to put such relevant questions as he may think necessary for the proper elicitation of the truth is at the end of the witness's evidence, and not during the course of examination or cross-examination'[1].


## Release of witness

The Crown should not release any witness cited by the prosecution but not called by the Crown, without the consent of the defence. This is because the defence has the right to call any witness who is on the Crown list or is in a notice of additional witnesses[2]. Once a witness has given evidence he may be released by the judge. If either party wishes the witness to continue to be available (perhaps, for example, for purposes of identification) this should be made clear to the judge so that the witness is not released. The judge may tell a witness who is being released, that he must not speak about the case to any witness who is still to give evidence.


## Recall of witness

At common law the judge has power to recall any witness at any time in order to clarify an ambiguity[3]. It has been held by the High Court that, in a summary case, the power may be exercised even during the defence speech to the court[4]. It is very doubtful whether a judge in a jury trial would be justified in recalling a witness during the defence speech to the jury. He should instead tell the jury that, if their recollection of the evidence differs from that of counsel or the solicitor for the defence, it is their recollection upon which they must rely.

If a judge does recall a witness in exercise of his common law power, he himself asks the witness whatever questions he considers appropriate. No doubt, if his questions elicited new matter from the witness, he would permit parties to ask further questions restricted to this new matter.

There is also a statutory right for a party to recall a witness with the leave of the judge[5]. The purpose of the recall is not confined to correcting omissions or clarifying ambiguities. Thus a witness who prevaricated in her evidence and was detained was allowed to be recalled, she having indicated her willingness to tell the truth[6]. Even a witness who has been charged with perjury following his original evidence may be recalled in terms of this provision[7]. Although it is not specifically stated in the section, it is probably implicit in it that recall of a witness thereunder must be before the close of the case of the party seeking the recall[8].


1  *Livingstone v HMA* (1974) SCCR Supp 68 at 69–70, per Lord Justice-Clerk Wheatley.
2  1995 Act, s 67(6).
3  *McNeilie v HMA* 1929 JC 50 at 53, 1929 SLT 145 at 147, per Lord Justice-General Clyde.
4  *Rollo v Wilson* 1988 SCCR 312, 1988 SLT 659: the ambiguity was whether or not a Crown witness had identified the accused.
5  1995 Act, s 263(5).
6  *Thomson v HMA* 1988 SCCR 354, 1989 SLT 22.
7  *Gall v HMA* 1992 JC 115, 1992 SCCR 447, 1993 SLT 290; *Birrell v HMA* 1993 SCCR 812.
8  *Thomson v HMA* 1988 SCCR 354 at 360 (note by Sheriff G H Gordon, editor of SCCR).

## Additional evidence

At any time before the commencement of the speeches to the jury the judge may permit the prosecutor or the defence to lead additional evidence[1] notwithstanding that the witness to be called or the production to be referred to is not included in the list appended to the indictment or in any notice lodged under section 67(5) (notice of additional witness or production for the Crown) or section 78(4) (notice of witnesses or productions for the defence) of the 1995 Act[2], or that a witness must be recalled[3]. Such additional evidence will be allowed, however, only when the judge (a) considers that it is prima facie material, and (b) accepts that, at the time when the jury was sworn[4], the evidence was not available and could not reasonably have been made available, or the materiality of the evidence could not have been foreseen by the party seeking to call the evidence[5]. The decision of the trial judge to refuse to allow additional evidence will not be reviewed by the appeal court on the basis that some explanation is available to the appeal court which was not given to the trial judge[6]. If a motion to lead additional evidence is granted, the judge may adjourn or postpone the trial before permitting the evidence to be led[7].

## Evidence in replication

After the close of the defence case and before the commencement of speeches to the jury[8], the judge may permit the prosecutor to lead additional evidence for the purpose of (a) contradicting evidence given by any defence witness which could not reasonably have been anticipated by the prosecutor, or (b) providing proof of a statement made by a witness on a previous occasion (under section 163(4) of the 1995 Act)[9].

As with the additional evidence mentioned in the preceding section, it is no bar to calling evidence under this section that the witness or production is not on any list or in any notice, or that a witness must be recalled[10]. Again, the judge may adjourn or postpone the trial before permitting the additional evidence to be led[11].

Evidence in replication is competent even where the evidence which it is sought to rebut has been elicited in cross-examination by a co-accused rather than in chief by the accused himself[12].

---

1  1995 Act, s 268(1).
2  1995 Act, s 268(3)(a).
3  1995 Act, s 268(3)(b).
4  1995 Act, s 268(5)(a).
5  1995 Act, s 268(2).
6  *Cushion v HMA* 1993 SCCR 356, 1994 SLT 410.
7  1995 Act, s 268(4).
8  1995 Act, s 269(4)(a).
9  1995 Act, s 269(1).
10  1995 Act, s 269(2)(a).
11  1995 Act, s 269(3).
12  *Sandlan v HMA* 1983 JC 22, 1983 SCCR 71, 1983 SLT 519. At the trial in this case the accused was himself permitted to be recalled in order to rebut evidence in replication, using the power to permit additional evidence under s 149(1) of the 1975 Act (now s 268(1) of the 1995 Act).

**Evidence of accused's criminal record**

There is a general prohibition against the leading of evidence about the criminal record (if any) of an accused[1]. Although the statutory provision does not say so explicitly, it is well established that the prohibition does not apply to the defence, and that there is nothing to stop an accused giving evidence about his own criminal record or eliciting evidence of it from some other witness, if he so desires[2]. There are special rules governing the accused himself being asked questions by the Crown or a co-accused about his character and criminal record, and these will be examined below[3].

There are exceptions to the general rule. It is always competent to prove a previous conviction if it is necessary to do so in order to establish part of the charge on which the accused is being tried[4]. Such a conviction may be proved by production of an extract signed by the clerk of the appropriate court provided that a copy of the extract has been served on the accused not less than fourteen days before the trial diet and the accused has not served a counter-notice denying that the conviction applies to him within seven days of the date of service of the copy on him[5].

There are also cases where the fact that an accused has a previous conviction may be referred to in the course of the evidence, although it is not necessary for the proof of the crime being tried as such, but is evidence of an incidental matter which is an essential part of the Crown case. So, where articles which an accused had been given on his release from prison were left by him on the same day at the scene of a crime, it was held admissible to lead evidence from the prison officer who had given him the articles (thus making it clear to the jury that he had just served a prison sentence)[6].

There are also relatively new statutory exceptions to the general rule. These were introduced in order to fill a perceived gap in the ability of the Crown to demonstrate an accused's bad character if his defence proceeded along certain lines. Up until the change in law, if an accused chose not to give evidence on his own behalf (in which case he could in certain circumstances be cross-examined about his character[7]) he was immune from any attack on his character. The position is now different. It is governed by section 270 of the 1995 Act. The section applies where[8]

'(a) evidence is led by the defence, or the defence asks questions of a witness for the prosecution, with a view to establishing the accused's good character or impugning the character of the prosecutor, of any witness for the prosecution or of the complainer[9]; or

(b) the nature or conduct of the defence is such as to tend to establish the accused's good character or to involve imputations on the character of the prosecutor, of any witness for the prosecution or of the complainer.'

1 1995 Act, s 101(1).
2 See below at p 163.
3 See below at pp 163, 164.
4 1995 Act, s 101(2)(b). This would apply, for example, in a charge of driving while disqualified, as it is necessary to prove that the accused has been disqualified. Such a charge is, however, tried separately from other charges in order that the jury may not be prejudiced. For an unusual example of evidence of a previous conviction being allowed under this provision see *Milne v HMA* 1995 SCCR 751, 1996 SLT 775, in which the accused was charged with perjury arising from his evidence in a previous trial where he had been charged with driving while disqualified.
5 1995 Act, s 286(1).
6 *HMA v McIlwain* 1965 JC 40, 1965 SLT 311. See also *Carberry v HMA* 1975 JC 40, 1976 SLT 38 and *Murphy v HMA* 1978 JC 1 (but note Lord Kissen's strong dissent in the latter case).
7 1995 Act, s 266(4). See below at pp 163, 164.
8 1995 Act, s 270(1).
9 That is the person against whom the offence is alleged to have been committed. For the purposes of this section it includes a victim who is deceased: 1995 Act, s 270(4).

If the section applies the prosecutor may apply to the court for permission to lead evidence[1]

> 'that the accused has committed, or has been convicted of, or has been charged with, offences other than that for which he is being tried, or is of bad character, notwith-standing that ... a witness or production concerned is not included in any list lodged by the prosecutor and that the notice required by sections 67(5) and 78(4) of this Act has not been given.'

An application by the prosecutor for permission must be made in the absence of the jury[2].

At the time of writing, there is no case law on the application of section 270 but it is suggested that the principles applicable to section 266(4) laid down in the case of *Leggate v Her Majesty's Advocate*[3] would be equally applicable here.

The effect of a breach of the prohibition on disclosure of previous convictions depends on the circumstances in which it occurs. If the prosecutor deliberately leads evidence that an accused has a criminal record, and the accused is convicted by the jury, the conviction will be quashed on appeal, even though the trial judge has directed the jury to ignore the disclosure[4]. However, if the disclosure has been the result of inadvertence or is accidental, then the conviction may be allowed to stand, provided that the judge has adequately directed the jury and there appears to have been no miscarriage of justice[5].

If previous convictions are disclosed and the trial judge concludes that the matter is too serious for him to remedy in his charge, he should probably desert the trial diet *pro loco et tempore*, reserving the right of the Crown to bring fresh proceedings against the accused[6]. If a conviction is quashed on appeal because of disclosure, it may be appropriate to allow a new trial[6].

## Evidence of crime other than that charged

The Crown can lead evidence relevant to the proof of a crime charged even though it may show or tend to show that the accused has committed a crime not charged, unless fair notice requires that the other crime should be charged or otherwise referred to in the indictment[7]. Fair notice will so require if (1) evidence sought to be led tends to show that the accused is of bad character and that the other crime is so different in time, place or character that the indictment does not give fair notice to the accused that evidence of that crime may be led; or (2) proof of the crime charged in the indictment requires proof that the accused committed the other crime[7].

---

1  1995 Act, s 270(2).
2  1995 Act, s 270(3).
3  *Leggate v HMA* 1988 SCCR 391, 1988 SLT 665. See below at p 164.
4  See eg *Graham v HMA* 1983 SCCR 314, 1984 SLT 67.
5  *Binks v HMA* 1984 JC 108, 1984 SCCR 335, 1985 SLT 59; *Deeney v HMA* 1986 SCCR 393. In certain special circumstances a conviction may be allowed to stand even if the trial judge has not dealt with the disclosure in his charge: *Fyfe v HMA* 1989 SCCR 429, 1990 SLT 50.
6  *Binks v HMA* 1984 JC 108, 1984 SCCR 335, 1985 SLT 59. For desertion *pro loco et tempore*, see below at p 176.
7  *Nelson v HMA* 1994 SCCR 192, 1994 SLT 389. This was a decision of a bench of five judges arising out of a trial for being concerned in the supply of controlled drugs. The evidence objected to related to the accused's obstructing the police by swallowing a substance believed to be a controlled drug, this being an offence under s 21 of the Misuse of Drugs Act 1971 which was not charged in the indictment. The conviction was upheld on appeal.

## Evidence of the accused

The accused who is standing trial is not obliged to give evidence[1]. Nor is he obliged to do anything during the course of the trial to assist the Crown, as, for example, by standing up in the dock in order that a witness may see his height[2]. The judge is entitled to comment on the accused's failure to give evidence, but must do so with discretion[3], although 'discretion' has on occasion been fairly liberally construed[4]. It used to be the law that the prosecutor was not permitted to comment on the failure of an accused to give evidence. This prohibition has now been removed[5]. However, it is expected that a prosecutor making such a comment will exercise restraint in the same way as is required of the judge.

The accused is always a competent witness in his own defence[6]. If he is the only defence witness who is to speak to the facts of the case, he should be called as the first witness for the defence[7].

The accused who gives evidence on his own behalf may be asked any question in cross-examination, notwithstanding that 'it' (by which is presumably meant the answer thereto) would tend to incriminate him of the offence charged[8].

The accused should give his evidence from the witness box and not the dock unless the judge directs otherwise[9]. Such a direction is likely to be given only if the judge were satisfied that there would be a serious security risk if the accused left the dock.

The accused has no right to make an unsworn statement but must give evidence on oath or affirmation[10]. If he gives evidence, then, like every other witness, he may be cross-examined on behalf of the other parties.

The accused should not be asked and is not required to answer questions tending to show that he has committed or been convicted of any offence other than that for which he is being tried, or is of bad character unless[11]:

'(a) the proof that he has committed or been convicted of such other offence is admissible evidence to show that he is guilty of the offence with which he is then charged; or

(b) the accused or his counsel or solicitor has asked questions of the witnesses for the prosecution with a view to establishing the accused's good character or impugning the character of the complainer[12], or the accused has given evidence of his own good character, or the nature or conduct of the defence is such as to involve imputations on the character of the prosecutor or of the witnesses for the prosecution; or

(c) the accused has given evidence against any other person charged in the same proceedings'.

---

1 1995 Act, s 266(2). An accused who pleads guilty before or in the course of a trial or who is acquitted in the course of a trial is a competent witness for the Crown against any co-accused against whom the trial proceeds: 1995 Act, s 266(10). See below at p 166.
2 *Beattie v Scott* 1990 JC 320, 1990 SCCR 296, 1991 SLT 110.
3 *Scott v HMA* 1946 JC 90.
4 See eg *McIntosh v HMA* 1997 SCCR 68.
5 Criminal Justice (Scotland) Act 1995, s 32 repealing the 1975 Act, s 141(1)(b).
6 1995 Act, s 266(1).
7 1995 Act, s 266(11).
8 1995 Act, s 266(3).
9 1995 Act, s 266(8).
10 *Gilmour v HMA* 1965 JC 45, 1966 SLT 198.
11 1995 Act, s 266(4).
12 As in the case of s 270 (see above at p 161), 'complainer' includes a victim who is deceased: 1995 Act, s 266(7).

Exceptions (a) and (c) are self-explanatory. There can obviously be no question of the court being asked to exercise a discretion whether or not to allow questioning in the case of exception (a). It has been held that the court has no discretion to refuse to allow the accused to be asked questions in the case of exception (c)[1]. The court has, however, a discretion whether or not to allow cross-examination of the accused in the case of exception (b)[2]. The prosecutor must apply to the judge outwith the presence of the jury for permission to cross-examine the accused in terms of (b)[3]. The first two parts of this exception (accused asking questions to establish his own good character, and himself giving evidence of his own good character) cause no difficulties. However, the interpretation of the remainder of this exception (nature or conduct of defence) and the exercise of discretion thereunder have been the subject of much judicial discussion. Matters have now been clarified, relatively speaking, by the decision in the seven-judge case of *Leggate v Her Majesty's Advocate*[4]. This case established the following propositions:

(1) If the nature or conduct of an accused's defence involves imputations on the character of Crown witnesses, the accused may be cross-examined as to his character. It is irrelevant whether or not it was necessary for the accused to conduct his defence in this way in order to establish it fairly.

(2) The accused may not be cross-examined as to his character when he merely asserts that a Crown witness was lying.

(3) The trial judge has a wide discretion to refuse to allow the accused to be cross-examined on character, and the fundamental test in exercising that discretion is fairness, having regard to the position of the accused on the one hand and the public interest in bringing wrongdoers to justice on the other. It is a significant factor in the exercise of that discretion whether the questions asked of the Crown witnesses were integral and necessary to the defence or were a deliberate attack on their character.

(4) When seeking permission to cross-examine on character, the prosecutor may refer to the date and general nature of the accused's criminal record, even though the judge is not normally entitled to have any knowledge of the accused's criminal record until the prosecutor moves for sentence following conviction at the trial[5].

The bar on questioning an accused about his character or record does not apply to questions asked in examination-in-chief by his own counsel or solicitor. It may sometimes be advantageous for an accused to make no secret of the fact that he has a record. For example, he may wish it to be known that, in the past, he has always pleaded guilty and ask the jury to infer his innocence from the fact that he is pleading not guilty on this occasion. Again, if he is a person with a record for dishonesty only and is on trial for a crime of violence, he may consider it beneficial to put before the jury that he is just a simple thief who would not harm anyone. It is often a question calling for nice judgment on the part of the advocate representing an accused whether or not to take from him that he has a record.

If the accused has no criminal record and is a person of good character, that should be brought out in evidence unless there is some very pressing reason to the contrary, and it is difficult to envisage what such a reason could be. It is, of course,

1 *McCourtney v HMA* 1977 JC 68, 1978 SLT 10.
2 1995 Act, s 266(5).
3 1995 Act, s 266(6).
4 *Leggate v HMA* 1988 SCCR 391, 1988 SLT 665.
5 1995 Act, s 101(3).

essential that the defence solicitor makes quite sure that his client *is* of good character. The fact that the prosecutor has not served a notice of previous convictions is not necessarily a guarantee of this. Convictions outwith the United Kingdom and appearances before a children's hearing for offences should not be overlooked as being relevant to the accused's character.

If an accused's bad character or criminal record is improperly disclosed to the jury as a result of questioning by the prosecutor, the same principles will apply as when his criminal record is disclosed in any other way[1]. The trial judge probably has the option of deserting the diet *pro loco et tempore* or carrying on and attempting to repair the damage when he comes to charge the jury[2].

In parenthesis it may be noted that, if an accused has a record, it is very unwise for the defence to leave the notice of previous convictions lying around where it may be visible to an observant member of the jury. Jury boxes in some courts are very close to the table where the defence advocate sits!

## Evidence of the accused's spouse

The spouse of an accused is a competent and compellable witness for the accused[3]. The spouse is a competent and compellable witness for either the prosecutor or the defence in a case of bigamy[4]. In all other cases the spouse is a competent witness for a co-accused and for the prosecutor[5], but cannot be compelled to give evidence for them unless that could have been done at common law[6]. There are in fact at common law no circumstances where the spouse of one accused could be a compellable witness for a co-accused. In the case of the Crown, however, the spouse of an accused is a compellable witness if the accused is charged with a crime committed against the spouse. This has been interpreted broadly to include not only acts of violence against the spouse, but also offences against the spouse's property[7]. If there are two accused and the Crown calls the spouse of one of them, he or she cannot be compelled to give evidence against *either* accused[8]. The privileges of a spouse do not attach to a person with whom the accused has lived, even for a long time, if they are not married to each other[9].

Even if the spouse is a compellable witness, he or she is entitled to refuse to disclose any communication made between the spouses during the marriage[10].

If a spouse is called as a witness in circumstances where he or she is not compellable the witness should be informed of this fact by the trial judge, and failure to do so may render the witness's evidence incompetent[11]. A spouse should also be advised by the judge of the privilege attaching to communications between spouses.

---

1 See above at p 162.
2 *Binks v HMA* 1984 JC 108, 1984 SCCR 335, 1985 SLT 59.
3 1995 Act, s 264(1)(a); *Hunter v HMA* 1984 JC 90, 1984 SCCR 306, 1984 SLT 434.
4 1995 Act, s 264(4).
5 1995 Act, s 264(1)(b).
6 1995 Act, s 264(2)(a).
7 *Harper v Adair* 1945 JC 21. However, vandalism of a house rented by the estranged wife of an accused does not amount to a crime committed against the spouse: *Hay v McClory* 1993 SCCR 1040, 1994 SLT 520.
8 *Bates v HMA* 1989 SCCR 338, 1989 SLT 701.
9 *Casey v HMA* 1993 SLT 33.
10 1995 Act, s 264(2)(b).
11 *Hay v McClory* 1993 SCCR 1040, 1994 SLT 520.

Neither the prosecutor nor a co-accused is entitled to comment on the failure of an accused's spouse to give evidence[1].

## Evidence of a co-accused

One co-accused is a competent witness for another co-accused, but is not compellable[2]. If one of two or more co-accused gives evidence on his own behalf, he may be cross-examined by the other accused[3]. However, if an accused gives evidence on his own behalf and is cross-examined by a co-accused, that co-accused is not then entitled also to call him as a witness[4].

It is now settled that it is not improper for the Crown to cross-examine one accused in order to obtain from him evidence incriminating another accused[5]. The co-accused who is thus incriminated is entitled to cross-examine the witness further on the evidence elicited by the Crown[5].

When one of two or more accused on the same indictment has pleaded guilty (even though not sentenced) or been acquitted or had the diet against him deserted, he is a competent and compellable witness for either the prosecutor or any other accused[6]. No notice of intention to call such a witness need be given, but the court may grant to any party an adjournment or postponement of the trial if it seems just to do so[6]. A co-accused is a competent witness under this provision, even though his plea of guilty was tendered at a section 76 diet prior to the trial diet, provided of course that he appears on the same indictment as that with which the trial is concerned[7]. It is no bar to a co-accused being called as a witness under this provision that he has heard part of the evidence in the case[8].

## Evidence in trials of sexual offences

There is a general prohibition[9] against an attack by the defence on the character of the complainer in a trial where the accused is alleged to have committed a sexual offence against the complainer. The actual offences to which the section applies are listed[10] and include offences against persons of either sex. The prohibition is against the defence asking questions designed to elicit or leading evidence tending to show that the complainer[11]:

(a)  is not of good character in relation to sexual matters;
(b)  is a prostitute or an associate of prostitutes; or
(c)  has at any time engaged with any person in sexual behaviour not forming part of the subject matter of the charge.

1   1995 Act, s 264(3).
2   1995 Act, s 266(9)(a).
3   1995 Act, s 266(9)(b).
4   1995 Act, s 266(9).
5   *Todd v HMA* 1984 JC 13, 1983 SCCR 472, 1984 SLT 123.
6   1995 Act, s 266(10).
7   *Monaghan v HMA* 1983 SCCR 524.
8   *HMA v Ferrie* 1983 SCCR 1.
9   1995 Act, s 274.
10  1995 Act, s 274(2). They are: rape, sodomy, assault with intent to rape, indecent assault, indecent behaviour, an offence under s 106(1)(a) or s 107 of the Mental Health (Scotland) Act 1984, and offences under the Criminal Law (Consolidation) (Scotland) Act 1995, ss 1 to 3, 5, 6, 7(2) and (3), 8, 13(5).
11  1995 Act, s 274(1).

The prohibition does not apply to questioning and evidence adduced by the Crown[1].

The general prohibition is subject to certain exceptions. The defence may apply to the court for permission to ask questions or lead evidence which would otherwise be forbidden by section 274, and the court must grant the application if it is satisfied[2]:

(a) that the questioning or evidence ... is designed to explain or rebut evidence adduced, or to be adduced, otherwise than by or on behalf of the accused;

(b) that the questioning or evidence ... (i) is questioning or evidence as to sexual behaviour which took place on the same occasion as the sexual behaviour forming the subject-matter of the charge, or (ii) is relevant to the defence of incrimination; or

(c) that it would be contrary to the interests of justice to exclude the questioning or, as the case may be, to admit the evidence.

Such an application by the defence must be made in court but in the absence of the jury, the complainer, any witness and the public[3]. Even if the application is granted, the court may limit the extent of the questioning or the evidence[4].

The judge may exclude the public from the court while the complainer is giving evidence in a trial of a sexual offence, in order to spare the complainer embarrassment and, as a result, make him or her more willing to give detailed evidence[5].

## Presence of witness in court

An expert witness (ie a witness called to give his opinion on a matter relevant to the case rather than to speak to a fact in the case) is usually permitted to remain in court while evidence of the facts is being given, if either party so moves[6]. However, the court always has a discretion in the matter. One expert should not be in court while another expert is giving evidence[6].

Witnesses to facts should not normally be in court before giving their evidence, but a witness may be permitted, on the motion of any party, to be in court prior to giving evidence 'if it appears to the court that the presence of the witness would not be contrary to the interests of justice'[7]. An example of this would be the mother of the complainer in a child abuse case, who was allowed to be present with her child while he was giving evidence, notwithstanding that she herself was subsequently to be called as a witness. The court would not, of course, permit her to be present during the child's evidence if there were any possibility of her own evidence becoming tainted by her hearing that of the child.

Even if a witness has, without permission, been in court prior to giving evidence, and a party is objecting to his being allowed to testify, the trial judge has a

---

1  1995 Act, s 274(4).
2  1995 Act, s 275(1).
3  1995 Act, s 275(3).
4  1995 Act, s 275(2).
5  1995 Act, s 92(3). The terms of the subsection suggest that the whole trial may be held *in camera* but in practice it is almost invariably only the evidence of the complainer which is so heard.
6  *Macdonald* p 295; *Renton and Brown* para 24–164.
7  1995 Act, s 267(1).

limited discretion whether to allow him to do so[1]. The discretion may be exercised in the witness's favour 'where it appears to the court that the presence of the witness was not the result of culpable negligence or criminal intent, and that the witness has not been unduly instructed or influenced by what took place during his presence, or that injustice will not be done by his examination' [1].

### Accused's counsel or solicitor as witness

The advocate or solicitor of an accused is a competent and compellable witness for the accused[2]. He may also be called by another party to the case, but, in that event, he cannot be compelled to disclose anything which he has learned in preparing the case[3]. The privilege of confidentiality is that of the accused and not of the lawyer, so that the lawyer must disclose information if his client wishes him to do so[3]. This privilege would probably not apply if the Crown were alleging that the advocate or solicitor were a party to a fraud or other illegal act by an accused[4], although in that event the witness might be entitled to refuse to answer questions on the ground of possible self-incrimination.

If an accused's lawyer is called as a witness on behalf of his own client, the confidentiality referred to above flies off[5].

The fact that the accused's counsel or solicitor has been in court and has heard the evidence in the case is no bar to his being called as a witness[6].

Under solemn procedure counsel or a solicitor should, of course, normally have advance warning of the fact that he may be called as a witness. He should therefore be able to arrange that another solicitor or counsel will act for the accused at the trial concerned. It is certainly undesirable that counsel or a solicitor who is conducting a trial should be a witness in it, and this should be avoided unless the circumstances are most exceptional.

### Objections to admissibility of evidence

If a witness is asked a question the answer to which is considered inadmissible by one of the parties in the case, that party must object to the question. If the questioner wishes to persist with his question, the judge directs the jury to withdraw. He then hears submissions from the objecting party and from the questioner and reaches a decision on the issue of admissibility. The jury is then brought back, and the examination of the witness continues.

An objection may be to a specific question, such as an accused being asked a question about his character by the prosecutor. The objection may also be to a 'line of examination' rather than to a single question. Thus, if it were sought to lead evidence about a search of premises which the defence maintained was illegal, it would be the line of examination in the sense of all questions about the search which would be objected to.

1 1995 Act, s 267(2). See *Heywood v Cavin* 1993 SCCR 663, 1994 SLT 315.
2 *Macdonald* p 294; *Renton and Brown* para 24–154.
3 *Macdonald* p 295.
4 *Micosta S.A. v Shetland Islands Council* 1983 SLT 483 at 485, per Lord President Emslie. Although this is a civil case there is no apparent reason in principle why what was said should not apply in a criminal case.
5 1995 Act, s 265(2).
6 *Macdonald* pp 294–5; *Renton and Brown* para 24–154.

If an objection is not taken timeously, the jury will, of course, hear the evidence, and, in any event, it cannot form the subject of a successful appeal unless the accused is without legal representation at his trial[1]. An objection should be taken by a party, but, in the case of a particularly blatant attempt to lead inadmissible evidence, the judge may, of his own volition, refuse to allow a line of questioning to be pursued, although this practice is not to be encouraged[2].

In certain circumstances the judge may require to hear evidence outwith the presence of the jury in order to decide whether or not evidence is admissible. This is what is known as 'a trial within a trial'. The cases in which it has occurred have been concerned almost exclusively with the admissibility of a statement allegedly made by an accused to the police, and the dispute has been as to whether the statement was fairly obtained. The procedure of a trial within a trial was introduced into Scotland by the case of *Chalmers v Her Majesty's Advocate*[3]. It has been much criticised since[4], partly because of the amount of time it allegedly wastes and partly because it is said to involve the judge in usurping the jury's function as the arbiter of facts. It is nevertheless still part of our procedure[5]. It is rare for a judge to exclude evidence following a trial within a trial, and the circumstances in which he is entitled to do so are limited.

'A judge who has heard the evidence regarding the manner in which a challenged statement was made will normally be justified in withholding the evidence from the jury only if he is satisfied on the undisputed relevant evidence that no reasonable jury could hold that the statement had been voluntarily made and had not been extracted by unfair or improper means'[6].

## Record of proceedings at judicial examination

The record of proceedings at any judicial examination of an accused must be on the Crown list of productions[7]. This record includes any declaration made by the accused as well as the questions and answers forming part of what is commonly called the judicial examination[8].

The record is usually read out to the jury by the clerk of court. It need not be sworn to by witnesses[9]. The record is almost invariably read to the jury before the prosecutor closes his case. If, for any reason, the Crown decides not to have it read, then it could be introduced as part of the defence case, the accused being entitled to put in evidence any Crown production[10].

Both the Crown and the defence have the right to apply to the court to have all or part of the record of the proceedings at a judicial examination excluded from the jury[11]. Such an application should be made at a first diet[12] in a sheriff court case or

---

1  1995 Act, s 118(8)(b).
2  *Kelso v HMA* 1990 SCCR 9.
3  *Chalmers v HMA* 1954 JC 66, 1954 SLT 177.
4  See eg *Hartley v HMA* 1979 SLT 26; *HMA v Whitelaw* 1980 SLT (Notes) 25; *HMA v Mair* 1982 SLT 471.
5  It was used eg in *Aiton v HMA* 1987 SCCR 252.
6  *Balloch v HMA* 1977 JC 23 at 28, 1977 SLT (Notes) 29 at 30, per Lord Justice-Clerk Wheatley.
7  1995 Act, s 68(1).
8  See above at pp 108–111.
9  1995 Act, s 278(1).
10  1995 Act, s 67(6).
11  1995 Act, s 278(2)(a).
12  See above at pp 132–134.

a preliminary diet[1] in a High Court case. At the hearing of any such application evidence may be led from any person who was present at any part of the judicial examination[2]. In practice there is very often agreement about what should be excluded (eg reference to a previous conviction), and there is no need for an application to the court to be made.

The evidential value of what an accused says at a judicial examination (or in any other previous statement about the crime charged) was considered in the case of *Morrison v Her Majesty's Advocate*[3]. The court (a bench of seven judges) held that where evidence is led by the Crown (or, without objection, by the defence) of a prior statement made by the accused which is capable of being both incriminatory and exculpatory, the whole statement is admissible as evidence of the facts contained in it and it is for the jury to consider whether they accept any part of it as truth[4]. The court also held that a prior statement made by an accused which was not to any extent incriminatory was admissible in evidence but only for the limited purpose of establishing that such a statement was made and that the accused had been consistent in what he said (if indeed that was the case). For example, it could demonstrate that the accused had made a statement consistent with innocence at an early stage of proceedings, or it could add to the weight and credibility of other exculpatory evidence in the case.

The fact that an accused did not answer any questions at a judicial examination is not something which should go against him at his trial[5] unless he has put forward a defence which he could have mentioned in answer to a question at the judicial examination[6]. In that event the prosecutor, the judge and any co-accused are entitled to comment on his failure to answer, and the jury is entitled to take account of it when weighing the evidence[7]. Any comment should, however, be restrained[8]. In deciding whether or not to comment the judge should have regard to the terms of the charge to which the question related[9]. In order to enable him to do that he should be provided by the prosecutor with the petition on which the accused appeared for judicial examination or a certified copy thereof[10], but there is no need for the petition or the certified copy to be included in any list of productions[11]. The petition is sufficient evidence of the terms of the charge[11].

## Undisputed evidence

If the parties have agreed evidence and incorporated the agreement in a joint minute or similar document[12] its terms are read to the jury. In the sheriff court this is done by the clerk of court. In the High Court it is usually done by junior counsel for the Crown. This normally happens at the end of the Crown case. A similar

1  See above at pp 135–137.
2  1995 Act, s 278(3).
3  *Morrison v HMA* 1990 JC 299, 1990 SCCR 235, 1991 SLT 57, overruling *Hendry v HMA* 1985 SCCR 274, 1986 SLT 186.
4  But see *Khan v HMA* 1992 JC 32, 1992 SCCR 146, 1993 SLT 172, in which it was suggested that this principle is not of universal application and that the test is ultimately one of fairness.
5  *Walker v HMA* 1985 SCCR 150.
6  *McEwan v HMA* 1990 SCCR 401.
7  1995 Act, s 36(8). See *Alexander v HMA* 1988 SCCR 542, 1989 SLT 193.
8  *McEwan v HMA* 1990 SCCR 401; *McGhee v HMA* 1991 JC 119, 1991 SCCR 510, 1992 SLT 2.
9  1996 Rules, r 5.5(4).
10  1996 Rules, r 5.5(6).
11  1996 Rules, r 5.5(5).
12  See p 129 above.

procedure is followed with a statement of uncontroversial evidence in terms of section 258 of the 1995 Act[1].

## Documentary evidence

Schedule 8 to the 1995 Act contains important provisions relating to documentary evidence in criminal proceedings, the details of which are not appropriate for a textbook such as this. It may, however, be noted that the Schedule provides that, generally speaking, copies of documents are acceptable as evidence in place of the originals if authenticated[2], and a statement in a business document is acceptable in place of oral evidence[3] if the document is appropriately certified[4]. The provisions of the Schedule are declared not to affect the operation of the Bankers' Books Evidence Act 1879[5]. This has been authoritatively interpreted as meaning that the Crown may choose whether to prove documents under the 1879 Act or under the provisions of the Schedule[6].

## Evidence by certificate

Apart from evidence which is admitted or agreed by the parties[7] and the evidence admissible in terms of Schedule 8 mentioned in the previous paragraph, the normal rule is that the only evidence which a jury may consider is oral evidence given in court[8]. However, there is statutory provision for evidence of certain routine matters to be presented to the jury in the form of a certificate[9]. This provision applies only to a limited number of specified statutory offences[10]. A certificate is admissible in evidence on behalf of either the Crown or the accused ('the first party') only if a copy of it has been served[11] on 'the other party' not less than fourteen days before the trial[12]. If the other party serves notice on the first party not more than seven days after service of the certificate (or later as the court may in special circumstances allow), that he is challenging anything in the certificate, then the certificate will not be sufficient evidence[13], and the first party must lead oral evidence in the usual way.

In terms of section 283 of the 1995 Act if the evidence in a case includes evidence of a video surveillance recording (ie a recording by a video camera in a fixed place[14]), a certificate purporting to be signed by a person responsible for the oper-

1 See pp 129–130 above.
2 1995 Act, Sch 8, para 1(1). The mode of authentication is provided by the 1996 Rules, r 26.1.
3 1995 Act, Sch 8, para 2.
4 1995 Act, Sch 8, para 3.
5 1995 Act, Sch 8, para 7(1)(b).
6 *Lord Advocate's Reference (No 1 of 1996)* 1996 SCCR 516, 1996 SLT 740.
7 1995 Act, s 256. See above at p 129.
8 This changed in respect of evidence of certain official documents when the 1997 Act, s 28 came into force on 1 August 1997. This in effect applies the provisions of the present 1995 Act, s 154, which apply only to summary proceedings (see p 214 below) to solemn proceedings also. See the Appendix at p 320 below.
9 1995 Act, s 280(1).
10 The statutes concerned are listed in the 1995 Act, Sch 9. This also specifies the matters which may be certified and the persons who 'may purport to sign certificates'. This Schedule was amended when the 1997 Act, s 30 came into force on 1 August 1997. See the Appendix at p 320 below.
11 'Served' may not necessarily mean that the certificate has actually to be handed to the other party: *Duffy v Normand* 1995 SCCR 538.
12 1995 Act, s 280(6)(a).
13 1995 Act, s 280(6)(b).
14 1995 Act, s 283(4).

ation of the system certifying the location of the camera, the nature and extent of the person's responsibility for the system, and that visual images recorded on a particular tape are images recorded at a specified time, date and place, is sufficient evidence of the matters contained in the certificate[1]. The provisions for service of the certificate and service of a counter-notice are exactly the same as those mentioned in the previous paragraph in connection with section 280[2].

There are similar provisions for evidence by certificate in relation to fingerprints but here the certificate must be signed by a person authorised by a chief constable[3]. If the certificate is served on all other parties not less than fourteen days before the trial diet, the sufficiency of the evidence contained therein is not open to challenge[4].

## Evidence by report

The 1995 Act contains provisions about evidence by report which are very similar to those about evidence by certificate[5]. A report purporting to be signed by two authorised (defined in the Act[6]) forensic scientists is sufficient evidence of its contents[7] provided that it has been served and there has been no counter-notice in exactly the same way as in the case of a certificate under section 280(1). This procedure is not always adopted, especially in solemn proceedings. It was not used by the procurator fiscal in the case of *David Balfour* where the terms of the report were agreed by joint minute.

There are similar provisions relating to reports by authorised forensic scientists about controlled drugs and medicinal products where no full analysis has been carried out[8]. These provisions may also apply to the oral evidence of such witnesses[9].

In the case of the report of an autopsy signed by two pathologists or forensic scientists the prosecutor may intimate, when lodging the report, that it is intended to call only one of the signatories, and his evidence will be sufficient unless the accused, not less than six days before the trial (or later in special circumstances), serves notice that he requires the attendance at the trial of the other signatory to the report[10]. Also in connection with the report of an autopsy it is presumed that the body identified in the report is the body of the deceased identified in the indictment unless the accused, not less than six days before the trial (or later in special circumstances), gives notice that the contrary is alleged[11].

## Evidence by letter of request and evidence on commission

There are two further exceptions to the general rule that only oral evidence is admissible in a criminal jury trial. First, if a witness is abroad (ie outside the United

---

1    1995 Act, s 283(1).
2    1995 Act, s 283(2).
3    1995 Act, s 284(1) as amended by the 1997 Act, s 47(4) with effect from 1 August 1997. See the Appendix at p 320 below.
4    1995 Act, s 284(2) as amended by the 1997 Act, s 47(4) with effect from 1 August 1997.
5    There may, however, be a distinction between evidence by certificate and evidence by report: *O'Brien v McCreadie* 1994 SCCR 516.
6    1995 Act, s 280(5).
7    1995 Act, s 280(4).
8    1995 Act, s 282(1), (3).
9    1995 Act, s 282(1).
10   1995 Act, s 281(2).
11   1995 Act, s 281(1).

Kingdom, Channel Islands and Isle of Man), the court in Scotland may issue a letter of request to a court or tribunal in the foreign country for it to examine the witness[1]. Secondly, if a witness in the United Kingdom, Channel Islands or the Isle of Man is too ill or infirm to attend court, or is normally resident abroad and is unlikely to be present in the United Kingdom, Channel Islands or Isle of Man at the time of the trial, the court may appoint a commissioner to take his evidence at any place within the United Kingdom, Channel Islands or Isle of Man[2].

An application for a letter of request or a commission is made by way of petition[3] to the court in which the trial is to take place (or the High Court if that is not yet known)[4]. The application must be intimated to all the other parties in the case[5]. The judge has a discretion whether or not to grant the application[6], but may grant it only if he is satisfied that (a) the evidence which it is averred the witness is able to give is necessary for the proper adjudication of the trial, and (b) there would be no unfairness to the other party were such evidence to be received in the form of the record of an examination conducted by the foreign court or the commissioner[7]. The opinion has been expressed in the High Court that letters of request should be granted only if the evidence to be obtained is formal[8].

The application may be made at any time before the jury is sworn[9] or, only in the case of evidence on commission, in exceptional circumstances, during the trial[10].

The record of the examination or commission, as the case may be, is read out to the jury by the clerk of court[11] after the party seeking to found on the evidence has so moved the court[12], and the judge may direct that the jury is to be provided with copies of the evidence[13].

## Television link evidence from abroad

Finally, in the field of evidence not given directly in court, notice must be taken of something which would not have been technically possible until very recently. This is the taking of evidence from a witness who is abroad by live television link[14]. Any witness who is outside the United Kingdom[15], other than the accused, may give evidence by television link if an application for a letter of request has been granted[16] and the court to which the application is made (the trial court) is satisfied as to the arrangements for the giving of evidence in this manner[17]. A letter of

1  1995 Act, s 272(1)(a). Detailed procedural rules are contained in 1996 Rules, rr 23.1–23.6.
2  1995 Act, s 272(1)(b). Detailed procedural rules are contained in 1996 Rules, rr 24.1–24.7.
3  1996 Rules, rr 23.1(1), 24.1(1).
4  1995 Act, s 272(1).
5  1996 Rules, rr 23.1(5)(a), 24.1(5)(a).
6  1996 Rules, rr 23.2(1), 24.2(1).
7  1995 Act, s 272(3).
8  *Muirhead v HMA* 1983 SCCR 133, 1983 SLT 545, per Lord Cameron. Cf *HMA v Lesacher* 1982 SCCR 418 (Sh Ct), in which a letter of request was granted for evidence which was very far from formal.
9  1995 Act, s 272(7)(a).
10  1995 Act, s 272(7).
11  1996 Rules, rr 23.6(3)(b), 24.7(3)(b).
12  1996 Rules, rr 23.6(1), 24.7(1).
13  1996 Rules, rr 23.6(3)(a), 24.7(3)(a).
14  1995 Act, s 273.
15  1995 Act, s 273(1)(a).
16  1995 Act, s 273(1)(b).
17  1995 Act, s 273(1)(c).

request must be addressed to the court or tribunal or other appropriate authority exercising jurisdiction in the country where the witness is ordinarily resident[1]. Application for evidence to be given in this way will be granted only if the judge to whom it is made is satisfied that the evidence which the witness will give is necessary for the proper adjudication of the trial[2], that the granting of the application would be in the interests of justice[3] and, in the case of an application by the prosecutor, that the granting of the application would not be unfair to the accused[4]. The procedural rules applying to conventional letters of request apply *mutatis mutandis* to letters of request in this field also[5].

## SUBMISSION OF NO CASE TO ANSWER

At the end of the Crown case the defence may submit to the judge that the accused has no case to answer in respect of both (a) an offence charged in the indictment and (b) any other offence of which he could be convicted under the indictment were the offence charged the only offence so charged[6].

It should be noted that a submission will be successful only if there is insufficient evidence to convict the accused of *any part* of an offence charged. Thus, in an indictment charging assault with intent to rape, if there were no evidence from which the jury would be entitled to infer the libelled intent, but there were sufficient evidence of assault, a submission would be rejected. It should also be noted that, for a submission to succeed, there must be no case to answer under both heads (a) and (b) of the subsection. Thus, if an accused were charged with robbery and there were insufficient evidence of that but there were sufficient evidence of theft, a submission would be rejected as a verdict of guilty of theft is competent on a charge of robbery[7]. However, if any part of an offence charged is essential to the whole offence, then a submission of no case to answer should be sustained if there is insufficient evidence in respect of that part only, notwithstanding that there may be sufficient evidence of other parts[8]. Note that the statutory provision refers to an 'offence' and not to a 'charge'. If the Crown chooses (as it sometimes does) to lump several offences into one charge, it is strongly arguable that a submission of no case to answer would be competent in respect of any *offence*[9].

The submission is heard by the judge outwith the presence of the jury[10]. The judge must hear argument from the party making the submission[11] and, apparently, from the prosecutor also, even though the judge is minded to reject the submission[12].

If the judge is satisfied that the evidence led by the Crown is insufficient in law to justify the accused being convicted under either head (a) or head (b) of the sub-

1   1995 Act, s 273(2).
2   1995 Act, s 273(3)(a).
3   1995 Act, s 273(3)(b)(i).
4   1995 Act, s 273(3)(b)(ii).
5   1996 Rules, ch 23.
6   1995 Act, s 97(1). For alternative verdicts see below at p 184.
7   1995 Act, s 64(6), Sch 3, para 8(3).
8   *Mackie v HMA* 1994 SCCR 277, 1995 SLT 110.
9   See *Cordiner v HMA* 1991 SCCR 652, 1993 SLT 2, especially per Lord McCluskey (p 671, p 9) and the commentary by Sheriff G H Gordon (editor of SCCR) at 1991 SCCR 673.
10   1995 Act, s 97(4).
11   *Taylor v Douglas* 1983 SCCR 323, 1984 SLT 69. This was a summary case, but the principle is the same.
12   *Stewart v Lowe* 1991 SCCR 317.

section he must acquit him of the offence in respect of which the submission has been made[1]. If there are any other charges in the indictment, the trial will proceed in respect of these[1].

Evidence is 'insufficient' when, even if it were accepted in its entirety, it would not entitle the court to proceed to conviction[2]. In other words, the court is concerned not with the credibility, reliability or acceptability of the evidence, but only with its sufficiency: not with its quality but with its quantity.

If the submission is rejected by the judge, the trial proceeds exactly as if no submission had been made[3].

The High Court has reserved its opinion on what the position would be if a judge wrongly rejected a submission of no case to answer, the trial proceeded, and the accused were convicted as a result of evidence given by himself, by a co-accused, or by some other defence witness[4].

# ABANDONMENT OF CHARGE BY THE CROWN; PLEA OF GUILTY BY ACCUSED

The Crown is master of the instance in a criminal trial, and the prosecutor has an unfettered discretion to abandon a charge and accept an accused's plea of not guilty to all or part of an indictment at any stage of a case. The judge has no authority to interfere in the exercise of the prosecutor's discretion. In practice the prosecutor may very well refer the question of whether or not to accept a plea of not guilty to some higher authority (the procurator fiscal in the case of a depute fiscal, or the home advocate depute or one of the law officers in the case of an advocate depute).

If the Crown abandons any offence charged in an indictment after a jury has been sworn, it used to be the case that the jury had to return a verdict of not guilty on that charge. This, however, is no longer the case. In such a situation the judge now acquits the accused of the offence concerned[5]. If there are any other offences charged in the indictment the trial proceeds in respect of them[5].

On the same basis, if an accused changes his plea to guilty at any stage of the trial after a jury has been sworn, it is the judge and not the jury who convicts the accused[6]. If there is any other offence charged in the indictment to which the accused still pleads not guilty the trial proceeds only in respect of that offence[7]. The accused is not sentenced until the trial is completed[8], but it is probably not competent for the court to allow the plea to be withdrawn once it has been recorded as the accused has already been 'convicted'[9].

1  1995 Act, s 97(2).
2  *Williamson v Wither* 1981 SCCR 214.
3  1995 Act, s 97(3).
4  *Little v HMA* 1983 JC 16, 1983 SCCR 56, 1983 SLT 489.
5  1995 Act, s 95(1).
6  1995 Act, s 95(2).
7  1995 Act, s 95(3)(a).
8  1995 Act, s 95(3)(b).
9  *Crossan v HMA* 1996 SCCR 279.

# ADJOURNMENT OF TRIAL AND DESERTION OF DIET

## Adjournment

Every trial must proceed from day to day until concluded unless it is adjourned over a day or days[1]. Whether or not to adjourn is within the discretion of the presiding judge[2]. If a trial is adjourned, it must be to a specified time and place. An adjournment to a later time on the same day is not usually minuted, but an adjournment to another date must be contained in an interlocutor duly signed[3].

If a trial is interrupted without being adjourned, the instance falls immediately[4]. However, this rule is subject to certain statutory exceptions. For example, a trial may be interrupted to take the verdict of a jury in another case[5], or to deal with a plea of guilty in another case[6].

If, as is very common, several cases are put down for a sitting of the court, the minute adjourning the case actually being tried normally adjourns that case and 'all remaining cases'. That is sufficient to keep alive all cases in the sitting (whether or not previously called) without each individual case being called[7].

## Desertion *pro loco et tempore*

The court may desert a diet of trial *pro loco et tempore* (ie for that particular time and place). The effect of such desertion is that the Crown may raise a fresh indictment against the accused or may, in certain circumstances, proceed against him at a later date on the same indictment[8].

The prosecutor is entitled to move the court to desert *pro loco et tempore* before the jury is sworn[9]. The court may, of its own volition, desert *pro loco et tempore* at any stage of the trial, and whether or not to do so is within the discretion of the presiding judge[10]. Circumstances in which such desertion is appropriate are, eg, the illness of an accused[11] or of a witness[12].

## Desertion *simpliciter*

When the court wishes, exceptionally, to bring the entire proceedings to an end, it may desert the diet *simpliciter*. The prosecutor is then barred from raising a fresh

---

1  1995 Act, s 91.
2  1995 Act, s 91; *Kyle v HMA* 1987 SCCR 116.
3  *Renton and Brown* para 18–18 founding on *Hull v HMA* 1945 JC 83; *Law and Nicol v HMA* 1973 SLT (Notes) 14.
4  *Law and Nicol v HMA* 1973 SLT (Notes) 14. The particular situation which arose in this case is now covered by the 1996 Rules, r 14.9.
5  1995 Act, s 102(1)(a).
6  1995 Act, s 102(2).
7  *Kiely v HMA* 1990 JC 264, 1990 SCCR 151, 1990 SLT 847.
8  1995 Act, s 81(1), (5). The accused must be served with another copy of the indictment within nine clear days after the date of the abortive trial diet, along with a notice to appear to answer the indictment at another diet (which may be in the same court or a different court), that diet to be not less than nine clear days after the date when notice was given.
9  *Renton and Brown* para 18–21 founding on *Ross* (1848) Ark 481 and *John Martin* (1858) 3 Irv 177.
10  *Mallison v HMA* 1987 SCCR 320.
11  *HMA v Brown and Foss* 1966 SLT 341.
12  *Farrell v HMA* 1984 JC 1, 1984 SCCR 301, 1985 SLT 58.

libel, unless the court's decision has been reversed on appeal[1]. However, a private prosecution may still be brought against the accused[2].

It is uncertain whether a diet may be deserted *simpliciter* in respect of only one charge on an indictment which contains several charges[3].

## Death or illness of presiding judge

If the presiding judge dies, is unable to proceed with a case because of illness, or is for some other reason absent, the clerk of court is given power to convene the court[4]. If no evidence has been led, he may adjourn the diet and any other diet appointed for that sitting to (i) a time later the same day, or a date not more than seven days later, when he believes a judge will be available; or (ii) a later sitting not more than two months after the date of the adjournment[5]. If evidence has been led, he may (i) adjourn the diet as in (i) above; or (ii) with the consent of the parties, desert the diet *pro loco et tempore*[6]. Where, evidence having been heard, the clerk adjourns the diet, the court may, at the adjourned diet, either further adjourn the diet or desert the diet *pro loco et tempore*[7]. If the diet is deserted *pro loco et tempore* in either of these situations specific power is given to the Lord Advocate to raise a fresh indictment[8].

# AMENDMENT OF INDICTMENT

It quite frequently occurs that the Crown seeks to amend the indictment either prior to the leading of evidence or, more commonly, in the course of the trial. The basic principle is clear:

> 'No trial shall fail or the ends of justice be allowed to be defeated by reason of any discrepancy or variance between the indictment and the evidence'[9].

This principle is amplified in the following subsection[10]:

> 'It shall be competent at any time prior to the determination of the case, unless the court see just cause to the contrary, to amend the indictment by deletion, alteration or addition, so as to –
> (a) cure any error or defect in it;
> (b) meet any objection to it; or
> (c) cure any discrepancy or variance between the indictment and the evidence.'

It is further provided that no amendment is permitted which changes the character of the offence charged[11].

1 1995 Act, s 81(3).
2 *X v Sweeney* 1982 JC 70, 1982 SCCR 161, 1983 SLT 48 sub nom *H v Sweeney*. For private prosecution, see ch 11.
3 *McMahon v Hamilton* 1992 JC 98, 1992 SCCR 351, 1992 SLT 242 (a summary case, but the principle must surely be the same).
4 1995 Act, s 87(1).
5 1995 Act, s 87(1)(a).
6 1995 Act, s 87(1)(b).
7 1995 Act, s 87(3).
8 1995 Act, s 87(4).
9 1995 Act, s 96(1).
10 1995 Act, s 96(2).
11 1995 Act, s 96(3).

It is clear that amendment will not be allowed in order to attempt to cure a fundamental nullity in an indictment or a charge. Thus, if no locus is stated for the offence, the prosecutor is not permitted to amend to insert one, a locus being essential in order to establish jurisdiction[1]. However, where the name of one of several accused was radically misstated in one of three charges in an indictment (having been correctly stated in the preamble and the remaining charges), the Crown was allowed to amend to correct the error[2].

Whether or not to allow an amendment is within the discretion of the trial judge, and the accused may be granted an adjournment or some other remedy if the judge considers that he may be prejudiced in his defence on the merits of the case as a result of the amendment[3].

An amendment is sufficiently authenticated by being initialled by the clerk of court[4].

## SPEECHES BY CROWN AND DEFENCE

At the conclusion of the evidence the prosecutor addresses the jury, followed by counsel or the solicitor for the accused, or the accused himself if he is unrepresented. The defence is always entitled to speak last[5]. If there are more than one accused, the normal practice is that the speeches follow the order in which they appear in the indictment.

It is no longer the case that the prosecutor is barred from commenting on the failure of the accused to give evidence[6], although comment on the failure of the accused's wife to give evidence is still prohibited[7]. The prosecutor may be permitted to comment on an accused's failure to answer a question at a judicial examination[8].

The speech to the jury is important as it enables each party to put forward to the jury the points most favourable to his case. Care should be taken in the preparation of a speech in order to ensure that it is presented in a logical and comprehensible way. It should not, of course, mention matters which were not led in evidence. As a general rule brevity is to be commended. It is probably advisable for the defence to mention any important Crown evidence and attempt to repudiate or explain it rather than simply to ignore it. When addressing a jury it is a good idea to watch the jury's reaction. If they start yawning, it is time to stop!

As the judge will direct the jury on the law, speeches should say as little about the law as possible, although some comment thereon is almost unavoidable. For example, it is usual for a prosecutor to tell the jury about the burden and standard of proof. Then too the jury is unlikely to understand what is involved in a special

---

1 *Stevenson v McLevy* (1879) 4 Couper 196, 6 R (J) 33. This was a summary case, but the principle is the same. A partial description of the locus will not suffice unles it makes it clear that it is within the jurisdiction of the court: *Yarrow Shipbuilders Ltd v Normand* 1995 SCCR 224, 1995 SLT 1215.
2 *Keane v HMA* 1986 SCCR 491, 1987 SLT 220. See also the cases cited in the context of amendment of a summary complaint below at p 218.
3 1995 Act, s 96(3).
4 1995 Act, s 96(4).
5 1995 Act, s 98.
6 1975 Act, s 141(1)(b) was repealed by the Criminal Justice (Scotland) Act 1995, s 32. See above at p 163.
7 1995 Act, s 264(3).
8 1995 Act, s 36(8). See above at p 109.

defence of self-defence unless some attempt to deal with the legal concept is made by the parties in their speeches[1]. It is good practice and good manners for an advocate to remind the jury that they *will* be directed on the law by the judge and that it is his direction which they must follow even if it differs from the view of the speaker.

It is, of course, open to either party to ask the judge to give a particular direction in law to the jury, for example, to the effect that part of a charge (eg the aggravation of an assault) has not been proved. However, it is not appropriate to do this in the course of a speech to the jury[2]. Nowadays, a request for directions is usually made in the absence of the jury prior to the speech by the prosecutor. It is helpful if the judge indicates whether or not he is prepared to give the requested direction, so that the parties may adapt their speeches accordingly. However, the judge is under no obligation to give such an indication. If an application for a direction is made before the prosecutor addresses the jury, there is an opportunity for a legal debate on the matter, provided that the judge is prepared to hear submissions from the parties. If, however, as sometimes happens, the defence does not make an application until after the prosecutor has spoken, there should be no debate as the prosecutor is *functus* (ie he has had his say).

## THE JUDGE'S CHARGE

The judge's primary task in charging the jury is to tell them what is the law which they must apply to the case[3]. He should tell the jury that the facts are for them. He should follow any advice given by the High Court on any particular point.

> 'When the High Court lays down what a trial judge ought to do when directing a jury on a particular point, the High Court expects that trial judges will follow the advice given to them'[4].

It seems now to be well settled that there is no duty on a judge to sum up the evidence.

> 'In our Scottish procedure the judge does not give a summing up, as is the practice south of the border, by rehearsing all the evidence. All that the judge is required to do is to make reference to such of the evidence as is necessary for the determination of the issues in the case, and he may do so on a broad canvas. All that is required in that situation is that he does it in an even-handed fashion so as not to give an advantage one way or the other'[5].

There is, it is true, a reference in an old statute to the judge's summing up the evidence[6], but it is suggested that this was probably an English importation which no longer has any place in our modern procedure.

The judge must tell the jury that the onus of proof is on the Crown, and he should direct them that the standard of proof is 'beyond reasonable doubt'. It is for each individual judge to decide how to tell the jury what is meant by reasonable

---

1 See the case of *David Balfour* above at pp 49–50.
2 *Collins v HMA* 1991 JC 204, 1991 SCCR 898, 1993 SLT 101.
3 *Hamilton v HMA* 1938 JC 134 at 144, 1938 SLT 333 at 337, per Lord Justice-General Normand.
4 *Smith v HMA* 1994 SCCR 72 at 79B, 1994 SLT 1161 at 1163J, per Lord Justice-Clerk Ross giving the opinion of the court.
5 *King v HMA* 1985 SCCR 322 at 328, per Lord Justice-Clerk Wheatley. See also *Douglas v HMA* 1990 SCCR 188, 1990 SLT 781; *Shepherd v HMA* 1996 SCCR 679.
6 Justiciary and Circuit Courts (Scotland) Act 1783, s 5.

doubt, but examples of commercial transactions are unlikely to be helpful, and it is advisable that judges should adhere to 'the traditional formula'[1]. It is not perhaps so easy to determine what *is* the traditional formula, but it is suggested that the sheriff in the case of *David Balfour*[2] dealt with the matter in a sufficiently traditional way[3].

The judge should tell the jury that they cannot find an accused guilty without corroborated evidence of the essential facts. He should direct them as to which are the essential facts and what evidence is capable of affording corroboration of them. It may, however, not be fatal for the judge to omit a direction about corroboration[4].

Where a particular piece of evidence is vital to the Crown case, the judge must so direct the jury and tell them that, if they do not accept that piece of evidence, they must acquit[5]. It is not proper for the judge to direct the jury that it is for *them* to decide which facts are crucial[6].

If identification is in issue it is usually appropriate for the judge to remind the jury of the possibility of mistaken identity and of the factors to which they might have regard in assessing the strength of identification evidence[7]. However, the matter is essentially one for the judge's discretion[8].

The judge should direct the jury on the legal meaning of the crime with which the accused is charged.

If inadmissible evidence has, through inadvertence, been heard by the jury, the judge should direct them to ignore it, although the omission of such a direction may not be fatal to a conviction[9].

If an accused gives evidence which is consistent with innocence, the jury should be told that, if they believe him or his evidence causes them to have a reasonable doubt, they must acquit. However, it may be sufficient if the jury is told that they must acquit if *any* evidence raises a reasonable doubt in their minds[10]. If an accused gives evidence in support of a special defence, the jury *must* be directed that, if they believe the accused, they must acquit[11].

In so far as a judge deals with the facts of the case, he must ensure that he does so accurately. A factual error in a charge may result in the conviction being quashed on appeal, notwithstanding that the judge has told the jury that it is *their* recollection of the evidence and not his which counts[12].

If there is more than one charge in the indictment, the judge must direct the jury that they should consider each charge separately and reach a verdict in respect of it. If there is more than one accused, the jury must be directed to consider the case against each accused separately.

---

1 *Shewan v HMA* 1989 SCCR 364.
2 See above at pp 51–52.
3 See also *McKenzie v HMA* 1959 JC 32 at 37, 1960 SLT 41 at 42, per Lord Justice-Clerk Thomson and *MacDonald v HMA* 1995 SCCR 663 at 671C, 1996 SLT 723 at 728C, per Lord Justice-Clerk Ross.
4 *Wilson v HMA* (1976) SCCR Supp 126; *Douglas v HMA* 1990 SCCR 188, 1990 SLT 781.
5 *McIntyre v HMA* 1981 SCCR 117.
6 *Dorrens v HMA* 1983 SCCR 407.
7 *McAvoy v HMA* 1991 JC 16, 1991 SCCR 123, 1992 SLT 46.
8 *Chalmers v HMA* 1994 SCCR 651.
9 *Jones v HMA* 1981 SCCR 192.
10 *Dunn v HMA* 1986 SCCR 340, 1987 SLT 295; *Mackie v HMA* 1990 SCCR 716; *Hughes v HMA* 1997 SCCR 277. See also *Harrison v HMA* 1993 SCCR 1087, which contains useful observations on what a judge should say to a jury in this context.
11 *Dunn v HMA* 1986 SCCR 340. See also *King v HMA* 1985 SCCR 322.
12 *Larkin v HMA* 1988 SCCR 30.

The judge should normally tell the jury of any alternative verdict of guilty which is open to them (eg reset in a case of theft)[1]. However, he should probably not mention an alternative verdict unless the matter has been raised by either the Crown or the defence[2].

The judge should take care not to make remarks in his charge which are prejudicial to the defence[3].

If the judge reaches the conclusion that there is insufficient evidence in law to support a finding of guilt on any charge, he must direct the jury to acquit the accused of that charge, even though the defence has not made a submission of no case to answer. Similarly, if there are any parts of a charge for which, in the opinion of the judge, there is insufficient evidence, he must direct the jury to delete these parts of the charge from any verdict of guilty which they may return.

The jury should be directed that it is not open to them to find an accused guilty of two separate statutory charges on the same evidence[4]. The reason for such a direction should be explained to the jury[5].

The jury should be told that there are three verdicts open to them: guilty, not guilty and not proven. The High Court has on several recent occasions remarked on the undesirability of attempting to explain to a jury the difference between not guilty and not proven as verdicts of acquittal[6]. This is quite astonishing. It displays an extraordinary lack of willingness on the part of the High Court to grasp the nettle of the inherent illogicality of two separate verdicts of acquittal in a legal system where the accused is presumed innocent until proved guilty[7].

The judge should direct the jury that they may reach a verdict either unanimously or by a majority, but that, if their verdict on any charge is to be guilty, there must be at least eight of them in favour of that verdict[8], and that this is so even if their number is reduced below fifteen[9]. It is inappropriate to direct a jury that they should spend a reasonable time trying to reach a unanimous verdict as there is no obligation on them to reach such a verdict[10]. It is apparently acceptable for a juror to abstain from voting[11], but it is submitted that it would not be appropriate to direct a jury to this effect.

Although it is not essential, it is good practice for a judge to tell a jury that they should elect one of their number as foreman or chancellor, to use the old Scottish (and perhaps more politically correct!) term. The foreman will act as chairman while the jury discuss their verdict, and will also give the verdict to the clerk when they return to court.

---

1 *Steele v HMA* 1992 SCCR 30.
2 *Allan v HMA* 1995 SCCR 234; *Hobbins v HMA* 1996 SCCR 637.
3 As in *Cooney v HMA* 1987 SCCR 60, where the sheriff made derogatory remarks about defence witnesses. The conviction was quashed. See also *McArthur v HMA* 1989 SCCR 646, 1990 SLT 451, and *Crowe v HMA* 1989 SCCR 681.
4 *Kyle v HMA* 1987 SCCR 116, 1988 SLT 601; *Fraser v HMA* 1994 SCCR 334.
5 *Erskine v HMA* 1994 SCCR 345.
6 *Affleck v HMA* 1987 SCCR 150; *Macdonald v HMA* 1989 SCCR 29, 1989 SLT 298; *Fay v HMA* 1989 SCCR 373, 1989 SLT 758; *Kerr v HMA* 1992 SCCR 281, 1992 SLT 1031; *MacDonald v HMA* 1995 SCCR 663, 1996 SLT 723. But see also *McNicol v HMA* 1964 JC 25, 1964 SLT 151; *Larkin v HMA* 1993 SCCR 715.
7 See the critical comments by Sheriff G H Gordon, editor of SCCR, at 1989 SCCR 378 and 1992 SCCR 289.
8 *Affleck v HMA* 1987 SCCR 150; *Glen v HMA* 1988 SCCR 37, 1988 SLT 369; *Allison v HMA* 1994 SCCR 464, 1995 SLT 24.
9 1995 Act, s 90(2).
10 *Crowe v HMA* 1989 SCCR 681, 1990 SLT 670.
11 *Allison v HMA* 1994 SCCR 464, 1995 SLT 24.

It used to be not uncommon for a judge, at the end of his charge, to ask the prosecutor and the defence lawyer whether they wished any further direction[1]. This practice was criticised by the High Court as undesirable[2] and has now largely been departed from. However, it is suggested that it is quite acceptable, indeed desirable, for either the prosecutor or the defence lawyer to draw the judge's attention to any obvious omission or error in his charge, provided that that is done with reasonable tact.

## SECLUSION OF THE JURY

It is generally undesirable to send a jury out to consider their verdict late on in the day, but the matter is essentially one for the discretion of the presiding judge[3]. When the jury retire, they are enclosed in a room by the clerk of court[4], and communication with them is excluded except in certain limited circumstances until they have reached their verdict[5]. Communication with the jury is confined to contact between them and the judge (or someone acting on his behalf, who would usually be the clerk of court) for certain specified purposes[5].

The judge may communicate with the jury for the purpose of giving them a further direction[6]. If the jury are to be given such a direction, they must be brought back into court. The clerk may not simply go to the jury room and give them the appropriate direction, even if he is acting on the judge's instructions[7]. This is because the whole trial must take place in the presence of the accused[8].

No juror may leave the jury room after the jury has been enclosed, other than to receive or seek a further direction from the judge, or to make a request about a matter relevant to the case or about certain other matters relating to the welfare of the jury[9]. An example of a matter relevant to the case would be a request to see one of the productions. Whether or not the jury should be allowed to see a production is a matter for the judge, whose discretion must be exercised in the interests of justice[10]. The judge should seek the views of parties on the matter[11].

The jury may be provided with food and drink while enclosed[12]. They may send and receive (through the medium of the judge or someone authorised by him) personal messages unconnected with the case[13]. They may be provided with medical treatment or other assistance which is immediately required by them[14]. A juror is

1 See eg *Alexander v HMA* 1988 SCCR 542, 1989 SLT 193 (a High Court judge); *Ralston v HMA* 1988 SCCR 590, 1989 SLT 474 (although the part of the charge concerned is not there reproduced) (a sheriff).
2 *Thomson v HMA* 1988 SCCR 534, 1989 SLT 170.
3 *Sinclair v HMA* 1991 SCCR 520, 1992 SLT 1093 (jury sent out at 3.50 pm and returning verdict at 6.09 pm).
4 1995 Act, s 99(1).
5 1995 Act, s 99(2).
6 1995 Act, s 99(3)(a).
7 *Cunningham v HMA* 1984 JC 37, 1984 SCCR 40, 1984 SLT 249; *McColl v HMA* 1989 SCCR 229, 1989 SLT 691.
8 1995 Act, s 92(1).
9 1995 Act, s 99(2)(b).
10 See eg *McMurdo v HMA* 1987 SCCR 343, 1988 SLT 234; *Bertram v HMA* 1990 SCCR 394.
11 *Martin v HMA* 1989 SCCR 546.
12 1995 Act, s 99(4)(a).
13 1995 Act, s 99(4)(c).
14 1995 Act, s 99(4)(d).

entitled to make a request to the judge with regard to any of these matters[1], and the judge may give the appropriate instruction[2].

A jury may be accommodated overnight if necessary, and the judge may give directions for their seclusion in such accommodation[3] (which is usually a hotel). Whether or not to arrange for the jury to be accommodated overnight is a matter for the judge's discretion. He should ask the jury whether they are likely to reach a verdict within a reasonable time, after having explained that no pressure is being put upon them to reach a verdict speedily, and that the interests of justice require that they should be given as much time as they need to decide on their verdict[4]. If the jury are accommodated overnight the judge should tell them not to discuss the case while they are outwith the jury room. If no accommodation is available the jury has to continue to deliberate until they have reached a verdict; they must not be allowed to go home for the night once they have retired to consider their verdict[5].

If the prosecutor or any other person enters the jury room while the jury is enclosed, or communicates with them in any way other than one of those authorised by the provisions discussed above, the accused must be acquitted[6].

The jury indicate that they have reached a verdict by ringing a bell or giving some other signal which is audible outside the jury room.

A juror must not give and should not be asked for information about anything which occurred while the jury was enclosed[7]. Any disobedience to this rule, whether by a juror or anyone else, is a contempt of court[7] which is punishable by imprisonment for a maximum period of two years or a fine or both[8].


# VERDICT


A jury may give their verdict without retiring[9], but in practice they usually retire to deliberate unless the verdict is a formal one directed by the judge.

When the jury return to court having indicated that they have reached a verdict, the clerk will ask: 'Who speaks for you?' or words to that effect. The foreman of the jury will identify himself or herself and will be asked by the clerk to stand up. The clerk will then ask the foreman whether the jury have reached a verdict. On receiving an affirmative answer, he will ask the foreman what the verdict is, separately in respect of each charge against each accused[10], and in each case whether the verdict is unanimous or by a majority[11].

If the verdict is guilty by a majority, it is competent for the judge to inquire what the majority is, and the opinion has been expressed by the High Court that, when

1  1995 Act, s 99(2)(b)(i).
2  1995 Act, s 99(4).
3  1995 Act, s 99(4)(b).
4  *McKenzie v HMA* 1986 SCCR 94, 1986 SLT 389; *Sinclair v HMA* 1996 SCCR 221, 1996 SLT 1127.
5  *Thomson v HMA* 1997 SCCR 121.
6  1995 Act, s 99(5).
7  Contempt of Court Act 1981, s 8(1).
8  Contempt of Court Act 1981, s 15(2).
9  1995 Act, s 100(3).
10  1995 Act, s 100(1). The subsection provides for the possibility of a written rather than an oral verdict, but the former is, in modern practice, virtually unknown.
11  1995 Act, s 100(2). For the difficulties which may arise in the case of a majority verdict see *Docherty v HMA* 1997 SCCR 345.

there is a majority verdict of guilty, the jury ought to be asked how many of them voted for guilty[1]. This opinion has, however, since been disapproved[2]. The view has been expressed that if there are less than eight votes for guilty but no majority for a finding of not guilty among those voting for acquittal, the proper course is to record the verdict as not proven[3]. It will, however, be only in a rare case that voting figures will be made known.

A verdict must be consistent with the indictment. A jury may delete certain parts of a charge and return a verdict of guilty to the remainder, provided that what is left is still a crime[4]. A jury may not, however, amend a charge. Thus, where an indictment charged an accused with assault by 'pulling' a quantity of hair and skin tissue from a woman's head, a verdict of guilty of assault by 'removing' the hair and skin tissue was held to be incompetent, as it proceeded upon an assumption that an instrument had been used, and that was not charged[5]. However, it is competent for a jury to substitute 'a sum of money' for a specific sum, or to reduce quantities of articles. Both are considered to amount to deletions of part of the charge.

A jury must not return a verdict of guilty to two separate statutory charges on exactly the same evidence[6].

By statute certain alternative verdicts are open to a jury, and they should, where appropriate, be directed about any such alternative in the course of the judge's charge. The more important alternatives[7] are:

(1)  On a charge of robbery, theft, embezzlement or fraud the accused may be convicted of reset[8];
(2)  On a charge of robbery, embezzlement or fraud the accused may be convicted of theft[9];
(3)  On a charge of theft an accused may be convicted of embezzlement or fraud[10];
(4)  On a charge of a completed crime the accused may be convicted of an attempt to commit that crime[11];
(5)  On a statutory charge the accused may be convicted of a common law crime, if the facts proved amount to the common law crime but not to the statutory charge[12], provided, of course, that the facts libelled in the charge are capable of amounting to a common law crime;
(6)  On a charge of rape an accused may be convicted of indecent assault or of various statutory sexual offences[13].

When the foreman of the jury has announced their verdict, the clerk of court records it. This may take some time, if the indictment is lengthy and there are

1   *McCadden v HMA* 1985 JC 98, 1985 SCCR 282, 1986 SLT 138.
2   *Pullar v HMA* 1993 JC 126, 1993 SCCR 514.
3   *Kerr v HMA* 1992 SCCR 281, 1992 SLT 1031.
4   1995 Act, s 64(6), Sch 3, para 9(2), (3); *Sayers v HMA* 1982 JC 17, 1981 SCCR 312, 1982 SLT 220.
5   *Blair v HMA* 1989 SCCR 79, 1989 SLT 459.
6   *Kyle v HMA* 1987 SCCR 116, 1988 SLT 601; *Fraser v HMA* 1994 SCCR 334.
7   For a comprehensive list see *Renton and Brown* paras 8–79 to 8–84.
8   1995 Act, s 64(6), Sch 3, para 8(2).
9   1995 Act, s 64(6), Sch 3, para 8(3).
10  1995 Act, s 64(6), Sch 3, para 8(4).
11  1995 Act, s 64(6), Sch 3, para 10(1).
12  1995 Act, s 64(6), Sch 3, para 14. This provision has resulted in the rather extraordinary consequence that a person accused of dangerous, or alternatively careless, driving in terms of ss 2 or 3 of the Road Traffic Act 1988, was convicted of a breach of the peace: *Horsburgh v Russell* 1994 SCCR 237, 1994 SLT 942.
13  Criminal Law (Consolidation) (Scotland) Act 1995, s 14.

several accused. The jury may be given a meal while their verdict is being recorded[1]. When the verdict has been recorded, the clerk reads it out, and the jury are asked to confirm that that is a 'true record of your verdict'.

If a jury return a verdict which is apparently incompetent, the judge should, before it is recorded, draw the attention of the jury to the defect in the verdict and invite them to reconsider it[2].

After the jury's verdict has been recorded, if it is a verdict of acquittal, the accused is discharged and is free to leave the dock.

Once the verdict has been recorded, the jury may be discharged, although it is common practice to postpone this until after the accused has been sentenced or the case has been adjourned for reports. If there are other cases to be tried at the sitting, the jurors may be told to return later to be available to be balloted for a further trial. When discharging a jury the judge usually thanks them for their services and may tell them where to go in order to claim any expenses to which they are entitled. If the trial has been exceptionally long or difficult, the judge may excuse the jurors from jury service for a specific period or even for life[3]. In any event a person who has attended for jury service (even if not selected to sit on a jury) has a right to be excused jury service for a period of five years[4].

## SENTENCE

If an accused is found guilty, the prosecutor moves for sentence.

> 'Even when a verdict of guilt has been returned and recorded, it still lies with the Lord Advocate whether to move the court to pronounce sentence, and without that motion no sentence can be pronounced or imposed'[5].

Thus, an accused was convicted of two charges in an indictment (murder and attempted murder), and the prosecutor moved for sentence on only the murder charge (as was then the practice if an accused were convicted of murder and another charge). The conviction on the murder charge was quashed on appeal. The accused went free as no sentence had been, or could be, passed on the remaining charge[6]. It is possible that the prosecutor may decide not to move for sentence at all. This might arise if an accused, who had been remanded in custody, were found guilty of only a minor charge. In such a situation the prosecutor might consider that he had already been sufficiently punished by having been remanded.

The exact words used by the prosecutor when moving for sentence are immaterial, provided that he makes it clear that he is inviting the court to pass sentence[7].

As the court must have regard to any period of time spent in custody on remand by an accused[8], it is proper for the prosecutor, when moving for sentence, to inform the judge of the date on which the accused was remanded and how long he

---

1  As in *Sayers v HMA* 1981 SCCR 312 (also reported on other matters in 1982 JC 17 and 1982 SLT 220).
2  *McGeary v HMA* 1991 JC 54, 1991 SCCR 203. See also *Ainsworth v HMA* 1996 SCCR 631.
3  Law Reform (Miscellaneous Provisions) (Scotland) Act 1980, Sch 1, Pt III.
4  Ibid.
5  *Boyle v HMA* 1976 JC 32 at 37, 1976 SLT 126 at 129, per Lord Cameron.
6  *Paterson v HMA* 1974 JC 35.
7  *Noon v HMA* 1960 JC 52, 1960 SLT (Notes) 51.
8  1995 Act, s 210(1).

has spent in custody. The prosecutor should, it is suggested, be in a position to inform the judge what is the maximum penalty for any statutory offence of which the accused has been convicted. This is both a courtesy and a help to the judge, and it is unfortunate that it is a practice which appears to have fallen into desuetude.

After the prosecutor has moved for sentence and produced any notice of previous convictions[1], counsel or the solicitor for the accused, or the accused himself if he is unrepresented, may address the court in mitigation of sentence. If the accused has pleaded not guilty and gone to trial, it is usual, and advisable, that the plea in mitigation should not refer to the facts of the crime. The personal circumstances of the accused should be given to the court. The accused's representative should, so far as possible, obtain independent confirmation of such matters as employment. Most courts are, without such confirmation, somewhat sceptical about the job due to start next Monday, not to mention the pregnant 'fiancée' or the ailing mother. Evidence in mitigation is competent, although not frequently led. There has in recent years grown up a practice in some sheriff courts of the sheriff being asked to read a letter from the accused himself. Although the judge is always entitled to have regard to such a letter, it is suggested that this is a practice which should not be followed. The accused's advocate is there to speak for him, and he can usually say much more effectively than the accused himself what requires to be said.

The prosecutor is entitled, indeed has a duty, to inform the court if the Crown disputes any of the information given in a plea in mitigation or considers it to be irrelevant[2].

Before passing sentence the judge may wish to order reports[3] or to obtain some other further information to enable him to decide on the appropriate sentence. He may adjourn the case for that purpose[4]. The accused may be remanded in custody, may be released on bail or may simply be ordained to appear[5]. An accused who is remanded in custody may appeal against the refusal of bail within 24 hours of being remanded[6]. If the accused is remanded in custody the adjournment must be for no longer than three weeks[7]. If, in error, the accused is remanded in custody for longer than three weeks, the instance of the case does not fall, and the Crown may appeal by advocation[8], asking the High Court to remit the case to the sheriff so that he may adjourn it to a date within the three-week period[9]. If the accused is granted bail or ordained to appear the adjournment should not exceed four weeks or, on cause shown, eight weeks[10]. The non-availability of a judge during the four-week period is sufficient 'cause' for extending the period to eight weeks[11]. The 'cause' need not be minuted but should be stated in open court[11]. An adjournment to allow evidence to be led in mitigation is covered by these time limits[12]. An

---

1   1995 Act, s 101(3). See above at p 122.
2   *HMA v Bennett* 1996 SCCR 331, 1996 SLT 662.
3   In the High Court a social enquiry report is normally prepared prior to the trial in any case where such a report is likely to be required before a custodial sentence may competently be imposed (see below at pp 223–224). In the sheriff court such a pre-trial report is never provided. Even in the High Court the judge may decide that a fuller report than that already prepared is necessary.
4   1995 Act, s 201(1).
5   1995 Act, s 201(2).
6   1995 Act, s 201(4).
7   1995 Act, s 201(3)(a).
8   See below at pp 291–292.
9   *Connolly v Normand, Normand v Connolly* 1996 SLT 1336.
10  1995 Act, s 201(3)(b).
11  *Hunter v Carmichael* 1995 SCCR 453, 1995 SLT 449.
12  *McCulloch v Scott* 1993 JC 31, 1993 SCCR 41, 1993 SLT 901.

adjournment to enable a case to be dealt with by a particular sheriff is probably not restricted by the time limits[1], nor is an adjournment to await the outcome of proceedings in another court[2], or an adjournment to have a hearing on objections to a list of previous convictions[3].

The court may also remand an accused for an inquiry into his physical or mental condition[4]. The remand may be in custody, or the accused may be placed on bail with a condition of attending for medical examination or residing in a particular institution[5]. Again there is a right of appeal against refusal of bail[6].

The accused must be present when sentence is passed[7], and the sentence must be pronounced in open court[8]. As has already been noted[9], a sheriff may remit an accused to the High Court for sentence if he considers that his powers are inadequate (ie that the sentence should be longer than three years' imprisonment)[10]. If two accused appear on the same indictment, and the sheriff considers that his powers of punishment are inadequate for the one but not for the other, he should nevertheless remit both in order that both may be sentenced by the same judge[11].

The subject of sentencing will be examined in detail in chapter 7.

1 *Normand v Humphrey* 1993 SCCR 140 (Sh Ct).
2 *Johnstone v Lees* 1993 SCCR 1050, 1994 SLT 551.
3 *Burns v Lees* 1994 SCCR 780.
4 1995 Act, s 200(1), (2).
5 1995 Act, s 200(6).
6 1995 Act, s 200(9).
7 *Hume* II 470; Alison *Practice* p 653; *Macdonald* p 349.
8 1995 Act, s 198(1).
9 See above at p 100.
10 1995 Act, s 195. The maximum sentence will be five years if the 1997 Act, s 13 comes into force. See the Appendix at p 318 below.
11 *HMA v Duffy* 1974 SLT (Notes) 46.

CHAPTER 6

# SUMMARY PROCEDURE

## INTRODUCTION

Summary procedure is the name given to the form of criminal procedure in which an accused, if he goes to trial, is tried by a judge or judges without a jury. The case of *Nicol Jarvie* described in chapter 2 is an example of summary procedure in the sheriff court. The two courts of summary jurisdiction are the sheriff court and the district court. The procedure is essentially the same in both courts. Many of the provisions of the 1995 Act are common to both summary and solemn procedure, but Part IX of the Act is concerned exclusively with summary proceedings.

In this chapter we shall examine the progress of a summary case from the time when the police make a report to the procurator fiscal to the conclusion of the trial. First, however, it is appropriate to discuss the composition, jurisdiction and powers of the courts of summary jurisdiction.

## THE SHERIFF COURT

The organisation, composition and territorial jurisdiction of the sheriff court in relation to solemn procedure were described in chapter 4[1]. What was said there applies equally to summary procedure.

Any common law crime may be prosecuted summarily in the sheriff court apart from those crimes for which the High Court has exclusive jurisdiction[2]. The crimes of uttering a forged document, wilful fire-raising, robbery, and assault with intent to rob, which were formerly triable only on indictment, may now be prosecuted summarily in the sheriff court[3]. Any statutory offence may be tried summarily in the sheriff court unless the statute specifically provides that it may be tried only on indictment[4].

The maximum power of sentence of a sheriff under summary procedure is usually what governs whether a case is brought summarily or on petition. The sheriff's powers (unless extended by statute) are: (a) to impose a fine not exceeding the prescribed sum[5] (£5,000 at the date of writing[6]); (b) to order the accused to find cau-

---

1 See above at pp 99, 100.
2 These are murder, treason, rape and breach of duty of magistrates: 1995 Act, s 3(6).
3 1995 Act, s 5(4).
4 For the mode of trial of statutory offences generally see the 1995 Act, s 292 and Sch 10.
5 1995 Act, s 5(2)(a).
6 1995 Act, s 225(8). In terms of s 225(4) the 'prescribed sum' may be altered by an order made by the Secretary of State.

tion (ie a sum of money as a guarantee) not exceeding the prescribed sum for his good behaviour for a period not exceeding twelve months[1]; (c) to impose a sentence of imprisonment in the event of the accused failing to pay a fine or find caution[2]; and (d) to impose a sentence of imprisonment of not more than three months[3]. The maximum period of imprisonment is extended to six months where a person is convicted of '(a) a second or subsequent offence inferring dishonest appropriation of property, or attempt thereat, or (b) a second or subsequent offence inferring personal violence'[4]. To bring into effect the increased power of sentence the accused must have been *convicted* of the previous offence prior to the commission of the later offence: it is not the date of commission of the previous offence which is to be looked at[5]. Of course, the sheriff also has power to pass many other forms of sentence, as will be discussed in the next chapter.

## THE DISTRICT COURT

District courts were established by the District Courts (Scotland) Act 1975 to replace the burgh courts, justice of the peace courts and various other courts of summary jurisdiction. The constitution, jurisdiction and powers of the district court are now mainly governed by the 1995 Act although certain provisions of the 1975 Act are still in force. The area of each local authority under the Local Government etc (Scotland) Act 1994 is a 'commission area'[6], and in each commission area there is a district court[7]. It is for the local authority to determine where and when the district court sits[7].

The judges of the district court are the justices of the peace for the relevant commission area or a stipendiary magistrate[8]. Justices of the peace are appointed by the Secretary of State[9]. A court may consist of one or more justices[10]. A stipendiary magistrate may be appointed by the local authority for the commission area[11]. He must be an advocate or solicitor of at least five years' standing[12]. At the time of writing the City of Glasgow is the only commission area with stipendiary magistrates.

A clerk of court must be appointed by the local authority. He must be an advocate or solicitor and acts as legal assessor as well as clerk[13].

---

1  1995 Act, s 5(2)(b).
2  1995 Act, s 5(2)(c). The maximum period of imprisonment which may be imposed as an alternative in respect of various sums is provided in s 219(2).
3  1995 Act, s 5(2)(d). This will be increased to six months if the 1997 Act, s 13 comes into force. See the Appendix at p 318 below.
4  1995 Act, s 5(3). This will be increased to twelve months if the 1997 Act, s 13 comes into force. See the Appendix at p 318 below. Attempting to pervert the course of justice by making threats of personal violence does not fall within the scope of the subsection: *Hemphill v Donnelly* 1992 SCCR 770. Nor does being in possession of an offensive weapon or reckless discharge of a firearm: *Sharp v Tudhope* 1986 SCCR 64.
5  *Sim v Lockhart* 1994 SCCR 243, 1994 SLT 1063.
6  1995 Act, s 6(6).
7  1995 Act, s 6(1).
8  1995 Act, s 6(2).
9  1995 Act, s 6(6) read in conjunction with the District Courts (Scotland) Act 1975, s 9.
10  1995 Act, s 6(6).
11  District Courts (Scotland) Act 1975, s 5(1).
12  District Courts (Scotland) Act 1975, s 5(2).
13  District Courts (Scotland) Act 1975, s 7(1).

The territorial jurisdiction of a district court is confined to its commission area[1], subject to a provision similar to section 9(4) of the 1995 Act to cover offences committed in several different commission areas[2]. Section 11(4) of the 1995 Act (thefts committed outside Scotland) applies to the district court as well as to the sheriff court[3]. A warrant granted by a district court may be executed anywhere in Scotland[4].

The type of common law crime which may competently be prosecuted in a district court consisting of justices is defined in a negative way, the relevant section of the 1995 Act[5] specifying crimes which may not be tried in such a court. The excluded crimes are: murder; culpable homicide; robbery; rape; wilful fire-raising or attempt thereat; theft by housebreaking; housebreaking with intent to steal; theft, reset, fraud, or embezzlement where the amount involved exceeds £2,500[6]; assault involving fracture of a limb; assault with intent to rape; assault to the danger of life; assault by stabbing; uttering forged documents; uttering forged banknotes; and offences under the Acts relating to coinage. If one of the excluded crimes comes before a district court, it should be remitted to the sheriff court[7]. The district court may also remit a case which *is* within its competence, if it considers that, 'in view of the circumstances of the case', it should be dealt with by the sheriff[8].

Any statutory offence triable summarily may be tried in a district court unless the statute provides otherwise[9]. The main category of exceptions is road traffic offences. In that regard a district court may try any offence for which a fixed penalty may be imposed and any other offence in respect of which a conditional offer may be sent[10]. Apart from that, a district court may not try any offence involving obligatory endorsement of a driving licence[11]. A district court may disqualify from driving under the 'totting up' procedure only[12].

The maximum powers of punishment of a district court consisting of justices (unless extended by statute) are: (a) to impose a sentence of imprisonment not exceeding 60 days[13]; (b) to impose a fine not exceeding level 4 on the standard scale (£2,500 at the date of writing)[14]; (c) to ordain the accused to find caution of an amount not exceeding level 4 on the standard scale for his good behaviour for a period not exceeding six months[15]; (d) to impose a sentence of imprisonment in the event of the accused failing to pay a fine or find caution[16].

It must be emphasised that the foregoing limitations on jurisdiction and powers apply only to courts consisting of justices. If a district court consists of a stipendiary

1   1995 Act, s 7(8)(a).
2   1995 Act, s 7(2). See the comments on s 9(4) at p 100 above.
3   See the comments on s 11 at pp 98–99 above.
4   1995 Act, s 297.
5   1995 Act, s 7(8).
6   The sum is described as level 4 on the standard scale (which is contained in s 225(2) of the 1995 Act). At the time of writing level 4 is £2,500.
7   1995 Act, s 7(9)(a), (10). Section 7(9) does not actually specify the sheriff court, referring only to 'a higher court', but the sheriff court is the only other court of summary jurisdiction.
8   1995 Act, s 7(9)(b), (10).
9   1995 Act, s 7(3).
10  Road Traffic Offenders Act 1988, s 10(1).
11  Road Traffic Offenders Act 1988, s 10(2).
12  Road Traffic Offenders Act 1988, s 35(6).
13  1995 Act, s 7(6)(a).
14  1995 Act, s 7(6)(b).
15  1995 Act, s 7(6)(c).
16  1995 Act, s 7(6)(d).

magistrate, it has the same jurisdiction and powers as a sheriff court sitting summarily[1]. If an accused pleads guilty before a lay justice, his case is adjourned for sentence and he then appears before a stipendiary magistrate, it is competent for the magistrate to impose a sentence exceeding 60 days' imprisonment[2].

## REPORT OF CRIME TO THE PROCURATOR FISCAL

The procurator fiscal is the prosecutor in both the sheriff court and the district court[3]. The great majority of cases which are to proceed in either of these courts are reported by the police to the fiscal. Other agencies[4] may also make reports to the fiscal but these form only a very small proportion of the total. The report may relate to an accused who has been arrested and detained in custody, or to one who has been arrested and released on an undertaking or on honour to attend a specified court[5]. Rather exceptionally it may relate to a case where, for some reason, the accused has not been in custody but will require to be arrested on a so-called 'initiating warrant' following preparation of a complaint[6]. However, by far the great majority of summary cases are those in which the accused has simply been told by the police that the circumstances of the alleged offence will be reported to the fiscal, and that, if proceedings are taken, the accused will be cited to attend court. A case which has started out on petition may be reduced to summary level and thereafter proceeds as a normal summary complaint[7]. The twelve-month time bar, which applies to solemn cases[8], does not affect such a case[9].

The police report as initially sent to the fiscal contains only a summary of the case against the accused and a draft charge or charges, together with a note of the accused's criminal record, if any. On the basis of this information the fiscal who receives the report must decide whether to prosecute the accused, and, if so, in which court to do so.

The fiscal may decide to offer the offender an opportunity to pay a fixed penalty[10]. Such an offer may be made in respect of any offence which could be tried in the district court with the exception of certain road traffic offences for which there are separate statutory provisions for fixed penalties[11]. In some courts it is not uncommon for a defence solicitor to approach the procurator fiscal on behalf of a client who has been charged by the police, suggesting the possibility of the case being disposed of by a fixed penalty. If the offender pays a fixed penalty no proceedings against him are competent[12], and there, is of course, no conviction recorded against him. Payment of a fixed penalty is enforced in the same way as

---

1  1995 Act, s 7(5).
2  *Main v Normand* 1996 SCCR 256; *Graham v Normand* 1996 SCCR 371, 1997 SLT 686.
3  1995 Act, s 6(3).
4  Eg SSPCA, Vehicles Inspectorate, Benefits Agency.
5  1995 Act, s 22(1). See above at p 89.
6  1995 Act, s 139(1)(b) provides for the granting of an initiating warrant. See above at p 87.
7  1995 Act, s 6(3).
8  1995 Act, s 65(1). See above at pp 117–118.
9  A decision of the High Court to the contrary in *Gardner v Lees* 1996 SCCR, 1996 SLT 342 was negatived by the Criminal Procedure and Investigations Act 1996, s 73, which introduced an amended s 65(1) to the 1995 Act.
10  1995 Act, s 302(1).
11  1995 Act, s 302(9)(a).
12  1995 Act, s 302(6).

payment of a fine except that imprisonment in default is replaced by recovery by civil diligence[1].

The decision whether or not to prosecute depends on a number of factors. The most important is likely to be the sufficiency of the evidence, but a decision may be taken that it would not be in the public interest to launch a prosecution because of the particular circumstances of the case. If an offence is triable in the district court, the decision whether to bring it there or in the sheriff court may depend on how serious an example of that type of offence it is and on the accused's criminal record.

Having taken a decision to prosecute, the fiscal prepares a complaint.


## THE COMPLAINT

The complaint is the document which contains the charge(s) against the accused under summary procedure. The form of complaint is standard[2]. The heading specifies the court in which the case is being brought. The complaint continues: 'The complaint of the Procurator Fiscal against ...'. The accused is then named and his address stated (and/or the fact that he is in custody). His date of birth is also usually stated. The next part of the complaint is the actual charge: 'The charge against you is ...'. Styles for most common law crimes and many (some rather out of date) statutory offences are given in Schedule 5 to the 1995 Act. A common law charge should be as nearly as may be in the form shown in the Schedule, and no further specification is required[3].

The complaint is signed by the procurator fiscal or one of his deputes[4]. An unsigned complaint is a nullity[5]. However, a complaint signed only on the first of two pages may proceed on the charges appearing on the first page[6]. If the principal complaint is lost, the case may proceed on a certified copy[7].

The provisions of Schedule 3 to the 1995 Act apply to complaints as well as to indictments[8], and the comments made thereanent in the previous chapter should be referred to[9]. In the case of statutory offences the Schedule provides specifically for complaints that

> 'the statement that an act was done contrary to an enactment shall imply a statement –
> (i)   that the enactment applied to the circumstances existing at the time and place of the offence;
> (ii)  that the accused was a person bound to observe the enactment;
> (iii) that any necessary preliminary procedure had been gone through; and
> (iv)  that all the circumstances necessary to a contravention existed.'[10]

1  1995 Act, s 303.
2  1995 Act, s 138(2); 1996 Rules, r 16.1(1); Form 16.1A. See the complaint in the case of *Nicol Jarvie* (at p 64 above).
3  1995 Act, s 138(2). See also *Anderson v Allan* 1985 SCCR 399. This case makes no reference to the principle of giving an accused fair notice. See the commentary by Sheriff G H Gordon (editor of SCCR) at 1985 SCCR 401. Contrast the position in the case of a statutory charge: see note 3 below at p 193.
4  1995 Act, s 138(1).
5  *Lowe v Bee* 1989 SCCR 476 (Sh Ct).
6  *Milne v Normand* 1993 SCCR 1058, 1994 SLT 760.
7  1995 Act, s 157(1).
8  1995 Act, s 138(4).
9  See above at pp 113–115.
10 1995 Act, ss 64(6), 138(4), Sch 3, para 12(a). These provisions apply only to the form of complaint and do not affect the onus of proof: *Donaldson v Valentine* 1996 SCCR 374, 1996 SLT 643.

The Schedule also provides that if the offence is alleged to be a contravention of subordinate legislation, it is implied that the statutory instrument concerned was duly made, confirmed, published and generally made effectual and was in force at the relevant time[1]. It further provides that

'where the offence is created by more than one section of one or more statutes or orders, it shall be necessary to specify only the leading section or one of the leading sections'[2].

Despite these provisions it is well established that an accused is entitled to fair notice of the case against him[3].

## CITATION

If an accused is in custody or attends as an 'undertaker' or on honour[4], he is served with the complaint and , if appropriate, a notice of previous convictions[5] by being handed them by a police officer[6]. However, the great majority of accused are cited to attend, and it is therefore appropriate to examine now the process of citation.

The court does not require to grant a warrant to cite. The 1995 Act is itself sufficient warrant[7]. The 1996 Rules provide for various forms to be used in connection with citation: the citation itself[8]; the form of notice of previous convictions[9]; the form of reply which an accused may use to plead to the complaint in writing rather than attending court[10]; and the means form in which an accused may provide information about his financial position, which will enable the court to fix an appropriate fine[11].

The 'form of citation' provides for a statement of the date and time when the case is to be heard[12] and the court in which the accused is to appear. It also contains advice about how to respond to the citation, indicating three possible ways: (1) to attend court personally; (2) to arrange for a lawyer or some other person to attend; (3) to write to the court, using the reply form and envelope provided. The form warns an accused that failure to respond at all may result in a warrant being issued for his arrest. Information about the availability of legal aid is included in the material sent with the complaint.

The 'form of reply to complaint' provides spaces for the accused to indicate whether he is pleading guilty or not guilty. If he is pleading guilty, it gives him an opportunity to admit or deny any previous convictions of which he has been given

---

1 1995 Act, ss 64(6), 138(4), Sch 3, para 12(a). These provisions apply only to the form of complaint and do not affect the onus of proof: *Donaldson v Valentine* 1996 SCCR 374, 1996 SLT 643.
2 1995 Act, ss 64(6), 138(4), Sch 3, para 12(b).
3 See eg *Blair v Keane* 1981 JC 19, 1981 SLT (Notes) 4; *Carmichael v Marks & Spencer plc* 1995 SCCR 781, 1996 SLT 1167.
4 1995 Act, s 22(1)(a).
5 1995 Act, s 166(2).
6 Strictly speaking, service is not necessary. It is sufficient that the terms of the complaint are read out to the accused when he first appears in court: 1995 Act, s 144(1)(b). In practice, however, an accused is always served with a complaint.
7 1995 Act, s 140(1).
8 1996 Rules, r 16.1(2); Form 16.1B.
9 1996 Rules, r 16.1(4); Form 16.1E.
10 1996 Rules, r 16.1(3)(a); Form 16.1C.
11 1996 Rules, r 16.1(3)(b); Form 16.1D.
12 The omission of the date of appearance makes the citation invalid: *Beattie v McKinnon* 1977 JC 64.

notice, although, if he does not expressly deny a conviction, he is deemed to have admitted it[1]. It provides a space for him to give any explanation which he may wish about the case. The form should be signed by the accused. Although the form is relatively simply set out and should be easy to understand, it is remarkable how often it is wrongly or misleadingly completed.

The means form emphasises that there is no obligation to provide the information requested. It contains spaces for details of the accused's income and expenditure to be stated together with details of his employment and dependants.

An accused must be cited at least 48 hours before he is due to appear in court[2].

There are various methods of citation, all of which may be effected by an officer of law[3]. An accused may be cited by having the citation delivered to him personally or left for him at his dwelling house or place of business with some person resident or employed there, or, where he has no known dwelling house or place of business, at any other place in which he may at the time be resident[4]. If the accused is employed on a vessel, the citation may be left with a person on board and connected with the vessel[5]. If the accused is a partnership, association or corporate body, the citation may be left at their ordinary place of business with a partner, director, secretary or other official, or they may be cited in the same way as if the proceedings were in a civil court[6]. If the accused is a body of trustees, the citation may be left with any one of them who is resident in Scotland or with their known solicitor in Scotland[7].

As an alternative to citation by an officer of law, the citation, signed by the prosecutor[8], may be sent by registered or recorded delivery post to the accused's dwelling house or place of business, or, if he has no known dwelling house or place of business, to any other place where he may at the time be resident[9]. If citation is by post, the provisions for trial in absence of a statutory offence[10] and granting a warrant for the accused's arrest on his failure to appear[11] do not apply, unless it is proved to the court that the accused actually received the citation or that the contents thereof came to his knowledge[12]. The accused's knowledge may be proved by production in court of any letter or other communication purporting to be written by him 'in such terms as to infer' (by which is surely meant 'in terms such as it may be inferred therefrom') that the contents of the citation came to his knowledge[13].

In the case of postal citation the period of notice (*induciae*) runs from 24 hours after the time of posting[14]. If the citation is actually received by the accused, it is the posting itself and not receipt by the accused which is the execution of citation[15]. However, if an attempted postal citation is returned by the post office marked 'not

1   1995 Act, s 166(4)(a).
2   1995 Act, s 140(2). The term *induciae* used in the section means a period of notice.
3   1995 Act, s 297(2). For the definition of 'officer of law' see s 307(1) discussed above at pp 120, 121.
4   1995 Act, s 141(1). See *Normand v Harkins* 1996 SCCR 355 (Sh Ct).
5   1995 Act, s 141(2)(a).
6   1995 Act, s 141(2)(b). For citation of a company in a civil court see I D Macphail *Sheriff Court Practice* (1988), ch 6, especially para 6–40.
7   1995 Act, s 141(2)(e).
8   1996 Rules, r 16.2(1).
9   1995 Act, s 141(3)(a).
10  1995 Act, s 150(5). See below at p 219 for trial in absence.
11  1995 Act, s 150(2).
12  1995 Act, s 140(4).
13  1995 Act, s 140(5).
14  1995 Act, s 141(6).
15  *Lockhart v Bradley* 1977 SLT 5.

known at this address', then there has been no valid execution of citation[1]. Postal citation is proved by production of a written execution signed by the person who signed the citation together with the relevant post office receipt[2].

## TIME LIMITS IN STATUTORY CASES

Some statutes provide for the commencement of proceedings within a certain time after the commission of the alleged offence[3], or after information sufficient to justify proceedings has come to the knowledge of the prosecutor or some other person[4]. In the latter case a certificate to the effect that the information has come to the prosecutor's knowledge within the relevant time may be typed on the complaint[5]. If there is no time limit imposed by the statute creating the offence for a statutory offence triable only summarily[6], a general time limit applies of six months after the date of the contravention concerned, or, in the case of a continuous contravention, within six months after the last date of such contravention[7]. In the case of a continuous contravention, if proceedings are commenced within six months after the last date, then the whole period of the offence may be included in the prosecution[7]. The prescriptive period is computed *de die in diem* and the day of the offence is excluded[8].

For the purpose of the six-month time limit proceedings are deemed to commence on the date when a warrant to apprehend 'or to cite an accused' is granted, provided that the warrant is executed without undue delay[9]. However, as has already been noted, a warrant to cite is unnecessary as the 1995 Act itself is sufficient warrant[10]. This provision has been interpreted as meaning the date when a diet is assigned (ie a date fixed when the case will call in court), to which the accused is then cited[11].

What constitutes 'undue delay' in executing a warrant is a question of fact, circumstances and degree, which is very much within the province of the court of

---

1 *Keily v Tudhope* 1986 SCCR 251, 1987 SLT 99.
2 1995 Act, s 141(7). Although this subsection refers to 'the form [of execution] prescribed by Act of Adjournal', there is at the time of writing no prescribed form.
3 See eg Firearms Act 1968, s 51(4) (four years); Misuse of Drugs Act 1971, s 25(5) (twelve months); Criminal Law (Consolidation) (Scotland) Act 1995, s 5(3) (unlawful sexual intercourse with girl aged over 13 but under 16) (one year).
4 See eg Road Traffic Offenders Act 1988, s 6 (six months from the date when evidence sufficient to warrant proceedings comes to the knowledge of the prosecutor); Social Security Act 1986, s 56(5)(a) (three months from the date on which evidence sufficient in the opinion of the Lord Advocate to justify proceedings comes to his knowledge, or twelve months from the commission of the offence, whichever is the later).
5 *Hampson v Carmichael* 1993 SCCR 1030, 1995 SLT 54. It may even be sufficient if the prosecutor submits a certificate of the appropriate date when the case first calls in court, although there is no authority on this point.
6 1995 Act s 292(1), (2) defines which offences are triable only summarily. Generally speaking an offence is triable only summarily if the only penalty provided by the statute is on summary conviction.
7 1995 Act, s 136(1).
8 *Lees v Lovell* 1992 JC 169, 1992 SCCR 557, 1992 SLT 967.
9 1995 Act, s 136(3). This provision has been held also to apply to a prosecution brought under a statute (Prevention of Corruption Act 1916, s 5(3)) which contains its own time limit: *Carmichael v Kennedy* 1991 JC 32, 1991 SCCR 145, 1992 SLT 583.
10 1995 Act, s 140(1).
11 Ie, under the 1995 Act, s 139(1)(a), which gives power to the court to assign a diet to which the accused may be cited.

first instance[1]. Much will depend on whether there has been any fault on the part of either the prosecutor or the accused. It has been held that a delay of only six days in citing an accused after the fixing of an assigned diet was 'undue' in the absence of any explanation by the Crown[2]. In another case, however, it was held that a similar delay of six days was *not* undue, the local practice with regard to citation having been followed[3]. At the other end of the scale a delay of fifteen months in executing a warrant to apprehend was held to be not undue where the delay was entirely due to the accused's own conduct[4]. Delay on the part of the sheriff clerk in issuing the warrant is not 'delay' within the meaning of the section as it does not imply fault on the part of the prosecutor[5]. It is not always necessary for the Crown to lead evidence to negative undue delay; an *ex parte* statement may suffice[6].

The period to be looked at in assessing whether there has been undue delay is the period between the grant of the warrant and its execution, and not the period between the end of the six months and the date of execution[7].

If a warrant to apprehend has been granted within the six months, and (as happens quite frequently) the accused attends court by arrangement without actually having been arrested, the requirement for execution without undue delay does not apply as there has been no execution of the warrant[8].

## UNDUE DELAY IN COMMENCING PROSECUTION

As is the case with proceedings on indictment undue delay in prosecuting a summary case may render proceedings incompetent if the result is substantial prejudice to the accused[9]. The principles are the same as for cases prosecuted under solemn procedure[10].

## WARRANT TO APPREHEND OR TO SEARCH

Relatively rarely, once a complaint has been prepared but before any further action has been taken on it, the prosecutor may seek to have the accused arrested rather than cited. The prosecutor may apply to a judge of the appropriate court for a warrant to apprehend[11]. The judge may grant a warrant if he considers it expedient [11].

---

1 *Beattie v Tudhope* 1984 SCCR 198, 1984 SLT 423. See also *Smith v Peter Walker & Son (Edinburgh) Ltd* 1978 JC 44; *McNeillie v Walkingshaw* 1990 SCCR 428, 1991 SLT 892; *Young v MacPhail* 1991 SCCR 630, 1992 SLT 98. If the facts are disputed, evidence should be heard: *McCartney v Tudhope* 1985 SCCR 373, 1986 SLT 159.
2 *Carmichael v Sardar & Sons* 1983 SCCR 433 (Sh Ct), a case in which the Crown marked an appeal, but did not proceed with it.
3 *Beattie v Tudhope* 1984 SCCR 198, 1984 SLT 423.
4 *Nicolson v Skeen* (1976) SCCR (Supp) 74.
5 *McGlennan v Singh* 1993 SCCR 341.
6 *Kennedy v Carmichael* 1991 SCCR 458.
7 *MacNeill v Cowie* 1984 SCCR 449, 1985 SLT 246; *McNeillie v Walkingshaw* 1990 SCCR 428, 1991 SLT 892.
8 *Young v Smith* 1981 SCCR 85, 1981 SLT (Notes) 101; *Chow v Lees* 1997 SCCR 253.
9 As in *Connachan v Douglas* 1990 JC 244, 1990 SCCR 101, 1990 SLT 563.
10 See above at p 138.
11 1995 Act, s 139(1)(b). See above at p 87 for the circumstances in which a warrant may be granted.

The prosecutor may also apply to a judge of the appropriate court at the same stage of proceedings for a warrant to search the accused's person, his dwelling house and repositories and any place he may be found, for anything likely to afford evidence of his guilt[1]. This power is not frequently used, but, if an application is made, the judge concerned should satisfy himself that there is good reason for granting the warrant. The legislation provides no criteria for assessing whether or not it is appropriate to grant a search warrant.

# FIRST CALLING IN COURT (FIRST DIET)

If the accused is in custody, he will, of course, be brought to court. If he is an undertaker[2], he must attend at the specified time. If, without reasonable excuse, he does not do so, he is guilty of an offence[3]. Those in custody and undertakers are entitled to the services of the legal aid duty solicitor, irrespective of their means[4]. Representation by the duty solicitor continues until the conclusion of the first diet (including any application for liberation) or, if the accused pleads guilty, until the case is finally disposed of[5]. An accused in custody or an undertaker is, of course, entitled to employ his own solicitor rather than the duty solicitor, if he wishes, but he will require to pay for the privilege.

A person who has been cited to a court need not attend in person. He may respond in writing[5], or he may be represented by a solicitor or by some other person 'who satisfies the court that he is authorised by the accused'[6]. An appearance cures any want of due citation or any informality therein[7].

An objection to the competency or the relevancy of the complaint[8] or the proceedings thereon (which includes a plea in bar of trial[9]), or a denial that the accused is the person charged by the police with the offence[10], must be stated before a plea is tendered by the accused or anyone on his behalf[11]. Such a preliminary objection may be disposed of at the first diet, but it is more usual for the case to be put down for a hearing at a later date, and it is usually reasonable to allow the prosecutor an adjournment to carry out any investigation which may be required[12]. There is a right of appeal to the High Court against the court's decision on a preliminary

---

1 1995 Act, s 139(1)(c). See above at pp 90, 91 for search warrants.
2 Under the 1995 Act, s 22(1)(a).
3 1995 Act, s 22(2).
4 Legal Aid (Scotland) Act 1986, s 22(1)(c); Criminal Legal Aid (Scotland) Regulations 1987, SI 1987/307, reg 5(1)(d).
5 1995 Act, s 144(2)(a). A plea of guilty by a company may be signed by an individual 'on behalf of' the company: *McGlennan v Beattie's Bakeries Ltd* 1992 SCCR 50, 1993 SLT 1109.
6 1995 Act, s 144(2)(b).
7 1995 Act, s 144(8). See *Kirkcudbright Scallop Gear Ltd v Walkingshaw* 1994 SCCR 372, 1994 SLT 1323.
8 The same principles of competency and relevancy apply to complaints as to indictments. See above at p 137.
9 *Normand v Rooney* 1992 JC 93, 1992 SCCR 336, 1992 SLT 275.
10 Under the 1995 Act, s 280(9) there is a presumption that the person who appears in answer to the complaint is the person charged with the offence by the police. The Crown is not deprived of this presumption even if the prosecutor seeks to have the accused identified in court: *Hamilton v Ross* 1991 JC 36, 1991 SCCR 165, 1992 SLT 384.
11 1995 Act, s 144(4).
12 *McGlennan v Johnston* 1991 SCCR 895.

objection, but such an appeal requires the leave of the court and must be taken within two days after the decision of the court[1]. If the preliminary objection is repelled, the accused may apply for leave to appeal only after stating how he pleads to the charge[2]. If a preliminary objection is not stated at the first diet, it may be stated at a later time only with leave of the court on cause shown[3]. Whether to allow a plea to be stated at a later stage is entirely within the discretion of the judge[4]. The fact that the accused was unrepresented at the first diet is invariably considered to be sufficient cause to allow him to state a preliminary objection at a later date. If a preliminary objection is taken at a later stage, even during a trial, an accused may appeal against a decision in favour of the prosecutor without waiting for the trial to be completed[5].

Assuming that there is no preliminary objection, the next stage is for the accused either to plead to the complaint or ask that it be adjourned (more commonly called 'continued') without plea[6]. The Act provides that if the accused is on bail or ordained to appear, no one period of adjournment may exceed 28 days[7], although a further adjournment without plea may be, and often is, sought and granted. If the accused is remanded in custody no one period of adjournment without plea may exceed seven days except on special cause shown[8], and the total period must not exceed 21 days[8]. If the accused is present and the case is not continued without plea, he must be called on to plead[9]. There is no provision for an accused to seek a continuation without plea in writing, but, in practice, it is common for the prosecutor to make such a motion at the request of the defence contained in a letter to the fiscal. If the accused is neither present nor represented when a case is continued without plea, the prosecutor must intimate the fact of the continuation and the date of the adjourned diet to him[10].

Not infrequently the fiscal asks for a case to be continued without plea where there has been no response from the accused but the fiscal has no reason to believe that he has not been cited. In such a situation, if it appears at the next calling of the case that the accused has in fact *not* been cited, the fiscal may seek an initiating arrest warrant on the same complaint under section 139(1)(b) of the 1995 Act, and the previous calling of the case is treated as if it had never happened[11].

If the accused has responded by means of the form of response which he received along with his citation, he should have indicated clearly whether he is pleading guilty or not guilty. If the accused is not present and is represented by a solicitor or other authorised person, he makes the plea on the accused's behalf. If the accused is present, whether or not he is represented by a solicitor or counsel, the strict rule is that he is required to state his plea himself[12]. There is power given to the court to accept a plea from a solicitor or counsel if the judge is satisfied that

---

1  1995 Act, s 174(1). Detailed rules for the appeal are provided in 1996 Rules, r 19.1.
2  1996 Rules, r 19.1(1). For the confused situation which can arise when this rule is not observed see *Lafferty v Jessop* 1989 SCCR 451, 1989 SLT 846.
3  1995 Act, s 144(5).
4  *Henderson v Ingram* 1982 SCCR 135.
5  *McLeay v Hingston (No 2)* 1994 SCCR 579, 1994 SLT 720.
6  1995 Act, s 195(1).
7  1995 Act, s 145(3).
8  1995 Act, s 145(2).
9  *McGlennan v Crawford* 1993 SCCR 621.
10  1996 Rules, r 18.1(3).
11  *Lees v Malcolm* 1992 JC 173, 1992 SCCR 589, 1992 SLT 1137; but see also *Heywood v McLennan* 1994 SCCR 1.
12  1996 Rules, r 18.1(1). See *McGowan v Ritchie* 1997 SCCR 322.

the accused is not capable of pleading personally[1]. However, it is fair to say that, in some courts at least, the rule requiring personal pleading by a represented accused is more honoured in the breach than in the observance. In these courts, in practice, a represented accused makes his plea personally only if the defence solicitor is having difficulty with his client and specifically requests that the court should take the plea from the accused himself. Otherwise the defence solicitor makes the plea on behalf of the accused[2].

## Plea of guilty

If the accused pleads guilty, a similar procedure is followed to that on a plea of guilty under solemn procedure[3], although neither the accused nor the judge signs the plea, and the prosecutor does not usually make any formal motion for sentence. He produces a notice of previous convictions, if any.

In the case of certain road traffic offences where the accused's driving licence must be endorsed, the licence should be produced to the court[4]. This is, first, so that the court may see what, if any, endorsements are already on the licence and thus take them into account when passing sentence[5]. Secondly, it is in order that the appropriate endorsement in the instant case may be added to the licence. If the licence is not produced, then, unless the accused satisfies the court that he has applied for a new licence and has not yet received it, the licence is suspended[6]. In practice a court may accept an undertaking by an accused to produce his licence later the same day or at a later date. If an accused claims to have mislaid his licence, the court may give him an opportunity to apply for a duplicate. If the accused, for whatever reason, does not produce a licence in court, the court is entitled to have regard to a computer print-out of the accused's record from the Driving and Vehicle Licensing Authority (DVLA)[7]. The accused must be asked if he admits the accuracy of the record[8], and, if any part of it is disputed, the prosecutor must prove it[9]. The view has been expressed that reference to the DVLA print-out is permitted only where the accused is or has been the holder of a driving licence[10], but it is submitted that the terms of section 32 of the Road Traffic Offenders Act 1988 are in fact wide enough to cover even the person who has never held a licence.

Except in the circumstances described in the previous paragraph, the court may not normally take account of previous convictions unless they are contained in a notice which has been served on the accused[11]. However, if an accused appears on a number of separate complaints only some of which are accompanied by notices of previous convictions, the court may have regard to any notice which is before it when disposing of a case for which there is no notice[12]. If the accused does not

1 1996 Rules, r 18.1(2).
2 This practice appears to be condoned by the High Court: *Crombie v Hamilton* 1989 SCCR 499; but see *McGowan v Ritchie* 1997 SCCR 322.
3 See above at pp 142, 143.
4 Road Traffic Offenders Act 1988, s 27(1).
5 1988 Act, s 31.
6 1988 Act, s 27(3).
7 1988 Act, s 32(2).
8 1988 Act, s 32(3).
9 1988 Act, s 32(5).
10 Road Traffic Encyclopedia (Sweet and Maxwell), para 4–1302, founding on the case of *Anderson v Allan* 1985 SCCR 262, which was decided on the basis of earlier legislation. See also Wheatley *Road Traffic Law in Scotland* (2nd edn, 1993), who appears not to take a categoric view on the matter.
11 1995 Act, s 166(2).
12 *Henderson v Heywood* 1992 SCCR 610.

admit a conviction, the prosecutor must prove it[1]. An erroneous notice of convictions may be amended[2].

After any necessary notice has been produced to the court the prosecutor usually narrates briefly the circumstances of the offence(s), although some statutory offences are so self-explanatory that little, if any, elaboration of the terms of the complaint is needed. The accused or his representative, if either of them is present, then makes a plea in mitigation. If the accused has pleaded guilty in writing, the court considers any explanation or mitigating circumstance which he may have provided and any information contained in his means form or other document. If there is any discrepancy between the account of events given by the Crown and that given by the defence, the same procedure should be followed as in a solemn case[3]. The court then usually proceeds to sentence. Alternatively, it may adjourn the case to obtain reports or (where the accused has not been present at the first diet) for the accused to appear personally at a subsequent diet[4]. If a case is adjourned for personal appearance but the accused fails to appear, it is still competent for the court to sentence him in absence[5]. If the court wishes to obtain reports, the accused may be remanded in custody even though he has not previously been in custody in connection with the case[6]. Such a remand is, however, relatively rare. The same time limits for periods of adjournment apply as in the case of solemn procedure[7].

An accused who has pleaded guilty may, in certain circumstances, be permitted to withdraw that plea and substitute a plea of not guilty[8]. It is, for example, not uncommon for an unrepresented accused to plead guilty, to have his case continued for a social enquiry report, and to give to the social worker an account of the offence which is inconsistent with guilt. In such a situation he would usually be allowed to change his plea. The court would also probably strongly advise him to consult a solicitor.


## Plea of not guilty

If an accused pleads not guilty, the prosecutor will almost certainly move the court to fix a diet of trial, although there are rare circumstances where the not guilty plea will be accepted. If the complaint contains more than one charge and a plea of guilty to part of the complaint is tendered and accepted but the Crown wishes to go to trial on any remaining charge, the case should be continued in respect of any charge to which a guilty plea has been tendered until the conclusion of the trial on any other charge[9]. A similar course should be followed where one of several accused pleads guilty and trial is fixed for the other accused, unless the case of the accused who has pleaded guilty is clearly separable from the case of the other accused. A continuation to await the outcome of a trial in these circumstances is

---

1   1995 Act, s 166(5).
2   1995 Act, s 159(1). There is no provision as there is in the case of solemn proceedings (1995 Act, s 101(5)) to the effect that an amendment to the notice of previous convictions must not be to the prejudice of the accused.
3   See above at p 143.
4   1995 Act, s 144(3)(b).
5   *Taylor v Lees* 1993 SCCR 947.
6   1995 Act, s 201(1).
7   1995 Act, s 201(3). See above at pp 186, 187.
8   *McClung v Cruickshank* 1964 JC 64; *Owens v Wilson* 1991 SLT 165.
9   *Cogan v Carmichael* 1993 SCCR 628, 1994 SLT 851.

not struck at by the restriction on adjournment for inquiries under section 201 of the 1995 Act[1].

In theory a trial may take place immediately after an accused has pleaded not guilty[2], unless the accused has appeared from custody. In that event he is entitled to have the case adjourned for at least 48 hours prior to the trial[3], unless it is necessary to secure the examination of witnesses who would not otherwise be available, in which case the trial may proceed at once or in less than 48 hours. In practice, however, a trial diet is fixed for some time ahead unless there are exceptional circumstances such as witnesses being due to go to sea or the like. In the normal case a trial should be fixed for the earliest practicable date[4]. If either the prosecutor or the defence has information to the effect that the trial is likely to be a long one, the clerk of court should be informed, in order that sufficient court time may be set aside.

## Intermediate diet

As well as a trial diet the court must now in virtually all cases fix an intermediate diet[5]. On joint application by the Crown and the defence the court may, if it considers it inappropriate to have an intermediate diet, refrain from fixing such a diet or discharge any such diet already fixed[6] but this is clearly intended to be the exception rather than the rule. The function of an intermediate diet is effectively the same as that of a first diet under solemn procedure[7]. The primary purpose is to ascertain whether the case is likely to proceed to trial on the date assigned for the trial diet, and in particular (a) the state of preparation of the parties, (b) whether the accused intends to adhere to his plea of not guilty, and (c) the extent to which each party has complied with the duty under section 257(1) of the 1995 Act to identify and agree uncontroversial evidence[8]. The court may ask each party any question for this purpose[9]. If the court concludes that the case is unlikely to proceed to trial on the assigned date it must 'unless having regard to previous proceedings in the case it considers it inappropriate to do so' postpone the trial diet[10], and may fix a further intermediate diet[11]. The court may also adjourn an intermediate diet[12].

The accused must attend an intermediate diet unless he is legally represented *and* the court considers that there are exceptional circumstances justifying his non–attendance[13]. In practice this means that the solicitor appearing for the accused at the first diet should move the court to dispense with his client's attendance at the

1 *Douglas v Jamieson, Douglas v Peddie* 1993 JC 201, 1993 SCCR 717, 1993 SLT 816.
2 1995 Act, s 146(2).
3 1995 Act, s 146(4).
4 *Heywood v Gray, Heywood v Ross* 1992 SCCR 635, 1993 SLT 541 sub nom *Heywood v Ross*.
5 1995 Act, s 148(1). On the face of it the subsection gives the court a discretion whether to fix an intermediate diet. However, in terms of s 148(7) the Secretary of State may prescribe the courts in which an intermediate diet is obligatory. The Secretary of State has made an order prescribing almost every court of summary jurisdiction in Scotland as such courts. The only exceptions are the sheriff courts in Kirkwall, Lerwick, Portree, Lochmaddy and Dornoch, and the district courts in Highland, Western Isles, Dumfries and Galloway and Scottish Borders.
6 1995 Act, s 148(1A) as inserted by s 148(7)(b).
7 See above at pp 132–134.
8 1995 Act, s 148(1).
9 1995 Act, s 148(4).
10 1995 Act, s 148(2)(a).
11 1995 Act, s 148(2)(b).
12 1995 Act, s 148(3).
13 1995 Act, s 148(5).

intermediate diet, giving reasons for the motion. A good reason for dispensing with attendance might be that the accused lived a considerable distance away from the court.

An intermediate diet is peremptory, and if it is not called, the instance falls[1].

The intermediate diet was introduced into summary procedure as a discretionary option in 1980, mainly with the intention of reducing the number of cases in which pleas of guilty were tendered on the day of the trial diet causing great inconvenience to witnesses and a considerable waste of court time. Regrettably, in many courts this intention was not fulfilled, and last minute changes of plea were still common even where there had been an intermediate diet. Whether the introduction of obligatory intermediate diets will produce a different effect remains to be seen.

At an intermediate diet an accused may plead guilty[2], in which case matters proceed exactly as if he had pleaded guilty at the first diet.

### Ordained, bailed or remanded

If a trial diet is fixed the question arises of what steps should be taken to ensure the accused's attendance at the later diet. In the great majority of cases he is simply ordained to appear. This means that he is told the date and time of the intermediate and trial diets and that he must appear at them. There are no conditions attached. If the accused fails, without reasonable excuse, to appear having been ordained, he is guilty of an offence punishable by a fine not exceeding level 3 on the standard scale[3] and to imprisonment not exceeding 60 days (in the district court) or three months (in the sheriff court)[4]. These penalties may be imposed in addition to any other penalty which the court may impose for the offence originally charged, notwithstanding that the normal maximum powers of the court may thereby be exceeded[5]. The accused may be dealt with for the offence of failing to appear either at the trial diet for the original offence or at a separate diet[6].

Alternatively, the accused may, provided that he is present in court, be released on bail[7]. The statutory provisions relating to bail which were discussed above[8] apply to summary proceedings as well as to solemn proceedings subject to certain minor modifications[9]. In the case of accused who have appeared from custody the Crown usually moves the court to admit to bail rather than to ordain to appear. Breach of any bail condition in connection with summary proceedings (including failure without reasonable excuse to appear at a diet but excluding the commission of an offence while on bail) is punishable with a fine not exceeding level 3 on the standard scale and imprisonment for 60 days (in the district court) or three months (in the sheriff court)[10]. These penalties may be imposed in addition to any other

1  *McDonald v Knight* 1990 SCCR 641.
2  1995 Act, s 148(6).
3  At the time of writing level 3 is £1,000.
4  1995 Act, s 150(8).
5  1995 Act, s 150(9).
6  1995 Act, s 150(10).
7  If a case, originally on petition, has been reduced to summary procedure, bail granted on the petition continues in force for the summary case: *McGinn v HMA* 1990 SCCR 170.
8  See above at pp 102–106.
9  Eg the power of a court of summary jurisdiction to grant bail is contained in the 1995 Act, s 23(6), whereas the power of a solemn court to do so is in s 23(1), (2).
10  1995 Act, s 27(1), (2).

penalty which the court may impose for the offence originally charged, notwith-standing that the normal maximum powers of the court may thereby be exceeded[1].

If the breach of bail conditions consists of the commission of an offence while on bail, this is libelled as an aggravation of the offence concerned, as is the case under solemn procedure[2], rather than as a separate offence[3]. The court is empow-ered to impose an additional penalty in such a case, this being a fine not exceeding level 3 of the standard scale and imprisonment for 60 days (district court) or six months (sheriff court)[4]. Such additional penalties may be imposed notwithstanding that the increased penalty would exceed the maximum penalty which the court could otherwise impose[4].

It is also competent, but only in the case of an accused appearing from custody, to remand him in custody for trial[5].

If an accused is remanded in custody for trial, his trial must be commenced[6] within 40 days after the first diet, failing which he must be liberated forthwith and 'shall be for ever free from all question or process for that offence'[7]. The 40-day period runs *de die in diem* and the day of the first calling is excluded[8]. This period may be extended by a sheriff (whether the case is in the district court or the sher-iff court), if he is satisfied that delay in the commencement of the trial is due to (a) the illness of the accused or of a judge; (b) the absence or illness of any necessary witness; or (c) any other sufficient cause which is not attributable to any fault on the part of the prosecutor[9]. Both the Crown and the defence have a right of appeal to the High Court against the sheriff's decision[10].

It is not uncommon that an accused is remanded in custody for trial and the trial then has to be adjourned for some reason with the accused being released on bail. If he fails to attend for the new trial date, he is likely subsequently to be arrested and again remanded in custody. It is important to remember that the previous period of remand counts towards the 40 days with the consequence that the new trial will have to be set down very promptly unless the sheriff is asked for and grants an extension of the 40-day period.

# LEGAL AID[11]

As we have seen, in a case under solemn procedure the decision whether or not to grant legal aid is for the court, and only the financial position of the accused is rel-

---

1  1995 Act, s 27(9).
2  See above at p 105.
3  1995 Act, s 27(3).
4  1995 Act, s 27(5).
5  1995 Act, s 146(6). It is not easy to reconcile the terms of this subsection with those of s 23(6) and (8) which appear to state that in a summary case a court has a discretion whether to remand an accused in custody whether or not he is already in custody at the time of any application for bail. It is not unknown for an accused who appears as an 'undertaker' in terms of s 22(1)(a) to be remanded in custody.
6  The commencement of the trial occurs when the first witness is sworn: 1995 Act, s 147(4).
7  1995 Act, s 147(1). The commencement of the trial stops the running of the 40 days; the accused may continue to be remanded in custody even though the trial is adjourned for a period of days.
8  *Hazlett v McGlennan* 1992 SCCR 799, 1993 SLT 74.
9  1995 Act, s 147(2).
10  1995 Act, s 147(3). 1996 Rules, r 17.1 and Form 17.1 apply to such appeals.
11  The statutory provisions for criminal legal aid will be substantially amended if the 1997 Act, Pt V comes into force. See the Appendix at p 319 below.

evant[1]. In summary proceedings the situation is quite different. The duty solicitor has responsibility for those in custody and undertakers until the end of the first diet or, in the case of a plea of guilty, ultimate disposal[2]. However, in the case of an accused pleading not guilty, or an accused pleading guilty who does not appear from custody or as an undertaker, the general rule[3] is that neither the court nor the duty solicitor is concerned in the provision of legal aid[4]. Instead, the body which determines eligibility for legal aid is the Scottish Legal Aid Board (usually abbreviated to 'SLAB').

The general rules for legal aid in summary cases are to be found in section 24 of the Legal Aid (Scotland) Act 1986. This provides that legal aid is to be made available in summary proceedings if the Board is satisfied that the accused could not afford to pay for representation himself 'without undue hardship to him or his dependants'[5], and 'that in all the circumstances of the case it is in the interests of justice that legal aid should be made available to him'[6]. The 'interests of justice' are not defined as such, but the Board is directed that the factors to be taken into account in determining whether it is in the interests of justice to grant legal aid include[7]:

(a) where the offence is such that if proved it is likely that the court would impose a sentence which would deprive the accused of his liberty or lead to loss of his livelihood;

(b) where the determination of the case may involve consideration of a substantial question of law, or of evidence of a complex or difficult nature;

(c) where the accused may be unable to understand the proceedings or to state his own case because of his age, inadequate knowledge of English, mental illness, other mental or physical disability or otherwise;

(d) where it is in the interests of someone other than the accused that the accused be legally represented;

(e) where the defence to be advanced by the accused does not appear to be frivolous;

(f) where the accused has been remanded in custody pending trial.

An accused must apply for legal aid in writing on the appropriate form[8]. Most solicitors practising in the criminal courts will have a supply of forms. Because the form is long and complex it is usually completed by the solicitor rather than by the accused. The accused must sign the form. The application must normally be submitted to the Scottish Legal Aid Board within 14 days after the accused has ten-

---

1  See above at pp 106, 107.

2  See above at p 197.

3  This is subject to one exception under the Legal Aid (Scotland) Act 1986, s 23(1)(b), which provides that the court may grant legal aid to a convicted accused who has not previously received a custodial sentence, and in respect of whom the court is now considering a custodial sentence. The financial criterion is the familiar one to the effect that the accused could not afford to pay for representation 'without undue hardship to him or his dependants'.

4  An accused who is pleading guilty but who is not eligible for legal aid in terms of s 23(1)(b) of the Legal Aid (Scotland) Act 1986 (see the previous footnote) may receive Advice and Assistance under the legal aid legislation. For details of this see C N Stoddart and H S Neilson *The Law and Practice of Legal Aid in Scotland* (4th edn, 1994), ch 5.

5  Legal Aid (Scotland) Act 1986, s 24(1)(a).

6  Legal Aid (Scotland) Act 1986, s 24(1)(b).

7  Legal Aid (Scotland) Act 1986, s 24(3).

8  Criminal Legal Aid (Scotland) Regulations 1987, SI 1987/307, reg 8(1)(a). See the case of *Nicol Jarvie* at pp 69–72 above.

dered a plea of not guilty[1]. This time limit does not apply if the Board considers that there is special reason to consider a late application[2]. Along with the form should be sent a copy of the complaint and evidence of the accused's income if he is working or, if he is receiving benefit, information about where he signs on for it.

If an accused is in custody and has actually applied for legal aid, then, even though his application has not yet been granted, legal aid is available to him up until the date when his application is finally determined by the Board[3] (and thereafter, of course, if his application is granted). Otherwise legal aid normally becomes available only from the date when the application is granted[4].

An accused whose application for legal aid has been refused may apply to the Board for a review[5].

If an accused, appearing unrepresented before a court for trial, has either not applied for legal aid or has been refused on the ground that it was not in the interests of justice, and the court considers that, owing to the exceptional circumstances of the case, it would be inequitable to proceed with the trial without the accused being represented, the court may adjourn the trial to enable the accused to apply for legal aid to the Board, and the Board must consider the application expeditiously[6]. In such a case legal aid is automatically available from the date of the making of the application until the date of its determination[7], so that the trial need not be adjourned for too long. The 14-day time bar on applying for legal aid does not affect such an application[8]. If, in such a case, the application is refused on the ground of means, the accused may be required to pay to the Scottish Legal Aid Fund the whole or part of what was paid out of the Fund for his representation[9].

Legal aid in a summary case normally covers only representation by a solicitor. If the accused wishes to employ counsel, he must apply for prior approval to the Board[10]. A similar rule applies if the accused wishes to make use of the services of an expert witness[11]. In either case, however, the Board may give retrospective approval, if it considers that there was special reason for prior approval not having been applied for[12].

# PREPARATION BY THE CROWN

In a summary prosecution the Crown does not normally obtain precognitions. Instead, the statements which the police have taken from witnesses prior to reporting the case to the procurator fiscal are used for the conduct of the trial. However,

---

1 Criminal Legal Aid (Scotland) Regulations 1987, reg 8(1)(b).
2 Criminal Legal Aid (Scotland) Regulations 1987, reg 8(2)(b).
3 Legal Aid (Scotland) Act 1986, s 22(1)(d)(ii). This provision exists in order to avoid summary trials of persons in custody having to be adjourned until the granting of a legal aid application.
4 But see also Legal Aid (Scotland) Act 1986, s 24(7).
5 Legal Aid (Scotland) Act 1986, s 24(5).
6 Legal Aid (Scotland) Act 1986, s 24(6).
7 Legal Aid (Scotland) Act 1986, s 24(7).
8 Criminal Legal Aid (Scotland) Regulations 1987, reg 8(2)(a).
9 Legal Aid (Scotland) Act 1986, s 24(8).
10 Criminal Legal Aid (Scotland) Regulations 1987, reg 14(1)(b).
11 Criminal Legal Aid (Scotland) Regulations 1987, reg 14(1)(c).
12 Criminal Legal Aid (Scotland) Regulations 1987, reg 14(2).

a case may already have been precognosced before the decision is taken to proceed summarily. The case may, for example, originally have been on petition, or it may have involved a sudden death and therefore have been reported, with precognition, to the Crown Office. The fiscal also has power, without applying to the court for a warrant to do so, to cite witnesses for precognition[1].

There is no obligation on the Crown to provide a list of prosecution witnesses to the defence, but, as a matter of courtesy, the fiscal will provide a list on request on the basis that the defence will reciprocate by providing a list of their witnesses to the Crown.

The statutory provisions regarding routine evidence[2] apply to summary proceedings as they do to solemn procedure. The prosecutor should consider whether evidence by certificate[3] or report[4] may be appropriate. A copy of the certificate or report must be served on the accused not less than 14 days before the trial[5]. The prosecutor must therefore make sure that the certificate or report is served in time if he wishes to avail himself of this facility. There are similar provisions for proof by certificate in certain statutes[6].

In the rare summary case where the accused has been the subject of a judicial examination the prosecutor must apply to the court if he wishes to have any part of the record thereof excluded from the evidence[7]. Except on cause shown, at least ten clear days' notice must be given to the court and to other parties[8].

The prosecutor must cite his witnesses. Citation may be by personal service or by leaving the citation with someone at the witness's dwelling house or place of business, or at a place where he is resident if he has no dwelling house or place of business[9]. If the witness is employed on a vessel, he may be cited by leaving the citation with a person on board and connected with the vessel[10].

Witnesses may also be cited by ordinary post[11]. In the case of postal citation the witness receives with the citation a form of acknowledgment which he must complete and return to the fiscal[12]. Postal citation of witnesses was introduced by the 1995 Act in order to reduce the amount of time spent by police officers (by whom witness citations were almost always served) in serving citations. How successful such citation will be remains to be seen.

The prosecutor should, of course, always be willing to discuss with the defence the possibility of agreeing any evidence and thus cutting down the number of witnesses.

---

1  1997 Act, s 57 amending the 1995 Act, s 140(1) and repealing s 140(3). See the Appendix at p 321 below.
2  1995 Act, s 280. See above at pp 171–172.
3  1995 Act, s 280(1).
4  1995 Act, s 280(4).
5  1995 Act, s 280(6)(a).
6  Eg Road Traffic Offenders Act 1988, s 16.
7  1995 Act, s 278(2)(b), (3).
8  1995 Act, s 278(4).
9  1995 Act, s 141(1).
10  1995 Act, s 141(2).
11  1995 Act, s 141(3)(b); 1996 Rules, r 16.6; Form 16.6A.
12  Form 16.6B.

# PREPARATION BY THE DEFENCE

Preparation by the defence for a summary trial should follow the same pattern as that for a solemn case[1].

Section 290 of the 1995 Act, allowing the defence to apply to the sheriff to order the prosecutor to hold an identification parade, is relevant to both solemn and summary proceedings[2]. It should be noted that even if the trial is to be in the district court, the application must still be made to the sheriff.

The statutory provisions regarding the duty to seek agreement of evidence[3] and uncontroversial evidence[4] apply to summary proceedings as they apply to solemn procedure.

The provision for precognoscing a witness on oath on behalf of the accused[5] also applies to summary proceedure.

Like the prosecutor, the defence may apply to the court to have all or part of the record of a judicial examination excluded from the evidence[6], and must, except on cause shown, give at least ten clear days' notice to the court and other parties of such an application[7]. As under solemn procedure such exclusion is usually agreed between prosecution and defence, and a formal application to the court is unnecessary.

The defence should make every effort to ensure that the case is fully prepared by the date of the intermediate diet, in order that it may be made clear to the court whether or not the trial is to proceed.

Defence witnesses may be cited in the same way as Crown witnesses[8], but, in the case of citation which is not by post, the person serving the citation would normally be a sheriff officer. Even though postal citation is competent[9], it is in most cases desirable to use the more formal method of citation by officer of court in order to ensure that the citation is effective. I understand that the Scottish Legal Aid Board usually pays for such citation without question.

# ALTERATION OF THE DIET

It quite frequently happens in a summary case that it is desired to change the date of a trial or other diet. The most common reason for this is that it is discovered, after a trial diet has been fixed, that an essential witness is to be unavailable on that date. The 1995 Act provides a convenient mechanism for changing a diet. All parties to a case (ie the fiscal and all accused) may apply to the court by written joint application to discharge a diet and fix an earlier diet in its place[10]. In practice a stan-

---

1 See above at pp 129–132.
2 The relevant rule is 1996 Rules, r 28.1. See above at p 95.
3 1995 Act, s 257. See above at p 129.
4 1995 Act, s 258. See above at p 125.
5 1995 Act, s 291(1). See above at pp 129–130. The 1996 Rules, ch 29 provides for the appropriate procedure.
6 1995 Act, s 278(2)(b), (3).
7 1995 Act, s 278(4).
8 Ie under 1995 Act, s 141. See above at p 206.
9 1995 Act, s 141(3)(b).
10 1995 Act, s 137(1).

dard form of joint petition is signed by the fiscal and by the defence solicitor (or by the accused himself if he is unrepresented), and the case then calls in court as soon as possible. When the case does call either party may move the court to fix a fresh diet of trial or whatever other diet is appropriate.

This procedure for accelerating a diet is also, of course, appropriate if, after a trial has been fixed, the accused decides to tender a plea of guilty. At the accelerated diet in such a case the plea is tendered, and the case then proceeds as if the accused had pleaded guilty at the first diet.

The prosecutor and the accused may also make a joint application to the court for postponement of a diet which has been fixed, and this may be made orally or in writing[1]. However, unlike the joint application for an accelerated diet described in the two preceding paragraphs, this application may be made only at a properly assigned diet of the case which has been duly called[2]. This may be either an intermediate diet or a trial diet. The application must be granted by the court unless there has been unnecessary delay on the part of one or more parties[3].

If the prosecutor wishes to postpone or accelerate a diet and an accused refuses to join with him in making a joint application[4], the prosecutor may apply to the court by way of an incidental application[5] for such a postponement or acceleration[6]. The court must give all parties an opportunity to be heard and may then discharge the diet and fix an earlier or later diet as the case may be[7].

An accused has a similar right to apply to the court for postponement or acceleration of a diet when the other parties are not prepared to join with him in an application[7]. Again, the court must give all parties an opportunity to be heard before deciding whether or not to grant the application[8].

# TRIAL DIET

## Plea in bar of trial

Many pleas in bar of trial[9] are really pleas to the competency of the proceedings (eg time bar) and should be treated as such[10]. However, a plea in bar of trial may depend on circumstances which have arisen only after service of a complaint, although the complaint itself is perfectly competent. For example, it may be submitted that there has been undue delay in actually bringing the case to trial, or that there has been prejudicial pre-trial publicity. It may be noted in passing that the court is less likely to sustain a plea in bar on the ground of pre-trial publicity in a summary case than it would be in a solemn case[11].

A plea in bar of trial should be stated when the case calls for trial, if it has not previously been stated.

1   1995 Act, s 137(2).
2   1996 Rules, r 16.7(1).
3   1995 Act, s 137(2).
4   Under either s 137(1) or s 137(2).
5   1995 Act, s 134; 1996 Rules, r 16.4(1); Form 16.4A.
6   1995 Act, s 137(4).
7   1995 Act, s 137(5).
8   1995 Act, s 137(5). 1996 Rules r 16.7(2) provides that Form 16.7 should be used for such an application.
9   See the comments on pleas in bar of trial in solemn procedure above at pp 137, 138, which apply equally to summary procedure.
10  See above at pp 197–198.
11  *Aitchison v Bernardi* 1984 SCCR 88, 1984 SLT 343.

## Defence of alibi

There is no general requirement to intimate a special defence in a summary trial. However, if an accused intends to found on an alibi, he must give notice to the prosecutor of the alibi, and of any witness who may be called to prove it, prior to the examination of the first prosecution witness[1]. The notice, which need not be in writing, should give particulars as to the time and place of the alibi[1]. It should be remembered that it is not a proper notice of an alibi to state the time as 'at the time when the crime was committed'. The notice should give specific times between which the accused was at a specific place or places. If notice of an alibi is given, the prosecutor is entitled, as of right, if he so desires, to an adjournment of the case[1].

## Call-over of trials

There are usually several cases put out for trial on the one day. The normal practice is that a call-over of cases takes place as soon as the court convenes, in order to ascertain which of the trials is actually going to proceed. Pleas of guilty are disposed of at this time, some cases may be adjourned to a later date and an arrest warrant may be granted for any accused who has failed to appear. A number of cases will be left in which it is clear that the trial is going to proceed. The court then adjourns for what should be a short time so that the prosecution and the defence may check that all witnesses have attended, the fiscal may decide on the order in which cases should be taken and consideration given to any other preliminary matters. Following the adjournment, if all goes according to plan, the court is able to proceed with the trials without further interruption. Unfortunately, things very often do not go according to plan. It is discovered that witnesses are missing or that there is some other reason why a trial cannot proceed. Not uncommonly the adjournment results in a plea of guilty to a modified charge being negotiated. It may even result in a plea of guilty as libelled because the accused, on learning that all the Crown witnesses are present, at last faces up to the realities of life! Whether the introduction of obligatory intermediate diets will affect this unsatisfactory situation is, sadly, doubtful.

This call-over procedure has no statutory authority, but is now widely accepted and has received the seal of approval from the High Court[2]. It enables witnesses in trials which are not to take place to be sent away rather than being kept waiting for the greater part of the day.

The call-over is not part of the trial[3].

## Conduct of the trial

The procedure in a summary trial is essentially the same as that in a solemn trial, although matters normally move somewhat more speedily. As in a solemn trial, there is no opening speech by the prosecutor.

1 1995 Act, s 149.
2 As eg in *Carmichael v Gilmour* 1995 SCCR 440 at 442E, 1995 SLT 1224 at 1225C, per Lord Justice-Clerk Ross.
3 *Deigan v Wilson* 1992 SCCR 840, 1993 SLT 522.

As a general rule no part of the trial should take place outwith the presence of the accused[1]. In certain limited circumstances a trial may proceed in his absence[2]. In addition, if an accused misconducts himself during the trial he may be removed 'for so long as his conduct makes it necessary'[3]. If he is unrepresented the court must appoint counsel or a solicitor to look after his interests during such absence[3].

## THE EVIDENCE

The comments about evidence under solemn procedure, which were made in chapter 5, are in the main equally applicable to summary proceedings although some of the statutory references are different. This section will accordingly deal only briefly with the topic, and reference should be made to chapter 5.

### Oath or affirmation

The form of oath or affirmation is the same as that under solemn procedure[4].

### Child witnesses

The provisions of the 1995 Act relating to the evidence of children[5] apply to summary procedure. The stage before which an application should normally be made to take a child's evidence on commission is before the first witness is sworn[6].

### Witnesses requiring interpretation

The same rules apply as under solemn procedure[7].

### Presentation of evidence

Even where there is no jury, care should be taken in the presentation of the evidence in a case. Where the court consists of lay magistrates matters may have to be spelt out more carefully than where there is a professional judge (sheriff or stipendiary magistrate). Even with the professional judge, however, it must be borne in

---

1 1995 Act, s 153(1). In *Brims v MacDonald* 1993 SCCR 1061, 1994 SLT 922, the sheriff visited the locus in a road traffic case. He had invited the parties to accompany him but the invitation was declined. On appeal the conviction was quashed on the ground that the inspection of the locus constituted part of the trial and had taken place outwith the accused's presence. Authority was given for a fresh prosecution.
2 1995 Act, s 150(5). See below at p 219.
3 1995 Act, s 153(2).
4 1996 Rules, r 18.2; Forms 14.5A and 14.5B.
5 1995 Act, s 271. See above at pp 148–151. These provisions have been extended to other categories of 'vulnerable' witnesses by the 1997 Act, s 29. See the Appendix at p 320 below.
6 1995 Act, s 271(1)(b).
7 See above at p 151.

mind that all he has seen of the case is the complaint, and the evidence should be presented in a clear and comprehensible way.

The comments in the previous chapter about leading questions[1], hearsay[2], examination-in-chief[3], cross-examination[4], re-examination[5] and questions by the judge[6] are all relevant to summary procedure also.

## Recall of witness

A judge has power at common law to recall any witness at any time in order to clarify an ambiguity. In a summary case this power may be exercised even during the submissions on the evidence by parties[7].

A judge may, on the motion of either party, permit a witness who has been examined already to be recalled[8].

## Additional evidence

The provisions in the 1995 Act regarding additional evidence[9] apply to summary procedure. Any motion to be allowed to lead additional evidence must be made before the prosecutor addresses the court on the evidence[10]. For the purposes of the section a trial commences when the first prosecution witness is sworn[11].

## Evidence in replication

The provisions in the 1995 Act regarding evidence in replication[12] apply to summary procedure. The time at which a motion to lead evidence in replication must be made is after the close of the defence evidence and before the prosecutor begins to address the court on the evidence[13].

## Evidence of accused's criminal record

The provisions of the 1995 Act regarding evidence of the accused's criminal record or character[14] apply to summary procedure.

---

1 See above at pp 152–153.
2 See above at pp 153–156.
3 See above at p 156.
4 See above at pp 156–158.
5 See above at p 158.
6 See above at pp 158–159.
7 *Rollo v Wilson* 1988 SCCR 312, 1988 SLT 659.
8 1995 Act, s 263(5).
9 1995 Act, s 268. See above at p 160.
10 1995 Act, s 268(1)(b).
11 1995 Act, s 268(5)(b).
12 1995 Act, s 269. See above at p 160.
13 1995 Act, s 269(4)(b).
14 1995 Act, s 270. See above at pp 161–162.

## Evidence of the accused

The provisions of the 1995 Act regarding the accused as a witness[1] apply to summary procedure.

## Evidence of the accused's spouse

The provisions of the 1995 Act regarding the accused's spouse as a witness[2] apply to summary procedure..

## Evidence of co-accused

The provisions of the 1995 Act regarding the evidence of a co-accused[3] apply to summary procedure.

## Evidence in trials of sexual offences

The provisions of the 1995 Act regarding evidence relating to sexual offences[4] apply to summary procedure.

## Presence of witnesses in court

The provisions of the 1995 Act regarding the presence of a witness in court before giving evidence[5] apply to summary procedure. There is no reason why the rule which permits an expert witness to be in court while evidence of the facts is being given, should not apply in summary cases as it does under solemn procedure.

## Accused's counsel or solicitor as witness

There is no specific authority on the subject of an accused's counsel or solicitor giving evidence in a summary trial, but it is submitted that there is no reason in principle why he should not, as in solemn procedure, be a competent witness, with the same restrictions on what he may be compelled to say[6]. If the solicitor is called as a witness on behalf of his own client, there is no confidentiality on a matter pertaining to the issue of the guilt of the accused[7].

A solicitor who is likely to be called as a witness should not, if at all possible, appear for the accused in the trial concerned.

---

1  1995 Act, s 266(1)–(8), (11). See above at pp 163–165.
2  1995 Act, s 264. See above at pp 165–166.
3  1995 Act, s 266(9), (10). See above at p 166.
4  1995 Act, ss 274, 275. See above at pp 166–167.
5  1995 Act, s 267. See above at pp 167–168.
6  See above at p 168.
7  1995 Act, s 265(2).

## Objections to admissibility of evidence

The same principles about objections to admissibility of evidence apply in summary as in solemn proceedings[1]. There is, of course, no question of a trial within a trial, although evidence relating to admissibility may have to be heard, eg as to service of a document. It is very important that an objection to the admissibility of evidence be stated timeously, as, if it is not, it cannot form the subject of a successful appeal unless the accused is without legal representation[2]. A party objecting has the right to have his objection noted in the record of proceedings[3]. If evidence is objected to, the court should not sustain the objection at that stage, but hear the evidence under reservation as to its competency[4]. In the event of a submission of no case to answer[5] by the accused the court should usually rule on questions of admissibility before hearing the submission[6].

## Record of proceedings at judicial examination

It will not often happen that an accused in a summary trial has been the subject of a judicial examination, but, where he has been, the record of the judicial examination is received in evidence without being sworn to by witnesses[7]. As has been noted above[8], both the prosecutor and the accused are entitled to apply to the court to have all or part of the record excluded from the evidence[9]. Except on cause shown, at least ten clear days' notice of the application must be given to the court and to all other parties[10].

What was said in the previous chapter[11] about the evidential value of anything said at judicial examination is relevant to summary proceedings as well as to solemn.

## Documentary evidence

Schedule 8 to the 1995 Act[12] applies to summary procedure.

## Evidence by certificate

The provisions of the 1995 Act regarding evidence by certificate[13] apply to summary procedure. It is common practice for the prosecutor, before he leads his first

---

1 See above at pp 168–169.
2 1995 Act, s 192(3)(b)(ii). See *West v McNaughtan* 1990 SCCR 439; *Jardine v Howdle* 1997 SCCR 294.
3 1995 Act, s 157(2). See *Macaulay v Wilson* 1995 SCCR 133, 1995 SLT 1070.
4 *Clark v Stewart* 1950 JC 8 at 11, 1949 SLT 461 at 463, per Lord Justice-General Cooper; *Heywood v Ross* 1993 SCCR 101 at 104C, 1994 SLT 195 at 197E, per Lord Justice-General Hope.
5 See below at p 215.
6 *Runham v Westwater* 1995 SCCR 356, 1995 SLT 835.
7 1995 Act, s 278(1).
8 See pp 206, 207.
9 1995 Act, s 278(2)(b).
10 1995 Act, s 278(4).
11 See above at p 170.
12 See above at p 171.
13 1995 Act, ss 280, 283, 284. See above at pp 171–172.

witness, to produce the appropriate certificate together with an execution of service thereof on the accused. The advantage of producing these at this stage and not later is that, if there is any defect in the certificate or the service, the prosecutor may apply to the court to desert the diet *pro loco et tempore*, whereas he can make no such application after the first witness has been sworn[1]. It also avoids the possibility of the certificate being overlooked[2].

### Evidence by report

The provisions of the 1995 Act regarding evidence by report[3] apply to summary procedure.

### Evidence by letter of request or on commission

In the sheriff court, but not in the district court, evidence by letter of request or on commission is competent as under solemn procedure[4]. The detailed procedural rules are the same as under solemn procedure[5]. An application for a letter of request must be made before the first witness is sworn[6]. An application to appoint a commissioner to take evidence should normally be made at that time also, but may be made during the course of the trial in exceptional circumstances[7].

### Television link evidence

There is no provision for the taking of evidence by live television link under summary procedure.

### Proof of official documents

Any letter, minute or other official document issuing from the office or in the custody of any of the departments of state or government in the United Kingdom is, in a summary prosecution, *prima facie* evidence of its contents without being spoken to by any witness, and a certified copy thereof is to be treated as equivalent to the original[8].

Any order by any of the departments of state or government or any local authority or public body made under statutory powers, or a print or copy of such an order, is to be received in a summary prosecution as evidence of the due making, confirmation and existence of the order[9] without prejudice to the possibility of its being challenged as *ultra vires*[10].

1   1995 Act, s 152(1).
2   As happened in *Evans v Wilson* 1981 SCCR 60.
3   1995 Act, ss 280–282. See above at p 172.
4   1995 Act, s 272(1).
5   1996 Rules, chs 23 and 24.
6   1995 Act, s 272(7)(b).
7   1995 Act, s 272(7).
8   1995 Act, s 154(1).
9   1995 Act, s 154(2).
10  1995 Act, s 154(3).

## Admissions by parties

Facts may be admitted by any party without proof, the terms of documents may be agreed and copies of documents may be held to be the equivalent of originals[1]. It is provided that such admissions and agreements should be made by lodging a minute with the clerk of court[2]. It is obviously desirable that as much as possible should be agreed in advance[3], in order to avoid the attendance of witnesses whose evidence is uncontroversial. For this reason it is very important that the defence solicitor and the fiscal discuss the case at an early stage, if at all possible before the intermediate diet.

## Advance evidence by defence witnesses

Although the normal rule is that the prosecutor calls all his witnesses before any defence evidence is led, there is a rarely used provision entitling the accused to apply to the court for permission to examine a witness prior to the prosecution evidence being concluded[4]. This facility would be useful, for example, if a defence witness were about to go abroad for a period. The provision appears to be wide enough to enable the defence witness either to be heard before any Crown evidence has been led, or to be interposed in the course of the Crown case. The accused is still permitted to lead further evidence in normal course at the conclusion of the Crown case[4].

From a practical point of view, where the defence wishes to call a witness such as a doctor, who does not wish to be kept waiting, the procurator fiscal may very well be willing to call the witness for the Crown. The witness may then be asked purely formal questions by the fiscal and the evidence which the defence wishes to take from him elicited in cross-examination. The Crown has, of course, a right to re-examine. This procedure is probably in fact more commonly used than the statutory procedure described in the preceding paragraph.

## No case to answer

There is provision for the making of a submission of no case to answer in a summary trial[5], which is, *mutatis mutandis*, in identical terms with those of the provision on the same subject under solemn procedure[6]. The comments on no case to answer in chapter 5[7] should be read as applying to summary procedure also. If the court rejects the submission of no case to answer and no defence evidence is led, the court is still obliged to hear submissions on the evidence if parties wish to make them[8].

1  1995 Act, s 256(1).
2  1995 Act, s 256(2).
3  The duty on each party to identify facts on which agreement may be reached under the 1995 Act, s 257 (see above at p 129) applies to summary procedure provided that the accused is legally represented: s 257(2).
4  1995 Act, s 146(9).
5  1995 Act, s 160.
6  1995 Act, s 97.
7  See above at pp 174–175.
8  *Duffin v Normand* 1993 SCCR 864.

## Abandonment

The most common way for a prosecutor to abandon a complaint is to refrain from having it called in court. This has the same effect as if the complaint were deserted *pro loco et tempore*[1], ie the instance in the case falls, although the prosecutor may thereafter raise a fresh complaint, assuming that it is not time-barred. As a matter of courtesy, a prosecutor who intends not to have a case called in court should inform the accused of his intention.

If the prosecutor decides to abandon a case after the trial has begun, he should do so by intimating to the court that he is not proceeding further and is prepared to accept a plea of not guilty. The court then returns a verdict to that effect.

## Adjournment of trial

A trial diet may be adjourned on the motion of either party or by the court of its own volition[2]. An adjournment may be applied for either before the trial has actually started or after some evidence has been led.

Whether or not to adjourn a trial is a matter for the discretion of the court, but a motion by the Crown should be refused only 'in the most serious circumstances and for the most compelling reasons'[3]. This is because the consequence of such a refusal is that the instance falls, and the Crown is barred from bringing a fresh prosecution. 'But at the same time this (the power to refuse a Crown motion for an adjournment) is a power which, in view of the possible consequences of its exercise to parties and to the public interest, must be exercised only after the most careful consideration, on weighty grounds and with due and accurate regard to the interests which will be affected or prejudiced by that exercise'[4]. Even fault on the part of the Crown may not be a sufficient reason for refusing an adjournment[5].

Only in exceptional circumstances should a prosecutor anticipate an adjournment of a trial by countermanding his witnesses[6]. Wherever possible a case should be accelerated under the provisions of section 137(1) of the 1995 Act, in order that the motion to adjourn may be made in sufficient time to enable witnesses to be cited or not as the case may be.

The same principles of balancing the interests of the parties and the interests of the public apply where the motion to adjourn is made by the defence. The conduct of the accused himself is a relevant factor. Thus, it is commonplace for a court to refuse to adjourn where the accused has done nothing about preparing for his defence, and then seeks an adjournment to enable him to do something about it. However, if he has instructed a solicitor and the latter is not immediately available when the trial diet calls, the court should at least adjourn until later in the day to

---

1   See below at p 217.
2   1995 Act, s 146(7).
3   *Tudhope v Lawrie* 1979 JC 44 at 48, 1979 SLT (Notes) 13 at 13, per Lord Cameron giving the opinion of the court.
4   *Tudhope v Lawrie* 1979 JC 44 at 49, 1979 SLT (Notes) 13 at 14.
5   *Tudhope v Mitchell* 1986 SCCR 45 (failure by Crown to cite witnesses). But see also *Timney v Cardle* 1996 SLT 376, where a sheriff's decision to allow a part-heard trial to be adjourned (for the fourth time) was overturned on appeal. For an example of a case where a Crown motion for adjournment of the whole trial was refused because the Crown had excused the attendance of two essential witnesses see *Heywood v L* 1996 SCCR 772 (Sh Ct) – the Crown did not appeal against this decision.
6   *Skeen v Evans* 1979 SLT (Notes) 55. See also *Rodger v Heywood* 1996 SCCR 788.

give the solicitor an opportunity to be present[1]. A motion by the defence to adjourn in respect of the absence of an essential witness who has not been cited is unlikely to be looked on with favour[2].

If a trial has commenced and cannot be completed in one day, it must be adjourned to a later date. It is, unfortunately, not uncommon in the busier courts for such an adjournment to be over a period of weeks.

On occasions, after the call-over of trials, it will be apparent that all the trials set down for that day cannot possibly proceed. It is then appropriate to adjourn one or more trials to a later date. Such trials should be given priority on that date.

## Desertion of the diet

As under solemn procedure[3], the court may desert a diet either *pro loco et tempore* or *simpliciter*. It is uncertain whether a complaint containing several charges may be deserted *simpliciter* in respect of only one charge[4].

The court may desert the diet *pro loco et tempore* of its own volition at any time, but the prosecutor may move for such a desertion only prior to the first witness being sworn[5]. Although a Crown motion to desert *pro loco et tempore* is normally granted without question, the decision is one for the discretion of the court, and such a motion may be refused if the court considers it inappropriate[6]. The effect of desertion *pro loco et tempore* is that the Crown may bring a fresh prosecution, provided that the case is not time-barred.

The power to desert the diet *simpliciter* of its own volition is rarely used by the court. It is appropriate only where it is desired to bring the case to an end for all time. If the diet is deserted *simpliciter*, the Crown may not bring a fresh prosecution.

If, at a trial diet, the Crown has moved the court to adjourn the trial or to desert the diet *pro loco et tempore*, and the court has refused to grant either motion, the court must desert the diet *simpliciter*[7], and the statute emphasises that the Crown may proceed no further[8]. This does not mean that, where the court has refused an adjournment, the Crown is not still entitled to move for desertion *pro loco et tempore*[9]. Whether such a motion would be granted is, however, a different question[9].

## Death, illness or absence of judge

In the event of a case being unable to proceed because of the death, illness or absence of the presiding judge, the clerk of court is given certain powers[10]. If the diet has not been called, he may convene the court and adjourn the diet[11]. If the

---

1 *Fraser v MacKinnon* 1981 SCCR 91; cf *Turnbull v Allan* 1989 SCCR 215, where an adjournment to a later date was refused, the case having been adjourned on three previous occasions. See also *Wilson v Lowe* 1991 JC 5, 1991 SCCR 77.
2 See eg *Milligan v Friel* 1994 SCCR 386.
3 See above at pp 176–177.
4 *McMahon v Hamilton* 1992 JC 98, 1992 SCCR 351, 1992 SLT 242.
5 1995 Act, s 152(1).
6 *Jessop v D* 1986 SCCR 716 (Sh Ct), 1987 SLT (Sh Ct) 115.
7 1995 Act, s 152(2).
8 1995 Act, s 152(3).
9 *Tudhope v Gough* 1982 SCCR 157 (Sh Ct).
10 1995 Act, s 151.
11 1995 Act, s 151(1)(a).

diet has been called but no evidence has been led, he may adjourn the diet[1]. If evidence has been led, he may either (i) with the agreement of the parties desert the diet *pro loco et tempore* or (ii) adjourn the diet[2]. If the diet is deserted *pro loco et tempore* under this provision any new prosecution must be brought within two months of the desertion notwithstanding that any other time limit has elapsed[3]. A new prosecution is brought when a warrant to arrest or to cite the accused is granted, provided that it is executed without undue delay[4].

## Amendment of complaint

There are provisions in Part IX of the 1995 Act relating to amendment of the complaint and the notice of previous convictions[5], similar to those in Part VII of the 1995 Act relating to amendment of an indictment[6]. The summary provisions have been interpreted as allowing a great deal of latitude to the Crown, although, even under summary procedure, an amendment cannot cure a fundamental nullity[7]. Thus a new locus may be added to a complaint provided that a locus is already stated[8], but, if there is no locus at all, that is fatal[9]. The name of a corporate body may be substituted for that of a non-existent body[10], and the name of an individual may be substituted for that of a non-existent corporate body with a similar name[11]. Although a charge is irrelevant, it may still be cured by amendment[12]. This extends even to the omission of the date of the alleged offence[13] and to a charge brought under a repealed statute[14] or under the wrong section of a statute[15]. However, as under solemn procedure, amendment is not permitted if it changes the character of the offence charged[16].

## Failure of accused to appear for trial

If an accused fails to appear for trial, the normal course is for the court to grant a warrant for his arrest on the motion of the prosecutor[17]. Alternatively, the court may fix a fresh trial diet, ordering the accused to attend and appointing intimation

---

1   1995 Act, s 151(1)(b).
2   1995 Act, s 151(1)(c).
3   1995 Act, s 151(2).
4   1995 Act, s 151(3). It is suggested that by 'warrant to cite' Parliament intended the assigning of a diet: see the comments above at p 195, footnote 11.
5   1995 Act, s 159.
6   1995 Act, s 96. See above at pp 177, 178.
7   Heading a sheriff court complaint with the name of a district court in the same sheriffdom is not a fundamental nullity: *Doonin Plant Ltd v Carmichael* 1993 SCCR 511, 1994 SLT 313.
8   *Craig v Keane* 1981 SCCR 166, 1982 SLT 198.
9   *Stevenson v McLevy* (1879) 4 Couper 196, 6 R (J) 33.
10  *Hoyers (UK) Ltd v Houston* 1991 JC 233, 1991 SCCR 919, 1991 SLT 934.
11  *Ralston v Carmichael* 1995 SCCR 729, 1996 SLT 301.
12  *Mackenzie v Brougham* 1982 SCCR 434, 1985 SLT 276; *Yarrow Shipbuilders Ltd v Normand* 1995 SCCR 224, 1995 SLT 1215.
13  *Duffy v Ingram* 1987 SCCR 286, 1988 SLT 226.
14  *Cook v Jessop* 1990 SCCR 211.
15  *Montgomery Transport Ltd v Walkingshaw* 1992 SCCR 17.
16  1995 Act, s 159(2). See eg *McArthur v MacNeill* 1986 SCCR 552, 1987 SLT 299. But see also *Fenwick v Valentine* 1993 SCCR 892, 1994 SLT 485.
17  1995 Act, s 150(3).

of the diet to be made to him[1], which may be done by an officer of law, or by letter sent by registered or recorded delivery post[2].

Exceptionally, the trial may proceed in the absence of the accused. This is possible only when the accused is charged with a statutory offence which does not carry a sentence of imprisonment, or if the statute concerned authorises procedure in the absence of the accused[3]. The court, before proceeding to trial in absence, must be satisfied that the accused has been duly cited or has received intimation of the diet of trial[3]. Evidence against the accused must be led, unless the statute under which he is charged authorises conviction in default of appearance[4]. The court may allow the absent accused to be represented by an authorised solicitor, 'if it shall judge it expedient'[5], although it is difficult to envisage circumstances where it could be considered inexpedient for the accused to be represented. The provision for trial in absence is rarely used. Obvious difficulties would arise if the identity of the accused were in issue.

As has already been noted, an accused who fails without reasonable excuse to attend any diet of which he has been given due notice is guilty of an offence[6].

## Speeches

At the end of the evidence it is normal for both the prosecutor and the defence to address the court. Speeches in summary trials are usually much briefer than those in jury trials. They may deal with both the facts and the law, but care should be taken to distinguish between the two, especially when addressing a lay court.

## Verdict

The court normally returns its verdict immediately after hearing the speeches. A lay court may adjourn to discuss the case if it consists of more than one justice. Again in the case of a lay court the justice or justices may wish to seek advice on the law from the clerk and adjourn for that purpose. A justice should ensure that any comment which he makes to the clerk of court is not overheard and possibly misconstrued[7]. Even a sheriff or stipendiary magistrate may wish to take time to consider the evidence or the law and may adjourn in order to do so, either until later in the same day or until a later date.

As in a case under solemn procedure, the court may find the accused guilty or not guilty or the charge not proven. The same alternative verdicts (eg guilty of theft on a complaint charging robbery) are open to a summary court as to a court of solemn jurisdiction[8].

---

1   1995 Act, s 150(2).
2   1995 Act, s 150(4).
3   1995 Act, s 150(5).
4   1995 Act, s 150(6).
5   1995 Act, s 150(7).
6   1995 Act, s 150(8). See above at p 202.
7   *Maxwell v Cardle* 1993 SCCR 15, 1993 SLT 1017; *McColligan v Normand* 1993 JC 88, 1993 SCCR 330, 1993 SLT 1026.
8   1995 Act, s 138(4), applying the provisions of Sch 3 to summary procedure. See above at p 184.

If a summary court consists of more than one justice and the members of the court are evenly divided as to the guilt of the accused, the accused must be found not guilty[1].

## Sentence

If the verdict is one of guilty, the court proceeds to sentence or adjourns for reports in the same way as if the accused had originally pleaded guilty[2], having considered any notice of previous convictions and a plea in mitigation. As the court will have heard the evidence in the case, the prosecutor does not narrate the facts.

For obvious reasons, if the case is adjourned to obtain reports, the sheriff or justice who took the trial should, if at all possible, preside at the adjourned diet and pronounce sentence.

1    1995 Act, s 162.
2    See above at pp 199, 200.

# CHAPTER 7

# SENTENCING

## INTRODUCTION

Sentencing is one of the most difficult tasks which a judge has to carry out. Many judges would say that it was *the* most difficult. The task is difficult for a number of reasons. First, judges receive very little in the way of training with regard to sentencing, although this has improved to some extent in recent years. Secondly, there is a very wide range of disposals available to a court. Thirdly, there is very often a delicate question involved of balancing the interests of the public (or of the victim) on the one hand against the interests of the accused on the other[1].

Another major factor which, at least until relatively recently, added to the difficulty of the sentencer was the fact that the High Court of Justiciary in its appellate capacity was, on the whole, reluctant to lay down general principles of sentencing, preferring to adopt an ad hoc approach to individual cases and placing much weight on the discretion available to the judge at first instance. The court has, however, recently been less unwilling to offer guidance where it considered it appropriate. In *Her Majesty's Advocate v Lee*[2] Lord Justice-General Hope said[3]:

'The discretion which is given to a trial judge in matters of sentencing will always be respected by the appeal court. This is an important aspect of sentencing practice, as there are so many factors which may have to be taken into account in his consideration of the particular offence and the circumstances of the particular offender. But this discretion is not unlimited. Undue disparity between sentences is as undesirable as rigidity. Thus a sentence which is excessive may be reduced on appeal, and the appeal court now has power to increase sentences which are shown to be unduly lenient. It has not been the practice in Scotland for the appeal court to lay down sentencing guidelines. But decisions of the appeal court in appeals against sentence, especially those where it has held a sentence to be unduly lenient, do from time to time provide guidance as to what is or is not appropriate. A judge who fails to take account of that guidance cannot be said to have acted within the proper limits of his discretion as sentencer. He cannot complain if his sentence is challenged as being excessive or unduly lenient or, if he decides upon a non-custodial disposal which conflicts with that guidance, that disposal is challenged as inappropriate.'

---

1 It is not proper for the sentencing court to seek the views of the victim of a crime on the sentence to be imposed, although the attitude of the victim may be a relevant factor in some cases: *HMA v McKenzie* 1989 SCCR 587, 1990 SLT 28.
2 *HMA v Lee* 1996 SCCR 205, 1996 SLT 568.
3 *HMA v Lee* 1996 SCCR 205 at 212E, 1996 SLT 568 at 574F.

However, the importance of judicial discretion, especially in exercising leniency, was emphasised a short time later by the same judge in *Her Majesty's Advocate v McKay*[1] when he said[2]:

'We wish to make it clear to the Lord Advocate and to impress upon anyone else who may seek to press us in [the direction of mandatory minimum sentences] that this court will continue, so long as the power to do so rests with us, to assert the right of judges to exercise leniency in the matter of sentencing whenever this is appropriate. We shall also continue to assert their right to take account of exceptional circumstances in deciding not to impose immediate custodial sentences in cases where a custodial sentence would otherwise be inevitable.'

The 1995 Act contains provisions intended to encourage the High Court to provide guidance on sentencing. Section 118(7) provides that in disposing of an appeal against sentence under solemn procedure, whether by the accused or by the Crown, the High Court may 'pronounce an opinion on the sentence or other disposal or order which is appropriate in any similar case'. There is a similar provision for appeals under summary procedure[3]. In respect of both solemn and summary procedure it is provided that 'a court in passing sentence shall have regard to any relevant opinion pronounced' by the High Court under either the solemn or summary provisions just referred to[4]. It remains to be seen to what extent and with what effect the High Court will be prepared to provide sentencing guidelines.

The purpose of this chapter is to examine the various disposals which are open to a court and to comment briefly on them[5]. However, before embarking on this exercise, it would be as well to recall the maximum powers of the various courts. These powers are, of course, in the case of a statutory offence, always subject to any limitation imposed by the statute creating the offence.

The High Court's powers of sentencing are unlimited. It may impose imprisonment for any term up to and including life, and it may impose a fine of any amount.

The sheriff court, as a court of solemn jurisdiction, may impose imprisonment for a maximum period of three years[6], although a sheriff may remit an accused to the High Court for sentence if he considers that his powers of punishment are inadequate[7]. The sheriff in a solemn case may also impose an unlimited fine.

Sitting summarily a sheriff may normally impose a maximum period of three months' imprisonment[8]. However, this maximum period may be extended to six

---

1  *HMA v McKay* 1996 SCCR 410, 1996 SLT 697.
2  *HMA v McKay* 1996 SCCR 410 at 417E, 1996 SLT 697 at 700E. These comments were directed against the idea of mandatory minimum sentences. Such sentences will become part of our law if the 1997 Act, ss 1–3 come into force. See the Appendix at pp 321–322 below.
3  1995 Act, s 189(7).
4  1995 Act, s 197. In his commentary on the passage quoted above from the opinion of the Lord Justice-General in *HMA v Lee*, Sheriff G H Gordon (editor of SCCR) wryly remarks at 1996 SCCR 213F: 'The court's comments on guidelines anticipates ss 118(7), 189(7) and 197 of the [1995 Act], thus proving that, as everyone except Parliament knew, they were unnecessary.'
5  For a detailed examination of the subject of sentencing in Scotland see *Nicholson*. In this chapter attention is drawn, where appropriate, to possible changes in sentencing which may occur under the 1997 Act. It should be noted that there is one completely new disposal which will be available to the court if s 5 of the Act comes into force. This is the restriction of liberty order. See the Appendix at p 323 below.
6  1995 Act, s 3(3). This will increase to five years if the 1997 Act, s 13 comes into force. See the Appendix at p 318 below.
7  1995 Act, s 195.
8  1995 Act, s 5(2)(d). This will increase to six months if the 1997 Act, s 13 comes into force. See the Appendix at p 318 below.

months where the accused is convicted of '(a) a second or subsequent offence infer-ring dishonest appropriation of property, or attempt thereat, or (b) a second or sub-sequent offence inferring personal violence'[1]. The sheriff has power to impose a fine or to order the accused to find caution, in both cases for a sum not exceeding the 'prescribed sum'[2], which is £5,000 at the time of writing.

A district court consisting of a stipendiary magistrate has the same powers as those of a sheriff sitting summarily[3].

A district court consisting of one or more lay justices may imprison for a period not exceeding 60 days[4]. It may impose a fine or order the accused to find caution in a sum not exceeding level 4 on the standard scale[5], which is £2,500 at the time of writing.

# IMPRISONMENT

## General

Imprisonment is the only form of custodial sentence which may now be imposed on a person over 21 years of age[6]. No person under 21 can be sent to prison[7], but that does not of course mean that such a person cannot receive a custodial sen-tence[8]. A court of summary jurisdiction may not sentence a person to a period of imprisonment for less than five days[9], although there is a rarely used provision for offenders being detained for up to four days in authorised police cells[10].

## Restrictions on imprisonment

If a convicted person has not previously been sentenced to imprisonment or deten-tion[11] by a court in any part of the United Kingdom, he may not have a sentence of imprisonment imposed on him unless the court considers that no other method of dealing with him is appropriate[12]. For the purpose of determining whether any other method is appropriate, the court must obtain such information as it can about the offender's circumstances, and must also take into account any information which is before it concerning the offender's character and physical and mental con-dition[12]. For practical purposes the court obtains the necessary information by

---

1 1995 Act, s 5(3). This will increase to twelve months if the 1997 Act, s 13 comes into force. See the Appendix at p 318 below.
2 1995 Act, s 5(2)(a), (b). The prescribed sum is discussed below at p 233.
3 1995 Act, s 7(5).
4 1995 Act, s 7(6)(a).
5 1995 Act, s 7(6)(b), (c). The standard scale is discussed below at p 233.
6 Penal servitude and imprisonment with hard labour were abolished by the 1975 Act, s 221. Preventive detention and corrective training were abolished by the Criminal Justice (Scotland) Act 1980, Sch 8.
7 1995 Act, s 207(1).
8 For custodial sentences for those under 21 see below at pp 231–232.
9 1995 Act, s 206(1).
10 1995 Act, s 206(2)–(6).
11 Defined in 1995 Act, s 204(4). It excludes a suspended sentence of imprisonment (competent in England and Wales and in Northern Ireland but not in Scotland) which has not yet taken effect: s 204(4)(a).
12 1995 Act, s 204(2).

means of a social enquiry report (usually abbreviated to 'SER') prepared by a member of the local authority social work department, although the Act does provide that the information may be obtained 'otherwise'[1]. A court of summary jurisdiction must state its reason for holding that no sentence other than imprisonment is appropriate and that reason must be minuted in the record of proceedings[2].

If an offender such as is mentioned in the previous paragraph is not legally represented, there is a further restriction on a sentence of imprisonment being imposed on him. Such a sentence cannot be imposed unless he has either (a) applied for legal aid and had his application refused on financial grounds, or (b) having been informed of his right to apply for legal aid and having had the opportunity to apply, he has failed to do so[3]. It is not enough that the accused be offered an opportunity to seek legal advice: he must be informed of his right to apply for legal aid[4].

These restrictions on imprisonment do not apply in the case of a witness in a summary trial who is in contempt of court in terms of section 155(1) of the 1995 Act[5].

## Length of sentence

The length of a sentence of imprisonment will depend on a number of factors, including the gravity of the crime, the circumstances of the accused and his previous criminal record. The fact that the accused has co-operated with the authorities may mitigate a sentence[6].

An important provision introduced by the 1995 Act is that, in the case of a plea of guilty, the court, in determining what sentence to pass, may take into account the stage in the proceedings at which the accused indicated his intention to plead guilty and the circumstances in which that indication was given[7]. This provision effectively overrules a much criticised decision of the High Court which stated that it was objectionable to give a more lenient sentence for an early plea of guilty[8].

It is an irrelevant consideration that the case has been indicted in the High Court rather than the sheriff court[9].

A very short sentence of imprisonment has on occasions not found favour with the High Court[10].

## Consecutive or concurrent

If an accused appears on a number of charges, each possibly carrying a sentence of imprisonment, a question may arise as to whether the sentences should run con-

---

1   1995 Act, s 204(2).
2   1995 Act, s 204(3).
3   1995 Act, s 204(1).
4   *Milligan v Jessop* 1988 SCCR 137.
5   *Forrest v Wilson* 1993 SCCR 631, 1994 SLT 490.
6   *Cormack v HMA* 1996 SCCR 53.
7   1995 Act, s 196.
8   *Strawhorn v McLeod* 1987 SCCR 413.
9   *Khaliq v HMA* 1984 SCCR 212.
10  *McKenzie v Lockhart* 1986 SCCR 663 (14 days); *Kinney v Tudhope* 1985 SCCR 393 (21 days): the offender was under 21, so the sentence was detention rather than imprisonment, but the principle (in so far as there is one) is the same. Cf *Stirling v Stewart* 1988 SCCR 619 (30 days upheld as appropriate – also a case of an offender under 21).

secutively or concurrently. A similar question may arise if the accused is already serving a sentence of imprisonment: should any new sentence be consecutive to or concurrent with that already being served?

If an accused appears on several charges in the same indictment or complaint, he should normally be sentenced separately on each charge[1]. The law was until recently somewhat confused as to whether sentences should be concurrent or consecutive if the court was dealing with a number of crimes or offences which were all part of one incident or course of conduct. However, this has now been clarified by the decision of a bench of five judges[2]. This case is authority for the following propositions:

(1) A court is entitled at common law to give concurrent or consecutive sentences;

(2) Where two or more charges appear on one complaint or indictment, the highest custodial sentence which may competently be imposed is the maximum prescribed for the charge which carries the highest sentence;

(3) The same rule applies where different charges are contained in more than one complaint or indictment but fairness requires them to be treated as if they were one;

(4) Where two or more charges are contained in more than one complaint or indictment and fairness does not require that they be treated as one, it is competent to impose custodial sentences which add up to more than the maximum which could have been imposed in respect of one complaint or indictment;

(5) If the charges appear on separate complaints or indictments for techncial reasons (as, for example, if one of the charges is driving while disqualified), they should be treated as if they had appeared in one complaint or indictment so that the sentences in aggregate cannot exceed the limit of the court's sentencing power on one complaint or indictment;

(6) Where a number of charges appear on separate complaints or indictments and that is not because of merely technical reasons, the court should simply determine whether the sentences should be concurrent or consecutive. In doing so it may consider: (a) the overall effect of the sentence; (b) whether it appears to be equitable that the charges were brought on separate complaints or indictments having regard to the possibility that they might all have been on the same complaint or indictment; (c) whether charges relating to crimes committed on two or more separate occasions are to be disposed of at the same diet; (d) whether the accused has gained an improper or illegitimate advantage because the complaints or indictments are being heard together; and (e) whether the accused has brought about or contributed to the situation in which a series of complaints or indictments are being dealt with at the same diet or on the same day (as, for example, by failing to attend court for disposal on previous occasions);

(7) There is no absolute rule to the effect that sentences have to be concurrent if charges arise out of the same course of conduct: it is in the court's discretion whether to impose a concurrent or consecutive sentence or, indeed, a cumulo sentence, bearing in mind that separate sentences may be required for statutory offences and that, if a cumulo sentence is imposed, all the charges stand or fall together in the event of an appeal;

1 *Caringi v HMA* 1989 SCCR 223, 1989 SLT 714 (common law charges). The principle had been established for statutory charges much earlier: *Seaton v Allan* 1973 JC 24, 1974 SLT 234.
2 *Nicholson v Lees* 1996 SCCR 551, 1996 SLT 706. See also *Howard v HMA* 1997 SLT 575.

(8) Where two or more offences are truly distinct in nature or arise at different times and at different places, the court may well consider that consecutive sentences are appropriate.

If an accused commits an offence while on bail or otherwise breaches a bail order or fails to attend a diet, the general rule is that in the first case the sentence which would otherwise be imposed for the offence should be increased[1], and that in the latter cases a consecutive sentence should be imposed[2]. In all cases what would otherwise be the maximum sentence available to the court may be exceeded[3].

If an accused has been sentenced to life imprisonment, any other sentence imposed at the same time or subsequently should be concurrent and not consecutive[4].

If an accused is already serving a sentence of imprisonment at the time of being sentenced, it is a matter for the judge's discretion whether the new sentence should be concurrent or consecutive[5], but the new sentence should not normally be consecutive when it is imposed for an offence known to be outstanding when the earlier sentence was passed[6]. The view is frequently expressed that, if a concurrent sentence is imposed, it is effectively no sentence at all. A consecutive sentence imposed on someone already in prison should be expressed as 'consecutive to the total period of imprisonment to which the prisoner is already subject' or 'to take effect on the expiry of all sentences previously imposed'[7].

It is not uncommon, especially where all the charges against an accused are common law and not statutory, to pass a cumulo sentence, ie one sentence covering all offences in the indictment or complaint instead of separate sentences for each offence, either concurrent or consecutive. It is competent to pass a cumulo sentence even where all the charges are statutory[8]. However, in such a case the sentencing judge should indicate what sentence each offence would have attracted if it had stood alone[8].

## Backdating of sentence

A sentence of imprisonment normally runs from the date of its imposition, but it may be backdated. In both solemn and summary cases the court is directed to 'have regard to any period of time spent in custody . . . on remand awaiting trial or sentence' when determining the period of imprisonment to impose[9]. The court must specify the date of commencement of the sentence[10]. This does not mean that a

---

1 In terms of the 1995 Act, s 27(3). See above at p 105. See *Hill v HMA* 1997 SCCR 376.
2 *Nicholson v Lees* 1996 SCCR 551, 1996 SLT 706.
3 1995 Act, s 27(5) (offence committed on bail); 1995 Act, s 27(9) (breach of bail condition); s 150(9) (failure to appear at diet in summary prosecution).
4 *McRae v HMA* 1987 SCCR 36; *McPhee v HMA* 1990 SCCR 313.
5 1995 Act, s 167(7) makes specific provision for a consecutive sentence in summary cases. The earlier sentence need not precede the finding of guilt or plea of guilty in the later case; it is enough that it precedes the later sentence: *Beattie v McGlennan* 1990 SCCR 497, 1991 SLT 384. There is no equivalent provision for solemn procedure, but the competence of a consecutive sentence under such procedure has never been questioned. In any event, even in a summary case the power to impose a consecutive sentence exists at common law: *Young v McGlennan* 1990 SCCR 373.
6 *McGill v HMA* 1996 SCCR 35.
7 *Moore v MacPhail* 1986 SCCR 169.
8 *McDade v HMA* 1997 SCCR 52.
9 1995 Act, s 210(1)(a).
10 1995 Act, s 210(1)(b).

sentence of imprisonment must always be backdated to the date of remand. All that is necessary is that the judge is informed of the period spent in custody and applies his mind to the question of how to take account of it. If a court does not backdate a sentence in the case of an accused who has been on remand, the reason for not doing so must be stated[1]. Whether to backdate or not is a question for the judge's discretion[2]. However, this is not to say that the High Court never interferes with a decision whether or not to backdate[3]. If an accused is convicted only of a charge to which he has previously been prepared to plead guilty, his sentence should be backdated at least to the date when he indicated his preparedness to plead guilty[4]. A similar principle applies if the Crown ultimately accepts a restricted plea of guilty tendered at an earlier stage of the proceedings[5]. If an accused is remanded in custody for a report to be obtained and the maximum sentence of imprisonment is then imposed, it need not necessarily be backdated to the date of remand[6].

The provisions requiring the sentencing judge to specify the date of commencement of the sentence and to give reasons for not backdating apply to a life sentence as much as to any other sentence[7].

## Imprisonment with another sentence

It is as a general rule very undesirable to impose a sentence of imprisonment at the same time as another non-custodial sentence. Thus imprisonment should not be imposed along with a probation order[8]. Nor is it appropriate to sentence an accused to imprisonment on one charge while at the same time deferring sentence on another charge[9]. However, in some cases the court may quite properly impose imprisonment on some charges and a fine on others for which imprisonment would be an incompetent disposal. In such circumstances it is usual for the accused to ask that no time be allowed for payment of the fine. This means that the alternative of imprisonment in default of payment may run concurrently with the sentence imposed on the other charges. Of course, if, in such a situation, the accused wishes to appeal against his sentence of imprisonment and is granted interim liberation meanwhile, then he should certainly ask for time to pay.

## Release from prison[10]

The provisions for release of prisoners are contained in Part I of the 1993 Act. Apart from those whose sentence is fixed by law (in practice those convicted of

---

1 1995 Act, s 210(1)(c).
2 *Muir v HMA* 1985 SCCR 402; *Dallas v HMA* 1992 SCCR 40.
3 Eg in *Callaghan v HMA* 1986 SCCR 563.
4 *Campbell v HMA* 1986 SCCR 403.
5 *Tulloch v Annan* 1991 SCCR 24.
6 *McDonald v Wilson* 1991 SCCR 61; *Brady v MacNeill* 1991 SCCR 234.
7 *Elliott v HMA* 1997 SCCR 111.
8 *Downie v Irvine* 1964 JC 52, 1964 SLT 205. But see *C v Lowe* 1990 SCCR 755, about which Sheriff G H Gordon (editor of SCCR) comments at 1990 SCCR 758: 'This case is interesting in that it suggests that there may be room for a disposal which combines a comparatively short period of imprisonment with a probation order.'
9 *Lennon v Copeland* 1972 SLT (Notes) 68.
10 The law on release from prison will be radically changed if the 1997 Act, Pt III, Ch I (ss 33–41) comes into force. See the Appendix at pp 324–325 below.

murder) there are four categories of prisoner: short-term, long-term, discretionary life prisoners and other life prisoners. There are different release provisions for each category.

### Short-term prisoners

A short-term prisoner is a prisoner who is serving a sentence of less than four years[1]. Such a prisoner is released unconditionally (unless subject to a supervised release order[2]) after serving one-half of his sentence[3].

In certain very limited circumstances a short-term prisoner may be released on licence[4] rather than unconditionally[5].

### Supervised release order[6]

Where a person is sentenced to imprisonment for a period of not less than twelve months but less than four years, the court may, on passing sentence, make a supervised release order 'if it considers that it is necessary to do so to protect the public from serious harm from the offender on his release'[7]. The order provides that for a specified period not exceeding twelve months[8] the offender is under the supervision of (in Scotland) a social worker or (in England or Wales) a probation officer[9] and must comply with (i) such requirements as may be imposed by the court in the order, and (ii) such requirements as the social worker or probation officer may reasonably specify 'for the purpose of securing the good conduct of the [offender] or preventing, or lessening the possibility of, his committing a further offence (whether or not an offence of the kind for which he was sentenced)'[10]. The offender must also comply with the 'standard requirements'[11]. These are: (i) to report to the supervising officer in a manner and at intervals specified by that officer; and (ii) to notify that officer without delay of any change of address[12].

Before making a supervised release order the court must obtain a report from a social worker[13].

When making a supervised release order the court must explain to the offender 'in as straightforward a way as is practicable, the effect of the order and the possible consequences for him of any breach'[14].

---

1  1993 Act, s 27(1).
2  In terms of the 1995 Act, s 209. See the next section.
3  1993 Act, s 1(1).
4  For release on licence see below at p 229.
5  In terms of the 1993 Act, s 3(1) (release on compassionate grounds) or s 16(7) (sentence imposed in respect of offence committed by released prisoner).
6  The scope of a supervised release order will be substantially extended if the 1997 Act, s 4 comes into force. See the Appendix at p 322 below.
7  1995 Act, s 209(1).
8  1995 Act, s 209(7).
9  1995 Act, s 209(3)(a).
10  1995 Act, s 209(3)(b).
11  1995 Act, s 209(3)(c).
12  1995 Act, s 209(4)(a); 1996 Rules, r 20.3; Form 20.3.
13  1995 Act, s 209(2).
14  1995 Act, s 209(5).

A supervised release order may be varied or amended on the application of the offender or of his supervising officer[1].

If an offender breaches a supervised attendance order the court may order him to be returned to prison for a period not exceeding the time between the first act constituting a breach and the date on which supervision under the order would have ceased[2]. Alternatively, the court may vary the order[3].

## Long-term prisoners

A long-term prisoner is one serving a sentence of four years or more[4]. Such a prisoner is released on licence after having served two-thirds of his sentence[5]. He may be released on licence after serving only one-half of his sentence if the Parole Board[6] so recommends and the Secretary of State accepts the recommendation[7]. A person released on licence must comply with such conditions as may be specified by the Secretary of State[8]. A licence (unless earlier revoked) expires when the whole period of the sentence has elapsed[9]. A licence may be revoked by the Secretary of State, in which case the offender is recalled to prison to serve the rest of his sentence[10]. However, the Secretary of State may normally revoke the licence only on the recommendation of the Parole Board[11] although, in a case of urgency where it is impracticable to await such recommendation, he may do so without it[12].

## Commission of offence by released prisoner

A prisoner (whether short-term or long-term) who has been released as described above and commits an offence punishable by imprisonment before the date on which he would (but for his release) have completed his sentence may in certain circumstances be returned to prison to serve a period equivalent to the balance of his sentence[13]. If the court which convicts him of the new offence is inferior to the court which imposed the original sentence it may refer the case to the superior court[14]. A court in England or Wales before which the offender is convicted of the new offence may refer the case to the Scottish court which imposed the original sentence[15].

In deciding whether to make an order for return to prison the court is entitled to take into account the whole history of the offender and not just the circumstances of the new offence[16].

1  1993 Act, s 15.
2  1993 Act, s 18(2)(a).
3  1993 Act, s 18(2)(b).
4  1993 Act, s 27(1).
5  1993 Act, s 1(2).
6  The Parole Board for Scotland is now constituted under the 1993 Act, s 20.
7  1993 Act, s 1(3).
8  1993 Act, s 12(1).
9  1993 Act, s 11(1).
10  1993 Act, s 17(1)(a), (5).
11  1993 Act, s 17(1)(a)(i).
12  1993 Act, s 17(1)(a)(ii).
13  1993 Act, s 16(1), (2)(a). See *McEleny* 1997 SCCR 297.
14  1993 Act, s 16(2)(b).
15  1993 Act, s 16(3).
16  *Lynch v Normand* 1995 SCCR 404.

## Discretionary life prisoners

A discretionary life prisoner is one 'whose sentence was imposed for an offence the sentence for which is not fixed by law' and in respect of whom the court has specified the period which should elapse before he may be considered for release[1]. In fixing the period the court should take into account the seriousness of the offence, or of the offence combined with other offences associated with it, and any previous convictions of the offender[2].

In the case of a discretionary life prisoner the Secretary of State must release him on licence if directed to do so by the Parole Board[3]. The Parole Board may give such a direction only if the Secretary of State has referred the prisoner's case to it and it is satisfied that it is no longer necessary for the protection of the public that the prisoner should be confined[4]. A prisoner may require the Secretary of State to refer his case to the Parole Board[5], but this is subject to certain limitations[6].

The licence of a prisoner serving a life sentence (unless revoked) remains in force until his death[7].

## Other life prisoners

If a prisoner, who is convicted of an offence the sentence for which is not fixed by law, is given a life sentence and the court decides not to recommend the period which should expire before release can be considered, which is very rare, the court must state its reasons for so deciding[8]. A prisoner in this category is not a discretionary life prisoner. He may be released on licence by the Secretary of State on the recommendation of the Parole Board but only after the former has consulted with the Lord Justice-General, whom failing the Lord Justice-Clerk, and the trial judge if he is available[9]. The Parole Board may not make a recommendation in such a case unless the Secretary of State has referred the case to the Board for advice[10].

## Sentence for murder

The sentence for murder in respect of a person over 21 is imprisonment for life[11]. When imposing such a sentence the judge is entitled to make a recommendation as to the minimum period which should elapse before the offender may be released on licence[12]. He must state his reasons for doing so[13]. It is undesirable for a judge to make a recommendation without defence counsel having had an opportunity to

1  1993 Act, s 2(1), (2).
2  1993 Act, s 2(2).
3  1993 Act, s 2(4).
4  1993 Act, s 2(5).
5  1993 Act, s 2(6).
6  1993 Act, s 2(7), which provides that two years must elapse after a previous reference has resulted in the prisoner's not being released. It also provides for the situation when the prisoner is serving a determinate sentence along with his life sentence.
7  1993 Act, s 11(2).
8  1993 Act, s 2(3).
9  1993 Act, s 1(4).
10  1993 Act, s 1(5).
11  1995 Act, s 205(1).
12  1995 Act, s 205(4).
13  1995 Act, s 205(5).

address him on the matter[1]. The judge should indicate to counsel if he is contemplating making a recommendation. A recommendation should normally be made only in an exceptional case as otherwise the hands of the Parole Board and the Secretary of State may be tied[2]. A recommendation should normally be for a period of not less than twelve years[3]. Although a life sentence for murder, being a sentence fixed by law, is not normally appealable[4], an appeal is competent against any such recommendation[5].

A person sentenced to life imprisonment for murder may be released on licence at any time by the Secretary of State on the recommendation of the Parole Board in the same way as any other life prisoner who is not a discretionary life prisoner[6]. His licence remains in force for the rest of his life[7] and may be revoked in the same way as that of an ordinary licensee[8].

# DETENTION OF YOUNG OFFENDERS

## General

In the case of an offender aged not less than sixteen but under 21 the only custodial sentence which a court may impose is detention in a young offenders' institution[9].

## Restriction on detention

As in the case of imprisonment, no person without legal representation may be sentenced to detention without either having been offered the opportunity to apply for legal aid or having been refused it on financial grounds[10].

There is a further restriction on detention. The court may not impose a sentence of detention unless it is of the opinion that no other method of dealing with the offender is appropriate[11]. The court must obtain such information as it can to enable it to form an opinion of this matter, and this may be obtained by means of a social enquiry report 'or otherwise'[12]. In practice a social enquiry report is invariably obtained. The court must also take into account any information before it concerning the accused's character and physical and mental condition[12]. There is some confusion as to whether appearances by an offender before a children's hearing may be taken into account when considering his character[13], but such appear-

---

1 *Murphy v HMA* 1995 SCCR 55, 1995 SLT 725.
2 *McGuire v HMA* 1995 SCCR 776, 1996 SLT 566.
3 *Casey v HMA* 1993 JC 102, 1993 SCCR 453, 1994 SLT 54. This case contains a useful examination of other cases where a recommendation has been made and discusses the type of case in which a recommendation is appropriate.
4 1995 Act, s 106(2).
5 1995 Act, s 205(6).
6 1993 Act, s 1(4). See above at p 230.
7 1993 Act, s 11(2).
8 See above at p 229.
9 1995 Act, s 207(1), (2), (5).
10 1995 Act, s 204(1).
11 1995 Act, s 207(3).
12 1995 Act, s 207(4).
13 In *Gibson v Annan* 1990 SCCR 519, it was held that appearances before a children's hearing were not relevant. The contrary view was taken in *Curran v Jessop* 1991 SCCR 150.

ances are probably a relevant part of the background information to which a court is entitled to have regard. The court must state the reason why no other disposal is appropriate, and, except in the case of the High Court, the reason must be minuted in the record of proceedings[1].

## Length of sentence, concurrent or consecutive, backdating of sentence, detention with another sentence

The comments made above[2] on all these topics with respect to imprisonment of adult offenders apply equally to the detention of young offenders.

### Release from young offenders' institution

Detention is the equivalent of imprisonment for an adult and the provisions of the 1993 Act mentioned above for those sentenced to a determinate period of imprisonment (with regard to short-term prisoners, long-term prisoners, release, supervised release orders, release on licence) apply to detainees in exactly the same way as they apply to prisoners[3].

### Sentence for murder

A person under eighteen who is convicted of murder is sentenced to be detained without limit of time and will be detained in such place and under such conditions as the Secretary of State may direct[4].

A person who is eighteen or over but under 21 who is convicted of murder is sentenced to be detained in a young offenders' institution and is liable to be detained for life[5].

As in the case of an adult offender, the judge may recommend a minimum period during which a young offender should be detained before being released on licence[6] and must state his reasons for doing so[7].

# FINES

### General

A fine is the most common sentence in courts of summary jurisdiction and is also relatively common in the sheriff court sitting as a court of solemn jurisdiction.

---

1  1995 Act, s 207(3).
2  See pp 224–227.
3  1993 Act, s 6(1)(a). See above at pp 228–229. These provisions will also be radically affected if the 1997 Act, Pt III, Ch I comes into force. See the Appendix at pp 324–325 below.
4  1995 Act, s 205(2).
5  1995 Act, s 205(3).
6  1995 Act, s 205(4). See above at pp 230, 231.
7  1995 Act, s 205(5).

It is not competent to impose both a fine and a sentence of imprisonment for the same common law offence[1]. A fine should not be imposed on one charge if the court is deferring sentence on another[2].

Like the length of a custodial sentence, the amount of a fine is governed by a number of factors, including the gravity of the offence. The value of goods stolen is not usually a factor to be taken into account when fixing the level of a fine, especially if the goods are recovered[3].

It is specifically provided that in determining the amount of a fine the court must take into consideration 'the means of the offender so far as known to the court'[4]. A fine which would have taken 90 weeks to pay by the instalments fixed (which were the most the accused could pay) was held to be excessive as being beyond his means[5]. If several accused are equally culpable but have substantially different means, the court is entitled to distinguish among them in fixing the amount of any fine[6]. The 'means of the offender' may include the means of a third party (eg an employer) who will actually be paying the fine[7].

## The standard scale and the prescribed sum

In order to avoid the necessity of regularly changing the actual amounts of the maximum fines for statutory offences as money loses its value, there was introduced the standard scale[8]. This lays down five levels of fine[9]. These are at present:

| Level 1 | £200 |
| Level 2 | £500 |
| Level 3 | £1,000 |
| Level 4 | £2,500 |
| Level 5 | £5,000 |

These sums may be altered by the Secretary of State by order if it appears to him that there has been a change in the value of money[10].

The same thinking is behind the fixing of 'the prescribed sum' as the maximum fine which may normally be imposed by a sheriff sitting summarily[11]. This is presently £5,000[12], and the sum may be altered by the Secretary of State by order if it appears to him that there has been a change in the value of money[13].

1 *McGunnigal v Copeland* 1972 SLT (Notes) 70; *Compton v O'Brien* 1994 SCCR 657.
2 *McElwaine v Cardle* 1993 SCCR 619.
3 *Donnelly v Wilson* 1991 SCCR 545.
4 1995 Act, s 211(7).
5 *Paterson v McGlennan* 1991 JC 141, 1991 SCCR 616, 1991 SLT 832. See also *Reynolds v Hamilton* 1994 SCCR 760, but contrast *Forsyth v Cardle* 1994 SCCR 769 where the fine, as reduced on appeal, would still take eight years to pay.
6 *Scott v Lowe* 1990 SCCR 15.
7 *St Clare v Wilson* 1994 SCCR 353, 1994 SLT 564.
8 Now contained in the 1995 Act, s 225(1).
9 1995 Act, s 225(2).
10 1995 Act, s 225(4), (5)(a).
11 1995 Act, s 5(2)(a).
12 1995 Act, s 225(8).
13 1995 Act, s 225(4), (5)(b).

## Exceptionally high maximum fines

Some statutes specify as the maximum fine payable on summary conviction a sum greater than the prescribed sum. The Secretary of State may by order amend such enactments to increase the amount of the maximum fine to take account of a change in the value of money or a change in the standard scale[1].

## Fines for statutory offences

In the case of a statutory offence triable only on indictment, or triable either on indictment or summarily which is actually tried on indictment, the court has an unlimited power to fine, notwithstanding that the statute concerned may provide a maximum fine[2]. If the statute makes no provision for a fine, but provides only for imprisonment, the court nonetheless has power to impose a fine[3].

In the case of a statutory offence, triable either on indictment or summarily, which is actually tried summarily, the provisions for calculating the maximum permissible fine in respect of contraventions of statutes passed prior to the introduction of the standard scale are complex[4], and the details are beyond the scope of this book. The practical effect is that all such fines are now stated in terms of the standard scale.

If the statutory offence is triable only summarily, the maximum fine which may be imposed is normally stated in the statute as a level on the standard scale. For contraventions of statutes passed prior to the introduction of the standard scale the penalties (all stated in terms of the standard scale) are now contained in Schedule 2 to the Criminal Procedure (Consequential Provisions) (Scotland) Act 1995.

## Remission of fines

All courts have power to remit a fine in whole or in part[5]. If a fine has been transferred for enforcement to a court other than that which imposed it[6], it is the court to which it has been transferred which has the power of remission[7]. Otherwise it is the court which imposed the fine[8], except if the fine was imposed by the High Court, in which case it is the court by which payment of the fine was first enforceable[9]. If the person fined is serving a custodial sentence for non-payment of the fine[10], the whole of the custodial alternative or a proportion thereof, as the case may be, is remitted if the fine or any part thereof is remitted[11]. An offender need not attend court to have his fine remitted[12]. Remission is normally the result of an application by an offender, but the court may remit a fine of its own volition.

1  1995 Act, s 226.
2  1995 Act, s 211(1), (2). This excludes offences normally triable only summarily but which may be tried on indictment by virtue of the 1995 Act, s 292(7).
3  1995 Act, s 199(2).
4  Criminal Procedure (Consequential Provisions) (Scotland) Act 1995, Sch 1, para 2. See *Renton and Brown* para 23–31.
5  1995 Act, s 213.
6  See below at p 241.
7  1995 Act, s 213(1)(a).
8  1995 Act, s 213(1)(b).
9  1995 Act, s 213(1)(b). For enforcement of fines imposed by the High Court see below at p 241.
10  See below at p 237 for custody for non-payment of a fine.
11  1995 Act, s 213(2).
12  1995 Act, s 213(3).

## Time for payment of fines

In the case of most fines the accused asks either for time to pay[1] or to be allowed to pay by instalments[2]. An offender may, of course, pay the whole fine at the time when it is imposed, if he wishes to do so. Payment by cheque is accepted, but the court then normally allows seven days for payment in order that the cheque may be cleared. An offender must be allowed at least seven days to pay either the whole fine or the first instalment thereof[3], unless (a) he appears to the court to possess sufficient means to enable him to pay forthwith; or (b) he states to the court that he does not wish time to pay; or (c) he fails to satisfy the court that he has a fixed abode; or (d) the court is satisfied for any other special reason that no time should be allowed[4]. If no time to pay is allowed, the court may immediately exercise its power to imprison for non-payment[5], but the reason for not allowing time to pay must be stated and recorded in the extract of the finding and sentence[6]. An offender who is not legally represented and who has not previously been sentenced to imprisonment or detention must not have an immediate alternative of imprisonment imposed with no time to pay, without having been given an opportunity of applying for legal aid[7]. The alternative of imprisonment may be made consecutive to a sentence of imprisonment imposed on the same day[8]. Any alternative imposed may also be made consecutive to a sentence already being served[9].

Where an offender is allowed time to pay or to make payment by instalments, it is possible at the same time to impose the alternative of imprisonment in default of payment (to act no doubt as an incentive to payment), but only in limited circumstances[10]. These are that the gravity of the offence, the character of the offender or 'other special reason' render it expedient that he should be imprisoned without further inquiry in default of payment[11]. It is not incompetent to impose an immediate alternative of imprisonment in respect of an offence which is not itself punishable by a sentence of imprisonment[12], but the alternative should be imposed in such a case only where the accused's record is such as to show that he is unlikely to pay a fine unless forced to do so[13].

An offender may apply to the court for further time to pay[14]. The application may be made orally or in writing[15]. The application should be made to the court which imposed the fine[16] or to any court to which the fine has been transferred for

1  1995 Act, s 214(1).
2  1995 Act, s 214(8).
3  1995 Act, s 214(1). There is no limit on the time which may be allowed for payment or over which instalments may be payable: *Johnston v Lockhart* 1987 SCCR 337. See also the cases cited in note 5 on p 233 above.
4  1995 Act, s 214(2). A court of summary jurisdiction has power to have an offender searched and any money found on him applied to payment of the fine imposed: 1995 Act, s 212(1).
5  See below at p 237.
6  1995 Act, s 214(2), (3).
7  1995 Act, s 204(1). The court has power to grant legal aid in such circumstances: Legal Aid (Scotland) Act 1986, s 23(1)(b).
8  *Young v McGlennan* 1990 SCCR 373.
9  *Russell v MacPhail* 1990 JC 380, 1990 SCCR 628, 1991 SLT 449.
10  1995 Act, s 214(4).
11  1995 Act, s 214(4). The reason must be stated. 'Nature of the offence' is not a relevant reason for imposing the alternative under this section: *Buchanan v Hamilton* 1988 SCCR 378.
12  *Kausen v Walkingshaw* 1990 SCCR 553.
13  *Paterson v McGlennan* 1991 JC 141, 1991 SCCR 616, 1991 SLT 832.
14  1995 Act, s 214(7).
15  1995 Act, s 215(4).
16  1995 Act, s 215(1).

enforcement purposes[1]. The court must allow further time unless it is satisfied that the offender's failure to pay has been wilful or that the offender has no reasonable prospect of being able to pay if further time is allowed[2]. A court has similar powers to vary instalments of a fine or to allow further time for payment of any instalment[3]. The offender need not attend court to have the instalments varied[3].

An offender who has been allowed time to pay a fine or to pay by instalments may be placed under the supervision of a social worker, either at the time of imposition of the fine or at a later time, 'for the purpose of assisting and advising the offender in regard to payment of the fine'[4]. This is commonly known as a fine supervision order (FSO). The supervision lasts until the fine is paid unless the fine is transferred[5] or the order is discharged[6]. This form of supervision is used especially in the case of offenders under 21, but may also be appropriate in the case of older offenders who are under some disability[7]. The amount of supervision provided varies considerably according to where the offender lives and the resources available to the local social work department.

If an offender has been fined and no alternative has been imposed at the same time as the fine, imprisonment in default cannot be imposed unless the offender attends court[8] on a subsequent occasion for the court to enquire 'into the reason why the fine has not been paid'[9]. Such enquiry is very often the subject of a separate sitting of the court known as a 'fines enquiry court' (FEC). The offender may be cited to attend for enquiry, or he may be arrested and brought before the court[10]. In practice an arrest warrant is issued only if the offender's whereabouts are unknown. If an offender, having been cited, fails to attend for enquiry into his means, a warrant to apprehend him may be issued[11] (and almost invariably is).

If an offender is under a fine supervision order, a report from his supervising social worker on the offender's conduct and means should be available to the court when he attends for fines enquiry[12]. The alternative of imprisonment should not be imposed unless the court has taken 'such steps as may be reasonably practicable' to obtain such a report (which may be oral)[12].

In the case of an offender under 21 the court must not impose the alternative for non-payment of a fine (which is not imprisonment but detention in a young offenders' institution)[13] unless either the offender has been placed on a fine supervision order or the court is satisfied that it is impracticable to place him under such supervision[14]. In practice this means that it is virtually impossible to impose the alternative of detention on a young offender without having first made a fine supervision order. Moreover, the restrictions on imposing detention on a young

---

1  1995 Act, s 215(2). For transfer of fine see below at p 241.
2  1995 Act, s 215(3).
3  1995 Act, s 214(9).
4  1995 Act, s 217(1).
5  1995 Act, s 217(3).
6  1995 Act, s 217(2).
7  See eg *Muirhead v Normand* 1995 SCCR 632.
8  The requirement to attend court does not apply if the offender is already in prison: 1995 Act, s 216(2).
9  1995 Act, s 216(1).
10  1995 Act, s 216(3).
11  1995 Act, s 216(4).
12  1995 Act, s 216(6).
13  1995 Act, s 218(2).
14  1995 Act, s 217(4).

offender contained in section 207(3) and (4) of the 1995 Act[1] also apply to detention as an alternative to a fine[2].

At a fines enquiry court (or any other court where enquiry is being made into the reason for non-payment of a fine) the offender is usually asked why he has not paid his fine, and what his income and expenditure are. The court will, of course, also have regard to the terms of any report which may be before it. Depending on the information which is given to the court from these sources, the offender may be allowed further time to pay, possibly with the alternative of imprisonment or detention being imposed in the event of future default[3]; or the alternative may be imposed with immediate effect[3]; or a supervised attendance order may be made[4].

Legal aid is not generally available for representation at a fines enquiry court. However, it is not uncommon for a solicitor to appear for a client at such a court – no doubt without payment.

## Custody for non-payment

The maximum alternative period of custody which may be imposed by a court for default in payment of a fine, whether at the time of imposition of the fine or at a later stage, varies according to the amount of the fine, and ranges from seven days for a fine of less than £200 to ten years for a fine of over £1,000,000[5]. If part of the fine has been paid, only a proportion of the alternative is served[6].

In the event of default by an offender on whom the alternative has been imposed the court grants a warrant for his arrest and imprisonment or detention. The warrant must specify the period during which he is to be detained[7]. If such a warrant has been issued, the offender may pay the full balance of the fine to the arresting officer, in which case the warrant will not be enforced[8]. The officer remits the fine to the clerk of the court which issued the warrant[8].

## Discretionary supervised attendance order

In 1990 there was introduced, as an alternative to custody in default of payment of a fine, an order called a supervised attendance order. The intention of doing this was to reduce the number of fine-defaulters going into custody. The statutory provisions for these orders are, somewhat confusingly, contained in both Part XI of the 1995 Act (the Part dealing with sentencing) and Schedule 7 thereto.

A supervised attendance order may be made only by a court which has been notified by the Secretary of State that arrangements have been made for the implementation of such orders[9]. At the time of writing not all courts in Scotland have such arrangements in operation, but I understand that it is the Government's inten-

1 See above at p 231.
2 *Divers v Friel* 1993 SCCR 394, 1994 SLT 247.
3 1995 Act, s 219(1)(b).
4 1995 Act, s 235. See below at pp 237–239.
5 1995 Act, s 219, which contains a full table of alternatives in sub-s (2). This table may be amended by order of the Secretary of State: 1995 Act, s 225(4), (5). If the 1997 Act, s 15 comes into force a court may, instead of imposing the alternative of custody, disqualify the offender from driving for a period not exceeding twelve months. See the Appendix at p 323 below.
6 1995 Act, s 219(4).
7 1995 Act, s 224.
8 1995 Act, s 218(3).
9 1995 Act, Sch 7, para 1(1)(a).

tion that they should be universally available some time in 1998. The statutory provisions for supervised attendance orders are quite similar to those for community service orders[1].

A supervised attendance order is an order requiring the offender to attend 'a place of supervision' for a stated period which must not be less than ten hours[2]. If the fine in respect of which the order is made does not exceed level 1 on the standard scale[3] the maximum number of hours is 50[4]. In any other case it is 100[5]. While at the place of supervision the offender must 'carry out such instructions as may be given to him by the supervising officer'[6].

A supervised attendance order is an option open to the court subject to certain conditions[7]. The conditions which must be satisfied before a supervised attendance order is made are: (a) that the offender is over eighteen years of age; (b) that he has failed to pay a fine or part thereof and the court would send him into custody if it did not make a supervised attendance order; and (c) that the court considers a supervised attendance order more appropriate than custody. A supervised attendance order cannot be made if the offender is already in prison[8].

Before making an order the court must explain to the offender 'in ordinary language' the purpose and effect of the order, the consequences of a breach and the fact that the order may be reviewed on application by the offender or the supervising officer[9]. Among the matters which must be explained to the offender are his obligation to notify any change of address and to notify changes in the times at which he usually works[10].

An order should be completed within twelve months of having been made[11], but there are provisions for extension of that time[12]. There are also provisions for the order being varied or revoked[13].

If a court receives a report that an offender is in breach of a supervised attendance order by failing to comply with any of its conditions it may grant a warrant for the offender's arrest or cite him to appear in court[14]. If the breach is proved (and the evidence of one witness is sufficient[15]), the powers of the court are limited. A supervised attendance order has the effect of discharging the fine in respect of which it is made[16]. This means that the only options which a court has in the event of breach of an order are either to revoke the order and impose a custodial sentence[17] or to vary the number of hours specified in the order[18]. If the court decides to impose a custodial sentence there is no obligation to relate that to what would have been the alternative for the original fine. The statutory provision is that the

---

1  See below at pp 251–255.
2  1995 Act, s 235(2).
3  For the standard scale see above at p 233.
4  1995 Act, s 235(2)(a)(i).
5  1995 Act, s 235(2)(a)(ii).
6  1995 Act, s 235(2)(b).
7  1995 Act, s 235(3).
8  1995 Act, s 235(4)(b).
9  1995 Act, Sch 7, para 1(2).
10  1995 Act, Sch 7, para 3(1).
11  1995 Act, Sch 7, para 3(2).
12  1995 Act, Sch 7, para 5(1)(a).
13  1995 Act, Sch 7, para 5(1)(b)–(d).
14  1995 Act, Sch 7, para 4(1).
15  1995 Act, Sch 7, para 4(3).
16  1995 Act, s 235(6).
17  1995 Act, Sch 7, para 4(2)(a).
18  1995 Act, Sch 7, para 4(2)(b).

court may impose 'such period of imprisonment . . . as the court considers appropriate'[1]. The maximum period which may be imposed is three months in the sheriff court and 60 days in the district court[2]. This means, of course, that an offender may end up serving a significant sentence of imprisonment for an offence for which a custodial sentence was not originally competent. Some may see this as a weakness of the supervised attendance order.

A supervised attendance order would normally be made immediately on default of payment. However, it is possible to make such an order to take effect in the event of future default in the same way as custody can be imposed in the event of future default[3]. Such an order would come into effect the day after a failure in payment[4]. If part of the fine has been paid, only a proportion of the original order rounded up or down to the nearest ten hours will apply, but the period cannot be reduced to less than ten hours[5]. I understand that the Scottish Office has expressed the view that this provision for a supervised attendance order in the event of future default is not restricted to those over eighteen years of age but is also available for sixteen and seventeen year olds. I suggest that this is not correct, having regard to the statutory provisions as a whole, but there is at the time of writing no authoritative decision on the matter[6].

## Mandatory supervised attendance order

The 1995 Act makes provision for a mandatory supervised attendance order in the event of failure to pay a fine in certain circumstances[7], but such orders apply only in courts which have been prescribed for the purpose[8]. At the time of writing no court has been so prescribed. I understand that none is likely to be so until 1999. The terms and conditions of a mandatory order are exactly as described in the preceding section save that it may be made only in the case of a fine (or an outstanding balance of a fine) not exceeding level 2 of the standard scale[9].

## Supervised attendance orders in place of fines for 16 and 17 year olds

Most 16 and 17 year olds are not eligible for State benefits. Therefore, if a person of that age offends it is very difficult to impose a fine, even though the offence itself and the offender's background would not justify any other penalty. In order to overcome this difficulty the 1995 Act introduced a special form of supervised attendance order for that group[10]. At the time of writing there is only a pilot scheme operating for such orders and that in only Dundee Sheriff Court and Dundee District Court.

---

1  1995 Act, Sch 7, para 4(2)(a).
2  1995 Act, Sch 7, para 4(2)(a).
3  1995 Act, s 237.
4  1995 Act, s 237(2)(a).
5  1995 Act, s 237(3).
6  My doubt on this matter appears to be supported by *Renton and Brown* paras 23–50 and 23–51.
7  1995 Act, s 235(1), (4).
8  1995 Act, s 235(4)(a).
9  1995 Act, s 235(4)(d).
10 1995 Act, s 236.

The section applies where a person of 16 or 17 is convicted by a court of summary jurisdiction 'and the court considers that, but for this section, the appropriate sentence is a fine'[1]. The court must determine the amount of the fine and consider whether the offender is likely to pay it within 28 days[2].

If the court considers that the offender *is* likely to pay within 28 days then it imposes a fine and makes a supervised attendance order in default of payment of the fine within that period[3]. In the event of the fine not having been paid in full within the 28 days such a supervised attendance order comes into force on the date specified in the order, which must be not less than 28 days after the making of the order[4]. The supervised attendance order is subject to the same proportional reduction in the event of part payment of the fine as is the case with a supervised attendance order made under section 237 of the 1995 Act (order made in the event of future default in payment)[5].

If the court, when considering whether or not to impose a fine, decides that the offender is *not* able to pay it within 28 days, then it makes a supervised attendance order straightaway[6]. Obviously a supervised attendance order made in these circumstances is virtually a punishment in itself rather as, in the normal case, an alternative to custody for non-payment of a fine.

There are two anomalous and worrying features of supervised attendance orders under section 236. First, the terms of section 211(7) of the 1995 Act appear to have been completely overlooked. That subsection, it will be recalled, provides:

> 'A court in determining the amount of any fine to be imposed on an offender shall take into consideration, amongst other things, the means of the offender so far as known to the court.'

How can a court determine the amount of the notional fine in terms of section 236(2) *and* comply with the terms of section 211(7) if it knows that the offender has no means at all? Surprisingly, although many of the sections of the Act applying to fines are stated not to apply to persons subject to section 236 orders[7], section 211(7) is not one of the excluded sections.

The second anomaly is that it seems distinctly possible that a section 236 supervised attendance order may lead to more, rather than fewer, young offenders going into custody because of the very limited options open to a court in the event of an offender breaching a supervised attendance order. As has been mentioned above[8], in the event of a breach, the only thing which a court can do other than impose a period of custody is to vary the number of hours specified in the order[9]. If an offender has been unable or unwilling to complete the order already made, he is unlikely to be able to complete a longer order. The court could vary the number of hours downwards, even possibly to nil, but this might be looked upon as a soft option which would not appeal to some courts.

It remains to be seen to what extent this no doubt well meant provision really meets the problem which it is intended to solve.

---

1   1995 Act, s 236(1).
2   1995 Act, s 236(2).
3   1995 Act, s 236(3).
4   1995 Act, s 236(4)(a).
5   1995 Act, s 236(5). For an order under s 237 see above at p 239.
6   1995 Act, s 236(6).
7   1995 Act, s 236(7) lists them.
8   At pp 238–239.
9   1995 Act, Sch 7, para 4(2).

## Transfer of fine orders

A fine may be transferred for the purposes of enforcement to a court other than that which imposed it, if the offender lives within the jurisdiction of the other court[1]. That court may be elsewhere in Scotland, or in England, Wales or Northern Ireland[1]. The order transferring the fine is known as a transfer of fine order[2]. The effect of the order is to transfer all functions of enforcement to the receiving court[3]. That court is responsible for remitting the fine, once paid, to the transferring court[4].

## Fines imposed by the High Court

A fine imposed by the High Court by way of sentence is remitted for enforcement to the sheriff court of the district where the offender resides[5], or, if the offender resides outwith Scotland, the sheriff court before which he was brought for examination in relation to the offence for which the fine was imposed[6]. In the latter case the fine may then be transferred to another court within the United Kingdom as described in the preceding section.

The above paragraph does not apply to a fine imposed by the High Court on an accused or a juror who fails to attend or to any forfeiture for non-appearance of a party, witness or juror in the High Court. Such penalties are payable to and recoverable by the Treasury unless the High Court orders otherwise[7].

## Recovery of fines by civil diligence

A court always has the power to order that a fine shall be recoverable by civil diligence[8], although in practice this power is rarely used except in the case of partnerships, limited companies and other corporate bodies. In such a case the finding of the court imposing the fine includes a warrant for civil diligence[9]. Diligence (arrestment or poinding) may then be executed in the same manner as on an extract decree in a civil summary cause[10]. Civil diligence is not competent after the offender has been imprisoned or detained for default in payment of his fine[11], but otherwise the two forms of enforcement are not mutually exclusive[12].

1  1995 Act, s 222(1).
2  1995 Act, s 222(2). Forms are specified in the 1996 Rules, r 20.9: Forms 20.9A, 20.9B, 20.9C.
3  1995 Act, s 222(3).
4  1995 Act, s 223(4).
5  1995 Act, s 211(4)(a).
6  1995 Act, s 211(4)(b).
7  1995 Act, s 211(5).
8  1995 Act, s 214(6).
9  1995 Act, s 221(1).
10  1995 Act, s 221(1). For execution of diligence see the Debtors (Scotland) Act 1987, Pts II and III.
11  1995 Act, s 221(3).
12  1995 Act, s 221(4).

# CAUTION

A court may order an offender to find caution[1] (ie a sum of money as a guarantee) for his good behaviour over a period of time. In solemn cases the court has power to order the finding of caution 'to such amount as the court considers appropriate', for good behaviour for a period not exceeding twelve months[2]. The district court has power to order an offender to find caution in a sum not exceeding level 4 on the standard scale, for his good behaviour for a period not exceeding six months[3]. In the case of the sheriff sitting summarily the maximum sum is the prescribed sum, and the maximum period is twelve months[4].

Almost all the provisions for payment and for enforcement of orders for caution are the same as those for fines[5]. The only important exceptions are that there is no provision for the payment of caution by instalments and that a supervised attendance order may not be imposed for default in payment.

There are certain additional provisions which apply to summary proceedings only. These are as follows: caution may be found by consignation of the amount with the clerk of court or by bond of caution (ie a written undertaking to pay the money)[6]; forfeiture of the caution (because of failure to be of good behaviour) may be granted on the motion of the prosecutor and, where necessary, a warrant granted for the recovery thereof[7]; and the court may, instead of ordering imprisonment in default of payment, order recovery by civil diligence[8].

If the offender remains of good behaviour throughout the period for which he has found caution, he is entitled to recover the sum paid together with any interest which may have accrued thereon.

In practice an order for caution is a relatively rare disposal of a case. It appears to be most popular in some district courts.

# COMPENSATION ORDER

## Scope

A compensation order is 'an order requiring [a person convicted of an offence] to pay compensation for any personal injury, loss or damage caused, whether directly or indirectly, by the acts which constituted the offence'[9]. An order is not competent where the victim suffers no physical injury but is only alarmed[10]. A compensation order may not be made in respect of loss suffered in consequence of the death of any person[11]. Nor may it be made in respect of injury, loss or damage due

---

1  Pronounced 'kayshun'.
2  1995 Act, s 227.
3  1995 Act, s 7(6)(c). Section 199(2)(c) confirms the power to order caution in the case of statutory offences.
4  1995 Act, s 5(2)(b). Section 199(2)(c) confirms the power to order caution in the case of statutory offences.
5  Ie 1995 Act, ss 214(1), 216, 219(2), 224.
6  1995 Act, s 168(2).
7  1995 Act, s 168(3).
8  1995 Act, s 168(4)(c).
9  1995 Act, s 249(1).
10  *Smillie v Wilson* 1990 SCCR 133, 1990 SLT 582.
11  1995 Act, s 249(4)(a).

to an accident arising out of the presence of a motor vehicle on a road except when a motor vehicle has been stolen or taken without authority and is recovered damaged, in which case the owner may be the beneficiary of a compensation order in respect of the damage[1].

When any property is dishonestly appropriated or unlawfully taken and used, or if a motor vehicle is taken without authority (in contravention of the Road Traffic Act 1988, section 178), and the property is recovered damaged, it is presumed that the damage was caused by the acts which constituted the offence, 'however and by whomsoever it was in fact caused'[2].

A court may normally make a compensation order instead of or in addition to imposing any other sentence, but not where it gives an absolute discharge[3] or defers sentence for good behaviour or on some other condition[4]. Nor may a court make a compensation order when it makes a probation order[5], but it is competent to make payment of compensation a condition of a probation order[6], which has the same practical effect as the making of a compensation order and is subject to many of the same statutory provisions[7].

## Amount

A compensation order may be made by all criminal courts. In the case of a court of solemn jurisdiction the amount which may be ordered to be paid as compensation is unlimited[8]. The maximum amount which may be ordered by a sheriff sitting summarily or a stipendiary magistrate is the prescribed sum[9]. In the case of a district court consisting of one or more lay justices, the maximum amount is level 4 on the standard scale[10]. In other words, the maximum amount in each case is the same as the maximum fine which may be imposed for a common law offence. As a court may impose a compensation order 'in addition' to other penalties[11], it is possible, at least in theory, for a court to impose both a maximum compensation order and a maximum fine, but this would, of course, be subject to the fact that the compensation order must be given priority over any fine[12].

A court must take into consideration an offender's means so far as known to it when determining whether to make a compensation order and the amount thereof[13], but any guidelines which may exist as to the time over which a person should be called upon to pay a fine[14] do not apply in the case of a compensation order[15]. There is no reason in principle why, in the case of a number of offenders, most of whom would not be able to pay, one of them who *has* the ability to pay

---

1  1995 Act, s 249(3), (4)(b).
2  1995 Act, s 249(3).
3  1995 Act, s 249(2)(a). For absolute discharge see below at pp 255–256.
4  1995 Act, s 249(2)(c). For deferred sentence see below at pp 256–257.
5  1995 Act, s 249(2)(b).
6  1995 Act, s 229(6). See below at p 248.
7  1995 Act, s 229(6) provides that ss 249(3)–(5), (8)–(10), 250(2), 251(1), (2)(b) and 253 apply to a probation order with a condition of compensation.
8  1995 Act, s 249(7).
9  1995 Act, s 249(8)(a).
10  1995 Act, s 249(8)(b).
11  1995 Act, s 249(1).
12  1995 Act, s 250(2). See below at p 245.
13  1995 Act, s 249(5).
14  See above at p 233.
15  *Ely v Donelly* 1996 SCCR 537; but see also *McEvoy v McGlennan* 1997 SCCR 385.

should not be given a compensation order[1]. If an offender is serving a custodial sentence, or is just about to serve one, no account should be taken, when assessing his means, of what he may earn if he obtains a job on his release[2].

Assessment of the amount of a compensation order from the point of view of the victim is not covered by the 1995 Act. In practice the procurator fiscal usually obtains information from the police about the loss suffered by a victim, or details of the injuries in personal injury cases. If the case proceeds to trial, the victim is able to give evidence about his loss. If there is a plea of guilty, there is usually no evidence led, although it would no doubt be possible for there to be a proof on the matter if the value of the loss stated by the prosecutor were challenged by the accused. It is probably the law that corroboration of the amount of a loss is not required[3].

A court may take a fairly broad approach to the amount of compensation[4], and precision such as has been required by the courts in England[5] is not necessary in Scotland.

The conduct of the victim is a relevant factor. If he has contributed to his loss, the amount of compensation may be reduced, and, if his behaviour has been such that he would not obtain an award from the Criminal Injuries Compensation Board, he should not benefit at all from a compensation order[6].

The fact that the victim has had to give evidence is not a factor to be taken into account when assessing the amount of a compensation order[7].

## Payment of compensation order

Payment is made to the clerk of court who must account for it to the victim[8]. The provisions relating to transfer of fines and payment of fines imposed by the High Court apply to compensation orders as if they were fines[9]. There are special rules governing compensation in favour of a person, eg a child, who is under a legal disability. The compensation is administered in the same way as an award made in favour of such a person in a civil case[10].

Payment by the offender may be made in exactly the same way as in the case of a fine, ie as a lump sum, or by instalments, or after a period of time[11].

1 *Notman v Henderson* 1992 SCCR 409.
2 1995 Act, s 249(6). See *Clark v Cardle* 1989 SCCR 92, where a compensation order of £500 payable at £3 per week on release from a six-month prison sentence was quashed on appeal as unreasonable, the accused having been given the maximum sentence of imprisonment. But see also *Collins v Lowe* 1990 SCCR 605, where a compensation order following imprisonment was upheld on appeal.
3 *Goodhall v Carmichael* 1984 SCCR 247. The uncertainty springs from the fact that the court issued no opinions. See also Docherty and Maher 'Corroboration and Compensation Orders' 1984 SLT (News) 125. Even if corroboration of loss were ever necessary, it is strongly arguable that it is no longer so since the coming into force of the Civil Evidence (Scotland) Act 1988, s 1, which abolished the need for corroboration in most civil proceedings.
4 See eg *Stewart v HMA* 1982 SCCR 203.
5 See eg *R v Vivian* [1979] 1 All ER 48, [1979] 1 WLR 291, [1978] RTR 106, (1978) 68 Cr App R 53; *R v Donovan* [1981] Crim LR 723.
6 *Brown v Normand* 1988 SCCR 229.
7 *Robertson v Lees* 1992 SCCR 545.
8 1995 Act, s 249(9).
9 1995 Act, s 252(2), applying ss 211(4), 222 and 223 to compensation orders.
10 1996 Rules, r 20.14(2).
11 1995 Act, s 252(2), applying ss 214 (with the exception of the provision for the imposition of imprisonment for future default) and 215 to compensation orders.

## Priority of compensation order over fine

If an offender's means are such that he cannot afford to pay both a compensation order and a fine, then, even though both penalties might have been appropriate, the court should make a compensation order rather than impose a fine[1].

If both a compensation order and a fine have been imposed in respect of the same offence or on different offences in the same proceedings, payments by the offender are appropriated first to the compensation order, and to the fine only after the compensation order has been paid off[2].

## Review of compensation order

A court may review a compensation order and remit it in whole or in part in the same way as it may review a fine[3]. The amount of a compensation order may also be reviewed in the light of the victim's loss turning out to be less than it was thought to be at the time when the order was made[4]. An application for such a review is made in writing to the clerk of the appropriate court who causes intimation to be made to the prosecutor, and the court may then dispose of the application after making such inquiry as it thinks fit[5]. The court to which application should be made is either the court which made the order or the court to which it has been transferred (provided that that is a court of summary jurisdiction in Scotland), or, in the case of a compensation order made by the High Court, the court by which the order was first enforceable[6].

## Enforcement of compensation order

The victim has no power to enforce a compensation order. Only the court may do so[7]. A compensation order is enforced in exactly the same way as a fine, and virtually all the provisions of the 1995 Act for enforcement of fines are applied to compensation orders[8]. There is only one notable exception. It is not competent to impose a period of imprisonment or detention in default of payment at the same time as actually making the compensation order[9]. A defaulter must therefore be summoned to a fines enquiry court before the alternative may be imposed.

Where an offender is subject to both a fine and a compensation order, the court may impose imprisonment or detention in respect of the fine and decline to do so in respect of the compensation order, but not vice versa[10]. Where imprisonment in default is imposed in respect of both a fine and a compensation order, the two sums are aggregated for the purpose of calculating the maximum period of custody which may be imposed[11].

1 1995 Act, s 250(1).
2 1995 Act, s 250(2).
3 1995 Act, s 256(2), applying s 213 to compensation orders. Any variation of the order may be made in chambers without attendance of the parties: 1996 Rules, r 20.15(2).
4 1995 Act, s 251.
5 1996 Rules, r 20.16.
6 1995 Act, s 251(2).
7 1995 Act, s 249(10).
8 1995 Act, s 252.
9 1995 Act, s 252(2), restricting the application of s 214.
10 1995 Act, s 252(3)(a).
11 1995 Act, s 252(3)(b).

### Effect of compensation order on damages in civil proceedings

The 1995 Act contains provisions[1] which are, in broad terms, to the effect that a person who receives an award of damages in a civil case and who has been the beneficiary under a compensation order in respect of the same incident, should not gain thereby. The amount of any payment made or to be made under a compensation order is set off against the amount of the damages payable. A similar principle is applied by the Criminal Injuries Compensation Board in respect of victims who make a claim and who have received compensation under a compensation order.

# PROBATION

## General

When an accused is convicted of any offence, other than one the sentence for which is fixed by law, the court may, instead of dealing with him in any other way, make him subject to a probation order. A probation order is an order 'requiring the offender to be under supervision for a period to be specified in the order of not less than six months nor more than three years'[2]. The court may make an order 'if it is of the opinion that it is expedient to do so (a) having regard to the circumstances, including the nature of the offence and the character of the offender; and (b) having obtained a report as to the circumstances and character of the offender'[2].

A probation order is usually made because the court considers that the offender is in need of some advice and guidance. It is used particularly in the case of young offenders and offenders with domestic difficulties, such as single parents. The person under whose supervision the offender will be is a social worker employed by the social work department of the local authority in whose area the offender lives (or a probation officer attached to a magistrates' court if the offender lives in England or Wales). The nature and degree of the supervision will vary according to the circumstances of the offender but in Scotland there are national standards laid down for the supervision of probation orders and probation is one of the local authority's functions which is wholly funded by central government.

## Social enquiry report

The social enquiry report (SER), which the court must obtain before making a probation order, is prepared by a social worker for the area where the offender lives (or by a probation officer if he lives in England or Wales).

The period for which a case may be adjourned in order to obtain such a report must not exceed three weeks if the offender is in custody[3]. In fact, in many courts if an accused is remanded in custody for a report, the case is adjourned for only two weeks. If the accused is not remanded in custody but is on bail or ordained to appear, the adjournment may be for a maximum of four weeks or, on cause shown, eight weeks[4].

1　1995 Act, s 253.
2　1995 Act, s 228(1).
3　1995 Act, s 201(3)(a).
4　1995 Act, s 201(3)(b). See above at pp 186–187.

A copy of the social enquiry report must be given by the clerk of court to the offender or his solicitor[1].

Although a written report is normal, it is possible for the court to receive an oral report if the circumstances make this appropriate.

A judge should not interview a social worker in private about the contents of a social enquiry report. If he requires further information, the proper course is either to speak to the social worker in open court in the presence of the accused or to ask for a supplementary report[2].

## Making the probation order

When a probation order is made the judge must explain to the offender in ordinary language what it means and what the consequences may be if he fails to comply with the order or commits a further offence[3]. The offender must agree to being placed on probation[3].

## Form and contents of the probation order

A probation order should be in the prescribed form[4]. It must name the local authority area in which the offender will be living and make provision for the offender to be under the supervision of a local social worker[4]. If the offender is to live outwith the jurisdiction of the court making the order, a court having jurisdiction in that area must be named (the 'appropriate court')[5]. The appropriate court will then require its local authority to arrange for supervision of the offender[5].

The order requires that the offender is: '(1) to be of good behaviour; (2) to conform to the directions of the supervising officer; (3) to inform the supervising officer at once if he changes his residence or place of employment'[6]. The court may add such other requirements according to the circumstances of the individual case which it considers to be 'conducive to securing the good conduct of the offender or for preventing a repetition by him of the offence or the commission of other offences'[7]. The 1995 Act provides for certain specific additional requirements which will now be examined, but these are by no means exhaustive.

After considering the offender's home surroundings, the court may require him to live at a particular place for a given period of time not exceeding twelve months[8].

If the offender is sixteen or more and has committed an offence punishable by imprisonment, he may be required, as a condition of probation, to perform a number of hours (between 80 and 240 in a summary case, between 80 and 300 in a solemn case) of unpaid work, in the same way as under a community service order[9]. This condition is not available to all courts: the court must have been notified by the Secretary of State that arrangements for the implementation of such a condition have been made for the area where the offender is to reside[10].

1  1995 Act, s 203(3).
2  *W v HMA* 1989 SCCR 461.
3  1995 Act, s 228(5).
4  1995 Act, s 228(3); 1996 Rules, r 20.10; Form 20.10A.
5  1995 Act, s 228(4).
6  1996 Rules, r 20.10; Form 20.10A.
7  1995 Act, s 229(1)(a).
8  1995 Act, s 229(2), (3).
9  1995 Act, s 229(4). For community service order see below at pp 251–255.
10  1995 Act, s 229(4)(b).

As has already been mentioned[1], an offender may be required to pay compensation as a condition of probation[2]. The date by which payment of compensation must be completed should be no later than either eighteen months from the making of the order or two months before the end of the period of probation, whichever is the earlier[3]. Either the offender or his supervising social worker may apply to the court to have the condition of compensation varied on a change of circumstances[4], for example, if the offender lost his job.

In the case of a person suffering from a mental disorder the court may make it a condition of a probation order that he receives medical treatment for a period not exceeding twelve months[5]. This condition will be discussed in chapter 9.

Examples of other conditions which might be appropriate in certain cases are attendance for alcohol counselling or at a drugs problem centre. The imposition of any additional conditions depends very much on the requirements of the individual offender and the facilities available in the area where he lives.

### Effect of probation order

A probation order counts as a conviction only for the purposes of the proceedings where it is made and of founding on it as a previous conviction in subsequent proceedings for another offence[6]. The offender's right to appeal against conviction is preserved[7]. The making of a probation order does not prevent the offender having his licence endorsed or being disqualified under the Road Traffic Acts 1988[8]. An exclusion order may be made against him[9].

### Amendment of probation order

The provisions for amendment of a probation order (and for its discharge) are, somewhat confusingly, contained in Schedule 6 to the 1995 Act rather than in Part XI where the provisions referred to so far appear.

If a probationer changes his residence, either he or his supervising social worker may apply to the court to have the probation order amended by substituting a different local authority area and a different court as the appropriate court[10]. The court has a discretion whether to grant such an application if made by the probationer, but must grant it if it is made by the social worker[10].

A probation order may also be amended by cancelling or by adding a requirement[11]. Again an application may be made to the court by either the probationer or his social worker[11]. There are three restrictions on the court's power of amendment: (1) the length of the order may not be reduced nor may it be extended

---

1  See above at p 243.
2  1995 Act, s 229(6).
3  1995 Act, s 229(7)(a).
4  1995 Act, s 229(7)(b).
5  1995 Act, s 230.
6  1995 Act, s 247(1).
7  1995 Act, s 247(3).
8  Road Traffic Offenders Act 1988, s 46(3).
9  Licensed Premises (Exclusion of Certain Persons) Act 1980, s 1(2)(c). For exclusion order see below at p 261.
10  1995 Act, s 231(1), Sch 6, para 2(1).
11  1995 Act, s 231(1), Sch 6, para 3(1).

beyond three years; (2) the twelve-month limit on a condition of residence or medical treatment for a mental condition may not be extended; and (3) a condition of medical treatment for a mental condition may be added only within the first three months of the order[1].

## Discharge of probation order

Both the probationer and his social worker have the right to apply to the court for the order to be discharged[2]. Applications by probationers themselves are rare. A discharge might be sought if the social worker considered that the objectives of probation had been achieved, for example if the main purpose of probation had been to enable the offender to sort out his financial situation, and this was done. On the other hand, discharge might be sought because the probationer had received a long prison sentence. The court is under no obligation to discharge an order, but it is relatively unusual for an application by a social worker to be refused.

## Failure to comply with a requirement of a probation order

If a probationer fails to comply with any requirement of an order, his social worker may apply to the court for what is commonly known as 'breach proceedings' to be taken. The usual procedure is for the social worker to submit a brief report to the court, describing the alleged breach and recommending whether or not proceedings should be taken. If the court decides to take the matter further, it may either have the offender cited to attend or grant a warrant for his arrest[3]. In some cases the judge may wish to discuss the case with the social worker before deciding whether to take breach proceedings.

When the offender appears before the court to answer the alleged failure to comply he may either admit it or deny it. If it is denied, evidence must be led to prove it to the satisfaction of the court. Such evidence is presented by the procurator fiscal, and the offender may, of course, himself give and lead evidence. The evidence of only one witness is sufficient to prove a breach[4].

If the failure to comply is proved or admitted, the court has a number of options. It may allow the probation order to continue and may express its displeasure at the breach by imposing a fine not exceeding level 3 on the standard scale (except where the breach consists of a failure to pay compensation)[5]. Next, it may sentence the offender for the original offence[6]. This has the effect of terminating the probation order[7]. Or the court may vary the requirements of the probation order, but may not extend it beyond three years[8]. Finally, the court may, while allowing probation to continue, make a community service order[9]. This last disposal is not the same as making unpaid work a condition of probation[10] as here there is a separate community service order, which runs in tandem with the probation order.

1  1995 Act, s 231(1), Sch 6, para 3(2).
2  1995 Act, s 231(1), Sch 6, para 1.
3  1995 Act, s 232(1).
4  1995 Act, s 232(3).
5  1995 Act, s 232(2)(a).
6  1995 Act, s 232(2)(b).
7  1995 Act, s 231(2).
8  1995 Act, s 232(2)(c).
9  1995 Act, s 232(2)(d). For community service order see pp 251–255 below.
10  See above at p 247.

## Commission of further offence

Although the commission of a further offence while on probation is clearly a failure to comply with the requirement to be of good behaviour, it is not subject to
the statutory provisions just described[1]. The normal practice is for the supervising
social worker to report the further offence (of which the probationer has been convicted by a court in any part of Great Britain[2]) to the court which is supervising the
probation order. The probationer may then be cited to attend court or a warrant
for his arrest may be granted[2]. When he appears before the court, either it may
allow probation to continue, or it may sentence him for the original offence[2].
There are no other options open to the court.

If, as often happens, a probationer is found guilty of a subsequent offence by the
court which made the probation order (or by the appropriate court to which the
order has been transferred), that court may take immediate cognisance of the
breach of probation by commission of another offence and deal with the offender
for both the new offence and the original offence[3]. In some courts with more than
one sheriff this power is not widely used as it is felt that it should be the sheriff who
made the probation order (rather than one of his colleagues) who decides whether
to allow it to continue or to bring it to an end in respect of a new offence. Even if
a judge is considering dealing with both offences, it would be normal for him to
obtain the views of the supervising social worker on the possibility of probation
being allowed to continue.

There are special provisions for an offence committed by a probationer subject
to the condition of performing unpaid work[4], if the offence is committed during
the period when he was subject to the requirement of unpaid work or within three
months following the expiry of that period[5], and the offence was committed in any
place where the unpaid work was being or had been performed[6]. Provided that
these circumstances are libelled in the indictment or complaint charging the
offence[7], the court must 'in determining the appropriate sentence for that offence
have regard to the fact that the offence was committed in those circumstances'[8].
Although it is not spelt out, it seems fairly clear that these are intended to be aggra-
vating circumstances with the consequence that the court is expected to impose a
more severe sentence than would have been the case if these circumstances had not
existed.

## Probation orders for offenders resident in England or Wales

A Scottish court has power to make a probation order in respect of someone aged
sixteen or more who lives in England or Wales[9]. There is no power to make an
order in respect of a person living in Northern Ireland.

1   1995 Act, s 232(6).
2   1995 Act, s 233(1).
3   1995 Act, s 233(2).
4   1995 Act, s 233(3)(a).
5   1995 Act, s 233(4)(a).
6   1995 Act, s 233(4)(b).
7   1995 Act, s 233(5).The fact that the offence was committed in the circumstances libelled will be held
    to be admitted unless challenged: 1995 Act, s 233(6) as inserted by the 1997 Act, s 26(1) with effect
    from 1 August 1997. See the Appendix at p 319 below.
8   1995 Act, s 233(3).
9   1995 Act, s 234.

The provisions governing probation orders for those in England and Wales are complex, and it is not intended to examine them in detail here. An offender will be under the supervision of a probation officer for the petty sessions area where he lives[1]. Breach of a requirement of probation may be dealt with by the English or Welsh magistrates' court[2], or the offender may be brought back to the Scottish court which made or amended the order for it to deal with the breach[3]. If the probationer commits a further offence while on probation, he may be brought back to the Scottish court which made the order for it to dispose of the case[4].

# COMMUNITY SERVICE ORDER

## General

When an offender aged sixteen or over is convicted of an offence punishable by a custodial sentence (except murder), the court may make a community service order, ie an order requiring him to perform unpaid work for a specified number of hours which must be not less than 80 nor more than 240 in the case of a summary prosecution or 300 in the case of proceedings on indictment[5]. These numbers of hours may be amended by order of the Secretary of State[6]. A community service order is specifically stated to be 'instead of ... a sentence of, or including, imprisonment or any other form of detention'[5]. It is therefore very much an alternative to custody, although the High Court has not been entirely consistent in upholding custodial sentences imposed when a community service order has been breached[7].

A court may make a community service order only where certain conditions are satisfied[8]. These are: (a) the offender consents; (b) community service is available in the area where the offender lives or is going to live; (c) the court is satisfied, as a result of a report from a social worker[9] (and if necessary hearing the social worker), that the offender is a suitable person for a community service order; and (d) that suitable work will be available for the offender.

## The making of the order

As in the case of probation the court must explain certain things about the order to the offender in ordinary language[10]. These are: (a) the purpose and effect of the order, especially the offender's obligations to report to his supervising social worker

1 1995 Act, s 234(1)(a).
2 Criminal Justice Act 1991, s 14(1), Sch 2 applied (in part) by the 1995 Act, s 234(5).
3 Criminal Justice Act 1991, s 14(1), Sch 2, para 3(3) applied by the 1995 Act, s 234(6).
4 1995 Act, s 234(7).
5 1995 Act, s 238(1) (as amended by the Community Service by Offenders (Hours of Work) (Scotland) Order 1996 (SI 1996/1938)).
6 1995 Act, s 238(5). There has already been one such order since the 1995 Act came into force – see the preceding note.
7 Compare *Dunsmure v Lowe* 1990 SCCR 524 (custodial sentence upheld) with *Rankin v McGlennan* 1990 SCCR 607 (three months' detention quashed and fine of £300 substituted) and *Simpson v HMA* 1990 SCCR 680 (six months' imprisonment quashed and a new community service order of 240 hours substituted).
8 1995 Act, s 238(2).
9 The offender or his solicitor must receive a copy of the report: 1995 Act, s 238(3).
10 1995 Act, s 238(4).

and notify him without delay of any change of address or change in the times at which he usually works[1], and the obligation to perform the specified number of hours work as directed by the supervising social worker[2]; (b) what may happen if the offender fails to comply with any of the requirements of the order; and (c) that the court has power to review the order at the request of either the offender or his supervising social worker.

A community service order is normally the only sentence which a court may impose for the offence concerned[3], but a court may also disqualify an offender[4], make an order for forfeiture[5], order the offender to find caution for his good behaviour[6], or make a compensation order[7]. It is not competent to make a community service order and impose a fine for the same offence[8]. However, if an accused appears on several charges, some of which could not be the subject of a community service order because they are not punishable by a custodial sentence, the court may impose a sentence such as a fine for these other offences while at the same time making a community service order in respect of the offences for which it is competent.

The order must: (a) specify the locality in which the offender resides or will reside when the order comes into force; (b) require the local authority for that locality to appoint or assign an officer (who will be a social worker) to supervise the order; and (c) state the number of hours of work which the offender must perform[9].

One community service order may be made to run concurrently with or consecutive to another community service order or a period of unpaid work as a condition of probation[10], provided that, at no time, the offender has an outstanding number of hours of work to complete which exceeds 240 (or 300 if the case is on indictment)[11].

The offender must be provided with a copy of the order[12].

## Performance of community service order

The hours of work must be performed within twelve months from the date of the order[13] unless it is extended[14]. The times of work must, so far as practicable, avoid any conflict with the offender's religious beliefs and any interference with the times, if any, at which he normally works or attends any educational establishment[15].

---

1   1995 Act, s 239(1)(a).
2   1995 Act, s 239(1)(b).
3   1995 Act, s 238(1).
4   1995 Act, s 238(7)(a). For disqualification see below at pp 261, 262.
5   1995 Act, s 238(7)(b). For forfeiture see below at pp 257–259.
6   1995 Act, s 238(7)(c). For caution see above at p 242.
7   1995 Act, s 249(1). For compensation order see above at pp 242–246.
8   *Kidd v Russell* 1993 SCCR 434, 1993 SLT 1028.
9   1995 Act, s 238(8).
10  See above at p 247.
11  1995 Act, s 238(9).
12  1995 Act, s 238(10)(a).
13  1995 Act, s 239(2).
14  See below at p 254.
15  1995 Act, s 239(3).

## Failure to comply with requirements of order

The procedures for breach of a community service order are very similar to those for failure to comply with the requirements of a probation order[1]. The normal practice is that the supervising social worker submits a 'breach report' to the 'appropriate court'[2], describing the failure to comply and recommending whether further action should or should not be taken. If the court decides to proceed, it may then cite the offender to attend or grant a warrant for his arrest[3].

When the offender appears in court he may either admit the failure to comply or deny it. In the latter case evidence must be led to prove the failure to the satisfaction of the court[4]. The evidence of one witness is sufficient to prove the breach[5]. If the breach is admitted or proved, the court may allow the order to continue with or without the imposition of a fine not exceeding level 3 on the standard scale[6], or it may revoke the order and deal with the offender for the original offence as if the order had not been made[7], or it may vary the number of hours, provided that the total does not exceed 240 (or 300 if the case is on indictment)[8].

An offender may still be dealt with for a failure to comply, even though more than twelve months have elapsed since the order was made and it has not been extended[9], but he may not be required to work after that period without an extension.

## Commission of offence while order in force

In this case differing from a probation order, the commission of a further offence while the offender is subject to a community service order is not a breach of the order. It is, rather surprisingly, not a condition of a community service order that the offender should be of good behaviour. However, as described above in the case of a probation order with a condition of unpaid work[10], the fact that an offence has been committed while the offender is subject to a community service order may be an aggravation of that offence. The circumstances which would amount to such an aggravation are that the offence was committed during the period of the community service order or within three months following its expiry[11], and that the offence was committed in any place where unpaid work under the order was being or had been performed[12]. If these circumstances are libelled in the indictment or complaint as applying to the offence[13] and the accused is convicted of it, the court must 'in determining the appropriate sentence for that offence, have regard to the

---

1 See above at p 249.
2 The High Court, if it has made the order, otherwise the sheriff or district court which has jurisdiction over the locality where the offender resides: 1995 Act, s 245(5).
3 1995 Act, s 239(4).
4 1995 Act, s 239(5).
5 1995 Act, s 239(6).
6 1995 Act, s 239(5)(a).
7 1995 Act, s 239(5)(b).
8 1995 Act, s 239(5)(c).
9 *HMA v Hood* 1987 SCCR 63.
10 See above at p 250.
11 1995 Act, s 241(2)(a).
12 1995 Act, s 241(2)(b).
13 1995 Act, s 241(3). The fact that the offence was committed in the circumstances libelled will be held to be admitted unless challenged: 1995 Act, s 241(4) inserted by the 1997 Act, s 26(2) with effect from 1 August 1997. See the Appendix at p 319 below.

fact that the offence was committed in those circumstances"[1]. Although this is clearly an aggravation of the offence, there is no provision for the court's being given additional sentencing powers to deal with it as is the case, for example, when an offence is committed while the offender is on bail[2].

## Amendment of community service order

Either the offender or his supervising social worker may apply to the appropriate court to have the community service order amended by (a) extending the period of twelve months during which the hours of work are to be completed; or (b) varying the number of hours, subject to the upper and lower limits of 240 (or 300) and 80 hours[3]. The court may grant the application if it appears 'that it would be in the interests of justice to do so having regard to the circumstances which have arisen since the order was made'[3]. Unless the application for amendment is by the offender himself he must be cited to attend court, and, if he fails to respond to the citation, the court may grant a warrant for his arrest[4].

If the offender has changed, or is going to change his residence, and community service for him is available in the new area, the court may (on the application of the offender) and must (on the application of the supervising social worker) amend the order to transfer it to the new locality[5].

## Revocation of community service order

A community service order may be revoked on the application of either the offender or his supervising social worker[6]. The order may be revoked without any further action being taken[7], or it may be revoked and the offender dealt with as if no order had been made[8]. As with amendment of the order, the court may revoke if it appears 'that it would be in the interests of justice to do so having regard to the circumstances which have arisen since the order was made'[9].

Circumstances in which an order might simply be revoked could be if the offender became seriously ill or received a very long prison sentence. Circumstances in which an order might be revoked and another sentence substituted could be that the offender had committed a further offence during the currency of the order or that, although he was not actually in breach of the order, it became clear that he was not a suitable candidate for community service.

If a court is contemplating revoking an order and substituting an alternative sentence, the offender must be cited to attend, and, if he fails to answer the citation, a warrant may be granted for his arrest[10].

1  1995 Act, s 241(1).
2  Under the 1995 Act, s 27(5). See above at p 105.
3  1995 Act, s 240(1).
4  1995 Act, s 240(3).
5  1995 Act, s 240(2).
6  1995 Act, s 240(1).
7  1995 Act, s 240(1)(c).
8  1995 Act, s 240(1)(d).
9  1995 Act, s 240(1).
10  1995 Act, s 240(3).

### Community service orders on offenders living in England, Wales and Northern Ireland

A Scottish court may make a community service order in respect of an offender living in England or Wales[1] or Northern Ireland[2]. The statutory provisions are complex, and it is not intended to examine them in detail here. Enforcement of the order is a matter for the 'home court' (the court for the petty sessions area (England and Wales) or district (Northern Ireland) of the offender's residence)[3]. In the event of a failure to comply with a requirement of the order, the home court may deal with the matter to the limited extent of varying the number of hours up to the limit which the original sentencing court could impose[4]. It may not revoke the order, whether with or without the substitution of an alternative sentence[4]. An order may be revoked (whether in respect of a breach or for any other reason) only by the court which made it, and the home court may require the offender's attendance at the sentencing court for that purpose[5]. The Scottish court has power to issue a warrant for the offender's arrest to ensure his attendance before it[6].

## ADMONITION

Both solemn and summary courts have the power to dismiss with an admonition a person convicted of an offence, 'if it appears to meet the justice of the case'[7]. An admonition is usually appropriate only if the offence is very minor or there are substantial mitigating circumstances. It is a disposal which is quite frequently used after sentence has been deferred for the accused to be of good behaviour and he has complied with that condition.

The offender is usually simply told: 'You are admonished'. What the court is, in effect, saying is: 'Go away. You are just being told off this time. Don't do it again'.

An offence for which an accused is admonished counts as a conviction for all purposes.

## ABSOLUTE DISCHARGE

### Nature of absolute discharge

An absolute discharge (which is an even more lenient disposal than an admonition) may be given by a court if it appears to the court, 'having regard to the circumstances, including the nature of the offence and the character of the offender, that it is inexpedient to inflict punishment and that a probation order is not appropriate'[8]. In a solemn case an absolute discharge follows conviction[9], while in a

---

1  1995 Act, s 242.
2  1995 Act, s 243.
3  1995 Act, s 244(2).
4  1995 Act, s 244(5)(a).
5  1995 Act, s 244(6).
6  1995 Act, s 244(7).
7  1995 Act, s 246(1).
8  1995 Act, s 246(2), (3).
9  1995 Act, s 246(2).

summary case the court gives an absolute discharge 'without proceeding to conviction'[1]. It is thus apparently incompetent to give an absolute discharge in a summary case where a person has been convicted and had sentence deferred for good behaviour or the like[2]. For this reason, if the defence solicitor is seeking to persuade the court that an absolute discharge is appropriate, he should make it clear that he does not wish sentence to be deferred for restitution or any other reason. Production of a receipt showing that restitution has already been made would be advisable in such a case!

Absolute discharge is a relatively rare form of disposal. The type of situation where a court might consider it appropriate could be where it felt that the prosecution should never really have been brought because of the triviality of the offence or for some reason peculiar to the offender[3].

### Effect of absolute discharge

An absolute discharge counts as a conviction only for the purposes of the proceedings where it is made and of founding on it as a previous conviction in subsequent proceedings for another offence[4]. The offender's right to appeal against conviction or a finding of guilt is preserved[5]. A person who has received an absolute discharge may also have his licence endorsed or be disqualified under the Road Traffic Acts 1988[6]. An exclusion order may be made against him[7]. He may not be made subject to a compensation order[8], but a suspended forfeiture order in the High Court or sheriff court[9], an order for forfeiture in the district court[10] or a confiscation order[11] may be made against him.

## DEFERRED SENTENCE

### General

All courts have the power to defer sentence following conviction[12]. Sentence may be deferred for any period and on any condition[12]. The most common condition on which sentence is deferred is that the accused should be of good behaviour. It is not desirable to defer sentence with a condition that the offender saves money towards a compensation order[13].

If an accused has been of good behaviour during the period of deferment, that should normally be reflected by the court's imposing a more lenient sentence than

1  1995 Act, s 246(3).
2  1995 Act, s 202(1) specifically provides for a court to defer sentence 'after conviction'.
3  For recent cases where the High Court has granted an absolute discharge on appeal see *Galloway v Mackenzie* 1991 SCCR 548 and *Kheda v Lees* 1995 SCCR 63.
4  1995 Act, s 247(1).
5  1995 Act, s 247(3).
6  Road Traffic Offenders Act 1988, s 46(3).
7  Licensed Premises (Exclusion of Certain Persons) Act 1980, s 1(2)(c). For exclusion order see below at p 261.
8  1995 Act, s 249(2)(a).
9  Proceeds of Crime (Scotland) Act 1995, s 21(1). See below at p 258.
10  Ibid, s 22(1). See below at pp 258–259.
11  Ibid, s 1(1). See below at pp 259–260.
12  1995 Act, s 202(1).
13  *Cameron v Webster* 1997 SCCR 228.

it might otherwise have done[1]. An admonition may be appropriate[2], but the court always has a discretion[3]. A judge should not tie his hands by promising a particular disposal in the event of an accused not behaving[4]. However, there is no reason why the likely consequences of offending should not be spelt out to the accused.

It is not appropriate to defer sentence on one charge while at the same time imposing a custodial sentence on another[5]. Nor should a fine be given on one charge and sentence deferred on another[6].

The High Court has stated that a sheriff who defers sentence should himself deal with the case at the end of the period of deferment if at all possible[7]. This may present a problem in the busier courts, especially with the increasing use of temporary sheriffs.

### Conviction of other offences during deferred sentence

If an accused, who is on deferred sentence, is, during the period of deferment, convicted of and dealt with by a court in any part of Great Britain for an offence committed during the period of deferment, the court which deferred sentence may have him brought before it immediately without waiting until the date to which sentence has been deferred, and it may cite the accused to attend or grant a warrant for his arrest for that purpose[8]. He may then be dealt with in any way which would have been competent at the end of the period of deferment[8]. Similarly, if an accused who is on deferred sentence is, during the period of deferment, convicted by the court which deferred sentence of an offence committed during the period of deferment, the case in which sentence was deferred may be accelerated from the deferment date, and both it and the new offence may be disposed of at the same time[9]. Surprisingly, both these provisions are used relatively infrequently.

# FORFEITURE

Several statutes make provision for forfeiture of specific items in the event of conviction of an offence committed under them[10].

In respect of certain road traffic offences punishable by imprisonment, including culpable homicide by the driving of a vehicle, a court may, on the application of the prosecutor, order forfeiture of the vehicle concerned[11].

---

1 See eg *McPherson v HMA* 1986 SCCR 278; *Main v Jessop* 1989 SCCR 437.
2 *Main v Jessop* 1989 SCCR 437; *Maxwell v MacPhail* 1990 SCCR 738.
3 *Linton v Ingram* 1989 SCCR 487.
4 *Cassidy v Wilson* 1989 SCCR 6.
5 *Lennon v Copeland* 1972 SLT (Notes) 68.
6 *McElwaine v Cardle* 1993 SCCR 619.
7 *Islam v HMA* 1989 SCCR 109; *Main v Jessop* 1989 SCCR 437. See also *Beattie v McGlennan* 1990 SCCR 497.
8 1995 Act, s 202(2).
9 1995 Act, s 202(3).
10 Eg Misuse of Drugs Act 1971; Salmon and Freshwater Fisheries (Protection) (Scotland) Act 1951.
11 Road Traffic Offenders Act 1988, s 33A.

There is also a general power given to courts of both solemn and summary juris-diction[1] (except the district court[2] for which there is a separate provision[3]) under Part II of the Proceeds of Crime (Scotland) Act 1995 to make an order in respect of any property (heritable or moveable) in the accused's ownership, possession or under his control at the time of the offence or of the accused's arrest, which the court is satisfied '(a) has been used for the purpose of committing, or facilitating the commission of, any offence; or (b) was intended by him to be used for that pur-pose'[4]. 'Facilitating the commission of an offence' includes 'the taking of any steps after it has been committed for the purpose of disposing of any property to which it relates or of avoiding apprehension or detention'[5]. The order made is a 'sus-pended forfeiture order'[4]. The statutory provisions concerning this order are com-plex and only a bare outline is given here[6].

If the prosecutor knows or reasonably suspects that the property concerned is owned by someone other than the accused he must inform the court of this fact and the order must name that person as a person having or suspected of having an interest in the property[7]. That person must then be notified by the prosecutor of the making of the suspended forfeiture order and of certain rights which he may have under the Act[8]. Property which is the subject of a suspended forfeiture order will, except in certain limited circumstances, be 'forfeited to and vest in the Crown'[9]. The court may make a compensation order as well as a suspended forfei-ture order and, in that event, may direct that the proceeds of sale of the property should first be directed towards satisfaction of the compensation order[10]. A sus-pended forfeiture order may be recalled or varied on the application of a person other than the accused[11]. It should be recalled if the prosecutor fails to satisfy the court that the owner or person having an interest knew that the property was being used in connection with the offence[12] or if the court is satisfied that the order for forfeiture would in the circumstances be excessive or inappropriate[13]. If the prose-cutor comes to believe that the person named in the order as owner or as having an interest does not in fact have an interest, he may apply to have the order var-ied[14]. If it transpires that property has been wrongly forfeited, application may be made to the court for its return or for compensation[15]. There is a right of appeal to the High Court in respect of recalls, variations and orders for return or compensa-tion[16].

The district court has power, in the same circumstances as those in which the sheriff court may make a suspended forfeiture order, to order the forfeiture of moveable property[17]. There are no provisions for variation or recall of this order.

1  Proceeds of Crime (Scotland) Act 1995, s 21(1).
2  Ibid, s 21(13).
3  Ibid, s 22. See below.
4  Ibid, s 21(2).
5  Ibid, s 21(5).
6  For a full account see *Renton and Brown* paras 23–76 to 23–92.
7  Proceeds of Crime (Scotland) Act 1995, s 21(4).
8  Ibid, s 21(10).
9  Ibid, s 24(1).
10  Ibid, s 21(9).
11  Ibid, s 25(1).
12  Ibid, s 25(2).
13  Ibid, s 25(3).
14  Ibid, s 25(5).
15  Ibid, s 26.
16  Ibid, s 27.
17  Ibid, s 22(1).

The court may order that the proceeds of sale should be first directed towards a compensation order[1].

## CONFISCATION

In terms of Part I of the Proceeds of Crime (Scotland) Act 1995 the High Court, the sheriff court and a district court consisting of a stipendiary magistrate have power to order confiscation of property which represents the proceeds of crime. Again, the statutory provisions are complex and only a bare outline is given here[2].

The provisions apply to all proceedings on indictment[3] but to summary proceedings only if the offence is punishable by a fine greater than level 5 of the standard scale or by imprisonment for longer than three months[4]. The provisions therefore apply only to summary cases where the sheriff's (or stipendiary magistrate's) usual sentencing powers[5] are increased.

The prosecutor must apply for the making of a confiscation order[6] and any such application should be made when the prosecutor moves for sentence in solemn proceedings[7], or following the conviction of the accused in summary proceedings[8]. A confiscation order may be imposed only if the court also orders some other disposal (including an absolute discharge)[9]. The court must determine the amount payable under a confiscation order before imposing a fine on the accused or making any order involving payment by him[10], and must take account of the order before imposing any fine or making any other order for payment[11]. Apart from that the order is to be left out of account in determining the appropriate sentence[11].

The provisions distinguish between the proceeds of a drug trafficking offence[12] and the proceeds of other crimes. In the case of the latter an order may be made only if the court is satisfied that the accused has benefited from the commission of the offence concerned[13]. In such a case the amount payable under the order is the lesser of (a) the amount of the benefit obtained from commission of the offence (together with other offences in certain circumstances) and (b) the amount that might be realised at the time when the order is made[14]. In the case of a drug trafficking offence the amount is not to exceed what the court assesses to be the value of the proceeds of the accused's drug trafficking or the amount which might be

1 Proceeds of Crime (Scotland) Act 1995, s 22(3).
2 For a full account see *Renton and Brown* paras 23–95 to 23–120.
3 Proceeds of Crime (Scotland) Act 1995, s 1(2)(a).
4 Ibid, s 1(2)(b). For the standard scale see p 233 above. At the time of writing level 5 is £5,000. There is no provision in the 1997 Act which would affect s 1(2)(b).
5 See above at pp 222–223.
6 Proceeds of Crime (Scotland) Act 1995, s 1(1).
7 Ibid, s 1(7)(a), which also provides that if the accused is remitted to the High Court for sentence the application should be made before sentence is pronounced. It is not clear whether this means that where there is a remit the application for an order must be made both in the sheriff court and in the High Court.
8 Proceeds of Crime (Scotland) Act 1995, s 1(7)(b).
9 Ibid, s 1(3).
10 Ibid, s 8(1).
11 Ibid, s 8(2).
12 Ibid, s 46(5) defines such an offence.
13 Ibid, s 1(4).
14 Ibid, s 1(6).

realised under the Act if that is less[1]. There are provisions for assessing the proceeds of drug trafficking[2] and for determining what is an accused's 'realisable property'[3]. There are provisions relating to gifts[4]. The court may postpone the making of a confiscation order for up to six months after the date of conviction in order to obtain further information to enable it to decide whether or not to make an order or to determine the amount of the order[5].

Other provisions in Part I of the Act relate to an increase in benefit or realisable property[6], the amount of realisable property being inadequate to meet the confiscation order[7], proceeds of a crime being discovered at a later date[8] and payment of interest[9]. The provisions relating to payment of fines are, with some exceptions, applied to payment of a confiscation order[10].

# RESTRAINT ORDER

In respect of both confiscation orders and suspended forfeiture orders the court is given power to make a 'restraint order' interdicting the person named in the order from dealing with certain property[11]. The object of such an order is the preservation of assets. Once again only an outline of the complex provisions is given here[12].

A restraint order is made not by a criminal court but by the appropriate court having civil jurisdiction. In the case where the criminal proceedings are in the High Court, that court is the Court of Session[13]. Where the criminal proceedings are in the sheriff court, that court is the sheriff sitting in his civil capacity[14]. The order may be made in respect of 'realisable property' in the context of a confiscation order[15] and 'forfeitable property' in the case of a suspended forfeiture order[16]. A restraint order may be varied or recalled[17]. The Court of Session may, on the application of the Lord Advocate, grant warrant for inhibition in respect of heritable realisable property affected by a restraint order[18], and the warrant has the same effect as inhibition on the dependence of an action for debt at the instance of the Lord Advocate[19]. A warrant for the arrestment of moveable property affected by a restraint order may be applied for by the prosecutor[20] and, if granted, has the same effect as arrestment on the dependence in an action for debt at the prosecutor's instance[21].

1 Proceeds of Crime (Scotland) Act 1995, s 1(5).
2 Ibid, s 3.
3 Ibid, s 4.
4 Ibid, ss 5, 6, 7. See *Rowan, Petrs (No 1)* 1997 SLT 667.
5 Ibid, s 10.
6 Ibid, s 11.
7 Ibid, s 12.
8 Ibid, s 13.
9 Ibid, s 15.
10 Ibid, s 14.
11 Ibid, s 28(1).
12 For a fuller account see *Renton and Brown* paras 23–89 and 23–117.
13 Proceeds of Crime (Scotland) Act 1995, s 28(7)(a).
14 Ibid, s 28(7)(b).
15 Ibid, s 29.
16 Ibid, s 30.
17 Ibid, s 31.
18 Ibid, s 32.
19 Ibid, s 32(1)(a).
20 Ibid, s 33(1).
21 Ibid, s 33(2).

# EXCLUSION ORDER

If a person is found guilty of an offence committed on licensed premises and the court is satisfied that, in committing the offence, he resorted to violence or offered or threatened to resort to violence, it may make an exclusion order[1]. This is an order prohibiting the offender from entering 'these premises or any other specified premises, without the express consent of the licensee of the premises or his servant or agent'. The order may be for any period not less than three months or more than two years[2].

An exclusion order may be imposed in addition to any other sentence, and is competent even if the offender is placed on probation or given an absolute discharge[3].

A person who enters premises in breach of an exclusion order is guilty of an offence and is liable to a fine not exceeding level 3 on the standard scale[4] and/or imprisonment for a term not exceeding one month[5]. The court convicting a person of such an offence may terminate the exclusion order or may vary it by deleting the name of any specified premises[6].

The licensee of premises may expel any person entering them in breach of an exclusion order and may call on the assistance of a police officer for that purpose[7].

# DISQUALIFICATION

## General

Under various statutes an offender may be disqualified from doing something which he could otherwise legally do. The most obvious example is disqualification for holding or obtaining a driving licence in terms of the Road Traffic Acts 1988, but an offender may also, for example, be disqualified from holding public office[8], or from keeping an animal[9]. If sentence is deferred in a case where disqualification is competent, the order for disqualification must usually be made at the date of sentencing and not at the date when sentence is deferred. However, interim disqualification from driving may be imposed when the case is adjourned or sentence is deferred in a case charging a road traffic offence[10]. Any period of disqualification subsequently imposed is treated as reduced by the period of interim disqualification[11].

---

1 Licensed Premises (Exclusion of Certain Persons) Act 1980, s 1(1).
2 Ibid, s 1(3).
3 Ibid, s 1(2).
4 £1,000 at the time of writing. For the standard scale see above at p 233.
5 Licensed Premises (Exclusion of Certain Persons) Act 1980, s 2(1).
6 Ibid, s 2(2).
7 Ibid, s 3.
8 Public Bodies Corrupt Practices Act 1889, s 2.
9 Protection of Animals (Amendment) Act 1954, s 1(1).
10 Road Traffic Offenders Act 1988, s 26(3).
11 Ibid, s 26(12).

### Disqualification under the Road Traffic Acts

It is not intended to examine disqualification from driving (as it is commonly called) in any detail here. Reference should be made to one of the specialist works on road traffic law[1]. However, the following points should be noted.

A court should not normally disqualify an offender without giving him an opportunity to make representations about disqualification, if disqualification is to any extent discretionary[2]. It happens quite often that an accused pleads guilty by letter to an offence for which disqualification is competent but not obligatory, and says nothing in mitigation in his letter. If the court is contemplating disqualification in such a case, the accused should be informed of this and given the opportunity of either appearing personally or stating mitigating circumstances in writing.

Where a court disqualifies an offender in respect of a number of offences committed at the same time, each offence has to be considered separately and the appropriate disqualification for *that* offence only imposed on each[3]. Some doubts were expressed as to whether this was still the law, given the provisions of a subsection of the Road Traffic Offenders Act 1988[4]. This appears to say that, when an offender is convicted on the same occasion of more than one offence involving obligatory or discretionary disqualification, not more than one disqualification must be imposed, and in deciding the period of disqualification the court must take into account all the offences. The problem is that this subsection is in the section dealing with the so-called 'totting up' provisions, where it makes little if any sense, and not in the preceding section where it would make perfect sense. Is it possible that an error has been made?

In addition to disqualification for an offence under the Road Traffic Acts 1988, the court also has power in certain circumstances to disqualify from driving in respect of common law offences. First, disqualification is competent but not obligatory in the case of theft of a motor vehicle[5]. Secondly, if a person is convicted of an offence (other than one triable only summarily), and the court is satisfied that a motor vehicle was used for the purpose of committing or facilitating the commission of that offence, the court may disqualify the offender from driving for such a period as it thinks fit[6]. In this context 'facilitating' has the same extended meaning as it has for the purposes of forfeiture[7].

## DEPORTATION

When a person over seventeen, who is not a British subject, is found guilty of an offence punishable with imprisonment in the case of someone over 21, the court

---

1 See eg J F Wheatley *Road Traffic Law in Scotland* (Law Society of Scotland/Butterworth, 2nd edn, 1993); Road Traffic Encyclopaedia (Sweet and Maxwell, looseleaf, regularly updated); Wilkinson's Road Traffic Offences (Longman Professional – new editions appear regularly).
2 *Stephens v Gibb* 1984 SCCR 195.
3 *McMurrich v Cardle* 1988 SCCR 20, which was decided under the former road traffic legislation. In *Patterson v Whitelaw* 1990 GWD 23-1308 (a case under the new legislation), *McMurrich* was affirmed and followed.
4 Road Traffic Offenders Act 1988, s 35(3).
5 Ibid, s 97(2), Sch 2, Pt II.
6 1995 Act, s 248(1). If the 1997 Act, s 15 comes into force a court may have power to disqualify from driving a person committing virtually any offence whether or not involving the use of a motor vehicle. See the Appendix at p 323 below.
7 1995 Act, s 248(3). See above at p 258.

may recommend that he be deported[1]. The power to recommend deportation may be exercised only by the High Court and the sheriff court[2]. The court may not recommend deportation unless the offender has received at least seven days' notice in writing stating that a person is not liable to deportation if he is a British subject[3]. After an accused has been found guilty the court may adjourn to enable such a notice to be served[4]. A recommendation for deportation may be made in the case of a person sentenced to life imprisonment[5]. An appeal against a recommendation for deportation is competent as an appeal against sentence[6].

There are restrictions on the making of a deportation order in respect of certain Commonwealth citizens and citizens of the Republic of Ireland[7].

Deportation may be recommended only in relation to a serious charge or series of charges, the test being whether to allow the offender to remain in this country would be contrary to the national interest[8]. In the case of a national of a country of the European Union, in terms of the provisions of the EC Treaty, a recommendation for deportation is justified only if the continued presence of the offender in the United Kingdom would be 'in addition to the perturbation of the social order which any infringement of the law involves, a genuine and sufficiently serious threat to the requirements of public policy affecting one of the fundamental interests of society'[9].

It should be remembered that it is not the court which makes the actual deportation order. The court merely recommends. The ultimate decision whether or not to deport is taken by the Home Secretary, and any order is made by him[10].

1 Immigration Act 1971, s 3(6), read in conjunction with s 6(3).
2 Immigration Act 1971, s 6(1).
3 Ibid, s 6(2).
4 Ibid. The adjournment may be under the 1995 Act, s 201(1).
5 Immigration Act 1971, s 6(4).
6 Ibid, s 6(5).
7 Ibid, s 7.
8 *Willms v Smith* 1982 JC 9, 1981 SCCR 257, 1982 SLT 163. See also *Faboro v HMA* 1982 SCCR 22 and *Salehi v Smith* 1982 SCCR 552.
9 *R v Bouchereau* [1978] QB 146, [1981] 2 All ER 924, [1978] 2 WLR 250, (1977) Cr App R 202. This was a decision of the Court of Justice of the European Communities.
10 Immigration Act 1971, s 5(1).

# CHAPTER 8

# APPEALS

## INTRODUCTION

Mention has been made in various parts of the text of appeals to the High Court of Justiciary in matters before final disposal of a case, such as bail[1] or decisions on competency and relevancy in summary cases[2]. This chapter is concerned primarily with appeals following final disposal, but other matters will be touched upon.

We shall first of all examine appeals in cases under solemn procedure, then appeals in cases under summary procedure. We shall then look briefly at appeal by advocation and appeal to the *nobile officium* of the High Court, both of which may apply to solemn and summary cases.

The High Court when acting as an appellate court is often called the Court of Criminal Appeal or the Justiciary Appeal Court, although these nomenclatures are not used in the current legislation.

## APPEALS UNDER SOLEMN PROCEDURE

### Scope of appeal

A person who has been convicted on indictment, whether in the High Court or the sheriff court, may, provided that he has been granted leave[3], appeal against conviction, conviction and sentence, or sentence alone[4]. There is no appeal against a sentence fixed by law[5]. 'By an appeal ... a person may bring under review of the High Court any alleged miscarriage of justice in the proceedings in which he was convicted, including any alleged miscarriage of justice on the basis of the existence and significance of additional evidence which was not heard at the trial and which was not available and could not reasonably have been made available at the trial'[6]. The only evidence which the court may consider in terms of this provision is evidence which was not available at the original trial and which could not reasonably have been made available at that trial[7].

1 See above at pp 103, 106.
2 See above at pp 197–198.
3 Under the 1995 Act, s 107. See below at pp 268, 269, 273.
4 1995 Act, s 106(1).
5 1995 Act, s 106(2).
6 1995 Act, s 106(3). The scope of this section has been extended by the coming into force of the 1997 Act, s 17 with effect from 1 August 1997. See the Appendix at p 325 below.
7 *Elliott v HMA* 1995 SCCR 280, 1995 SLT 612, a decision of a bench of five judges, disapproving the decision in *Church v HMA* 1995 SCCR 194, 1995 SLT 604.

## Legal aid

An appellant may apply for legal aid to the Scottish Legal Aid Board. Legal aid will be granted if leave to appeal has been granted in a case where leave is necessary[1], and, in any other case where the applicant for legal aid is the appellant, if 'the Board is satisfied that in all the circumstances of the case it is in the interests of justice that the applicant should receive criminal legal aid'[2]. If the Board has refused legal aid in a case where leave to appeal is not required, the High Court may determine that it is in the interests of justice that the appellant should receive legal aid, and the Board must then grant it[3]. If an appellant has had legal aid in the trial court, he does not require to qualify financially for the appeal[4], but otherwise he will receive legal aid only if he is unable to meet the expenses of the appeal without undue hardship to himself or his dependants[5].

The application for legal aid is signed by the appellant and must include a statement signed by or on behalf of the appellant's solicitor as to his willingness to act for the appellant[6]. It must also include a statement by the solicitor of the nature of the grounds of appeal where the solicitor is of the opinion that in all the circumstances they are substantial[7]. In cases of urgency legal aid may be granted even though the conditions specified in section 25(2) of the Legal Aid (Scotland) Act (ie that the appellant qualifies financially, that leave to appeal has been granted or that the Board is satisfied as to the interests of justice) are not satisfied[8]. Application may be made to the Board by telephone for such legal aid, which is granted only for a limited specified purpose[9]. Such a purpose could, for example, be lodging a note of appeal, obtaining counsel's opinion on the prospects of success in the appeal or making an application for interim liberation.

Article 6(3) of the European Convention on Human Rights provides: 'Everyone charged with a criminal offence has the following minimum rights: … (c) to defend himself in person or through legal assistance of his own choosing or, if he has not sufficient means to pay for legal assistance, to be given it free when the interests of justice so require.' A refusal of legal aid for an appeal against conviction in a case where a long sentence has been imposed may amount to a contravention of this provision[10].

## Appeals against conviction[11]

*Intimation of intention to appeal*

A person who wishes to appeal against conviction (whether or not appealing also against sentence) must lodge with the Clerk of Justiciary written intimation of his

---

1 Legal Aid (Scotland) Act 1986, s 25(2)(b).
2 Ibid, s 25(2)(c).
3 Ibid, s 25(2A).
4 Ibid, s 25(4).
5 Ibid, s 25(2)(a).
6 Criminal Legal Aid (Scotland) Regulations 1987, SI 1987/307, reg 13(1)(a), (b).
7 Ibid, reg 13(1)(c).
8 Ibid, reg 15(1).
9 Ibid, reg 15(2)(a).
10 *Boner v UK, Maxwell v UK* 1995 SCCR 1, a decision of the European Court of Human Rights.
11 With the coming into force of the 1997 Act, s 20 on 1 August 1997 there is now the possibility of an appeal being taken on behalf of a person who cannot himself pursue the appeal because he is dead. See the Appendix at p 327 below.

intention to appeal within two weeks of the final determination of the proceedings in the trial court[1]. 'Final determination' means the date when sentence is passed[2], except when sentence has been deferred for a period, in which case it is the date when sentence is first deferred[3]. The two-week period may be extended by a single judge of the High Court[4] on application by the appellant[5].

### Suspension of disqualification, forfeiture etc

Any disqualification, forfeiture or 'disability' to which a person is liable as a result of the conviction against which he seeks to appeal is in effect suspended, as soon as his intimation of intention to appeal is lodged, until his appeal is determined[6]. This does not apply where the statute under which disqualification or the like was imposed makes specific provision as to what should happen in the case of an appeal[7]. For example, in the case of someone disqualified from driving for a road traffic offence, there is no automatic suspension of disqualification, and application should be made to the trial court[8].

Where a fine has been imposed or a compensation order made, nothing can be done to enforce payment until the appeal has been determined[9], and if some payment towards a compensation order has been made, the clerk of court must not pay it to the person entitled to payment until that time[10].

Where leave to appeal is refused[11], an appeal is 'determined', in the case of refusal by a single judge where there is no further application to the High Court, on the fifteenth day after the date of intimation of refusal to the appellant or his solicitor[12]. Where there is an application to the High Court which is refused, it is determined on the day two days after intimation of the refusal[13].

### Note of appeal

Within six weeks of lodging his intimation of intention to appeal the appellant must lodge a note of appeal with the Clerk of Justiciary[14]. This must contain a full statement of all the grounds of appeal[15]. An appellant will not be allowed to found on a ground of appeal not stated in the note except by leave of the High Court on cause shown[16]. The period of six weeks may be extended by the Clerk of

---

1   1995 Act, s 109(1). The form of intimation is Form 15.2A: 1996 Rules, r 15.2(1). Forms are available from the Clerk of Justiciary who should also provide all other forms in connection with appeals to courts and prisons: 1995 Act, s 127.
2   1995 Act, s 109(4).
3   1995 Act, s 109(5). There is no reason why the trial court should not pass sentence at the end of the period of deferment, even if the case is then still under appeal: *McRobbie v HMA* 1990 SCCR 767.
4   1995 Act, s 103(5)(a).
5   1995 Act, s 111(2). The form of application is Form 15.2C: 1996 Rules, r 15.2(3). There is a right of appeal to a bench of three judges from a refusal by the single judge: 1995 Act, s 103(2), (6).
6   1995 Act, s 121(1)(b), (2)(b). With the coming into force of the 1997 Act, s 24 on 1 August 1997 an applicant may now apply to the court for suspension of other sentences. See the Appendix at p 326 below.
7   1995 Act, s 121(3).
8   Road Traffic Offenders Act 1988, s 39(2).
9   1995 Act, s 121(4)(a).
10  1995 Act, s 121(4)(b).
11  See below at p 268.
12  1996 Rules, r 15.13(a).
13  1996 Rules, r 15.13(b).
14  1995 Act, s 110(1). The form of note is Form 15.2B: 1996 Rules, r 15.2(2).
15  1995 Act, s 110(3). It is essential that the grounds of appeal are fully stated. Otherwise the court may not entertain the appeal: *Smith v HMA* 1983 SCCR 30; *Mitchell v HMA* 1991 SCCR 216.
16  1995 Act, s 110(4).

Justiciary[1]. This is to ensure that the appellant is able to see the transcript of the judge's charge to the jury before he lodges his note of appeal. The six-week period (or the longer period prescribed by the Clerk of Justiciary) may be extended by a single judge of the High Court[2] on application by the appellant[3].

### Judge's report

On receipt of the note of appeal the Clerk of Justiciary sends a copy of it to the trial judge[4]. As soon as reasonably practicable thereafter the judge should provide the Clerk of Justiciary with a report giving his opinion on the case generally and on the grounds contained in the note of appeal[5]. The judge must comment on the grounds of appeal[6]. Such a report used to be confidential to the High Court and was not seen by either the appellant or the respondent. Now, however, a copy of the report must be sent to the appellant or his solicitor and to the Crown Agent[7]. If the case is not a normal appeal, but has been referred to the court by the Secretary of State under section 124(3) of the 1995 Act[8], a copy of the judge's report is also sent to the Secretary of State[9]. The High Court may hear and determine an appeal without a report[10].

In addition to the above-mentioned provision for the trial judge providing a report, the High Court is given specific power to order the trial judge to provide a report 'giving the judge's opinion on the case generally or in relation to any particular matter specified in the order'[11]. Any such report must also be made available to the parties[12]. This power was introduced for the first time by the 1995 Act. It is presumably intended to cover the situation where the trial judge's original report does not cover a matter raised during the course of the appeal hearing.

The trial judge may be required by the High Court to produce any notes taken by him at the trial[13]. This requirement is very seldom made, which is perhaps just as well, considering the illegibility in some cases of such notes, including those of the present writer!

### Bail

An appellant may apply to the High Court for bail pending his appeal[14]. The bail application is considered by a single judge[15], but the appellant may appeal against a refusal of bail to a bench of three judges[16]. A bail application is usually lodged along with or after the note of appeal but it may be considered by the High Court before the lodging of the note of appeal provided that the application sets out the grounds

---

1  1995 Act, s 110(2).
2  1995 Act, s 103(5)(a).
3  1995 Act, s 111(2). The form of application is Form 15.2C: 1996 Rules, r 15.2(3). There is a right of appeal to a bench of three judges from a refusal by the single judge: 1995 Act, s 103(2), (6).
4  1995 Act, s 110(1).
5  1995 Act, s 113(1).
6  *McPhelim v HMA* 1996 SCCR 647, 1996 SLT 992.
7  1995 Act, s 113(2).
8  See below at p 276.
9  1995 Act, s 113(2)(c).
10  1995 Act, s 113(3).
11  1995 Act, s 298(1).
12  1995 Act, s 298(2).
13  1996 Rules, r 15.7.
14  1995 Act, s 112(1), (3). The form is Form 15.2D: 1996 Rules, r 15.2(4).
15  1995 Act, s 103(5)(c).
16  1995 Act, s 103(2), (6).

of appeal[1]. If bail is granted the appellant must appear personally for the hearing of the appeal unless the High Court directs otherwise[2]. If the appellant fails to attend personally, the court may dismiss the appeal[3]. Alternatively, it may be dealt with in his absence[4].

### Leave to appeal

No appeal against conviction will be considered by the High Court unless leave to appeal has been granted[5]. The requirement for leave was introduced by the 1995 Act with the intention of reducing the workload of the criminal appeal court. Some would argue that, even though the court itself now has to consider a substantially smaller number of appeals, the burden has simply been shifted to those judges who deal with the 'sift' (as the consideration of whether to grant leave has come to be called).

Each case in which a note of appeal against conviction has been lodged is considered by a single judge of the High Court[6]. The judge has before him the note of appeal, the trial judge's report and (if appropriate) a transcript of the judge's charge to the jury[7]. In an appeal from a sheriff and jury case the judge also has the certified copy or record of the proceedings at the trial[8]. Having considered these, 'if he considers that the documents ... disclose arguable grounds of appeal' the judge must 'grant leave to appeal and make such comments in writing as he considers appropriate'[9]. Otherwise he must refuse leave to appeal and give reasons in writing for refusal[10]. If the appellant was sentenced to imprisonment but was released on bail pending appeal, a warrant for his arrest is granted[11].

Within fourteen days of refusal by the single judge the appellant may apply 'to the High Court' for leave to appeal[12]. This second application, in the case of an application which includes an appeal against conviction, is considered by three judges[13]. If, 'after considering the documents [which were before the single judge] and the reasons for refusal' the court considers that there are arguable grounds of appeal, it grants leave to appeal and makes such comments in writing as it considers appropriate[14]. In any other case it refuses leave and gives reasons in writing[15]. If the appellant was sentenced to imprisonment but was released on bail pending appeal, a warrant for his arrest is granted[16].

Any judge considering whether to grant leave to appeal may remit the case to the trial judge for a supplementary report 'to be produced by him as soon as is reasonably practicable on any matter with respect to the grounds of appeal'[17].

1   1995 Act, s 112(2)(b).
2   1995 Act, s 112(3).
3   1995 Act, s 112(4)(a).
4   1995 Act, s 112(4)(b).
5   1995 Act, s 106(1).
6   1995 Act, s 107(1).
7   1995 Act, s 107(2)(a), (c), (d).
8   1995 Act, s 107(2)(b).
9   1995 Act, s 107(1)(a).
10   1995 Act, s 107(1)(b)(i).
11   1995 Act, s 107(1)(b)(ii).
12   1995 Act, s 107(4). This period cannot be extended by the *nobile officium* of the High Court: *Connolly, Petr* 1997 SCCR 205, 1997 SLT 689.
13   1995 Act, s 103(2).
14   1995 Act, s 107(5)(a).
15   1995 Act, s 107(5)(b)(i).
16   1995 Act, s 107(5)(b)(ii).
17   1996 Rules, r 15.14.

All consideration of whether to grant leave to appeal, whether before a single judge or three judges, is in chambers and outwith the presence of the parties[1].

The comments in writing made by the single judge or the three judges when granting leave to appeal may specify the arguable grounds of appeal on the basis of which leave has been granted, whether these are contained in the note of appeal or not[2]. When this is done the appellant may not put forward any other ground of appeal except with the leave of the High Court on cause shown[3]. An application for such leave must be made not less than seven days before the date fixed for the hearing of the appeal[4] and must within the same period be intimated to the Crown Agent[5].

All decisions on the question of leave to appeal (with reasons in the case of a refusal) must be intimated by the Clerk or Justiciary to the parties 'forthwith'[6].

### Intimation of hearing

If leave to appeal is granted the Clerk of Justiciary gives notice of the date of the appeal hearing to the Crown Agent and to the appellant or his solicitor[7]. The appellant's solicitor (or the appellant himself if he is unrepresented) must lodge three copies of the appeal for the use of the court within seven days before the hearing[8]. The appellant is entitled to be present at the hearing if he wishes[9], and should appear in ordinary civilian clothes rather than in prison uniform[10].

### Failure of appellant to attend

If the appellant fails to attend or to be represented at the hearing of the appeal, and no case or argument in writing[11] has been timeously lodged, the court must dispose of the appeal as if it had been abandoned[12].

### Abandonment of appeal

An appellant may abandon his appeal against conviction by lodging a notice of abandonment with the Clerk of Justiciary, and the appeal is then deemed to have been dismissed[13]. A person who has appealed against both conviction and sentence may abandon his appeal against conviction and proceed only with the appeal against sentence[14].

### Hearing of appeal

The hearing of an appeal against conviction usually takes place before a bench of three judges and cannot be considered by less than that number[15], but a bench of

1  1995 Act, s 107(6).
2  1995 Act, s 107(7).
3  1995 Act, s 107(8).
4  1995 Act, s 107(9)(a).
5  1995 Act, s 107(9)(b).
6  1995 Act, s 107(10).
7  1995 Act, s 117(9).
8  1996 Rules, r 15.8(1).
9  1995 Act, s 117(3).
10  1995 Act, s 117(6).
11  In terms of the 1995 Act, s 115. See below at p 270.
12  1995 Act, s 120(1). For abandonment of appeals see the next paragraph.
13  1995 Act, s 116(1). The form is Form 15.6: 1996 Rules, r 15.6.
14  1995 Act, s 116(2).
15  1995 Act, s 103(2).

five or seven judges may be convened when it is desired to reconsider an earlier decision of the court[1]. A quorum of the High Court (ie usually three judges) is bound by the previous decision of a court of equal size; a decision of a court of equal number can be reviewed only by a larger court[2].

The appeal is almost invariably conducted by means of oral debate, but there is a rarely used provision for an appellant to present his argument in writing[3]. At least four days prior to the hearing of the appeal notice of his desire to present a written argument must be made to the Clerk of Justiciary[4], three copies of the argument must be lodged with the Clerk of Justiciary[5] and a copy of the intimation, case and argument must be sent to the Crown Agent[6]. Unless the High Court directs otherwise, the respondent does not make a written reply, but responds orally[7]. If the appellant presents a written argument, he is not entitled also to make oral submissions except with the leave of the court[8].

### Powers of the High Court

The court is given various powers for the purposes of an appeal under section 106(1) of the 1995 Act[9]. These powers (which apply to appeals against both conviction and sentence) are:

(a)  to order the production of any document or other thing connected with the proceedings[10];

(b)  to hear any additional evidence relevant to any alleged miscarriage of justice or order such evidence to be heard by a judge of the High Court or by such other person as it may appoint for that purpose;

(c)  to take account of any circumstances relevant to the case which were not before the trial judge[11];

(d)  to remit to any fit person to enquire and report in regard to any matter or circumstance affecting the appeal[12];

(e)  to appoint a person with expert knowledge to act as assessor to the High Court in any case where it appears to the court that such expert knowledge is required for the proper determination of the case.

---

1  Eg *Templeton v McLeod* 1985 SCCR 357, 1986 SLT 149 (five judges): overruled by *Leggate v HMA* 1988 SCCR 391, 1988 SLT 665 (seven judges). For a recent example of a five judge case see *Elliott v HMA* 1995 SCCR 280, 1995 SLT 612, which disapproved *Church v HMA* 1995 SCCR 194, 1995 SLT 604.

2  *Elliott v HMA* 1995 SCCR 280, 1995 SLT 612.

3  1995 Act, s 115.

4  1995 Act, s 115(1)(a).

5  1995 Act, s 115(1)(b).

6  1995 Act, s 115(1)(c).

7  1995 Act, s 115(3).

8  1995 Act, s 115(4).

9  1995 Act, s 104(1).

10  There is separate provision (1995 Act, s 94(1)) for production of the transcript of the shorthand or tape-recorded record of a trial.

11  The opinion has been expressed that this provision is designed only for appeals against sentence: *Rubin v HMA* 1984 SCCR 96 at 107, 1984 SLT 369 at 371, per Lord Justice-General Emslie.

12  For a recent example of use of this power see *Crossan v HMA* 1996 SCCR 279. It would be competent under this provision to order an enquiry into allegations of prejudice on the part of a juror notwithstanding the terms of the Contempt of Court Act 1981, s 8: *McCadden v HMA* 1985 SCCR 282, 1986 SLT 138.

*Additional evidence*

The High Court may bring under review any alleged miscarriage of justice including any alleged miscarriage of justice on the basis of the existence and significance
of additional evidence which was not heard at the trial subject to certain detailed
conditions[1].

The law on the subject of additional evidence before the High Court on appeal
and its effect was clarified by the case of *Cameron v Her Majesty's Advocate*[2]. This
established the following propositions. Where the appeal court is satisfied that, if
the original jury had heard the new evidence, they would have been bound to
acquit, the court will quash the conviction. Where the appeal court is satisfied that
the additional evidence is at least capable of being described as important and reliable evidence which would have been at least likely to have had material bearing
on, or a major part to play in, the jury's determination of a critical issue at the trial,
it will be open to the court to hold that a conviction returned in ignorance of that
evidence represents a miscarriage of justice, and to set aside the verdict and authorise a new prosecution[3].

Since *Cameron* there have been further developments in the law in this field. It
is not necessary that the appeal court has to find the new evidence credible: it is
sufficient if it finds that it is *capable* of being found credible and reliable by a reasonable jury properly directed[4]. Evidence which was not in existence at the time
of the trial may still constitute additional evidence within the meaning of section
106(3)[5]. The additional evidence need not be evidence which would have been
relevant and admissible at the original trial. Thus, evidence which has become
admissible only as a result of a change in the law after the date of the original trial
may be founded upon for the purposes of this section[6]. An appeal based on additional evidence is competent even though the appellant has pleaded guilty before
the trial court[7].

The court will never entertain an appeal based on the proposition that a witness
who has given evidence at a trial merely wishes to change his story: that is not additional evidence within the meaning of section 104(1)(b)[8].

An application to the court to hear fresh evidence should be supported by a precognition from the witness concerned. That precognition should be taken by a
qualified solicitor[9].

Additional evidence may be led before the appeal court itself (although this
rarely if ever occurs) or before a single judge or before another person appointed
by the High Court[10] (eg a sheriff principal). The evidence is taken by examination
and cross-examination in the normal way[11]. The fact that the court has ordered

1  1995 Act, s 106(3), (3A)–(3D). The scope of this provision has been extended with the coming into
   force of the 1997 Act, s 17 on 1 August 1997. See the Appendix at p 325 below.
2  *Cameron v HMA* 1987 SCCR 608, 1988 SLT 169.
3  See below at pp 272–273.
4  *Church v HMA* 1996 SCCR 29, 1996 SLT 383 sub nom *Church v HMA (No 2)*; *Mitchell v HMA* 1996
   SCCR 477, 1996 SLT 1339.
5  *McLay v HMA* 1994 SCCR 397, 1994 SLT 873 (a five judges case).
6  1995 Act, s 106(3B) inserted by the 1997 Act, s 17(1) effectively overruling *Conway v HMA* 1996
   SCCR 569, 1996 SLT 1293. See the Appendix at pp 325–326 below.
7  *Carrington v HMA* 1994 SCCR 567, 1995 SLT 341.
8  *Mitchell v HMA* 1989 SCCR 502.
9  *Allison v HMA* 1985 SCCR 408.
10  1995 Act, s 104(2).
11  1995 Act, s 104(3).

additional evidence to be heard does not prevent it from considering an objection to the admissibility of that evidence at the stage when it is sought to be led[1].

## Disposal of appeals against conviction

There are three ways in which the appeal court may dispose of an appeal against conviction[2]. It may affirm the verdict of the trial court[3]; or it may set aside the verdict and either quash the conviction or substitute an amended verdict of guilty[4] (provided that such a verdict would have been competent before the trial court[5]); or it may set aside the verdict and grant authority to bring a new prosecution[6]. If the court sets aside a verdict it may quash the sentence imposed on the indictment and substitute another (but not more severe) sentence[7].

The only ground of appeal now is that there has been a miscarriage of justice[8]. It has been held that, even if a miscarriage of justice has occurred, the verdict will not necessarily be set aside if the miscarriage of justice is not such as to warrant quashing the conviction[9].

## Authorisation of new prosecution

If a new prosecution is authorised by the appeal court, proceedings therein must be commenced within two months of the date on which authority was granted[10]. Proceedings are commenced on the date when a warrant to apprehend or to cite the accused is granted 'where such warrant is executed without unreasonable delay', and otherwise on the date when the warrant is executed[11]. In this context 'unreasonable' may probably be equiperated with 'undue' in section 136(3) of the 1995 Act (six-month time-bar for certain summary statutory prosecutions[12]). It has been held in the sheriff court that a challenge to the competency of the proceedings may be made at the committal stage[13]. If proceedings are not commenced within the two months, the setting aside of the verdict by the appeal court has the effect of an acquittal[14]. The other time limits applying to proceedings on indictment do not, however, apply here[15].

The new prosecution may be for the same offence as was originally charged or for any similar offence arising out of the same facts[16], provided that the accused is not charged with an offence more serious than that of which he was convicted in

---

1   *Perrie, Petr* 1991 SCCR 475, 1992 SLT 655. See also *Perrie v HMA* 1991 JC 27, 1991 SCCR 255, 1992 SLT 651.
2   1995 Act, s 118(1).
3   1995 Act, s 118(1)(a).
4   1995 Act, s 118(1)(b).
5   1995 Act, s 118(2).
6   1995 Act, s 118(1)(c).
7   1995 Act, s 118(3). See *Caringi v HMA* 1989 SCCR 223, 1989 SLT 714.
8   1995 Act, s 106(3).
9   *McCuaig v HMA* 1982 JC 59, 1982 SCCR 125, 1982 SLT 383.
10  1995 Act, s 119(5). If the new proceedings are commenced timeously and then deserted *pro loco et tempore* the Crown may re-indict even though more than two months have passed: *McPhelim v HMA* 1997 SCCR 87.
11  1995 Act, s 119(8). Warrant to cite in this context means a warrant granted under the 1995 Act, s 66(1): *McPhelim v HMA* 1997 SCCR 87.
12  *Friel v Mailley* 1993 SCCR 928 (Sh Ct). For s 136(3) see above at pp 195, 196.
13  *Friel v Mailley* 1993 SCCR 928 (Sh Ct).
14  1995 Act, s 119(9).
15  1995 Act, s 119(4).
16  1995 Act, s 119(1).

the earlier trial[1]. In the event of his being convicted at the new trial, no sentence may be pronounced which could not have been pronounced on conviction under the earlier proceedings[2].

A new trial has most frequently been authorised where the miscarriage of justice has been procedural rather than going to the merits of the case[3]. However, even though a conviction is quashed on a procedural matter it does not necessarily mean that a new prosecution will be authorised[4]. The fact that the principal prosecution witness is a child is a factor to be taken into account when deciding whether or not to authorise a new prosecution[5].

## Appeals against sentence by the accused

The procedure for appealing against sentence only (which includes absolute discharge or admonition[6], probation or community service[7], and any order deferring sentence[8]) in solemn proceedings is very similar to that for appealing against conviction, except that there is no intimation of intention to appeal. The first document lodged is a note of appeal, and that must be lodged with the Clerk of Justiciary within two weeks of the imposition of the sentence appealed against[9]. Thereafter the procedure regarding bail, application for extension of time and the trial judge's report is exactly the same as in the case of appeals against conviction.

As with appeals against conviction, an appeal against sentence cannot be considered unless leave to appeal has been granted[10]. The provisions for considering whether leave to appeal should be granted are also similar except that if the application proceeds beyond the single judge it is considered not by three judges but by only two[11].

If leave to appeal is granted the provisions about fixing a hearing and the hearing itself are similar to those for an appeal against conviction but the hearing may take place before a court consisting of only two judges[12].

The provision about abandonment of an appeal[13] applies equally to an appeal against sentence. However, it is particularly important in the case of an appeal against sentence to lodge a proper notice of abandonment. The court may well not permit the appeal to be abandoned at the bar without proper notice having been given, as it is may be considering increasing the sentence[14].

After hearing the appeal the court may affirm the sentence[15] or it may quash it and pass another sentence which may be more or less severe[16]. Cases of a sentence

---

1 1995 Act, s 119(2).
2 1995 Act, s 119(3).
3 Eg *Mackenzie v HMA* 1982 SCCR 499, 1983 SLT 220; *Cunningham v HMA* 1984 JC 37, 1984 SCCR 40, 1984 SLT 249.
4 *McColl v HMA* 1989 SCCR 229, 1989 SLT 691.
5 *Farooq v HMA* 1991 SCCR 889, 1993 SLT 1271.
6 1995 Act, s 106(1)(c).
7 1995 Act, s 106(1)(d).
8 1995 Act, s 106(1)(e).
9 1995 Act, s 110(1)(a).
10 1995 Act, s 106(1).
11 1995 Act, s 103(3).
12 1995 Act, s 103(3).
13 1995 Act, s 116(1).
14 *Ferguson v HMA* 1980 JC 27, 1980 SLT 21.
15 1995 Act, s 118(4)(a).
16 1995 Act, s 118(4)(b).

being increased are not common, but they do occur[1]. In the case of an appeal from a sentence imposed in the sheriff court the appeal court may even impose a sentence which would have been beyond the powers of the sheriff[2].

## Appeals against sentence by the Crown

Since 1993 the Crown has had a right to appeal against a sentence imposed on an accused on the ground that it is 'unduly lenient'[3]. This provision is now contained in section 108 of the 1995 Act[4]. It is not only against what is strictly a 'sentence' that this right of appeal exists, but also the making of a probation order or community service order[5], admonition or absolute discharge[6], and deferment of sentence[7]. The Crown also has a right of appeal against sentence on a point of law[8]. The Crown does not require to obtain leave to appeal.

Appeal is by note of appeal which must be lodged with the Clerk of Justiciary within four weeks of the passing of the sentence against which appeal is taken[9]. The Crown does not have any right to apply for an extension of this period[10].

An appeal against sentence by the Crown, unlike appeals against sentence by an accused, may not be heard by a court of only two judges[11]: there must be three to make a quorum[12]. It is not competent for the Crown to present an appeal in writing[13].

The provisions described above for the trial judge's report[14], fixing a hearing[15] and abandonment of appeal[16] apply to appeals by the Crown as they apply to appeals by accused.

The possible disposals open to the Court in the case of an appeal by the Crown are the same as in an appeal by an accused[17], although it is of course very unlikely in practice that the court would reduce the sentence under appeal.

Even though at the time of writing there have been relatively few reported cases of appeals against sentence by the Crown some established principles have already been laid down by the appeal court. The most important case so far is probably *Her Majesty's Advocate v Bell*[18] in which the court made the following comments[19]:

---

1 Eg *Ferguson v HMA* 1980 JC 27, 1980 SLT 21; *Donnelly v HMA* 1988 SCCR 386.
2 *Connelly v HMA* 1954 JC 90, 1954 SLT 259.
3 Introduced by the 1993 Act, s 42(1).
4 The scope of an appeal under s 108 has been extended by the coming into force of the 1997 Act, s 21 on 1 August 1997. See the Appendix at p 326 below.
5 1995 Act, s 108(a)(ii).
6 1995 Act, s 108(a)(iii).
7 1995 Act, s 108(a)(iv).
8 1995 Act, s 108(b).
9 1995 Act, s 110(1)(b).
10 1995 Act, s 111(2) applies only to appeals by an accused.
11 1995 Act, s 103(3) applies only to appeals by an accused.
12 1995 Act, s 103(2).
13 1995 Act, s 115(1) specifically excludes appeals by the Lord Advocate.
14 1995 Act, s 113. See p 267 above.
15 1995 Act, s 117. See p 269 above.
16 1995 Act, s 116. See p 269 above.
17 1995 Act, s 118(4).
18 *HMA v Bell* 1995 SCCR 244, 1995 SLT 350.
19 *HMA v Bell* 1995 SCCR 244 at 250D, 1995 SLT 350 at 353H, per Lord Justice-General Hope.

'It is clear that a person is not to be subjected to the risk of an increase in sentence just because the appeal court considers that it would have passed a more severe sentence than that which was passed at first instance. The sentence must be seen to be unduly lenient. This means that it must fall outside the range of sentences which the judge at first instance, applying his mind to all the relevant factors, could reasonably have considered appropriate. ... Undue leniency will be easier to detect in some cases than in others. A non-custodial disposal may be seen clearly to be unduly lenient in a case where, on any reasonable view of the matter, the only appropriate disposal was a custodial one. A very short term of imprisonment may be seen clearly to be unduly lenient where the sentence normally imposed for the particular offence, in analogous circumstances, is a very long one. Extreme cases of that kind will be relatively easy to identify. ... Where the issue is as narrow a one as we think it is in this case, it will be appropriate to identify the purpose which is sought to be achieved by declaring the sentence unduly lenient. This is a relevant factor, as the appeal court has a discretion as to whether or not to pass a different sentence if it is satisfied that the original sentence was unduly lenient. But it is not obliged to impose a more severe sentence if, in all the circumstances, it does not consider this appropriate. It should and will do so if a more severe sentence is necessary for the protection of the public, or because the offence is a very serious one and a more severe sentence is required in order to provide guidance to sentencers generally.'

This is not the only case in which the point has been made that, even if the appeal court considers that a sentence is unduly lenient, it will not necessarily increase it[1].

The court has emphasised the importance of the Crown's proceeding on accurate information in an appeal against sentence, especially in view of the fact that the Lord Advocate, unlike an accused, does not require to seek leave to appeal[2]. In at least one case there is a suggestion that the Crown should appeal only where a matter of principle is involved[3].

The appeal court will not entertain an appeal based on an argument about the admissibility or relevance of evidence which was taken into account by the trial judge and which was not challenged by the Crown before him[4].

## Time spent pending appeal

If an appellant is released on bail pending appeal, then time spent on bail does not count towards any custodial sentence which may still exist following the determination of the appeal[5]. If an appellant is not released on bail, or if bail is recalled at any stage, the period spent in custody pending appeal will count as part of a custodial sentence unless the court directs otherwise[6]. If an appellant is in custody on another matter pending his appeal, his sentence in the appeal case will run from the date when his appeal is determined or abandoned[7]. The same rules apply *mutatis mutandis* to a convicted person against whose sentence the Crown appeals[8].

---

1   See also *HMA v McVey* 1995 SCCR 706, 1996 SLT 1080.
2   *HMA v McKay* 1996 SCCR 410, 1996 SLT 697. See also *HMA v Ross* 1996 SCCR 107, 1996 SLT 729.
3   *HMA v Gordon* 1996 SCCR 274.
4   *HMA v Bennett* 1996 SCCR 331, 1996 SLT 662.
5   1995 Act, s 125(1).
6   1995 Act, s 125(2).
7   1995 Act, s 125(3)(b).
8   1995 Act, s 125(1), (2), (3).

### Reference by the Secretary of State[1]

The Secretary of State for Scotland may refer a case to the High Court at any time, whether or not there has already been an appeal in the case[2]. The reference is to be heard and determined as if it were an appeal[3]. This power is relatively rarely used but would obviously be beneficial, for example, in a case where there has been an unsuccessful appeal and new evidence emerges.

In dealing with a reference by the Secretary of State the court is not confined to answering the particular question to which the Secretary of State has drawn attention but *is* confined to considering only the matters raised by an appellant in his grounds of appeal[4].

### Reference by the Lord Advocate

Although there is no right of appeal by the Crown against the verdict of a jury, there has since 1980 been provision for the Lord Advocate, in effect, to have it declared that the trial court has gone wrong in law. The actual provision[5] is to the effect that, when a person tried on indictment is acquitted of a charge, the Lord Advocate may refer a point of law which has arisen in relation to that charge to the High Court for their opinion.

A copy of the reference and intimation of the date of the hearing must be given to the former accused[5]. The latter is entitled to appear personally or by counsel at the hearing. If he elects to do so, he must intimate that fact to the Clerk of Justiciary no later than seven days before the date of the hearing[6]. If he does not so intimate, he is not entitled to appear or to be represented at the hearing except by leave of the court on cause shown[6]. Representation by counsel is paid for by the Crown[7]. If the former accused does not appear and is not represented, the court appoints counsel to act as *amicus curiae*[8].

Whatever the court may decide in the reference, the acquittal of the former accused is not affected[9].

# APPEALS UNDER SUMMARY PROCEDURE

### Legal aid

The provisions for Legal Aid in summary appeals are the same as those for Legal Aid in solemn appeals[10].

---

1 If the 1997 Act, s 25 comes into force a Scottish Criminal Cases Review Commission with power to refer cases to the High Court will be created. See the Appendix at p 327 below.
2 1995 Act, s 124(1), (3).
3 1995 Act, s 124(3).
4 *Beattie v HMA* 1995 SCCR 93, 1995 SLT 275.
5 Now contained in the 1995 Act, s 123(1).
6 1995 Act, s 123(2).
7 1995 Act, s 123(4).
8 1995 Act, s 123(3).
9 1995 Act, s 123(5).
10 See above at p 265.

## Scope of appeal

An accused who has been convicted in summary proceedings may appeal against conviction, conviction and sentence, or sentence alone[1], provided that leave to appeal has been granted[2]. The prosecutor may appeal against an acquittal on a point of law only[3]. He may also appeal against a sentence on a point of law[4]. The prosecutor may appeal against sentence on the ground of undue leniency[5]. No leave to appeal is required in the case of a prosecutor. An appeal by an accused or by the prosecutor against an acquittal may bring under review of the High Court any alleged miscarriage of justice in the proceedings, including, in the case of an appeal by an accused any alleged miscarriage of justice on the basis of the existence and significance of additional evidence which was not heard at the trial subject to certain detailed conditions[6].

An appeal against conviction (whether with or without an appeal against sentence) by an accused and appeals by a prosecutor against an acquittal or against sentence on a point of law are normally by way of stated case[7]. An accused may also, in certain limited circumstances, appeal against conviction and/or sentence by bill of suspension[8]. A prosecutor may also, again in certain limited circumstances, appeal by bill of advocation[8]. Both of these methods of appeal will be discussed below[9]. It must be stressed that stated case is the normal appeal procedure. Bills of suspension and advocation are the exception.

## Appeal by stated case by accused

### Time of application

The appellant must apply for a stated case by lodging an application with the clerk of the summary court within one week of final determination of the proceedings in that court[10]. At the same time a copy of the application should be sent to the respondent or his solicitor[11].

'Final determination' normally means the date when sentence is passed in open court[12]. However, if sentence has been deferred, and the appeal is against conviction only, or by the prosecutor against an acquittal of an accused who has been convicted (and had sentence deferred) on another charge, 'final determination' means the date when sentence is first deferred[12]. It should be noted that in the case of an appeal against conviction where sentence has been deferred in a summary

1  1995 Act, s 175(2)(a).
2  1995 Act, s 180 governs leave to appeal against conviction, and s 187 leave to appeal against sentence.
3  1995 Act, s 175(3)(a).
4  1995 Act, s 175(3)(b).
5  1995 Act, s 175(4), brought into effect in respect of sentences imposed on or after 1 November 1996 by the Prosecutor's Right of Appeal in Summary Proceedings (Scotland) Order 1996, SI 1996/2548.
6  1995 Act, s 175(5), (5A)–(5D). The scope of this provision has been extended with the coming into force of the 1997 Act, s 17 on 1 August 1997. See the Appendix at pp 325–326 below.
7  1995 Act, s 175(7).
8  1995 Act, s 191.
9  See below at pp 286–288, 291–292.
10  1995 Act, s 176(1)(a). The form of application is 1996 Rules, r 19.2(1); Form 19.2A.
11  1995 Act, s 176(1).
12  1995 Act, s 194(3).

case, it is not competent to pass sentence while the appeal is pending[1]. The position is different in a solemn case[2].

The application must actually be received by the clerk of the summary court within the week: it is not enough that it is posted within that time[3].

If an application is refused as not being in proper form, a second application may competently be lodged provided that this is done within the week[4].

On application by an appellant the High Court may allow a further period of time for lodging an application for a stated case[5]. Such an application falls to be treated in the same way as a bail appeal[6], ie it is normally heard by a single judge, although he may remit it to a bench of three[7]. The High Court may dispense with a hearing or order such enquiry as it thinks fit[8].

### Contents of application

The application for a stated case must contain a full statement of all the matters which the appellant wishes to bring under review and should state whether it includes an appeal against sentence[9]. It is absolutely essential that this requirement for a full statement is complied with. If it is not, the trial court may be entitled to refuse to state a case[10]. The reason for the requirement is so that the trial judge may be in no doubt as to what the issues are and should thus be able to make appropriate findings in fact[11].

If the application does contain a full statement of what it is desired to bring under review, a case must be stated, notwithstanding that the trial judge may consider what is said to be irrelevant[12].

What is contained in the application may be amended or added to during the period of adjustment of the draft stated case[13].

### Bail

If the appellant is in custody, the trial court may grant him bail pending the appeal[14]. An application for bail must be disposed of within 24 hours after the making of the application[15]. It has been suggested that the 24-hour period commences when the application is actually presented to the court and not when it is lodged with the clerk of court[16], and this is surely correct. The Act is silent on what should happen if the application is not disposed of within 24 hours.

---

1  *Valentine v Parker* 1992 SCCR 695.
2  *McRobbie v HMA* 1990 SCCR 767. See above at p 266.
3  *Elliot, Applicant* 1984 JC 37, 1984 SCCR 125, 1984 SLT 294.
4  *Singh, Petr* 1986 SCCR 215, 1987 SLT 63.
5  1995 Act, s 181(1). There is no prescribed form, but the application must be made in writing to the Clerk of Justiciary: s 181(2).
6  1995 Act, s 181(3).
7  See *Elliot, Applicant* 1984 JC 37, 1984 SCCR 125, 1984 SLT 294.
8  1995 Act, s 181(3)(a), (b).
9  1995 Act, s 176(1)(b).
10  *Dickson v Valentine* 1988 SCCR 325, 1989 SLT 19 (the only ground stated was 'The sheriff erred in law' without further specification): *McQuarrie v Carmichael* 1989 SCCR 371 (the ground was 'Police evidence at the time of the trial which was untrue, namely the evidence of senior officer').
11  *Durant v Lockhart* 1986 SCCR 23, 1986 SLT 312.
12  *McDougall, Petr* 1986 SCCR 128; *McTaggart, Petr* 1987 SCCR 638.
13  1995 Act, s 176(3). For adjustment of the draft case see below at p 281.
14  1995 Act, s 177(1).
15  1995 Act, s 177(2).
16  *Renton and Brown* para 31–15.

The appellant may appeal to the High Court against the decision on bail of the trial court within 24 hours of the decision being given[1]. The appeal may be heard by a single judge of the High Court[1].

If an appellant, having been granted bail and having been subsequently imprisoned for another offence, abandons his appeal, the trial court may order that his sentence for the original offence should run from a particular date, which must not be later than the expiry of the sentence subsequently imposed[2].

An appellant who has been granted bail should appear at the hearing of his appeal. If he fails to do so, the appeal court may dispose of the appeal as if it had been abandoned[3]. Alternatively, on cause shown, it may permit the appeal to be heard in the absence of the appellant[4].

Intimation of the date of hearing the appeal is sent to the address specified in the bail order as the domicile of citation. If the accused changes his address without applying to have his domicile of citation altered and, as a result, does not appear for his appeal, the appeal will almost certainly be refused for want of insistence and will not be reinstated[5].

## Suspension of disqualification

If an appellant has been disqualified from driving and the appeal includes an appeal against the disqualification, he may apply to the trial court for the disqualification to be suspended pending the appeal. This application should be made together with the application for a stated case[6]. The trial court may grant or refuse the application and must do so within seven days of its being made[7].

If the application is refused, the appellant may apply to the High Court for suspension of the disqualification[8]. The application may be heard by a single judge, whose decision is not open to review[9].

## Suspension of forfeiture etc

If an appellant was, on conviction, disqualified (other than from driving) or had property ordered to be forfeited, the disqualification or forfeiture may be suspended at the discretion of the trial court, pending the appeal[10]. This provision does not apply in the case of disqualification or forfeiture under any statute which makes specific provision for suspension pending appeal[11]. It is now competent to suspend a community service order pending an appeal[12]. However, a fine or compensation order made in respect of an accused who has appealed will not be enforced until the determination of the appeal[13].

1  1995 Act, s 177(3).
2  1995 Act, s 177(6). If the trial court is contemplating making the sentence run from a date later then that of abandonment of the appeal, it should give the appellant the opportunity of making representations: *Proudfoot v Wither* 1990 SCCR 96, 1990 SLT 742.
3  1995 Act, s 192(2)(a).
4  1995 Act, s 192(2)(b).
5  *McMahon v MacPhail* 1991 SCCR 470.
6  1996 Rules, r 19.9(1). There is no prescribed form of application.
7  1996 Rules, r 19.9(2).
8  1996 Rules, r 19.9(3). The application is by note: in Form 19.9.
9  1996 Rules, r 19.9(10).
10  1995 Act, s 193(1). The right to apply for suspension of a sentence has been extended with the coming into force of the 1997 Act, s 24 on 1 August 1997. See the Appendix at p 326 below.
11  1995 Act, s 193(2).
12  1995 Act, s 121A(1),(4) inserted by the 1997 Act, s 24(1) effectively overruling *Farmer v Guild* 1991 SCCR 174, 1992 SLT 320. See the Appendix at p 326 below.
13  1995 Act, s 193(3).

*Draft stated case*

A draft stated case must be prepared within three weeks of the final determination of the proceedings which are the subject of the appeal[1]. This time limit may be extended by the sheriff principal of the sheriffdom where the trial court is situated, if the trial judge is temporarily absent from duty, is a temporary sheriff or is a justice of the peace[2]. This may be done retrospectively[3]. In the case of an appeal from a sheriff court the draft case is prepared by the sheriff[4]. In the case of an appeal from a district court the draft case is prepared by the clerk of court[5], except where the judge is a stipendiary magistrate, in which case he prepares the draft himself[6].

The form prescribed for a stated case[7] provides only a bare outline. The case must 'set forth the particulars of any matters competent for review which the appellant desires to bring under the review of the High Court and of the facts, if any, proved in the case, and any point of law decided, and the grounds of the decision'[8].

The usual form of case starts with a statement of the charge(s) in the case (although these should not necessarily be set out in full[9]) and a summary of the procedure up to and including the trial. It then has a statement of the facts found to be proved or admitted. There is then usually a note giving the court's reasons for reaching the conclusion which it did, with particular reference to the points raised in the application for the stated case. Finally it poses a question or questions of law for the opinion of the High Court. The questions asked will depend on the issues raised by the appeal. They might, for example, be concerned with the sufficiency of evidence, with the admissibility of evidence, or whether the court was entitled to draw an inference of guilt from the stated facts.

If the appeal is against a decision of the court finding no case to answer in terms of section 160 of the 1995 Act[10], there should be no findings in fact, but the evidence led should be set out together with any inference drawn therefrom[11]. However, if a submission of no case to answer was rejected, defence evidence was led, the accused was convicted and then appeals against his conviction on the basis that the submission was wrongly rejected, the stated case must contain findings in fact based on the *whole* evidence as well as setting out the Crown evidence and any inferences drawn therefrom[11]. If, the submission having been rejected, no defence evidence was led, the stated case should contain findings in fact together with a note of the evidence on which these findings are based[11].

The draft case and a duplicate thereof are issued to the appellant and the respondent respectively, or to their solicitors[12].

1   1995 Act, s 178(1).
2   1995 Act, s 194(2).
3   *Burns v Lees* 1992 SCCR 244, 1992 SLT 1112 sub nom *Burns v Lowe*.
4   1995 Act, s 178(1)(b).
5   1995 Act, s 178(1)(a).
6   1995 Act, s 178(1)(b).
7   1996 Rules, r 19.2(2); Form 19.2B.
8   1995 Act, s 178(2). The grounds should be fully set forth on any important issue: *Petrovich v Jessop* 1990 SCCR 1, 1990 SLT 594.
9   *Friel v Initial Contract Services Ltd* 1993 SCCR 675 at 680D, 1994 SLT 1216 at 1220B, per Lord Justice-Clerk Ross.
10  See above at p 215.
11  *Wingate v McGlennan* 1991 SCCR 133, 1992 SLT 837.
12  1995 Act, s 178(1).

## Adjustment of draft case

Within three weeks from the issue of the draft case each party must send to the clerk of court and to the other parties or their solicitors a note of any adjustment which he wishes to be made[1]. Adjustments may be proposed to the findings in fact and, in certain circumstances, to the judge's note[2]. The questions in law may also be adjusted. If an issue is not raised in the course of adjustment, the High Court may not allow it to be argued in the appeal[3]. If he has no adjustments to propose, the appellant *must* intimate that fact to the clerk of court within the period for adjustment[4]. The reason for emphasising this point is that, if the appellant does not send any proposed adjustments or intimate that he has none, he is deemed to have abandoned his appeal[5].

On application by either party to the High Court the time limit of three weeks may be extended[6]. The provisions for disposing of such an application are the same as those for an application to extend the period for lodging an application for a stated case[7].

During the three-week period (or any extension thereof granted by the High Court) the appellant may also make amendments or additions to his application for a stated case[8]. Any such amendments or adjustments must be intimated to the respondent or his solicitor[8].

## Hearing on adjustments

If adjustments have been proposed, or if the trial judge wishes to make any alteration to the draft stated case (eg to take account of an amendment or addition to the application for a stated case by the appellant), a hearing must be fixed within one week of the expiry of the period for adjustment (either original or extended as the case may be)[9]. The hearing must take place even if one or more of the parties is neither present nor represented[10].

At the hearing the judge must consider representations made to him about the adjustments or his own proposed alterations. If he rejects any adjustment, that fact must be recorded in the minute of proceedings[11]. The final version of the stated case must have appended to it the terms of any rejected adjustment together with a note of any evidence rejected by the judge which is alleged to support that adjustment, and the reasons for his rejection of the adjustment and evidence[12].

The High Court may take account of a rejected adjustment[13]. If a judge wrongly rejects a question proposed at adjustment, the High Court may allow the question to be argued at the appeal[14].

At the hearing on adjustments, if an alteration proposed by the judge is not accepted by all parties, that must be recorded in the minute of proceedings[15].

---

1  1995 Act, s 179(1).
2  *Ballantyne v Mackinnon* 1983 SCCR 97; *McDonald v Scott* 1993 JC 54, 1993 SCCR 78.
3  *McLeod v Campbell* 1986 SCCR 132.
4  1995 Act, s 179(1).
5  1995 Act, s 179(3).
6  1995 Act, s 181(1).
7  See above at p 278.
8  1995 Act, s 176(3).
9  1995 Act, s 179(4).
10  1995 Act, s 179(5).
11  1995 Act, s 179(6)(a).
12  1995 Act, s 179(7)(a).
13  1995 Act, s 182(5)(f). See *Wilson v Carmichael* 1982 SCCR 528.
14  *O'Hara v Tudhope* 1986 SCCR 283, 1987 SLT 67.
15  1995 Act, s 179(6)(b).

If, at the conclusion of the hearing, there is any finding in fact which any party maintains is not supported by evidence, the judge must append to the case a note of the evidence upon which he bases that finding[1].

*Signing and lodging of stated case*

Within two weeks of the date of the hearing on adjustments the judge must finalise and sign the case, which must have appended to it the items referred to in the preceding section of this chapter[2]. The clerk of court sends a copy of the case to the parties or their solicitors and transmits the trial court process to the Clerk of Justiciary[3]. Within one week of receiving the case the appellant or his solicitor must have it lodged with the Clerk of Justiciary[4]. If this is not done, the appeal is deemed to have been abandoned[5], subject to the appellant's right to apply to the High Court to have the time extended[6]. The provisions for disposing of such an application are the same as those for an application to extend the time for lodging an application for a stated case[7].

If the appellant's solicitor does not practise in Edinburgh, he may appoint an Edinburgh solicitor 'to carry out the duties of solicitor to the appellant in relation to' the appeal[8]. The appellant will continue to deal with his local solicitor. The Edinburgh solicitor is concerned only with what requires to be done in Edinburgh.

*Leave to appeal*

As in the case of appeals under solemn procedure, no appeal against conviction in a summary case will be considered by the High Court unless leave to appeal has been granted[9]. The statutory provisions relating to leave to appeal in summary cases are essentially the same as those for solemn cases.

Each case in which a stated case has been lodged is considered by a single judge of the High Court[10]. The judge has before him the stated case and the trial process from the lower court[11]. Having considered these, 'if he considers that the documents ... disclose arguable grounds of appeal' the judge must 'grant leave to appeal and make such comments in writing as he considers appropriate'[12]. Otherwise he must refuse leave to appeal and give reasons in writing for refusal[13]. If the appellant was sentenced to imprisonment but was released on bail pending appeal, a warrant for his arrest is granted[14].

Within fourteen days of refusal by the single judge the appellant may apply 'to the High Court' for leave to appeal[15]. This second application, in the case of an application which includes an appeal against conviction, is considered by three judges[16]. If, 'after considering the documents [which were before the single judge]

1  1995 Act, s 179(7)(b).
2  1995 Act, s 179(7).
3  1995 Act, s 179(8).
4  1995 Act, s 179(9).
5  1995 Act, s 179(10).
6  1995 Act, s 181(1).
7  See above at p 278.
8  1996 Rules, r 19.11(1).
9  1995 Act, s 175(2).
10  1995 Act, s 180(1).
11  1995 Act, s 180(2)(a), (b).
12  1995 Act, s 180(1)(a).
13  1995 Act, s 180(1)(b)(i).
14  1995 Act, s 180(1)(b)(ii).
15  1995 Act, s 180(4).
16  1995 Act, s 173(1).

and the reasons for refusal' the court considers that there are arguable grounds of appeal, it grants leave to appeal and makes such comments in writing as it considers appropriate[1]. In any other case it refuses leave and gives reasons in writing[2]. If the appellant was sentenced to imprisonment but was released on bail pending appeal, a warrant for his arrest is granted[3].

All consideration of whether to grant leave to appeal, whether before a single judge or three judges, is in chambers and outwith the presence of the parties[4].

The comments in writing made by the single judge or the three judges when granting leave to appeal may specify the arguable grounds of appeal on the basis of which leave has been granted, whether these are contained in the note of appeal or not[5]. When this is done the appellant may not put forward any other ground of appeal except with the leave of the High Court on cause shown[6]. An application for such leave must be made not less than seven days before the date fixed for the hearing of the appeal[7] and must within the same period be intimated to the Crown Agent[8].

All decisions on the question of leave to appeal (with reasons in the case of a refusal) must be intimated by the Clerk or Justiciary to the parties 'forthwith'[9].

## Abandonment of appeal

An appellant may abandon his appeal at any time. Before the stated case is lodged with the Clerk of Justiciary, abandonment is effected by lodging with the clerk of the trial court a minute signed by the appellant or his solicitor. The minute may either be written on the complaint or lodged as a separate document[10]. Such abandonment is without prejudice to any other competent mode of appeal, review, advocation or suspension which may be open to the appellant[10]. After the case has been lodged with the Clerk of Justiciary the statute does not make it clear how the appeal should be abandoned, but it is suggested, by analogy with the procedure described in the next paragraph, that a minute of abandonment should be lodged with the Clerk of Justiciary. The lodging of the case with the Clerk of Justiciary means that the appellant is deemed to have abandoned any other form of appeal, except for suspension or advocation under section 191 of the 1995 Act[11].

An appellant who has appealed against both conviction and sentence may abandon his appeal against conviction and proceed with an appeal against sentence only[12]. The abandonment is effected by minute[13] lodged with the clerk of the trial court[14], or, if the case has already been lodged with the Clerk of Justiciary, the minute is to be lodged with him[15].

1  1995 Act, s 180(5)(a).
2  1995 Act, s 180(5)(b)(i).
3  1995 Act, s 180(5)(b)(ii).
4  1995 Act, s 180(6).
5  1995 Act, s 180(7).
6  1995 Act, s 180(8).
7  1995 Act, s 180(9)(a).
8  1995 Act, s 180(9)(b).
9  1995 Act, s 180(10).
10  1995 Act, s 184(1).
11  1995 Act, s 184(2).
12  1995 Act, s 175(8).
13  1996 Rules, r 19.6(2). The form of minute is Form 19.6.
14  1996 Rules, r 19.6(3).
15  1996 Rules, r 19.6(4).

## Hearing of the appeal

Usually three judges sit to hear an appeal by stated case, but, as under solemn procedure, a larger court may be convened if it is desired to reconsider an earlier decision. The hearing is conducted by oral debate. There is no provision for written argument being submitted to the court.

## Limitations of the hearing

At the hearing of the appeal the appellant may, as a general rule, found only on what is contained in his original application for a stated case together with any duly made amendment or addition thereto[1]. This rule does not apply where either the single judge or the High Court has specified a ground as an arguable ground of appeal following the sift[2]. The High Court may also allow an appellant to found on a matter not contained in his original application, if he shows cause why he should be allowed to do so[3]. If the appellant has referred in his application for a stated case to an alleged miscarriage of justice which, for whatever reason, the trial court is unable to take into account when stating the case, the High Court may nevertheless have regard to that allegation at the hearing of the appeal[4].

## Powers of the High Court

The High Court is given various powers for the purposes of an appeal by stated case[5]. These powers are:

(a)  to order the production of any document or other thing connected with the proceedings;

(b)  to hear any additional evidence relevant to any alleged miscarriage of justice, or to order such evidence to be heard by a judge of the High Court or by such other person as it may appoint for that purpose[6];

(c)  to take account of any circumstances relevant to the case which were not before the trial judge[7];

(d)  to remit to any fit person to enquire and report in regard to any matter or circumstance affecting the appeal[8];

(e)  to appoint a person with expert knowledge to act as assessor to the High Court in any case where it appears to the court that such expert knowledge is required for the proper determination of the case;

(f)  to take account of any matter proposed in any adjustment rejected by the trial judge and of the reasons for such rejection;

(g)  to take account of any evidence contained in a note either of evidence rejected by the trial judge or of evidence upon which the trial judge based a finding in fact which has been challenged by any party[9].

---

1  1995 Act, s 182(3).
2  1995 Act, s 182(4).
3  1995 Act, s 182(3).
4  1995 Act, s 182(2).
5  1995 Act, s 182(5).
6  In *Marshall v MacDougall* 1986 SCCR 376, 1987 SLT 123, the High Court remitted the case to the sheriff principal to hear evidence. The court may take account of additional evidence without having it actually led, if the Crown agrees that it is correct: *Marshall v Smith* 1983 SCCR 156.
7  See eg *Marshall v Smith* 1983 SCCR 156.
8  See eg *Marshall v MacDougall* 1986 SCCR, 1987 SLT 123. The High Court remitted the case to the sheriff principal to hear evidence and to make further enquiries.
9  See eg *Wilson v Carmichael* 1982 SCCR 528.

The High Court may also remit the stated case back to the trial court so that it may be amended and returned to the High Court[1]. Alternatively, the High Court may itself make the amendment and proceed to hear the case as amended[2].

## Disposal of appeal by stated case

There are four ways in which the High Court may dispose of an appeal by stated case by an accused[3]. First, it may remit the case to the trial court with its opinion and a direction as to what the trial court should do[4]. Secondly, the High Court may affirm the verdict of the trial court[5]. Thirdly, it may set aside the verdict and either quash the conviction or substitute an amended verdict of guilty[6] (which must be one which was competent to the trial court on the complaint[7]). Finally, the High Court may set aside the verdict of the trial court and grant authority to bring a new prosecution[8]. The provisions for a new prosecution[9] are virtually identical with the equivalent provisions under solemn procedure[10]. If the court orders that the appellant should be detained pending the new trial, the detention cannot be for more than 40 days[11].

If the court sets aside a verdict of guilty, it may quash the sentence imposed on the complaint and substitute another (but not more severe) sentence[12].

If the appellant has appealed against both conviction and sentence, the High Court deals with that part of the appeal concerning sentence in the same way as if it were an appeal against sentence alone[13].

If an appeal by the Crown against an acquittal is successful, the High Court has three available options[14]. First, it may itself convict and sentence the respondent[15], but may not impose any sentence which would have been beyond the powers of the trial court[16]. Secondly, it may remit the case to the trial court with a direction to convict and sentence the respondent[17]. The respondent must attend any diet in the trial court which is fixed for that purpose[17]. Thirdly, the High Court may simply remit the case to the trial court with its opinion[18].

If an appellant, who received a custodial sentence but was released on bail pending his appeal, loses his appeal, the High Court may grant a warrant for his arrest

1  1995 Act, s 182(6).
2  *O'Hara v Tudhope* 1986 SCCR 283, 1987 SLT 67, where the sheriff had rejected a question in law, and the High Court allowed it to be added and then argued.
3  1995 Act, s 183(1).
4  1995 Act, s 183(1)(a). In *Aitchison v Rizza* 1985 SCCR 297, the court remitted the case to the sheriff so that he could hear evidence which he had wrongly excluded. See also *Heywood v Ross* 1993 SCCR 101, 1994 SLT 195.
5  1995 Act, s 183(1)(b).
6  1995 Act, s 183(1)(c).
7  1995 Act, s 183(2).
8  1995 Act, s 183(1)(d).
9  1995 Act, s 185.
10  1995 Act, s 119. See above at pp 272–273.
11  1995 Act, s 185(10).
12  1995 Act, s 183(4).
13  1995 Act, s 183(3).
14  1995 Act, s 183(6).
15  1995 Act, s 183(6)(a).
16  1995 Act, s 183(7).
17  1995 Act, s 183(6)(b).
18  1995 Act, s 183(6)(c).

and imprisonment or detention[1]. The warrant specifies the term of custody which must not, of course, exceed the unexpired part of the sentence originally imposed[1]. If such an appellant, having been released on bail, subsequently receives a custodial sentence for another offence and is actually serving that sentence when his appeal against conviction is refused, the High Court has the same power as the trial court would have had on abandonment of the appeal[2]. This means that the High Court may direct that the unexpired part of the original sentence is to begin from a given date not later than the end of the sentence actually being served.

### Expenses

In an appeal by stated case the High Court has power to award such expenses in respect of the proceedings before it and before the trial court as it thinks fit[3]. Full expenses may be awarded[4], but in practice expenses are almost invariably modified. If (which is very unlikely) the expenses were not modified or the exact amount thereof not determined by the High Court, the account of expenses would be taxed by the Auditor of the Court of Session as if it were a Court of Session account[5].

## Appeal by stated case by prosecutor

The provisions for appeal by a prosecutor against an acquittal or, on a point of law, against sentence are *mutatis mutandis* identical with those for appeal against conviction by an accused[6] save that a prosecutor does not require to obtain leave to appeal[7].

## Appeal by bill of suspension

### When appropriate

An accused may, in certain circumstances, appeal against his conviction by bill of suspension. He may do so 'where an appeal [by stated case] would be incompetent or would in the circumstances be inappropriate'[8]. The ground of appeal under a bill of suspension is 'an alleged miscarriage of justice in the proceedings'[9]. If an appellant has already taken an appeal by stated case, he may not proceed with an appeal on the same ground by bill of suspension until the appeal by stated case has been fully disposed of or abandoned, unless he has obtained leave of the High Court[10].

Appeal by bill of suspension is appropriate 'when some step in the procedure has gone wrong or some factor has emerged which satisfies the court that a

---

1  1995 Act, s 183(10)(a).
2  1995 Act, s 183(10)(b). The power of the trial court on abandonment is set forth in s 177(6). See above at p 279.
3  1995 Act, s 183(9).
4  As in *Walker v Linton* (1892) 3 White 329, 20 R (J) 1.
5  Courts of Law Fees (Scotland) Act 1895, s 3.
6  1995 Act, s 176(1).
7  1995 Act, s 175(3).
8  1995 Act, s 191(1). For a full discussion of the circumstances where a bill of suspension is competent and appropriate see *Renton and Brown* paras 33–01 to 33–08.
9  1995 Act, s 191(1).
10  1995 Act, s 191(2).

miscarriage of justice has taken place resulting in a failure to do justice to an accused'[1]. It is, for example, appropriate if the appeal is based on alleged oppression or irregular conduct on the part of the trial court[2]. A bill of suspension is also appropriate, and indeed the only competent method of appeal against conviction, if the trial judge dies before signing a stated case or is precluded by illness or some other cause from doing so[3].

## Time

There is no time limit for appealing by way of bill of suspension, although it is obviously desirable to do so as soon as possible after conviction[4].

## Bail

An appellant who has received a custodial sentence and who is taking an appeal by bill of suspension may apply for bail. He does so by craving interim liberation in the bill, which is then, strictly speaking, a bill of suspension and liberation.

## Form

The bill of suspension is in form[5] rather similar to a writ or petition in civil proceedings. It begins by narrating the fact of the appellant's conviction and sentence. Then come the craves, which would usually be for (1) warrant to serve a copy of the bill on the respondent; (2) warrant ordaining the clerk of the trial court to transmit the process to the Clerk of Justiciary; (3) suspension of the conviction and sentence; (4) liberation and interim liberation; and (5) expenses. Next there is a statement of facts which should be in separate numbered articles, as in the condescendence of an initial writ or summons. Finally, there are pleas in law. The bill is signed by the appellant or by his counsel or solicitor.

## Further procedure

The bill is lodged with the Clerk of Justiciary who places it before a single judge of the High Court in order to obtain the warrant to serve. The bill may be served by any officer of law[6]. If the bill craves interim liberation or interim suspension of any order (for example disqualification), the judge before whom it is placed assigns a diet at which counsel for both the appellant and the respondent may be heard[7]. Interim suspension of disqualification from driving may be applied for as in an appeal by stated case[8] but is subject to certain special rules. The application is made in the prayer of the bill[9] and does not take effect until the bill has been served on the respondent, and the principal bill has been exhibited to the clerk of the trial court and returned to the Clerk of Justiciary[10].

1 *MacGregor v McNeill* 1975 JC 57 at 60, 1975 SLT (Notes) 54 at 55, per Lord Justice-Clerk Wheatley.
2 Eg *Fraser v MacKinnon* 1981 SCCR 91; *Hawthorn v MacLeod* 1986 SCCR 150, 1986 SLT 657.
3 1995 Act, s 176(4). See *Brady v Barbour* 1994 SCCR 890, 1995 SLT 223, a case where a temporary sheriff failed to produce a stated case despite repeated requests.
4 In *McPherson v Henderson* 1984 SCCR 294, it was sought to suspend a conviction and sentence imposed nearly twenty years previously. Although the bill was refused, it was not suggested that it was incompetent because of the delay. Delay may, however, result in the bill being held to be incompetent on the ground of acquiescence: *Love v Wilson* 1993 SCCR 325, 1993 SLT 948.
5 A form of bill of suspension is given in *Renton and Brown* App A, Form 5.
6 1995 Act, s 192(5).
7 1996 Rules, r 19.15.
8 See above at p 279.
9 1996 Rules, r 19.10(1).
10 1996 Rules, r 19.10(2).

*Answers*

After the bill has been served on the respondent he may, and usually does, lodge answers to it. The answers are in similar form to defences in a civil action. Each statement of fact is answered, and the respondent appends appropriate pleas in law.

*Edinburgh solicitor*

The same provisions about appointing an Edinburgh solicitor and his duties apply to bill of suspension procedure as to stated case procedure[1].

*Hearing*

The hearing takes the same form as in an appeal by stated case. The High Court has many of the same powers as in such an appeal[2]. These powers include the hearing or ordering to be heard of additional evidence[3], and the power to remit to a fit person (such as the sheriff principal) to make enquiry into any matter[4]. In disposing of the appeal the High Court may, as well as simply quashing the conviction, grant authority to the prosecutor to bring a new prosecution[5]. It may also, when quashing a conviction, quash a sentence and substitute another sentence[6]. The High Court has power to award expenses in the same way as in an appeal by stated case.

## Consent by prosecutor to set aside conviction

In an appeal against conviction, whether by stated case or bill of suspension, the prosecutor may indicate his consent to the conviction being set aside as soon as the appeal is intimated to him[7]. The prosecutor's consent is intimated by a minute which must set forth the grounds why he considers that the conviction cannot be maintained[8]. The decision whether to set aside the conviction remains with the High Court, but is taken by a single judge[9]. If the conviction is set aside, the appellant is entitled to 'such expenses ... both in the High Court and in the inferior court as the judge may think fit'[10]. If the High Court refuses to set the conviction aside, the appeal may proceed along the usual course[11].

Even if no appeal has been taken by an accused, if the prosecutor is at any time not prepared to maintain the conviction, he may lodge a minute with the trial court seeking to have it set aside[12]. The procedure is then the same as that described in the preceding paragraph.

1  1996 Rules, r 19.11(2). See above at p 282.
2  1995 Act, s 191(3).
3  1995 Act, s 182(5)(b), applied by s 191(3) to bills of suspension.
4  1995 Act, s 182(5)(d), applied by s 191(3) to bills of suspension.
5  1995 Act, s 191(3), applying ss 183(1)(d) and 185 to bills of suspension.
6  1995 Act, s 191(3), applying s 183(4) to bills of suspension.
7  1995 Act, s 188(1)(a).
8  1995 Act, s 181(2). See *MacRae v Hingston* 1992 SCCR 911, 1992 SLT 1197.
9  1995 Act, s 188(4).
10  1995 Act, s 188(4)(a)(i).
11  1995 Act, s 188(5).
12  1995 Act, s 188(1)(b).

## Appeals against sentence by the accused

*Bill of suspension*

Appeal against sentence by bill of suspension is competent if the appeal is based on an alleged fundamental irregularity relating to the imposition of the sentence[1]. However, such an appeal is not common. The procedure is the same as in a bill of suspension appealing against conviction[2]. As such an appeal is at common law rather than statutory, the powers of the court are wider than in the case of an appeal by note of appeal. The court may, for example, remit to the lower court 'to proceed as accords'[3].

*Note of appeal*

The usual method of appealing against sentence in a summary case is by means of a note of appeal[4], which must state the ground of appeal[5]. As in the case of an appeal against conviction by stated case the appeal may proceed only with leave of the High Court[6].

An accused who wishes to appeal against a court's finding that he was properly served with a notice of previous convictions must do so by note of appeal, as in an appeal against sentence, and not by stated case, even though evidence may have been led before the lower court[7].

*Time limits and procedure*

The note of appeal must be lodged with the clerk of the trial court within one week of the date of imposition of the sentence which is appealed against[8]. When he receives the note the clerk of court must send a copy of it to the respondent and obtain a report from the judge who imposed the sentence appealed against[9].

The judge *must* submit a report, even if the grounds of appeal are inadequate[10].

Within two weeks of the date of the sentence the clerk of court must send the process in the case, including the note of appeal and the judge's report, to the Clerk of Justiciary[11]. A copy of the judge's report must, at the same time, be sent to the respondent[12].

This period of two weeks may be extended by the sheriff principal of the sheriffdom where the trial court is situated if the sentencing judge is temporarily absent from duty, is a temporary sheriff or is a justice of the peace[13]. This extension may be granted retrospectively[14]. If the judge does not provide a report within the

1  1995 Act, s 175(9).
2  See above at pp 286–288.
3  *Martin v Crowe* 1992 SCCR 388.
4  1995 Act, ss 175(9), 186(1). The form is 1996 Rules, r 19.3(1); Form 19.3A.
5  1995 Act, s 186(1). The ground of appeal must be specific and not something vague such as 'severity of sentence': High Court Practice Note of 29 March 1985 (reproduced in *Renton and Brown* App E at p 726). See *Campbell v MacDougall* 1991 SCCR 218.
6  1995 Act, s 175(1)(b), (c).
7  *Cowan v Guild* 1991 SCCR 424, 1992 SLT 939.
8  1995 Act, s 186(2)(a).
9  1995 Act, s 186(3).
10  *Henry v Docherty* 1989 SCCR 426, 1990 SLT 301.
11  1995 Act, s 186(4)(a).
12  1995 Act, s 186(4)(b).
13  1995 Act, s 186(5).
14  *Burns v Lees* 1992 SCCR 244, 1992 SLT 1112 sub nom *Burns v Lowe*.

appropriate time, the High Court may extend the time for furnishing it, or it may proceed to deal with the appeal without a report[1].

As in the case of an appeal against conviction, the appellant may apply to the High Court for an extension of the time for lodging a note of appeal against sentence[2].

### Leave to appeal

The provisions for leave to appeal against sentence in a summary case[3] are *mutatis mutandis* identical with those for leave to appeal against sentence in a solemn case[4]. The single judge before whom the application is put considers the note of appeal, the judge's report, and the other documents in the case[5]. If the application is refused by the single judge it may go before two judges[6].

### Abandonment of appeal

An appeal against sentence may be abandoned at any time prior to the hearing of the appeal. This is done by way of a minute signed by the appellant or his solicitor[7]. The minute should be lodged with the Clerk of Justiciary[8], unless the process has not yet been sent to him, in which case it should be lodged with the clerk of the trial court[9].

### Bail

The appellant may apply for bail pending the hearing of his appeal in the same way as if he were appealing against conviction[10].

### Hearing and disposal of appeal

An appeal against sentence may be heard by a quorum of only two judges[11]. The court, when hearing the appeal, has the same powers to order production of documents, hear evidence and cause enquiry to be made as it has in the case of an appeal against conviction[12].

The Court will not usually entertain any submission in mitigation which could have been stated before the sentencing court but was not[13].

The High Court may affirm the sentence appealed against[14]. Or it may quash it and pass a different sentence, whether more or less severe[15], provided that it may not impose a sentence which would have been outwith the competency of the sentencing court[16]. Where an appellant has been sentenced on more than one charge,

---

1  1995 Act, s 186(7).
2  1995 Act, s 181(1) applied to appeals against sentence by s 186(8). See also 1996 Rules, r 19.4(2).
3  1995 Act, s 187.
4  See above at p 273.
5  1995 Act, s 187(1)(a).
6  1995 Act, s 173(2).
7  1995 Act, s 186(9).
8  1995 Act, s 186(9)(b).
9  1995 Act, s 186(9)(a).
10  1995 Act, s 186(10), applying s 177 to appeals against sentence.
11  1995 Act, s 173(2).
12  1995 Act, s 186(10), applying s 182(5)(a)-(e) to appeals against sentence.
13  Eg *Stewart v Carnegie* 1988 SCCR 431.
14  1995 Act, s 189(1)(a).
15  1995 Act, s 189(1)(b).
16  1995 Act, s 189(2).

the High Court has no power to alter the sentence on a charge against the sentence for which no appeal has been taken[1]. If the appellant remains liable to a custodial sentence following the appeal, identical provisions apply as in the case of an unsuccessful appeal against conviction[2].

The High Court has power to award expenses in an appeal against sentence[3].

### Appeals against sentence by the Crown

The prosecutor in a summary case may appeal against any sentence imposed on a point of law[4]. He may also appeal against a sentence or other order (such as a probation order or an absolute discharge) on the ground of undue leniency[5].

An appeal against sentence on a point of law is by way of stated case[6], and the provisions described above[7] for appeal by stated case apply save that the prosecutor does not require leave to appeal[8].

An appeal against sentence on the ground of undue leniency is taken by note of appeal[9]. The provisions described above for an appeal against sentence by an accused apply *mutatis mutandis* save that the prosecutor does not require leave to appeal[10].

## ADVOCATION

### General

The right of appeal by way of bill of advocation is preserved by the 1995 Act for both solemn and summary proceedings[11].

### Advocation in solemn proceedings

Under solemn procedure advocation is a method of appeal available to bring to the High Court for review the decision of any solemn court of first instance, including the High Court sitting as a trial court[12]. It cannot be used to review a verdict of acquittal by a jury, but may be appropriate for appealing against an alleged irregu-

---

1 *Allan, Petr* 1993 JC 181, 1993 SCCR 686, 1994 SLT 229.
2 1995 Act, s 189(4). See above at pp 285–286.
3 1995 Act, s 189(3).
4 1995 Act, s 175(3)(b).
5 1995 Act, s 175(4), brought into effect in respect of sentences imposed on or after 1 November 1996 by the Prosecutor's Right of Appeal in Summary Proceedings (Scotland) Order 1996: SI 1996/2548. The prosecutor's right of appeal has been extended further with the coming into force of the 1997 Act, s 21 on 1 August 1997. See the Appendix at p 326 below.
6 1995 Act, s 176(1).
7 See above at pp 277–286.
8 1995 Act, s 175(3).
9 1995 Act, s 175(9).
10 1995 Act, s 175(4).
11 Section 131 (solemn procedure); s 191 (summary procedure). For a full discussion of advocation see *Renton and Brown* paras 33–19 to 33–22.
12 1995 Act, s 131(1).

larity in the court of first instance[1]. It cannot be used in the course of a trial[2]. However, it is competent as a means of reviewing the decision of a trial court to refuse to adjourn a trial which has commenced, with the consequence that if the bill of advocation is passed the trial must continue[3].

Advocation may be used by an accused to correct an irregularity in preliminary solemn proceedings but only if the irregularity is of such a nature that grave injustice would result, which could not reasonably be rectified by an appeal against conviction[4].

Advocation as a method of appeal in solemn proceedings is relatively rare. It might have been thought that it would almost disappear with the introduction of first and preliminary diets and the provisions for appeals therefrom[5]. This is not, however, the case. The right of appeal by advocation from such diets is specifically preserved[6] and is used, for example, when for, whatever reason, the Crown has failed to comply with the very rigid time limit[7] which applies to the normal statutory appeals from such diets[8].

## Advocation in summary proceedings

In summary proceedings a bill of advocation is considered primarily to be the prosecution counterpart of a bill of suspension for the defence[9]. Like suspension advocation may be brought where an appeal by stated case would be incompetent or inappropriate, and the ground for bringing it is an alleged miscarriage of justice[9].

However, advocation in summary proceedings is also a remedy open to an accused, if he wishes to appeal on the ground of an irregularity allegedly occurring during the currency of a case[10]. Suspension is not competent prior to conviction[11].

A bill of advocation is in similar form to that of a bill of suspension, and the respondent may lodge answers to it. The powers of the High Court in hearing a bill of advocation in summary proceedings are identical with those in hearing a bill of suspension[12]. The Court may, if it quashes an acquittal, grant authority to the prosecutor to bring a new prosecution[13].

1 Eg *HMA v Walker* 1981 JC 102, 1981 SCCR 154, 1981 SLT (Notes) 3 (a case dealing with the application of the 80-day rule). See also *HMA v McKenzie* 1989 SCCR 587, 1990 SLT 28, a very unusual case where the Crown brought a bill of advocation between a plea of guilty and sentence.
2 *HMA v Thomson* 1994 SCCR 40, 1994 SLT 354. See 1994 SCCR pp 45-46 for an interesting discussion on advocation by Sheriff G.H. Gordon, editor of SCCR.
3 *HMA v Khan* 1997 SCCR 100.
4 *Khalid v HMA* 1994 SCCR 47, 1994 SLT 357; *McKenna v HMA* 1994 SCCR 51, 1994 SLT 362.
5 1995 Act, s 74. See above at pp 134–135, 137.
6 1995 Act, s 74(1)(b).
7 1995 Act, s 74(2)(b).
8 See eg *HMA v Sorrie* 1996 SCCR 778, 1997 SLT 250.
9 1995 Act, s 191(1).
10 As in *Platt v Lockhart* 1988 SCCR 308, 1988 SLT 845; *Runham v Westwater* 1995 SCCR 356, 1995 SLT 835.
11 *Durant v Lockhart* 1985 SCCR 72, 1985 SLT 394.
12 1995 Act, s 191(3). See above at p 288.
13 1995 Act, s 183(1)(d) applied to advocation by s 191(3).

# APPEAL TO THE *NOBILE OFFICIUM* OF THE HIGH COURT

There is at common law a 'long stop' right of appeal to the *nobile officium* of the High Court of Justiciary.

'It is neither necessary nor desirable to attempt to lay down comprehensively the circumstances in which application may appropriately be made to the *nobile officium*. ... . Suffice it to say that it is well recognised that this court has a power to provide a remedy for all extraordinary or unforeseen occurrences in the course of criminal business'[1].

'The jurisdiction which this court is empowered to exercise under the *nobile officium* exists for the purpose of preventing injustice or oppression. Its scope is limited by the principle which is now well settled that the power will only be exercised where the circumstances are extraordinary or unforeseen, and where no other remedy or procedure is prescribed by the law'[2].

This form of appeal is not appropriate or competent if there is statutory provision for the eventuality concerned. Thus, where an appellant had applied in terms of the statutory provisions for an extension of time to lodge a stated case, and his application had been refused, it was held incompetent for him to apply to the *nobile officium* for an extension of time[3].

The High Court has held an application to the *nobile officium* to be competent in the following circumstances: to seek the release of a witness who had been arrested for non-attendance at a trial[4]; where a sheriff refused to state a case in an appeal by the Crown, to direct him to do so[5]; to authorise a medical examination of a child in local authority care on behalf of a person accused of assaulting him[6]; to recall a pretended desertion of the diet in a High Court trial and allow the jury to be excused and a new jury to be empanelled[7]; to seek bail for an accused on a murder charge[8]; to appeal against a sentence for contempt of court in solemn proceedings in the sheriff court[9]; to reinstate an appeal which had been abandoned as a result of incomplete and inaccurate advice[10].

An application to the *nobile officium* is made by petition[11], and the respondent may lodge answers[12]. The application is heard by a bench of at least three judges.

---

1 *Hughes, Petr* 1989 SCCR 490 at 497, 1990 SLT 142 at 145, per Lord Justice-Clerk Ross.
2 *Macpherson, Petr* 1989 SCCR 518 at 522, per Lord Justice-General Hope.
3 *Berry, Petr* 1985 SCCR 106. See also *Windsor, Petr* 1994 SCCR 59, 1994 SLT 604; *Connolly, Petr* 1997 SCCR 205, 1997 SLT 689.
4 *Gerrard, Petr* 1984 SCCR 1, 1984 SLT 108.
5 *MacDougall, Petr* 1986 SCCR 128.
6 *K, Petr* 1986 SCCR 709.
7 *Hughes, Petr* 1989 SCCR 490, 1990 SLT 142.
8 *Welsh, Petr* 1990 SCCR 763, 1992 SLT 903.
9 *George Outram & Co Ltd v Lees* 1992 JC 17, 1992 SCCR 120, 1992 SLT 32.
10 *McIntosh, Petr* 1995 SCCR 327, 1995 SLT 796.
11 See the cases cited in this section of the chapter (ie Appeal to the *Nobile Officium* of the High Court) for the form which the petition may take.
12 As in *Hughes, Petr* 1989 SCCR 490, 1990 SLT 142.

CHAPTER 9

# MENTALLY DISORDERED PERSONS IN THE CRIMINAL COURTS

## INTRODUCTION

Sadly it is not uncommon for the criminal courts to have before them persons suffering from some form of mental disorder, a term which is used as meaning 'mental illness or mental handicap however caused or manifested'[1]. In some contexts the more old fashioned terms 'insane' and 'insanity' are used.

In this chapter we shall examine briefly the procedures for dealing with those suffering from mental disorder at various stages of the proceedings. As the statutory provisions for both solemn and summary procedure are substantially the same[2], both forms of procedure will be examined together.

## AT FIRST APPEARANCE IN COURT

If the procurator fiscal has reason to believe that an accused person is suffering from mental disorder, he must bring before the court any evidence which he may have of that person's mental condition[3].

If a person is charged in the district court with an offence punishable with imprisonment, and he appears to the court to be suffering from mental disorder, he must be remitted to the sheriff court[4]. The reason for this is that the sheriff court has powers of disposal for such persons which are not available to the district court[5].

Before trial a court may remand an accused in hospital rather than in prison if he appears to be suffering from mental disorder[6]. The court must have medical evidence (either written or oral) before it can make such a remand[7]. The accused will be detained in the hospital if he appears to be suffering from a mental disorder such as would justify his admission to hospital under Part V of the 1984 Act[8], which is

---

1  1984 Act, s 1(2). This definition is effectively incorporated into the 1995 Act by references to the 1984 Act in various sections.
2  The provisions are contained in Pt VI of the 1995 Act. These provisions will undergo some substantial changes if the 1997 Act, ss 6–12 come into force. See the Appendix at pp 327–329 below.
3  1995 Act, s 52(1).
4  1995 Act, s 58(10).
5  Hospital order and guardianship order under the 1995 Act, s 58(1). See below at pp 300–303.
6  1995 Act, s 52(1).
7  1995 Act, s 52(5).
8  1995 Act, s 52(3).

the part dealing with compulsory admission to hospital. If the hospital reports to the court that the accused is not suffering from such a mental disorder, the court may then remand him in prison or deal with him in some other way[1].

## INSANITY IN BAR OF TRIAL

If a person is unable, because of mental disorder, to plead or to give instructions for his defence, he cannot go to trial. If the prosecutor does not accept the position, a plea in bar of trial must be taken. The statutory provision uses the terms 'insane' and 'insanity' in this connection[2]. Insanity in bar of trial may be proved by the written or oral evidence of two medical practitioners[3].

Under solemn procedure the normal provisions for a plea in bar of trial apply. Thus, in a case which is indicted in the sheriff court, notice of the plea should normally be given to the court and the other parties at least two days before the first diet[4]. In a case which is indicted in the High Court notice of the plea should normally be given at least ten days prior to the trial date[5] so that a preliminary diet may be ordered[6]. It is possible, however, that the mental condition of the accused may change and that the plea in bar may be tendered only at the trial diet or even in the course of the trial.

In a summary case, notice of the plea in bar of trial must be given before the first prosecution witness is called[7]. The notice must include the names of the witnesses by whom the accused proposes to prove his unfitness to plead[7].

Under both solemn and summary procedure the court may adjourn for investigation before making a finding of unfitness to plead[8]. Evidence of the accused's fitness to plead may be led in his absence if it appears to the court that it is not practicable or appropriate for him to be in court and if no objection is taken by him or on his behalf[9].

If a plea in bar of trial on the ground of insanity is sustained the prosecutor may simply move the court to desert the diet *pro loco et tempore*[10]. If this is not done, the court must (a) make a finding that the accused is insane so that the trial cannot proceed and state the reasons for that finding[11]; (b) discharge the trial diet and order that an 'examination of facts' be held under section 55 of the 1995 Act[12]; and (c) remand the accused in custody or on bail or, if certain conditions are satisfied, commit him to hospital under a 'temporary hospital order'[13].

1 1995 Act, s 52(4).
2 1995 Act, s 54.
3 1995 Act, s 54(1). The requirements of the 1995 Act, s 61 must be satisfied with regard to the medical evidence. See below at p 304. See *Stewart v HMA* 1997 SCCR 330.
4 1995 Act, s 71(2).
5 1995 Act, s 72(1)(b), (6)(b).
6 For preliminary diet see above at pp 135–137.
7 1995 Act, s 54(7).
8 1995 Act, s 54(3).
9 1995 Act, s 54(5).
10 1995 Act, s 54(2). For desertion *pro loco et tempore* see above at p 176.
11 1995 Act, s 54(1)(a).
12 1995 Act, s 54(1)(b). For examination of facts see the next section of this chapter.
13 1995 Act, s 54(1)(c).

The conditions for making a temporary hospital order are (i) that two medical practitioners[1] have certified that the accused is suffering from mental disorder of a nature or degree which warrants his admission to hospital under Part V of the 1984 Act[2], and (ii) that a hospital is available for his admission and suitable for his detention[3]. A temporary hospital order may at any time be reviewed by the court making it on the ground that there has been a change in circumstances[4]. Following such a review the court may revoke the order if it considers that it is no longer required, and remand the accused in custody or on bail[5]. Alternatively, it may confirm or vary the order[6] or revoke the order and make such other order as it thinks fit[7].

## EXAMINATION OF FACTS

The procedure of an examination of facts was introduced by the 1995 Act in order to remedy the injustice which existed under the former law whereby a person found insane in bar of trial was, without any proof that he had committed the act or omission with which he had been charged, effectively treated as if he had been found guilty and was committed to hospital. Under the new procedure the court must be satisfied that the accused did commit the act or omission before it can proceed further.

An examination of facts should be ordered as soon as a plea in bar of trial on the ground of insanity is sustained provided that the diet is not deserted *pro loco et tempore*. In solemn proceedings this may be at the trial diet or even in the course of the trial. In a summary case, however, a plea in bar must be taken before the first witness is sworn[8]. If the examination of facts is ordered at the trial diet the court may proceed to hear evidence there and then[9]. If evidence has already been heard in the case, the court may take that evidence into consideration along with any other evidence which may be led[10]. If the plea in bar of trial has been sustained at a first diet or preliminary diet, then a diet will be fixed for the examination of facts and witnesses will be cited to it in the normal way, the warrant for citation of witnesses to the trial being sufficient warrant to cite to an examination of facts[11].

The examination of facts may proceed in the absence of the accused if it is not practical or appropriate for him to attend and there is no objection taken by him or on his behalf[12]. In any case in which an examination of facts is ordered, if an accused is unrepresented the court must appoint counsel or a solicitor to represent his interests[13]. The rules of evidence and procedure at an examination of facts should be as nearly as possible the same as those at a trial[14].

---

1   The requirements of the 1995 Act, s 61 must be satisfied with regard to the medical evidence. See below at p 304.
2   1995 Act, s 54(1)(c)(i).
3   1995 Act, s 54(1)(c)(ii).
4   1995 Act, s 54(4).
5   1995 Act, s 54(4)(a).
6   1995 Act, s 54(4)(b)(i).
7   1995 Act, s 54(4)(b)(ii).
8   1995 Act, s 54(7).
9   1995 Act, s 56(1).
10   1995 Act, s 55(1).
11   1995 Act, s 56(2).
12   1995 Act, s 55(5).
13   1995 Act, s 56(3).
14   1995 Act, s 55(6).

The purpose of an examination of facts is to ascertain whether the accused committed the act or omission with which he is charged. The evidence led is therefore likely to be much the same as that which would be led if the case proceeded to trial in the normal way. The court must determine two questions: (1) whether it is satisfied beyond reasonable doubt, as respects any charge in the indictment or complaint, that the accused did the act or made the omission constituting the offence[1]; and (2) whether it is satisfied on balance of probabilities, that there are no grounds for acquitting him[2]. If the court is satisfied on both these matters it must make a finding to that effect[3]. If the court is not so satisfied it must acquit the accused[4], but if it is satisfied that he did commit the act or omission but was insane at the time, the court must state whether the acquittal is on the ground of insanity[5]. This provision is presumably stated in this way to allow, for example, for an accused being found to have attacked someone but to have done so in self-defence.

If the accused is found to have committed the act or omission and there are no grounds for acquitting him (ie the requirements of section 55(1) are fulfilled) or if he is acquitted on the ground of insanity (in terms of section 55(4)) certain consequences follow and these are discussed below. If he is acquitted on any other ground (in terms of section 55(3)) then that has the same effect as an acquittal following a trial.

## INSANITY AS A DEFENCE

If an accused is insane at the time of doing something which would be criminal if he were sane, he is entitled to be acquitted on the ground of insanity.

### Solemn procedure

Under solemn procedure insanity at the time is a special defence. If the case is indicted in the sheriff court the special defence must be lodged at or before the first diet[6]. If it is a High Court case notice of the special defence must normally be given not less than ten clear days before the trial diet[7]. The jury should be directed that, if they acquit the accused, they must declare whether he was acquitted on account of his insanity at the time[8]. An accused acquitted on the ground of insanity may be dealt with in a number of different ways as discussed below[9].

### Summary procedure

In a summary case there is no provision for the lodging of a special defence prior to the trial but it is suggested that it would be a sensible precaution for the defence

1 1995 Act, s 55(1)(a).
2 1995 Act, s 55(1)(b).
3 1995 Act, s 55(2).
4 1995 Act, s 55(3).
5 1995 Act, s 55(4).
6 1995 Act, s 78(3)(b). See above at p 131.
7 1995 Act, s 78(3)(a). See above at p 131.
8 1995 Act, s 54(6)(a).
9 See the next section of this chapter.

solicitor to intimate at the intermediate diet[1] that it will be submitted that the accused was insane at the time of the alleged offence. If the court is satisfied on the evidence that this is indeed the case and the accused is not acquitted on any other ground, he is acquitted on the ground of insanity[2]. As in the case of solemn procedure there are a number of disposals open to the court[3].

## DISPOSAL WHERE ACCUSED FOUND TO BE INSANE

A person who is acquitted on the ground of insanity, whether following an examination of facts (in terms of section 55(3) and (4)) or following trial (in terms of section 54(6)) and a person who is insane in bar of trial but whom the examination of facts has found to have committed the act or omission and for whom there are no grounds of acquittal (in terms of section 55(1) and (2)) are both dealt with in the same way[4].

In any case where the accused was charged with a crime other than murder the court has a choice from a number of disposals. First it may make an order that he be detained in a specified hospital[5]. This has the same effect as a hospital order under section 58(1) of the 1995 Act[6]. Secondly, the order for detention in hospital may have added to it an order that he is to be subject to the special restrictions set out in section 62(1) of the 1984 Act[7]. This has the same effect as a restriction order under section 59(1) of the 1995 Act[8]. Thirdly, the court may place the person under the guardianship of a local authority or of a person approved by a local authority[9]. This has the same effect as a guardianship order under section 58(1) of the 1995 Act[10]. Fourthly, the court may make a supervision and treatment order[11]. Fifthly, the court may make no order[12].

If the offence with which the person was charged is murder the court must order that he be detained in hospital as a restricted patient[13].

### Supervision and treatment order

A supervision and treatment order was introduced into Scotland for the first time by the 1995 Act. Unlike a hospital order (with or without a restriction order) and a guardianship order it is not available after a finding of guilt. It is available only if an accused is found to be insane in bar of trial (and it is proved that he committed the act or omission with which he was charged) or is found not guilty on the

---

1  For intermediate diet see above at pp 201–202.
2  1995 Act, s 54(6)(b).
3  See the next section of this chapter.
4  1995 Act, s 57(1).
5  1995 Act, s 57(2)(a).
6  See below at pp 300–301 for hospital order.
7  1995 Act, s 57(2)(b). The 1984 Act, s 62(1) places severe restrictions on the circumstances in which a patient may be given leave of absence, transferred or discharged.
8  See below at p 301 for restriction order.
9  1995 Act, s 57(2)(c).
10 See below at p 303 for guardianship order.
11 1995 Act, s 57(2)(d). See the next section of this chapter for supervision and treatment order.
12 1995 Act, s 57(2)(e).
13 1995 Act, s 57(3), applying s 57(2)(a) and (b).

ground of insanity[1]. The statutory provisions relating to such an order are contained in Schedule 4 to the 1995 Act[2].

A supervision and treatment order has some similarities to a probation order[3]. It requires the 'supervised person' to be under the supervision of a social worker (the 'supervising officer') for a specified period not exceeding three years[4], to comply during that period with instructions given to him by that social worker[5], and 'to submit during that period to treatment by or under the direction of a medical practitioner with a view to the improvement of his mental condition'[6]. The treatment may be out-patient treatment at a named institution[7], or treatment by a named practitioner[8], and arrangements for the treatment may be varied by a medical practitioner with the consent of the supervised person[9]. The order may also include a requirement as to the residence of the supervised person[10]. If the residence is in an institution the period of such residence must be specified in the order[11].

Before making an order the court must be satisfied of certain matters. These are:

(1) that having regard to all the circumstances of the case, the making of such an order is the most suitable means of dealing with the person[12]; and

(2) that the mental condition of the person is (i) such as requires and may be susceptible to treatment but (ii) is not such as to warrant the making of an order under section 57(2) of the Act which is the equivalent of either a hospital order or a guardianship order[13]; and

(3) that the social worker intended to be nominated in the order as supervising officer is willing to undertake the supervision[14]; and

(4) that arrangements have been made for the intended treatment[15].

As in the case of a probation order the court must, when making a supervision and treatment order, explain certain things to the supervised person 'in ordinary language'[16]. These are the effect of the order[17] and that the sheriff court for the area where the supervised person will live ('the relevant sheriff court'), has power to review it on the application of either the supervised person or the supervising officer[18].

The court must be satisfied of the matters specified in items (1) and (2) on the written or oral evidence of two medical practitioners approved for the purpose of sections 20 or 39 of the 1984 Act[19].

1 1995 Act, s 57(2)(d).
2 1995 Act, s 57(5).
3 For probation order see above at pp 246–251.
4 1995 Act, Sch 4, para 1(1)(a).
5 1995 Act, Sch 4, para 1(1)(b).
6 1995 Act, Sch 4, para 1(1)(c).
7 1995 Act, Sch 4, para 4(2)(a).
8 1995 Act, Sch 4, para 4(2)(b).
9 1995 Act, Sch 4, para 4(3), (4).
10 1995 Act, Sch 4, para 5(1).
11 1995 Act, Sch 4, para 5(4).
12 1995 Act, Sch 4, para 2(1)(a).
13 1995 Act, Sch 4, para 2(1)(b).
14 1995 Act, Sch 4, para 2(2)(a).
15 1995 Act, Sch 4, para 2(2)(b).
16 1995 Act, Sch 4, para 3(2).
17 1995 Act, Sch 4, para 3(2)(a).
18 1995 Act, Sch 4, para 3(2)(b).
19 1995 Act, Sch 4, para 2(1)(b). The approval referred to is approval by a health board of the practitioner as having special experience in the diagnosis or treatment of mental disorder.

Either the supervising officer or the supervised person may apply to the relevant sheriff court to revoke the order. The order will be revoked if 'having regard to circumstances which have arisen since the order was made, it would be in the interests of the health or welfare of the supervised person that the order should be revoked'[1]. There is also provision for the order being amended, either on a change of address by the supervised person[2], or for amendment of a non-medical require-ment[3], or for amendment of a medical requirement[4]. In the two former cases appli-cation may be made by either the supervising officer or the supervised person[5]. In the latter case application may be made only on the application of the supervising officer following a report from the doctor in charge of the case[6].

## DISPOSAL AFTER FINDING OF GUILT

If a mentally disordered person is found guilty of committing an offence or pleads guilty, there are certain disposals open to the court[7] as well as the various forms of sentence discussed in chapter 7. These disposals, which will now be examined, are: hospital order (with or without a restriction order); guardianship order; probation with a condition of treatment.

Before deciding on the appropriate disposal the court may adjourn the case for inquiries with the accused remanded in custody, on bail or ordained[8]. Alternatively, if the court wishes specifically to have the accused's mental condi-tion investigated it may continue the case for a period not exceeding three weeks for this purpose[9]. The accused may be remanded in custody, realeased on bail or committed to hospital[10]. However, committal to hospital is possible only if the court is satisfied on the written or oral evidence of a medical practitioner that the accused appears to be suffering from a mental disorder and that a hospital is avail-able for his admission and suitable for his detention[10].

### Hospital order

A hospital order is an order for the admission of a person to a specified hospital and his detention there[11]. The practical effect of the order is that the accused is in the same position as a person admitted to hospital as a compulsory patient under Part V of the 1984 Act, except that the accused's nearest relative may not order his dis-charge[12].

---

1  1995 Act, Sch 4, para 6.
2  1995 Act, Sch 4, para 7.
3  1995 Act, Sch 4, para 8.
4  1995 Act, Sch 4, para 9.
5  1995 Act, Sch 4, paras 7(2), 8(1).
6  1995 Act, Sch 4, para 9(1).
7  If the 1997 Act, ss 6 and 7 come into force the court will be able to make a new order in the shape of a 'hospital direction'. See the Appendix at p 327 below.
8  In terms of the 1995 Act, s 201. See above at pp 186–187.
9  1995 Act, s 200(2).
10  1995 Act, s 200(2)(b).
11  1995 Act, s 58(1). If the 1997 Act, s 9 comes into force the order may specify a 'hospital unit'. See the Appendix at p 328 below.
12  1984 Act, s 60(2).

A hospital order may be made by both the High Court and the sheriff court in the case of an accused found guilty of an offence (other than an offence for which the sentence is fixed by law) punishable by imprisonment[1]. In the case of a summary prosecution the court may make a hospital order without convicting the accused[2]. The court must be satisfied that the accused is suffering from mental disorder of a nature or degree which makes it appropriate for him to receive medical treatment in hospital, that it is necessary for the health or safety of the accused or for the protection of other persons that he should receive such treatment, and that treatment cannot be provided unless he is detained in hospital[3].

The court must have evidence from two doctors, which may be either written or oral[4].

If the court has satisfactory medical evidence, then it may make a hospital order if it 'is of opinion, having regard to all the circumstances including the nature of the offence and the character and antecedents of the offender, and to the other available methods of dealing with him, that the most suitable method of disposing of the case' is by making the order[5]. The court must also be satisfied that there will be accommodation for the accused in the specified hospital within 28 days of the date of the order being made[6].

The hospital specified in the hospital order should not be a State hospital unless the court is satisfied from the medical evidence that 'the offender, on account of his dangerous, violent or criminal propensities, requires treatment under conditions of special security, and cannot suitably be cared for in a hospital other than a State hospital'[7].

## Restriction order

A hospital order is usually not subject to any restriction. This means in effect that an accused may be discharged from hospital when the hospital doctors consider that he no longer requires compulsory treatment. However, a court may direct that an accused be subject to a restriction order, in which case his discharge from hospital is strictly controlled[8].

A restriction order may be made only if 'it appears to the court, having regard to (a) the nature of the offence with which [the accused] is charged; (b) the antecedents of the [accused]; and (c) the risk that as a result of his mental disorder he would commit offences if set at large, that it is necessary for the protection of the public from serious harm so to do'[9]. The restriction order may be without limit of time[9].

A restriction order may not be made unless the doctor approved by the Health Board[10] has given evidence orally in court[11].

1 1995 Act, s 58(1).
2 1995 Act, s 58(3).
3 1984 Act, s 17(1), applied by 1995 Act, s 58(1)(a)(i). Section 17(1) contains further provisions and its exact terms should be studied.
4 1995 Act, s 58(1)(a). The requirements of the 1995 Act, s 61 must be satisfied with regard to the medical evidence. See below at p 304.
5 1995 Act, s 58(1)(b).
6 1995 Act, s 58(4).
7 1995 Act, s 58(5).
8 For the restrictions on discharge see the 1984 Act, ss 62–68.
9 1995 Act, s 59(1).
10 See the section 'Requirements for Medical Evidence' at p 304 below.
11 1995 Act, s 59(2).

## Other orders with hospital order

A court which makes a hospital order may not impose a sentence of imprisonment or a fine, or make a probation order or a community service order in respect of the offence concerned, but it may make any other competent order[1]. For example, the court may disqualify from driving.

## Interim hospital order

The courts have a limited power to have an offender detained in hospital for a reasonably lengthy period in order that it may be established whether a hospital order would, at the end of the day, be appropriate. This is called an interim hospital order. Such an order is competent only where there is reason to suppose that any hospital order ultimately made would specify a State hospital[2], and therefore applies only to offenders of dangerous, violent or criminal propensities. An interim hospital order authorises the offender's admission to a State hospital, or such other hospital as for special reasons the court may specify[3], and his detention there for a specific period not exceeding twelve weeks[4].

The order may be renewed for further periods of not more than 28 days at a time if it appears to the court on the written or oral evidence of the responsible medical officer[5] that the continuation of the order is warranted[6]. It may not, however, continue in force for more than six months in all[7]. An interim hospital order may be renewed without the offender being in court provided that he is legally represented and that his representative has an opportunity to be heard[8].

As in the case of a hospital order evidence from two doctors is required[9], but one of the doctors must be employed by the hospital which is to be specified in the order[10].

The court must be satisfied that there will be accommodation available for the offender in the specified hospital within 28 days of the making of the order[11].

When making an interim hospital order the court may not impose a custodial sentence or a fine or make a probation order or community service order, but it may make any other order which it has the power to make[12].

Interim hospital orders are made relatively infrequently, but are useful in cases where it is desired to carry out an assessment of an offender over a period of time longer than the three weeks usually allowed for obtaining a medical report[13].

1 1995 Act, s 58(8).
2 1995 Act, s 53(1)(b)(ii).
3 1995 Act, s 53(1).
4 1995 Act, s 53(6)(a).
5 'Responsible medical officer' is defined in the 1984 Act, s 59(1)(a), applied by the 1995 Act, s 307(1).
6 1995 Act, s 53(6)(b). See also the 1996 Rules, r 7.1; Forms 7.1 A and B.
7 1995 Act, s 53(6). If the 1997 Act, s 11 comes into force the maximum period will be extended to twelve months. See the Appendix at p 328 below.
8 1995 Act, s 53(7).
9 1995 Act, s 53(1).
10 1995 Act, s 53(2).
11 1995 Act, s 53(3).
12 1995 Act, s 53(4).
13 1995 Act, s 200(2).

## Guardianship order

If a person is found guilty of an offence punishable by imprisonment, and the court is satisfied that he is 'suffering from mental disorder of a nature or degree which warrants his reception into guardianship'[1], it may make a guardianship order. This is an order placing the offender under the guardianship of a specified local authority or of a specified person approved by a local authority[2]. The provisions for guardianship orders are, *mutatis mutandis*, the same as those for hospital orders[3].

Guardianship orders are made less frequently than are hospital orders, but provide a useful way of disposing of a case where it is possible for the offender to remain at liberty rather than being confined in hospital. A guardianship order is probably more likely to be used in the case of a person suffering from mental handicap than in the case of someone suffering from mental illness.

## Probation with a condition of treatment

There is specific provision in the 1995 Act for an offender to be placed on probation with a condition that he must submit to treatment for his mental condition[4].

The court must have evidence from one doctor that the mental condition of the offender is such as requires and may be susceptible to treatment but is not such as to warrant his detention under a hospital order[5]. The doctor who provides the evidence must be approved by a Health Board as having special experience in the diagnosis or treatment of mental disorder[5]. Certain of the general provisions relating to medical evidence for those suffering from mental disorder apply[6].

The probation order must specify whether the treatment is to be as an in-patient or out-patient at a named hospital, or by or under the direction of a named doctor or chartered psychologist[7]. The requirement for treatment must be for a specific period not exceeding twelve months[8]. Before making the order the court must be satisfied that arrangements for the treatment have been made[9].

Provision is made for variation of the conditions of treatment subject to agreement by the probationer and his supervising social worker without the necessity of returning to court[10].

All the provisions relating to probation orders in general[11] apply to an order with a condition of treatment. The order may be varied and discharged in the same way as any other probation order, but may not be varied so as to extend the period of treatment beyond twelve months[12].

---

1 1984 Act, s 36(a), applied by 1995 Act, s 58(1)(a).
2 1995 Act, s 58(1).
3 1995 Act, s 58 applies to both forms of order.
4 1995 Act, s 230.
5 1995 Act, s 230(1).
6 1995 Act, s 230(8) applying s 61(3)–(5). For the general provisions see the next section of this chapter.
7 1995 Act, s 230(2).
8 1995 Act, s 230(1).
9 1995 Act, s 230(3).
10 1995 Act, s 230(4), (5), (6), (7).
11 See above at pp 246–251.
12 1995 Act, s 231(1), Sch 6, para 3(2)(b).

# REQUIREMENTS FOR MEDICAL EVIDENCE

The 1995 Act contains important provisions about the medical evidence which a court must have before it can find an accused person insane in bar of trial or make a hospital order, guardianship order or interim hospital order[1]. 

There must be evidence from two medical practitioners and at least one of them must be approved by a health board as having special experience in the diagnosis or treatment of mental disorder[2]. The evidence must include a statement as to whether the person giving evidence is related to the accused or has any pecuniary interest in the admission of the accused to hospital or his reception into guardianship[3]. Although a written report is sufficient evidence the court may insist on oral evidence being given[4]. Both doctors must agree that the accused is suffering from the same form of mental disorder (either mental illness or mental handicap)[5]. 

The accused's legal representative is entitled to see a copy of any written medical report[6]. If the accused is unrepresented, the substance of the report must be disclosed to him (or to his parent or guardian if he is under sixteen)[7]. The accused may insist on oral evidence being given by a doctor who has submitted a written report, and he may lead evidence in rebuttal[8]. The court may adjourn the case to give the accused time to consider any medical report[9]. An accused is entitled to have a medical examination in private for the purpose of obtaining rebuttal evidence[10].

# APPEALS

An accused has the right to appeal against a hospital order, an interim hospital order (but not a renewal thereof), a guardianship order or an order restricting discharge, in the same way as against any sentence[11]. 

In an appeal against conviction (whether under solemn or summary procedure), if the High Court finds that the accused committed the act charged but was insane at the time, it may substitute a verdict of acquittal on the ground of insanity and deal with the accused as if he had been acquitted on the ground of insanity by the trial court[12].

---

1   The provisions in the 1995 Act, s 61(3)–(5) described below apply also to the making of a probation order with a condition of treatment. See the previous section of this chapter.
2   1995 Act, s 61(1). If the 1997 Act, s 10 comes into force there will be a general requirement that one of the practitioners should be employed in the hospital which is to be specified in the order. See the Appendix at p 328 below.
3   1995 Act, s 61(2).
4   1995 Act, s 61(3).
5   1995 Act, s 58(7).
6   1995 Act, s 61(4)(a).
7   1995 Act, s 61(4)(b).
8   1995 Act, s 61(4)(c).
9   1995 Act, s 61(4).
10  1995 Act, s 61(5).
11  1995 Act, s 60.
12  1995 Act, s 118(5).

# CHAPTER 10

# CHILDREN IN THE CRIMINAL COURTS

## INTRODUCTION

The great majority of children under sixteen who commit offences in Scotland do not appear in court at all. They are dealt with under the children's hearing system, the statutory provisions for which are now contained in Chapters 2 and 3 of Part II of the Children (Scotland) Act 1995[1]. The sheriff court has a limited involvement in the hearing system in respect that proof may be led before a sheriff if the ground of referral to the hearing is not accepted and in certain other circumstances[2]. There is an appeal to the sheriff against the decision of a hearing[3]. There is a further appeal from the sheriff to the sheriff principal on a point of law or in respect of any irregularity in the conduct of the case[4]. There is a further right of appeal to the Court of Session, either directly from the sheriff or, with leave of the sheriff principal from him[5]. The hearing system is, however, outwith the scope of this book[6]. This chapter will deal briefly with the relatively rare situation when a child does appear in court, accused of having committed an offence.

## DETENTION AND ARREST

The general law of detention and arrest applies to children. In addition there are certain special rules applying only to children.

If a child is arrested or detained under section 14 of the 1995 Act[7], his parent should be informed of the fact without delay[8]. The parent must then be allowed access to the child, unless he too is suspected of being involved in the crime, in which case access may be refused[9]. Access may be restricted in the interests of furthering the investigation of the case or the well-being of the child[10].

---

1 A child is defined for the purposes of these provisions as a person under sixteen years of age, subject to an extension to the age of eighteen if the child is under supervision by direction of a children's hearing and in certain other limited circumstances: Children (Scotland) Act 1995, s 93(2)(b).
2 Ibid, s 65(7), (9).
3 Ibid, s 51(1).
4 Ibid, s 51(11)(a).
5 Ibid, s 51(11)(b).
6 For a detailed examination of the hearing system and its relationship with the court see B Kearney *Children's Hearings and the Sheriff Court* (1987). I understand that a second edition is presently (1997) in preparation.
7 See above at pp 82–85.
8 1995 Act, s 15(4). 'Parent' includes a guardian or a person having actual custody of the child: s 15(6).
9 1995 Act, s 15(4)(b).
10 1995 Act, s 15(5).

A child who has been arrested should normally be released on an undertaking being given by him or his parent or guardian that he will attend court for his case to be heard[1]. The decision whether or not to release the child must be taken by an officer of the rank of inspector or above, or by the officer in charge of the police station to which the child has been brought[2]. The child will not be released if '(a) the charge is one of homicide or other grave crime; or (b) it is necessary in his interest to remove him from association with any reputed criminal or prostitute; or (c) the officer has reason to believe that his liberation would defeat the ends of justice'[3].

If the child is not liberated, he should be detained in a place of safety other than a police station[4] unless a police officer (of the rank of inspector or above or the officer in charge of the police station to which the child is brought) certifies '(a) that it is impracticable to do so; (b) that he is of so unruly a character that he cannot safely be so detained; or (c) that by reason of his state of health or of his mental or bodily condition it is inadvisable so to detain him'[5]. The certificate must be produced to the court before which the child is brought[5]. If the child continues to be detained, but it is decided not to proceed with the charge against him, the Principal Reporter[6] must be informed, and the child may then be dealt with under the hearing system[7].

## PROSECUTION

No child under the age of eight may be prosecuted as it is conclusively presumed that such a child cannot be guilty of any offence[8].

No child under sixteen may be prosecuted except on the instructions of the Lord Advocate or at his instance[9]. Thus a private prosecution[10] against a child would not be competent. The Lord Advocate from time to time issues general directions to fiscals about the prosecution of children. Such general directions are sufficient to comply with the statutory requirement[11]. If it is wished to challenge the competency of proceedings against a child on the ground of lack of authority

---

1  1995 Act, s 43(1). If the child fails without reasonable excuse to attend court, the person giving the undertaking is guilty of an offence punishable by a maximum fine not exceeding level 3 on the standard scale: s 43(6). With the coming into force of the 1997 Act, s 55 on 1 August 1997 a child who has been arrested may now be liberated unconditionally. See the Appendix at p 329 below.
2  1995 Act, s 43(1). In practice the officer in charge of a police station may be a sergeant or even, exceptionally, a constable.
3  1995 Act, s 43(3).
4  1995 Act, s 43(4). A place of safety is '(a) a residential or other establishment provided by a local authority; (b) a community home within the meaning of s 53 of the Children Act 1989; (c) a police station; or (d) a hospital, surgery or other suitable place, the occupier of which is willing temporarily to receive the child' (Children (Scotland) Act 1995, s 93(1), applied by 1995 Act, s 307(1)).
5  1995 Act, s 43(4).
6  The Principal Reporter is the person concerned with the administration of the hearing system: Children (Scotland) Act 1995, s 40. In practice the duties of the Principal Reporter are delegated to local reporters.
7  1995 Act, s 43(5).
8  1995 Act, s 41.
9  1995 Act, s 42(1).
10 See below at pp 312, 313.
11 *McGuire v Dean* 1973 JC 20, 1974 SLT 229 sub nom *M v Dean*.

from the Lord Advocate, this must be done at the appropriate time for pleas to the competency[1].

A child may be prosecuted only in the High Court and the sheriff court[2].


# APPEARANCE IN COURT

A child must be prevented from associating with any adult charged with an offence other than that with which the child himself is charged, while at a police station, while being conveyed to or from court and while waiting before or after attendance at court[3]. In practical terms this means that if a child is in custody, he must be kept in a separate cell. If the child is cited to attend court or attends on undertaking, he should wait in a separate room for his case to be called and should not be in the courtroom where other accused wait for the calling of their cases. A female child must at all these times be under the care of a woman[4].

A child's parent or guardian is under an obligation to attend the court, unless the court is satisfied that it would be unreasonable to require his attendance[5]. To this end the police officer arresting a child or the officer in charge of the police station where the child is brought must cause the parent or guardian to be warned to attend court[6]. The attendance of a child's parent is not required if the child has been removed from the parent's custody or charge by a court order[7].

When a child is to be brought before a court, the chief constable for the area where the offence is alleged to have been committed must notify the local authority (in practice the social work department) for the area in which the court will sit, of the time and place of the child's appearance and of the nature of the charge against him[8]. The local authority must then carry out investigations and furnish the court with a report on the child's background[9].


# PROCEDURE IN COURT

## Restrictions on reporting

In both solemn and summary proceedings there is a restriction on the reporting by the press and other media of proceedings in court involving any child under sixteen[10]. The restriction is against publication of the name, address or school or of any particulars calculated to lead to the identification of any such child concerned

---

1 *McGuire v Dean* 1973 JC 20, 1974 SLT 229 sub nom *M v Dean*. For the time when pleas to the competency should be made see the 1995 Act, ss 71(2), 72(6), 144(4).
2 1995 Act, s 42(1).
3 1995 Act, s 42(9).
4 1995 Act, s 42(10).
5 1995 Act, s 42(2). The parent or guardian concerned is the parent who has parental responsibilities or parental rights (under the Children (Scotland) Act 1995, ss 1(3) or 2(4)) or the guardian having actual possession and control of the child (s 42(5)).
6 1995 Act, s 42(3).
7 1995 Act, s 42(6).
8 1995 Act, s 42(7).
9 1995 Act, s 42(8).
10 1995 Act, s 47.

in the proceedings, whether he be the accused, the complainer or a witness[1]. The restriction extends to publication of any picture including the child[2]. If the only involvement of a child under sixteen is as a witness (other than a complainer), and no accused in the case is under sixteen, the restriction applies only if the court so directs[3]. At any stage of the proceedings the court may direct that the statutory restrictions should be dispensed with, either completely or partially, if it is satisfied that it is in the public interest to do so[4]. The Secretary of State has a similar power after proceedings have been completed[5]. The dispensing power of the court has on occasion been used to permit the media to identify a child found guilty in a particularly bad case. It is advisable that the trial court should direct that the dispensing power should not take effect until after the expiry of any period within which an appeal may be lodged.

Any person who contravenes this statutory requirement is guilty of an offence punishable by a fine not exceeding level 4 on the standard scale[6].

## Remand or committal for trial or sentence

In both solemn and summary proceedings it may happen that a child who is awaiting trial or in respect of whom, after conviction, the court has adjourned the case to obtain reports, is neither released on bail nor ordained to appear. Such a child should not normally be committed to prison. Instead he should be committed to the local authority in whose area the court is situated[7], either, if the court so directs, in secure accommodation[8], or 'in a suitable place of safety chosen by the local authority'[9]. Exceptionally, if the child is over fourteen years of age and is certified by the court to be 'unruly or depraved' and the court has been notified that a remand centre is available, he may be committed to such a centre[10]. If no remand centre is available (and at the time of writing there is no such centre in Scotland), then he can be committed to prison[10]. Committal to a remand centre or to prison may be revoked by 'the sheriff' if he is satisfied that detention therein is no longer necessary[11]. This provision appears to imply that the matter should be dealt with by a sheriff even though the committal may have been by the High Court. If a child of fourteen years or over has been committed to a local authority and 'it appears to the court that he is unruly or depraved', the committal to the local authority may be revoked and the child may be committed to a remand centre (if such exists) or to prison[12].

1  1995 Act, s 47(1).
2  1995 Act, s 47(2).
3  1995 Act, s 47(3)(a).
4  1995 Act, s 47(3)(b).
5  1995 Act, s 47(3)(c).
6  1995 Act, s 47(4).
7  1995 Act, s 51(1)(a). With the coming into force of the 1997 Act, s 56 on 1 August 1997 the court is not now restricted to committing a child to the local authority of the area in which it sits. See the Appendix at p 329 below.
8  1995 Act, s 51(1)(a)(i). 'Secure accommodation' is defined in the Children (Scotland) Act 1995, s 93(1) as a residential establishment approved by the Secretary of State in accordance with certain regulations 'for the purpose of restricting the liberty of children'.
9  1995 Act, s 51(1)(a)(ii).
10  1995 Act, s 51(1)(b).
11  1995 Act, s 51(4).
12  1995 Act, s 51(3).

## Summary proceedings

Certain provisions apply only when a child is charged on summary complaint and not when he appears on petition or indictment.

When a child appears as an accused on a summary complaint the sheriff should either sit in a different court room or building from that in which he normally sits to conduct criminal business, or on a day when other courts in the building are not engaged in criminal proceedings[1]. The only persons entitled to be in court during the hearing of such a case are (a) members and officers of the court; (b) parties to the case, their legal representatives, and witnesses and other persons directly concerned in the case (this would, of course, include the parents of the child); (c) bona fide reporters of the press or news agencies; (d) such other persons as the court may specially authorise[1]. These restrictions do not apply where a child appears charged jointly with a person who is not a child[2]. It has been held that the provisions are directory only and not mandatory; breach of the restrictions does not nullify the proceedings[3].

The court must take steps as far as possible to prevent children attending sittings of the court from mixing with one another[4].

There are detailed provisions in the 1996 Rules governing the appearance of a child who is without legal representation[5]. These are not examined here as it must be very seldom nowadays that a child would appear in court unrepresented. It is to be hoped that, if he did so, the sheriff would use his powers under the legal aid legislation to allow the child to apply for legal aid[6].

# DISPOSAL OF CASE AGAINST A CHILD

## Summary proceedings

In a summary case the terms 'conviction' and 'sentence' should not be used in relation to a child. Instead the terms 'finding of guilt' and 'order' are appropriate[7].

## Reference to 'the panel'

If a child, who is not subject to a supervision requirement from a children's hearing, is found guilty or pleads guilty under either solemn or summary procedure, the court may, instead of dealing with the case itself, remit the case to the reporter to arrange for the disposal of the case by a children's hearing[8]. This is popularly known as remitting the case to 'the panel'. Alternatively, the court may request the reporter to arrange a hearing to provide the court with advice as to the treatment

---

1  1995 Act, s 142(1).
2  1995 Act, s 142(5).
3  *Heywood v B* 1994 SCCR 554.
4  1996 Rules, r 6.6(1).
5  1996 Rules, rr 6.3, 6.4.
6  Legal Aid (Scotland) Act 1986, s 24(6). See above at p 205.
7  1995 Act, s 165.
8  1995 Act, s 49(1)(a).

of the child[1]. Once the advice has been obtained the court may dispose of the case itself or remit to the hearing itself for disposal[2].

If a child who is subject to a supervision requirement from a children's hearing[3] pleads or is found guilty in the sheriff court, the court must, before dealing with the child, obtain the advice of a children's hearing[4]. It may then dispose of the case itself or remit to the hearing for disposal[5]. The High Court has the option whether or not to obtain such advice[6].

### Non-custodial disposal

A child may be given an absolute discharge or admonition, may be placed on probation[7], and may be fined in the same way as an adult offender. A child may not be imprisoned in default of payment of a fine, but may be detained for a period not exceeding one month in a place chosen by the local authority in whose area the court is situated[8]. As with any other offender under 21, the alternative of detention may not be imposed in the case of a child unless he has been under supervision in respect of the fine or the court is satisfied that it is impracticable to place him under supervision[9].

A court may order the parent or guardian of a child to find caution for the child's good behaviour[10]. The parent or guardian must be given the opportunity to be heard[11], unless he or she has been required to attend court and has failed to do so[12].

### Custodial disposal: solemn procedure[13]

If a court of solemn jurisdiction convicts a child of a crime other than murder[14] and is of opinion that no other method of dealing with him is appropriate, it may sentence him to be detained for a specified period[15]. A sheriff may sentence a child to detention for more than three years under this provision[16]. Detention without limit

1  1995 Act, s 49(1)(b).
2  1995 Act, s 49(2). With the coming into force of the 1997 Act, s 23 on 1 August 1997 a child is now given a right of appeal against a decision to remit him to a hearing for disposal. See the Appendix at p 326 below.
3  Children (Scotland) Act 1995, s 70(1).
4  1995 Act, s 49(3)(b).
5  1995 Act, s 49(3).
6  1995 Act, s 49(3)(a).
7  Procedure for breach of probation in the case of a child who is unrepresented is governed by the 1996 Rules, r 6.5.
8  1995 Act, s 216(7).
9  1995 Act, s 217(4).
10  1995 Act, s 45(1).
11  1995 Act, s 45(2).
12  1995 Act, s 45(3).
13  If the 1997 Act, Pt III, Ch I comes into force there will be major changes in the provisions for the release of children sentenced to custodial disposals. See the Appendix at pp 324–325 below for changes relating to adult prisoners. Some of these will apply also to children.
14  For murder, see the 1995 Act s 205(2), commented on above at p 232.
15  1995 Act, s 208.
16  The limitation on a sheriff's power of sentencing contained in the 1995 Act, s 3(3) refers only to imprisonment, and there is no equiparation of detention of a child under s 208 to imprisonment, as there is in the case of detention of a young offender under s 207(2).

of time is competent[1], even though this effectively amounts to a life sentence[2]. The place and conditions of detention will be as directed by the Secretary of State[3].

The Secretary of State may, on the recommendation of the Parole Board, release the child from detention on licence at any time prior to the expiry of the period specified by the court[4]. Otherwise the provisions for release of a child[5] are *mutatis mutandis* the same as those for an adult offender[6].

## Custodial disposal: summary procedure[7]

A child who has pleaded guilty or been found guilty under summary procedure in the sheriff court of an offence in  respect of which it is competent to impose imprisonment on a person aged 21 or more[8] may be ordered to be detained in residential care by the appropriate local authority[9] for a specified period not exceeding one year[10]. The local authority has the same powers and duties in respect of the child as if the child were under supervision following a children's hearing[11]. A child should be released after having been detained for not more than half of the period specified in the court's order[12], and such release may be under supervision and subject to conditions[12]. If a child who has been released is found guilty of an offence committed during the period when he would have been detained if not released, the court sentencing him may instead of or in addition to sentencing him for the new offence order that he be returned to the residential accommodation and serve the balance of his original sentence[13].

---

1  *K v HMA* 1991 SCCR 703, 1993 SLT 237.
2  1993 Act, s 6(1)(b)(ii).
3  1995 Act, s 208.
4  1993 Act, s 7(2). A similar provision applies to a child detained without limit of time: ibid, s 6(2).
5  1993 Act, s 7.
6  See above at pp 227–231.
7  If the 1997 Act, Pt III, Ch I comes into force there will be major changes in the provisions for the release of children sentenced to custodial disposals. See the Appendix at pp 324–325 below for changes relating to adult prisoners. Some of these will apply also to children.
8  1995 Act, s 44(2).
9  The 'appropriate local authority' is the local authority for the area where the child usually resides, or, if he does not reside in Scotland, the area where the offence was committed: 1995 Act, s 44(11).
10  1995 Act, s 44(1).
11  1995 Act, s 44(3).
12  1995 Act, s 44(6)(a).
13  1995 Act, s 44(8).

# CHAPTER 11

# PRIVATE PROSECUTION

In Scotland private prosecution is rare, and therefore the topic will be dealt with here relatively briefly.

## SOLEMN PROCEDURE

This century there have been only two occasions when a private prosecution has been allowed under solemn procedure[1].

### Competency

In order to bring a private prosecution a person must be able to maintain that the alleged crime amounts to a wrong towards him personally[2]. Not entirely convincingly the High Court has held that perjury, even though it may have resulted in a person being wrongly convicted or suffering some other form of injury, can never be the subject of a private prosecution as it is essentially a crime against public justice[3]. Even though a person holds office in an organisation whose members may be harmed by the alleged crime, he is not entitled to bring a private prosecution to protect the members. Thus the vice-president of a union of boys' clubs was not allowed to prosecute a bookseller for selling an allegedly obscene book, which he feared could corrupt members of the clubs[4].

The potential private prosecutor must apply to the Lord Advocate for his concurrence in the prosecution[5]. If the Lord Advocate refuses his concurrence, the High Court may authorise the private prosecution to proceed without it[6]. The fact that the Crown has abandoned its right to prosecute is no bar to a private prosecution[7].

A private prosecution under solemn procedure is probably competent only in the High Court[8].

1  *J & P Coats Ltd v Brown* (1909) 6 Adam 19, 1909 SC (J) 29, 1909 1 SLT 432; *X v Sweeney* 1982 JC 70, 1982 SCCR 161, 1983 SLT 48 sub nom *H v Sweeney* (popularly known as 'the Glasgow rape case').
2  *J & P Coats Ltd v Brown* (1909) 6 Adam 19 at 37, 1909 SC (J) 29 at 33, 1909 1 SLT 432 at 437, per Lord Justice-Clerk Macdonald.
3  *Trapp v M, Trapp v Y* 1971 SLT (Notes) 30; *Meehan v Inglis* 1975 JC 9, 1974 SLT (Notes) 61.
4  *McBain v Crichton* 1961 JC 25, 1961 SLT 209..
5  *J & P Coats Ltd v Brown* (1909) 6 Adam 19 at 37, 1909 SC (J) 29 at 33, 1909 1 SLT 432 at 437, per Lord Justice-Clerk Macdonald.
6  As in both the cases which have gone ahead this century (see note 1 above).
7  *X v Sweeney* 1982 JC 70, 1982 SCCR 161, 1983 SLT 48 sub nom *H v Sweeney*.
8  *Dunbar v Johnston* (1904) 4 Adam 505, 7 F (J) 40.

It has been held that, although the twelve-month time-bar under section 65(1) of the 1995 Act[1] does not apply to a private prosecution, it is not appropriate to authorise a private prosecution after a long lapse of time[2]. However, the opinion was expressed in the same case that the 110-day rule under section 65(4)(b)[3] may apply to such a prosecution[4].

### Procedure

An application for a private prosecution is made to the High Court by a bill for criminal letters. This should be supported by productions and precognitions. If the bill is passed (ie the application is granted), criminal letters are issued[5]. The case then proceeds to trial before a jury like any other High Court case except that the prosecutor is not, of course, represented by Crown Counsel.

### Expenses

An unsuccessful private prosecutor may be found liable in expenses[6].

## SUMMARY PROCEDURE

There is now no such thing as a private prosecution in the strict sense under summary procedure[7].

---

1  See above at pp 117–118.
2  *C v Forsyth* 1995 SCCR 553, 1995 SLT 905.
3  See above at p 119.
4  *C v Forsyth* 1995 SCCR 553 at 565E, 1995 SLT 905 at 911E, per Lord Justice-Clerk Ross.
5  See *X v Sweeney* 1982 SCCR 161 at 178–80, for the form of criminal letters.
6  *Hume* II, 127; Alison *Principles* p 113. See also *Gallacher, Petr* 1990 JC 345, 1990 SCCR 492, 1991 SLT 371.
7  The 1975 Act, s 462(1) included 'private prosecutor' in its definition of 'prosecutor' for summary proceedings. The 1995 Act, s 307(1) omits 'private prosecutor' in its definition of 'prosecutor' for summary proceedings. This is in contrast to the definition of the same term for solemn proceedings in s 307(1) which does include 'private prosecutor'.

CHAPTER 12

# REFERENCES TO THE EUROPEAN COURT

## THE TREATIES AND THE COURT

As the United Kingdom is a member of the European Union it is bound by the three Community Treaties[1]. The Court of Justice of the European Communities (usually referred to as 'the European Court') which sits in Luxembourg, is vested with the duty of ensuring that the law is observed in the interpretation and application of the Treaties[2]. The Court has authority to give preliminary rulings on the interpretation of community law[3]. A question of law may be referred to the European Court for such a ruling by a Scottish court[4].

This chapter will examine the procedure for such references from courts of both solemn and summary jurisdiction and from the High Court sitting in its appellate capacity.

## SOLEMN PROCEDURE

The procedure for referring a question to the European Court is laid down in Chapter 31 of the 1996 Rules[5].

Notice of intention to raise the question must be given to the trial court and to the other parties no later than fourteen days after service of the indictment[6]. Consideration of the matter is then reserved to the trial diet[7], and the court may order that no jurors or witnesses should be cited to that diet[8]. At the trial diet the

---

1 The treaties are those setting up the European Coal and Steel community (ECSC), the European Economic Community (EEC) and the European Atomic Energy Community (Euratom). The EEC was renamed the European Community (EC) by the Treaty on European Union ('the Maastricht Treaty') which came into force on 1 November 1993. The relevant United Kingdom legislation is the European Communities Act 1972.
2 ECSC Treaty, art 31; EC Treaty, art 164; Euratom Treaty, art 136.
3 ECSC Treaty, art 41; EC Treaty, art 177; Euratom Treaty, art 150.
4 In the case of a question arising under the ECSC Treaty, art 41, a reference to the European Court is obligatory. A reference is also obligatory if the question arises before a court from which there is no appeal: EC Treaty, art 177, and Euratom Treaty, art 150. Thus, in the present context, a reference is obligatory from the High Court in its appellate capacity.
5 1996 Rules, rr 31.1, 31.2, 31.5–31.7.
6 1996 Rules, r 31.2(1).
7 1996 Rules, r 31.2(2).
8 1996 Rules, r 31.2(3).

court may determine the question itself or may decide that a preliminary ruling should be sought from the European Court[1]. If the court determines the question itself, the accused is called on to plead (if appropriate) and the trial may thereafter proceed, provision being made for extension of time limits and the like[2].

If the court decides that a preliminary ruling should be sought, it must give its reasons for doing so[3]. The proceedings are thereafter continued from time to time as necessary[4]. The reference is in a form similar to a stated case and includes the question or questions on which the preliminary ruling is sought[5]. The court may give directions to the parties about the drafting and adjustment of the reference[6]. When the reference is in its final form the court approves its terms and orders that it be transmitted to the Registrar of the European Court with other parts of the process[7]. The order approving the reference should be made in open court or intimated to the parties[8].

When the ruling has been made by the European Court and been received by the clerk of the trial court, that court gives directions as to further procedure in the light of the ruling, and these directions are intimated to the parties together with a copy of the ruling[9].

There is a right of appeal to the High Court in its appellate capacity against an order making a reference to the European Court. The appeal must be taken within fourteen days of the order being made[10].

# SUMMARY PROCEDURE

The procedure for referring a question to the European Court from a court of summary jurisdiction is also laid down in Chapter 31 of the 1996 Rules[11].

Notice of intention to raise a question must be given before the accused is called on to plead to the complaint[12]. The court may then hear parties immediately or it may adjourn to a later date in order to do so[13]. After hearing submissions the court may determine the question itself or may decide that a preliminary ruling should be sought[14]. If the court decides to determine the question itself, the accused is called on to plead (where appropriate) and the case thereafter proceeds in the usual way[15].

---

1 1996 Rules, r 31.2(4).
2 1996 Rules, r 31.2(5), (6), (7).
3 1996 Rules, r 31.5(1)(a).
4 1996 Rules, r 31.5(1)(b).
5 1996 Rules, Form 31.5. For an example of the form of reference, see *Gewiese v Mackenzie; Mehlich v Mackenzie* 1984 SCCR 130, 1984 SLT 449.
6 1996 Rules, r 31.5(2)(a), (b).
7 1996 Rules, r 31.5(2)(c).
8 *HMA v Cowie, HMA v Wood* 1990 JC 281, 1990 SCCR 195 sub nom *HMA v Wood, HMA v Cowie* 1990 SLT 798 sub nom *HMA, Petr,* in which it was held that the *nobile officium* of the High Court could be used to extend the period of appeal under the equivalent of the 1996 Rules, r 31.7 where no intimation had been made.
9 1996 Rules, r 31.6.
10 1996 Rules, r 31.7(1). The procedure in such an appeal is governed by the remaining paragraphs of r 31.7. See *HMA v Cowie, HMA v Wood* 1990 JC 281, 1990 SCCR 195 sub nom *HMA v Wood, HMA v Cowie* 1990 SLT 798 sub nom *HMA, Petr.*
11 1996 Rules, rr 31.3, 31.5-31.7.
12 1996 Rules, r 31.3(1).
13 1996 Rules, r 31.3(3).
14 1996 Rules, r 31.3(4).
15 1996 Rules, r 31.3(5).

If the court decides to seek a preliminary ruling, the procedure is identical with that under solemn procedure[1].

There is a right of appeal to the High Court against an order making a reference to the European Court. The appeal must be taken within fourteen days of the order being made[2].

## REFERENCES BY THE HIGH COURT IN APPEALS

If in the course of an appeal to the High Court, whether under the 1995 Act, or by bill of suspension or advocation, or by petition to the *nobile officium*, a question of Community law arises, the High Court *must* make a reference to the European Court for a preliminary ruling[3]. This may take some time[4].

---

1  1996 Rules, rr 31.5–31.7.
2  1996 Rules, r 31.7(1). The procedure in such an appeal is governed by the remaining paragraphs of r 31.7. In *Wither v Cowie; Wither v Wood* 1990 SCCR 741, 1991 SLT 401 sub nom *Wither v Cowie* a suggestion that the rule allowing an appeal to the High Court against a reference by a sheriff (now r 31.7(1)) was *ultra vires* of the High Court was rejected.
3  1996 Rules, r 31.4.
4  In *Walkingshaw v Marshall* 1991 SCCR 397, 1992 SLT 1167, the sheriff repelled a plea to the competency of a complaint on 22 September 1987. The accused appealed. On 23 November 1988 the High Court referred the case to the European Court. That court issued its decision on 13 November 1990. On 10 January 1991 the High Court allowed the appeal and remitted the case to the sheriff.

# THE CRIME AND PUNISHMENT (SCOTLAND) ACT 1997

This Act, which received the Royal Assent on 21 March 1997, contains many provisions which, if brought into force, would make radical changes to some of the subjects discussed in this book. The Act is unusual in respect that, with very limited exceptions relating to the police which are not relevant to the subject matter of the book, its provisions are to come into force only 'on such day as the Secretary of State may by order made by statutory instrument appoint, and different days may be appointed for different purposes'[1]. The reason for this is, I understand, that the Act went through all its Parliamentary stages at relatively high speed shortly before Parliament was prorogued in preparation for the general election of 1 May 1997. The Opposition was prepared to co-operate with the Government only on the basis that none of the potentially controversial provisions of the statute would be brought into force before the election. At the time of writing the main text it was not known which provisions would be brought into force. It may well be that some of them will remain permanently unimplemented.

This situation presented a problem. I felt that I could not completely ignore the existence of the Act, tempting though that was! It seemed probable that at least some of its provisions would come into force while readers were using this book, and it is important that they should not be misled. I decided to solve the problem as best I could by providing this appendix to the book. In it I have attempted fairly briefly to summarise the provisions of the 1997 Act which seem to impinge to any substantial extent on the text of the preceding chapters. By means of references to this appendix in the footnotes to these chapters I have tried to draw attention to matters which are likely to be affected if certain parts of the 1997 Act ever come into force. I hope that this will be of some assistance to readers. The problem was compounded when, at the proofreading stage, a commencement order *was* produced[2].

I have tried, so far as possible, to deal with the topics covered by the Act in the same order as that in which they are presented in the main text.

## TAKING OF FINGERPRINTS AND OTHER IMPRESSIONS AND SAMPLES

### Obtaining of fingerprints etc[3]

Section 18 of the 1995 Act is amended by introducing a provision that a constable may 'require [a person arrested or detained] to provide him with' what are now

---

1 1997 Act, s 65(2).
2 The Crime and Punishment (Scotland) Act 1997 (No 1 Commencement and Transitional Provisions) Order 1997, SI 1997/1712, brought some sections into force on 1 August 1997. These are noted in the Appendix and throughout the main text.
3 The provisions referred to in this paragraph came into force on 1 August 1997.

described as 'relevant physical data'[1] and 'the person so required shall comply with that requirement'[2]. A constable may use reasonable force in taking any relevant physical data or securing a person's compliance with a requirement to provide[3].

## Samples from persons convicted of sexual and violent offences

If a person has been sentenced to imprisonment for 'a relevant offence'[4] and was serving that sentence any time during the five years before the coming into force of section 48 of the 1997 Act[5] or thereafter[6], a constable is empowered to take from that person or require him to provide 'such relevant physical data as the constable reasonably considers appropriate'[7]. In addition, an officer of a rank no lower than inspector may authorise the taking from such a person of any of the samples mentioned in section 18(6) of the 1995 Act[8]. These samples include hair, nail clippings, body fluid taken from an external part of the body and a saliva swab[9].

# POWERS OF THE SHERIFF AND DISTRICT COURTS

## Sentencing powers of sheriff under solemn procedure

The maximum sentence of imprisonment which may be imposed by a sheriff in solemn proceedings is increased from three years to five years[10].

## Sentencing powers of sheriff under summary procedure

The maximum sentence of imprisonment which may be imposed by a sheriff in summary proceedings is doubled[11]. This means that in a 'normal' case the sheriff may imprison for six months. In an aggravated case under section 5(3) of the 1995 Act he may impose a maximum sentence of twelve months. These increased powers also apply to a stipendiary magistrate sitting in the district court[12].

---

1 Defined as fingerprint, palm print, print or impression from some other external part of the body and 'record of a person's skin on an external part of the body created by a device approved by the Secretary of State': 1995 Act, s 18(7A) inserted by the 1997 Act, s 47(1).
2 1995 Act, s 18(2) as amended by the 1997 Act, s 47(1).
3 1995 Act, s 19B inserted by the 1997 Act, s 48(2).
4 1995 Act, s 19A(6) inserted by the 1997 Act, s 48(2) gives an extensive list of sexual and violent offences which are 'relevant offences'.
5 1995 Act, s 19A(1)(c).
6 1995 Act, s 19A(1)(a), (b).
7 1995 Act, s 19A(2)(a).
8 1995 Act, s 19A(2)(b).
9 1995 Act, s 18(6).
10 1997 Act s 13(1)(a) amending the 1995 Act, s 3(3), (4) and inserting a new s 3(4A); 1997 Act, s 13(3) amending the 1995 Act, s 195(2); and 1997 Act, s 13(4) amending the Criminal Procedure (Consequential Provisions) (Scotland) Act 1995, Sch 3, para 12(3).
11 1997 Act, s 13(2) amending the 1995 Act, s 5(2)(d), (3).
12 1995 Act, s 7(5).

# CRIMINAL LEGAL ASSISTANCE

Part V of the 1997 Act makes substantial changes to the provisions for legal aid in criminal cases, including registration of all solicitors who are to provide criminal legal assistance[1] and provision for a pilot 'public defender' scheme[2]. The details are outwith the scope of this Appendix.

# SOLEMN PROCEEDINGS[3]

## List of jurors

An accused is entitled to have a list of jurors provided to him only on the day of his trial[4]. Neither the accused nor anyone acting on his behalf is permitted to make a copy of that list[5], and the list must be returned to the clerk of court after the oath has been administered to the jury[6]. To fail to comply with this provision is an offence punishable by a fine not exceeding level 1 on the standard scale[7].

# EVIDENCE[8]

## Proof of commission of offence in course of unpaid work

If an offender is sentenced to perform unpaid work either under a community service order or as a condition of a probation order and he commits an offence in certain circumstances which amount to an aggravation of that offence[9], the fact that the offence *was* committed in the relevant circumstances is to be held as admitted unless challenged[10]. The challenge is to be made by giving notice of preliminary objection under section 72(1)(b) of the 1995 Act in the case of solemn procedure[11], and by preliminary objection before recording of a plea in the case of summary proceedings[12].

## Proof of age

The age of any person specified in an indictment or complaint is to be held as admitted unless challenged[13]. The challenge is to be made by giving notice of preliminary objection under section 72(1)(b) of the 1995 Act in the case of solemn

1  1997 Act, s 49 inserting a new  Part IVA in the Legal Aid (Scotland) Act 1986.
2  1997 Act, s 50 inserting a new s 28A in the Legal Aid (Scotland) Act 1986.
3  The provisions referred to in this section of the Appendix came into force on 1 August 1997.
4  1997 Act, s 58(3) inserting a new s 85(2A) in the 1995 Act.
5  1995 Act, s 85(2B)(a) inserted by the 1997 Act, s 58(3).
6  1995 Act, s 85(2B)(b) inserted by the 1997 Act, s 58(3).
7  1995 Act, s 85(2C) inserted by the 1997 Act, s 58(3).
8  All the provisions referred to in this section of the Appendix came into force on 1 August 1997.
9  1995 Act, ss 233(4) and 241(2). See above at pp 250, 253–254.
10  1997 Act, s 26 inserting new ss 233(6) (probation order) and 241(4) (community service) in the 1995 Act.
11  1995 Act, ss 233(6)(a), 241(4)(a).
12  1995 Act, ss 233(6)(b), 241(4)(b).
13  1997 Act, s 27 inserting a new s 255A in the 1995 Act.

procedure[1], and, in summary proceedings, by preliminary objection before recording of a plea or by objection at such later time as the court may in special circumstances allow[2].

### Evidence from certain official documents

Section 154 of the 1995 Act (which provides that in summary proceedings certain official documents are *prima facie* evidence of their contents without being proved) is repealed[3], but a virtually identical section is created which applies to both solemn *and* summary proceedings[4]. The scope of this relaxation of the strict rules of evidence is thus significantly extended.

### Evidence of vulnerable persons

The provisions for taking the evidence of children contained in section 271 of the 1995 Act are extended to the taking of evidence of any 'vulnerable person'[5]. 'Vulnerable person' is defined as being a child and 'any person of or over 16 years: (i) who is subject to an order made in consequence of a finding of a court in any part of the United Kingdom that he is suffering from mental disorder within the meaning of [certain mental health statutes]; or (ii) who is subject to a transfer direction under [certain mental health statutes]; or (iii) who otherwise appears to the court to suffer from significant impairment of intelligence and social functioning'[6].

### Routine evidence

Schedule 9 to the 1995 Act (which provides for proof of certain matters by certificate) is amended in certain respects[7].

### Proof of convictions in solemn proceedings

Section 101(5) of the 1995 Act (which provides that an amendment made to a notice of previous convictions shall not be to the prejudice of the accused) is repealed[8].

### Proof of fingerprints etc

Evidence that fingerprints or indeed any 'relevant physical data'[9] were taken from a particular person may be given by certificate signed by 'a person authorised in that behalf by a chief constable' instead of by two constables[10].

1 1995 Act, s 255A(a).
2 1995 Act, s 255A(b).
3 1997 Act, s 28(1).
4 1997 Act s 28(2) inserting a new s 279A in the 1995 Act.
5 1997 Act, s 29 substituting a new s 271 in the 1995 Act.
6 1995 Act, s 271(12) (as substituted).
7 1997 Act, s 30.
8 1997 Act, s 31.
9 Defined in 1995 Act, s 18(7A) as inserted by the 1997 Act, s 47(1)(d).
10 1997 Act, s 47(4) amending the 1995 Act, s 284.

## Precognitions

The 1995 Act is made sufficient warrant for citation of witnesses for precognition whether or not any person has been charged with the offence in relation to which the precognition is taken[1]. The requirement that a judge should grant a warrant to cite a witness for precognition is repealed[2].

A witness who has been cited for precognition and who either fails without reasonable excuse to attend, or refuses to give information within his knowledge, is guilty of an offence punishable by a fine not exceeding level 3 on the standard scale or imprisonment for not more than 21 days[3].

# SENTENCING

## Mandatory life sentences

The Act provides for a mandatory life sentence in the event of an accused being convicted of any of a category of offences (a 'qualifying offence') if he has previously been convicted in Scotland in the High Court, or in England or Northern Ireland, of any of the offences in that category (a 'qualifying offence' if the conviction was in Scotland, a 'relevant offence' if the conviction was in England or Northern Ireland)[4]. The category of offences includes culpable homicide, attempted murder, rape, aggravated assault, robbery involving a firearm, certain sexual offences, and their equivalents under English and Northern Irish law[5]. The trial judge is given a limited discretion not to pass a life sentence if his opinion is 'that it would be in the interests of justice ... to pass a sentence other than' a life sentence[6]. A previous conviction for the purposes of this provision includes a finding of guilt where the offender was admonished or placed on probation[7].

There is a right of appeal by an offender against the judge's refusal to exercise his discretion[8], and the Crown is given a right of appeal against the judge's exercise of discretion in favour of the offender[9]. There are also provisions for appeal where the conviction laying the foundation for the mandatory sentence is quashed on appeal[10].

## Mandatory sentences for drug trafficking

It is provided that a person convicted in the High Court of trafficking in a class A drug who has been convicted on two previous occasions of offences of trafficking in a class A drug in any part of the United Kingdom in any court must be sentenced to a minimum period of seven years' imprisonment or detention[11]. Again the trial

---

1  1997 Act, s 57(2)(a) amending the 1995 Act, s 140(1).
2  1997 Act, s 57(2)(b) repealing the 1995 Act, s 140(3).
3  1997 Act, s 57(1) inserting a new s 67A in the 1995 Act.
4  1997 Act, s 1(1) inserting a new s 205A in the 1995 Act.
5  1997 Act, s 1(2) inserting a new Sch 5A in the 1995 Act.
6  1995 Act, s 205A(3).
7  1997 Act, s 3 inserting a new s 205C(1) in the 1995 Act.
8  1997 Act, s 18(1) inserting a new s 106(1)(bb) in the 1995 Act.
9  1997 Act, s 18(2) inserting a new s 108A in the 1995 Act.
10 1997 Act, s 19 inserting a new s 106A in the 1995 Act.
11 1997 Act, s 2(1) inserting a new s 205B in the 1995 Act.

judge is given a limited discretion to pass a lesser sentence if it is his opinion 'that there are specific circumstances which - (a) relate to any of the offences or to the offender; and (b) would make [the mandatory minimum] sentence unjust'[1]. If the offender pleads guilty to the class A trafficking offence the mandatory minimum sentence is reduced to five years, two hundred and nineteen days[2]. A previous conviction for the purposes of this provision includes a finding of guilt where the offender was admonished or placed on probation[3].

There is a right of appeal by an offender against the judge's refusal to exercise his discretion[4], and the Crown is given a right of appeal against the judge's exercise of discretion in favour of the offender[5]. There are also provisions for appeal where one of the convictions laying the foundation for the mandatory sentence is quashed on appeal[6].

## Supervised release order

The scope of a supervised release order is widened. Such an order is no longer to be confined to sentences of four years or less.

In the event of an offender receiving a determinate sentence after having been convicted on indictment of an offence which is a 'qualifying offence' for the purpose of a mandatory life sentence he *must* be made subject to a supervised release order[7]. The court may decline to make an order in such a case only if it is of opinion 'that there are exceptional circumstances which justify its not making' the order[8]. As with other mandatory sentences both the accused and the Crown are given rights of appeal against the refusal or otherwise to exercise this limited discretion[9].

In any other case where an offender receives a determinate sentence, whether in solemn or summary proceedings, a court may make a supervised release order 'if it considers that it is necessary to do so to protect the public from serious harm from the offender'[10].

The maximum length of a supervised release order is to depend on the nature of the offence of which the accused was convicted. If the offence is a non-sexual 'qualifying offence' or some offence which is not a qualifying offence at all, a supervised release order is to be for a period 'of not less than three months; and not exceeding whichever is the greater of two years or one quarter of the full sentence of imprisonment from which the person is being released'[11]. If the offence is a sexual 'qualifying offence' then the period is not less than three months and not exceeding ten years[12].

1   1995 Act, s 205B(3).
2   1997 Act, s 2(2) inserting a new s 196(2) in the 1995 Act.
3   1997 Act, s 3 inserting a new s 205C(1) in the 1995 Act.
4   1997 Act, s 18(1) inserting a new s 106(1)(bb) in the 1995 Act.
5   1997 Act, s 18(2) inserting a new s 108A in the 1995 Act.
6   1997 Act, s 19 inserting a new s 106A in the 1995 Act.
7   1997 Act, s 4(2) substituting a new s 209(1)(a) in the 1995 Act.
8   1997 Act, s 4(2) inserting a new s 209(1A) in the 1995 Act.
9   1997 Act, s 18(1), (2) inserting new ss 106(1)(bb) and 108A in the 1995 Act.
10  1997 Act, s 4(2) substituting a new s 209(1)(b) in the 1995 Act.
11  1997 Act, s 4(3), (5) amending s 209(7) and adding s 209(9)(a) in the 1995 Act.
12  1997 Act, s 4(3), (5) amending s 209(7) and adding s 209(9)(b) in the 1995 Act.

## Restriction of liberty order

A restriction of liberty order is a completely new form of disposal. It applies to any offender over the age of sixteen years who is convicted of an offence the sentence for which is not fixed by law[1]. The order 'may restrict the offender's movements to such extent as the court thinks fit'[2]. It may include a provision 'requiring the offender to be in such place as may be specified for such period or periods [not exceeding twelve hours in any one day] in each day or week as may be specified'[3] or a provision 'requiring the offender not to be in such place or places, or such class or classes of place or places, at such time or during such periods, as may be specified[4]. The order may be for a maximum period of twelve months[5]. A restriction of liberty order may be imposed along with a probation order[6], and some of the provisions for a restriction of liberty order are modelled on those for probation orders[7].

The Secretary of State is empowered to prescribe which courts may make restriction of liberty orders[8], what method of monitoring compliance may be specified[9], and the class or classes of offenders in respect of whom orders may be made[10].

There is provision made for monitoring compliance with the order[11], including what is described as 'remote monitoring'[12], but what is perhaps better known as 'electronic tagging'.

An offender who is in breach of a restriction of liberty order may be fined an amount not exceeding level 3 on the standard scale[13].

## Extension of power to impose disqualification from driving

Courts are given power to disqualify an offender from driving for any offence whatsoever[14]. Disqualification may be in addition to or instead of any other penalty[15]. The Secretary of State may prescribe which courts or class of courts should exercise this power[16].

If an offender has been fined and fails to pay the fine, a court may, instead of imposing a period of imprisonment, disqualify him from driving for a maximum of twelve months[17]. Again the Secretary of State may prescribe which court or class of court should exercise this power[18].

1 1997 Act, s 5 inserting a new s 245A(1) in the 1995 Act. New ss 245B–245I make further provisions for restriction of liberty orders.
2 1995 Act, s 245A(2).
3 1995 Act, s 245A(2)(a).
4 1995 Act, s 245A(2)(b).
5 1995 Act, s 245A(3).
6 1995 Act, s 245D.
7 See eg 1995 Act, ss 245A(4) (making the order), 245E (variation of order), 245F (breach of order).
8 1995 Act, s 245A(8)(a).
9 1995 Act, s 245A(8)(b).
10 1995 Act, s 245A(8)(c).
11 1995 Act, s 245B.
12 1995 Act, s 245C.
13 1995 Act, s 245F(2)(a).
14 1997 Act, s 15(1) inserting a new s 248A in the 1995 Act.
15 1995 Act, s 248A(1). If the offence carries a sentence fixed by law disqualification may be imposed in addition to such a sentence: 1995 Act, s 248A(2).
16 1997 Act, s 15(1) inserting a new s 248C(1) in the 1995 Act.
17 1997 Act, s 15(1) inserting a new s 248B in the 1995 Act.
18 1997 Act, s 15(1) inserting a new s 248C(1) in the 1995 Act.

# IMPRISONMENT

## Designated life prisoners

Changes are made to the rules governing release of certain categories of those sentenced to life imprisonment for crimes other than murder except where the murder was committed when the offender was under the age of eighteen years, these including those sentenced under the mandatory provision introduced by the 1997 Act. Such prisoners are referred to as 'designated life prisoners'[1] instead of 'discretionary life prisoners'[2]. The practical effect of these changes is unlikely to be great.

## Release from prison

The automatic right to remission of one half or one third of a sentence is abolished[3] as is the distinction between long-term and short-term prisoners[4]. Instead a prisoner is to be entitled to release before the end of the period actually stated as his sentence only if he behaves well in prison. The new provisions are relatively complex but in essence mean that a prisoner serving a sentence of more than two months[5] is entitled to a certain number of 'early release days' if his behaviour attains the prescribed minimum standard[6] and to extra early release days if his behaviour exceeds that standard[7]. The maximum number of early release days which a prisoner may be awarded during his first two months in prison[8] is twelve, and he will be awarded these provided that his behaviour attains the prescribed minimum standard[9]. He is not eligible to any extra early release days during this period. Thereafter, the maximum number of early release days which he may be awarded for attaining the prescribed minimum standard during any two-month period[10] is six[11], and to earn more early release days his behaviour must exceed that standard[12].

Provision is made to take account of a prisoner who has been on remand prior to sentence[13].

The early release provisions are applied to fine defaulters and those imprisoned for contempt of court[14], children[15] and those detained because they are liable to be removed from the United Kingdom[16].

A prisoner who has been released early because he has gained early release days and who is convicted of an offence punishable by imprisonment during either a period when he is subject to a supervised release order or a period representing one

1  1997 Act, s 16 amending the 1993 Act, s 2.
2  The term 'discretionary life prisoner' disappears from the 1993 Act. See the 1997 Act, Sch 1, para 14(8), (10).
3  1997 Act, Sch 3 repealing the 1993 Act, s 1(1)–(3).
4  1997 Act, Sch 1, para 14(16) amending the 1993 Act, s 27(1).
5  1997 Act, s 34(1). A prisoner serving a sentence of two months or less is apparently not to be entitled to any remission.
6  1997 Act, s 34(2), (3)(a).
7  1997 Act, s 34(3)(b).
8  1997 Act, s 34(8).
9  1997 Act, s 34(2).
10  1997 Act, s 34(8).
11  1997 Act, s 34(3)(a).
12  1997 Act, s 34(3)(b).
13  1997 Act, s 35.
14  1997 Act, s 39(1).
15  1997 Act, s 39(2).
16  1997 Act, s 40.

sixth of the term of imprisonment to which he was originally sentenced, may be ordered to be returned to prison to serve the balance of that sentence as well as or instead of any other sentence for the new offence[1].

The fact that a released prisoner commits an offence during the period representing one sixth of the term of imprisonment to which he was originally sentenced may amount to an aggravation of the new offence and a factor to which the sentencing court should have regard[2]. Written notice of the fact that the new offence was committed during the relevant period must be given to the accused[3]. If the new offence carries a fixed penalty the sentencing court has additional powers: in the case of a fine to increase it by an amount equivalent to level 3 of the standard scale[4]; and in the case of imprisonment to increase the sentence by six months in the case of the High Court and sheriff court[5], and by 60 days in the case of the district court[6].

# APPEALS[7]

### Right of appeal against conviction

The 1997 Act extends the right of appeal against conviction in the case of both solemn and summary proceedings.

In the case of solemn proceedings a miscarriage of justice in respect of which an appellant may bring a conviction under review is to include a miscarriage based on 'the jury's having returned a verdict which no reasonable jury, properly directed, could have returned'[8].

In the case of both solemn and summary proceedings the right of appeal relating to new evidence is amended. An alleged miscarriage of justice may be brought under review on the basis of the 'existence and significance of evidence which was not heard at the original proceedings'[9]. Such evidence may, however, found an appeal only in certain circumstances. First, there must be a reasonable explanation of why it was not heard[10]. Secondly, if the new evidence is from a person or of a statement by a person who gave evidence at the original proceedings, and that evidence is different from the evidence then given, it may not found an appeal unless there is a reasonable explanation as to why the evidence was not then given, and that explanation is itself supported by independent evidence[11]. In both these cases, if the explanation for the evidence not having been given at the original proceed-

---

1  1997 Act, s 37.
2  1997 Act, s 38(1).
3  1997 Act, s 38(2).
4  1997 Act, s 38(4)(a).
5  1997 Act, s 38(4)(b)(i).
6  1997 Act, s 38(4)(b)(ii).
7  All the provisions referred to in this section of the Appendix, with the exception of s 25 (Scottish Criminal Cases Review Commission) and the reference to a restriction of liberty order in s 24, came into force on 1 August 1997.
8  1997 Act, s 17(1) amending the 1995 Act, s 106(3).
9  1997 Act, s 17(1) amending the 1995 Act, s 106(3) in the case of solemn proceedings; and 1997 Act, s 17(2) amending the 1995 Act, s 175(5) in the case of summary proceedings. The 1997 Act, s 17 introduces new subsections to the 1995 Act, ss 106 and 175, which are referred to in the following footnotes.
10  1995 Act, s 106(3A) for solemn proceedings; 1995 Act, s 175 (5A) for summary proceedings.
11  1995 Act, s 106(3C) for solemn proceedings; 1995 Act, s 175(5C) for summary proceedings. 'Independent evidence' is defined as evidence which was not heard at the original proceedings, which is from a source independent of the person who gave evidence at the original proceedings, and which is 'accepted by the court as being credible and reliable': 1995 Act, ss 106(3D), 175(5D).

ings is that the evidence was not then admissible, the appeal court may admit it if it is admissible at the time of the appeal and 'it appears to the court that it would be in the interests of justice to do so'[1].

### Right of appeal by prosecutor

The right of a prosecutor to appeal against an acquittal in summary proceedings on a point of law[2] is extended to the effect that in such an appeal 'a prosecutor may bring under review of the High Court any alleged miscarriage of justice'[3].

The right of appeal of a prosecutor to appeal against a sentence or its equivalent is extended for both solemn and summary proceedings. In addition to the existing provisions[4] the prosecutor is given the right to appeal against: a decision not to make a supervised release order; a decision not to make a non-harassment order[5]; and a decision to remit to the Principal Reporter[6]. The ground of appeal in these new cases is that the decision was 'inappropriate'[7].

### Right of appeal by accused against decision to remit to children's hearing

In both solemn and summary proceedings an accused child is given the right to appeal against a remit by a court to a children's hearing for disposal under section 49(1)(a) or (7)(b) of the 1995 Act[8]. It seems improbable that this right of appeal will be extensively used.

### Suspension of sentences pending determination of appeal

In the case of both solemn and summary proceedings the court is given power to suspend the operation of certain sentences pending the outcome of an appeal by either the convicted person or the prosecutor[9]. The sentences to which this provision applies are: a probation order; a supervised attendance order on a 16 or 17 year old in terms of section 236(6) of the 1995 Act; a community service order; and a restriction of liberty order[10]. The suspension is discretionary and may be made only on the application of the appellant[11].

1   1995 Act, s 106(3B) for solemn proceedings; 1995 Act, s 175(5B) for summary proceedings.
2   In terms of the 1995 Act, s 175(3).
3   1997 Act, s 17(2) inserting a new s 175(5E) in the 1995 Act.
4   Contained in the 1995 Act, s 108(1) (solemn proceedings) and 1995 Act, s 175(4) (summary proceedings).
5   A non-harassment order  was introduced by the Protection from Harassment Act 1997, s 11 inserting a new s 234A in the 1995 Act. The section came into force on 16 June 1997: Protection from Harassment Act 1997 (No 1 Commencement) Order 1997, SI 1997/1418.
6   1997 Act, s 21(1) amending the 1995 Act, s 108(1) for solemn procedure and 1997 Act s 21(2) amending the 1995 Act, s 175(4) for summary procedure.
7   1997 Act, s 21(1) inserting a new s 108(2) in the 1995 Act for solemn procedure and 1997 Act s 21(2) inserting a new s 175(4A) in the 1995 Act for summary procedure.
8   1997 Act, s 23 amending 1995 Act, ss 106(1) (solemn proceedings) and 175(2) (summary proceedings).
9   1997 Act, s 24(1) inserting a new s 121A in the 1995 Act for solemn proceedings and 1997 Act, s 24(2) inserting a new s 193A in the 1995 Act for summary proceedings.
10   1995 Act, ss 121A(4) (solemn procedure) and 193A(4) (summary procedure).
11   1995 Act, ss 121A(1) (solemn procedure) and 193A(1) (summary procedure).

## Transfer of rights of appeal of deceased person

If a person dies who is in the course of an appeal or who, if he had lived, might have instituted an appeal, the court may authorise another person to pursue the appeal[1]. Such a person may be the executor of the deceased or a person who otherwise appears to the court to have a legitimate interest[2]. Any application by such a person must be made within three months of the death of the deceased or 'at such later time as the court may, on cause shown, allow'[3].

## Scottish Criminal Cases Review Commission

A new Part XA of the 1995 Act provides for the creation of this Commission[4]. The provisions relating to the Commission are complex, extending to twelve new sections and a new schedule of eleven paragraphs in the 1995 Act. In essence the Commission is given power to refer a case to the High Court[5] if it believes that a miscarriage of justice may have occurred and that it is in the interests of justice that a reference should be made[6].

# MENTALLY DISORDERED OFFENDERS

## Hospital direction

The 1997 Act introduces a new disposal called a 'hospital direction'[7]. A hospital direction may be made in addition to any sentence of imprisonment imposed and authorises the admission to and detention of an offender in a specified hospital[8]. Medical evidence of mental disorder from two medical practitioners is required before a hospital direction can be made[9]. A State hospital should be specified in a hospital direction only in exceptional circumstances[10]. There is a right of appeal against the making of a hospital direction[11]. A hospital direction may be made in the case of a young offender[12], but not in the case of a child[13].

Substantial amendments are made to the 1984 Act to take account of the introduction of a hospital direction[14].

1  1997 Act, s 20 inserting a new s 303A in the 1995 Act.
2  1995 Act, s 303A(4).
3  1995 Act, s 303A(2).
4  Inserted by the 1997 Act, s 25(1).
5  1995 Act, s 194B(1).
6  1995 Act, s 194C.
7  1997 Act, ss 6, 7 inserting new s 59A in the 1995 Act and a new s 62A in the 1984 Act and making various other amendments to both Acts.
8  1995 Act, s 59A(1).
9  1995 Act, s 59A(3).
10  1995 Act, s 59A(4).
11  1997 Act, s 6(2) amending the 1995 Act, s 60.
12  1997 Act, s 6(4) inserting a new s 207(4A) in the 1995 Act.
13  1997 Act, s 6(2).
14  1997 Act, s 7.

## Remand in hospital

Section 70 of the 1984 Act is amended to permit a remand in a private hospital[1].

## Power to specify hospital unit

The power to specify a particular hospital[2] is extended to a power to specify a particular hospital unit[3], this being defined as 'any part of a hospital which is treated as a separate unit'[4].

## Medical evidence

There is introduced a general requirement that in cases where the evidence of two medical practitioners is required[5] at least one of these practitioners should be employed at the hospital which is to be specified in the order or direction concerned[6].

## Interim hospital orders

The maximum length of an interim hospital order is increased from six months to twelve months[7].

## Right of appeal by prosecutor against making of hospital order etc

The prosecutor is given a right of appeal against the making of a hospital order, guardianship order, restriction order or hospital direction, and their equivalents in the case of a person acquitted on the ground of insanity[8]. The appeal may be on the ground that the disposal was 'inappropriate'[9] or on a point of law[10].

## Early release provisions for mentally disordered offenders

The changes referred to above relating to release of prisoners[11] are applied to mentally disordered offenders who are either transferred to hospital during the course of a prison sentence[12] or who are made the subject of a hospital direction[13]. For the

---

1   1997 Act, s 8.
2   In terms of the 1995 Act, ss 57(2), 58, 59A and 71.
3   1997 Act, s 9(1).
4   1997 Act, s 9(3).
5   Under the 1995 Act, ss 53(1), 54(1)(c), 58(1)(a) and 59A(3)(a), (b).
6   1997 Act, s 10 amending the 1995 Act, ss 53 and 61.
7   1997 Act, s 11 amending the 1995 Act, s 53.
8   1997 Act, s 22 inserting a new s 60A in the 1995 Act.
9   1995 Act, s 60A(2)(a).
10   1995 Act, s 60A(2)(b).
11   See above at pp 324–325.
12   Under the 1984 Act, s 71.
13   See above at p 327.

purpose of calculating the date of release of such an offender, time spent in hospital is to be treated as time spent in prison with the maximum number of early release days which could have been awarded[1].

# CHILDREN AND YOUNG PERSONS[2]

### Arrest of child

A child who is arrested may be liberated unconditionally as well as (under the present law) on a written undertaking by him or his parent[3].

### Remand of child or young person

A child who is committed to the care of a local authority need not (as under the present law) be committed to the care of the local authority in whose area the court is situated but may be committed to the care of a local authority which the court 'considers appropriate'[4]. Such local authority may be the local authority for the area in which the court is situated or the local authority for the area in Scotland where the child is usually resident or, if the child is subject to a supervision requirement, the supervising local authority[5].

A person over the age of sixteen years who is under supervision may, instead of being remanded in prison, be committed to the local authority which the court considers appropriate[6].

---

1  1997 Act, s 41(2).
2  All the provisions in this section of the Appendix came into force on 1 August 1997.
3  1997 Act, s 55(2) amending the 1995 Act, s 43(1), (6).
4  1997 Act, s 56(2) amending the 1995 Act, s 51(1).
5  1995 Act, s 51(4A) inserted by the 1997 Act, s 56(4).
6  1995 Act, s 51(1)(aa) inserted by the 1997 Act, s 56(2)(b).

# Index

**Letter of request**
evidence by, 172–173, 214
**Lodgment**
productions, 123
**Lord Advocate**
public prosecution of crime, responsibility
    for, 80
reference by, 276

**Magistrate**
arrest warrant, power to grant, 86–87
search warrant, power to grant, 90–91
**Mentally disordered person**
appeal by, 304
criminal court, in –
    appeal, 304
    facts, examination of, 296–297
    first appearance, 294–295
    generally, 294
    guilt, disposal after finding of –
        generally, 300
        guardianship order, 303
        hospital order –
            generally, 300–301
            interim, 302
            other orders with, 302
        probation with condition of
            treatment, 303
        restriction order, 301
    hospital direction, 327–329
    insanity –
        bar of trial, in, 295–296
        defence, as –
            generally, 297
            solemn procedure, 297
            summary procedure, 297–298
        disposal, 298
        supervision order, 298–299
        treatment order, 300
medical evidence, requirements for, 304
**Multiple accused**
indictment, essentials of, 113
**Murder**
arrest, procedure after, 88
sentence for –
    imprisonment, 230–231
    young offender, detention of, 232
solicitor, involvement of, 92–93

**No case to answer**
submission of, 174–175, 215

**Oath**
precognition on, 111
solemn procedure, 148
summary procedure, 210
**Offence**
bail condition, breach of, 104–105

**Offence** – *contd*
district court, prosecution in, 190
sexual, evidence in trial of, 166–167, 212
statutory, fine for, 234
**Offender**
resident in England or Wales –
    community service order, 255
    probation order, 250–251
young. *See* YOUNG OFFENDER
**Ordained to appear**
trial diet, 202–203
**Order**
attendance, 237–240
bail, 17, 106
caution, for, 242
community service. *See* COMMUNITY
    SERVICE ORDER
compensation. *See* COMPENSATION ORDER
deportation, 262–263
exclusion, 261
fine, transfer of, 241
guardianship, 303
hospital. *See* HOSPITAL ORDER
probation. *See* PROBATION
restriction, 301

**Palmprints**
detainee, of, taking of, 84
records, destruction of, 85
**Party**
admission by, 215
**Penalty**
fixed, 191–192
**Petition**
arrest warrant, power to grant, 86–87
**Piracy**
High Court of Justiciary, jurisdiction of,
    98
**Place**
indictment, essentials of, 115
**Pleading**
bar of trial, plea in, 208
guilty, plea of, 199–200
jury trial, 144–145
not guilty, plea of, 200–201
**Police**
arrest. *See* ARREST
detention –
    Criminal Procedure (Scotland) Act 1995 –
        section 13, under, 85–86
        section 14, under, 82–85
    *David Balfour*, case of, 1–17
investigation of crime by, 80
questioning by, 80–82
search. *See* SEARCH
**Precognition**
Crown witness, of, by defence, 124–125